THE LINCOLN-DOUGLAS DEBATES

ABRAHAM LINCOLN   STEPHEN A. DOUGLAS

THE LINCOLN STUDIES CENTER EDITION

THE
LINCOLN-DOUGLAS
DEBATES

Edited by Rodney O. Davis and Douglas L. Wilson

PUBLISHED BY

THE KNOX COLLEGE LINCOLN STUDIES CENTER

AND THE UNIVERSITY OF ILLINOIS PRESS

URBANA AND CHICAGO

October 6, 2008

Dear Frank,

Inasmuch as the book cover contains a strongly worded suggestion that your interest in the life and career of Abraham Lincoln should not be ignored, we had but little choice in our selection of this gift for you as our house guest.

Dad and Roberta

Library of Congress Cataloging-in-Publication Data
Lincoln, Abraham, 1809–1865.
The Lincoln-Douglas debates / edited by
Rodney O. Davis and Douglas L.
Wilson. — Lincoln Studies Center ed.
p.   cm. —
(The Knox College Lincoln Studies
Center publication series)
Includes bibliographical references and index.
ISBN-13 978-0-252-03355-1 (cloth : alk. paper)
ISBN-10 978-0-252-03355-8 (cloth : alk. paper)
1. Lincoln-Douglas Debates, Ill., 1858.
2. United States—Politics and government—1857–1861.
I. Douglas, Stephen Arnold, 1813–1861.
II. Davis, Rodney O. III. Wilson, Douglas L.
IV. Knox College (Galesburg, Ill.).
Lincoln Studies Center. V. Title.
E457.4.L7754   2008
973.6'8—dc22   2008006405

CONTENTS

PREFACE

The Knox College Lincoln Studies Center Publication Series was established for the purpose of making important sources for the study of Abraham Lincoln available to twenty-first-century readers. In this, the second volume in the series, the subject is the celebrated 1858 debates between Lincoln and his longtime adversary, Stephen A. Douglas. Those debates were the highlight of an intensely contested senatorial campaign in Illinois, and they proved consequential in the elevation of Abraham Lincoln to national prominence and the presidency two years later. But the debates have long since ceased to be self-explanatory. To be accessible and fully appreciated by contemporary readers, they need to be placed in their historical context, just as the disparate newspaper texts that originally recorded them require editorial treatment and illumination. This edition has been designed to address these basic needs and to provide, by a number of different means, the necessary historical orientation, as well as a fuller and more accurate account of the speeches.

First-time readers typically find the Lincoln-Douglas debates to be something quite different from what they expected. Though high-minded discussions of such things as the morality of slavery are certainly present, these debates are also rife with petty partisanship, contrived accusations, and blatant attempts to stigmatize one's opponent or to place him on the defensive. They feature positions that, however politically permissible or even necessary in Illinois in 1858, may now seem offensive or even repugnant. Moreover, they are replete with references to individuals, events, and circumstances that were then common knowledge but are now unfamiliar. To help students and other readers navigate the antebellum world of Lincoln and Douglas and to provide necessary information and background, the editors have included three kinds of reading aids: introductions, annotations, and an extensive glossary of people, issues, and events.

The speeches given by Douglas and Lincoln in the seven joint debates were reported by two Chicago newspapers in what were represented as verbatim accounts. But these newspapers, like almost all of their time and place, were unabashedly partisan and made no secret of their devotion to one of the candidates, and little pretense at objectivity. Unsurprisingly, the "verbatim" reports of the speeches printed in these two papers are markedly divergent. This edition differs from its predecessors in attempting, by means of a critical process, to reconcile many of the disparities in the two versions of each speech and to arrive at a more reliable account of what was actually said.

The work on this edition, more than on any project the editors have undertaken, has been markedly divided. The historical commentary—the general introduction, the introductions to the individual debates, the annotations, and the glossary—are almost exclusively the work of Rodney O. Davis. The preparation of the critical text, including the textual introduction and notes, is the work of Douglas L. Wilson.

During the course of this project, the editors have amassed a number of debts to people and institutions, most of which are described elsewhere. But a special acknowledgement seems in order for the unstinting support afforded the Lincoln Studies Center by its host institution, Knox College. For the past several years, the editors have been privileged to work at the very site of the fifth Lincoln-Douglas debate with the constant aid and encouragement of President Roger Taylor and Dean Lawrence Breitborde. They are also pleased to pay special tribute to the extraordinary contribution of their dedicated student assistant, Andrew J. Christen, whose four years in the service of this edition are gratefully acknowledged.

GENERAL INTRODUCTION

The Lincoln-Douglas debates have been models for interactive political discourse in this country for nearly half a century, since the Kennedy-Nixon campaign of 1960. For a century longer than that they have been known as constituting one of the great events in American political history. They now exist as veritable icons of our democratic political culture, venerated and emulated especially at election times, but the significance of the debates is far more substantial than their mere iconic status would suggest. At their 150th anniversary, it is especially appropriate to consider the debates as prime documents of a former political era that was a watershed in the development of American institutions. They are thus time-bound, but they are also timeless in their relevance to issues constantly recurring in democratic societies.

Though the immediate field of contention between Lincoln and Douglas was a statewide race for a seat in the United States Senate, their campaign attracted nationwide attention, far more than any other state-level contest ever had, for the issues they considered were national as well as local, involving the expansion of slavery into the territories and the rights of African Americans, slave or free, in this country. David Herbert Donald has pointed out that the debates thus represented a choice between two radically different views of the American experience, manifest in the debaters' contradictory views of the meaning of the Declaration of Independence. To Lincoln, the declaration's affirmation that "all men are created equal" applied, at least in their possession of inalienable natural rights, to all human beings, whereas to Douglas that affirmation referred only to whites. Restated, the debates offered a choice between the values of majority rule, as advocated by Stephen Douglas, and minority rights, as defended by Lincoln. As Donald says, Douglas would allow almost no limit to what a popular majority could do, while Lincoln "felt passionately that no majority should have the power to limit the most fundamental rights of a minority to life, liberty and the pursuit of happiness."[1] The problem of a majority tyrannizing over a minority can be considered a moral problem, in Lincoln's estimation almost literally involving the

---

1. David Herbert Donald, *Lincoln* (New York: Simon and Schuster, 1994), 222, 226–27.

supposed right of a majority to do wrong, and that it is a central and constantly recurring difficulty in a democracy was abundantly illustrated in the debates.

To Lincoln, the expansion of the wrongful and tyrannical institution of slavery could not be tolerated in a nation dedicated to the pursuit of inalienable natural rights. It was thus a legitimate topic of political discourse at all levels. To Douglas, the morality of slavery was not a matter of congressional concern and should thus not even be discussed in the debates by candidates for congressional office, but the extension or limitation of the peculiar institution were legitimate considerations for local political action. Politicizing a moral issue, such as the persistence or expansion of African American slavery, or otherwise involving the rights of slaves or of African Americans generally or of any other minority in other times, is invariably a dangerous tactic in a democracy, especially if a moral infraction can also be identified with specific classes of people or geopolitical regions.

The debates also afford to contemporary readers insight into the career, ideas, and skills not only of our greatest political leader but also those of his foil, Stephen A. Douglas, at the time "the most prominent, most controversial political leader in the United States,"[2] without whose opposition Abraham Lincoln's rise to national prominence might never have happened. They dramatize a campaign in which Lincoln attained a national reputation, and as a result of which Douglas's political prospects were seriously eroded. Furthermore, because of the careful language Lincoln in particular had sometimes used on racial matters, and the unguarded language of Douglas, the debates afford to a contemporary reader real insight into the gradations of popular sentiment at the time on the volatile subjects of slavery and the rights of blacks, into important components of antebellum popular culture, in other words. Put yet another way, they afford current readers a notion of the great obstacles faced by the proponents of black freedom in Illinois (or America) before the Civil War. And the size of the debate crowds and the byplay between debaters and spectators attest to the vigor of American democracy in the nineteenth century. These and other issues raised by the Lincoln-Douglas debates can therefore be considered both time bound and of great historical interest, and timeless and still open. The editors consider that these reasons justify this new, extensively annotated edition of the debates, containing a critical text that we believe enables today's reader to come closer to experiencing the words that were actually spoken by Abraham Lincoln and Stephen A. Douglas than has been possible with previous editions.

✳ ✳ ✳

---

2. Robert W. Johannsen, *Stephen A. Douglas* (Urbana: University of Illinois Press, 1997), viii.

Knowing the Illinois backgrounds of the contestants, and the immediate context of the debates, is essential to their being understood by current readers. The
debates had a prehistory of at least four years, in which Abraham Lincoln and
Stephen A. Douglas were both involved. But the personal connection of Lincoln
and Douglas was much longer than that. Indeed, throughout their long acquaintance, from the early 1830s through the 1850s, the relationship of Douglas and
Lincoln to one another can be thought of as that of opposite numbers, or perhaps
even of significant others. Lincoln was a Kentucky and Hoosier Whig and later
Republican, who became morally opposed to slavery. Douglas was a Vermont
Yankee Jacksonian Democrat, publicly indifferent to slavery, though he is privately quoted to have had no use for it.[3] As a Whig, Lincoln took the hard road
politically in Illinois, which was long an overwhelmingly Jacksonian state, but
Douglas took the easier road immediately in Illinois politics, ingratiating himself with the Democratic establishment upon his first arrival, and then climbing
the political ladder. Lincoln's career in politics had reached the limit possible for
a Whig in Illinois by the end of his congressional term in 1849: leadership of a
hopelessly permanent Whig minority in the lower house of the state legislature,
and one term in Congress from the only consistently safe Whig district in the
state. Douglas constantly moved up politically, through administrative positions
and the Illinois legislative and judicial branches to multiple terms in the federal
House of Representatives and Senate. He had been seriously considered presidential timber by the Democrats at their national convention in Cincinnati in 1856,
and he was definitely construed to be the greatest man in Illinois when he and
Lincoln contested Douglas's Senate seat two years later. Surveying his own political career with only a little exaggeration, Lincoln famously admitted to himself
in 1856 that "with me, the race of ambition has been a failure—a flat failure; with
him [Douglas] it has been one of splendid success."[4]

   In the American democracy, the successful politician is one whose motives
and positions best coincide with those of the electorate that he or she aspires to
represent, and of Lincoln and Douglas, the latter for long was more clearly the
articulator of the dominant spirit of his time. In his early career he supported the
classic Jacksonian skepticism toward banks and corporations. He was a strong
nationalist in the sense that he considered the central American concern to be

---

3. George Murray McConnell, "Recollections of Stephen A. Douglas," *Transactions of the
Illinois State Historical Society,* 1900, 49. For an exhaustive recent discussion of SAD's attitude
toward slavery, see Graham A. Peck, "Was Stephen A. Douglas Antislavery?" *Journal of the
Abraham Lincoln Association* 26 (2005), 1–21. Peck's answer to his own question is "no."

4. "Fragment on Stephen A. Douglas" [December 1856?], in Roy P. Basler et al., eds.,
The Collected Works of Abraham Lincoln (New Brunswick: Rutgers University Press, 1953),
2:382–83.

the occupation of the American West by a self-governing people of European ancestry, before which all other issues, including slavery, were simply subordinate. In Congress he was in the forefront of American projects to annex Oregon, Texas, and California, and he proposed the construction of a transcontinental railroad even before the United States possessed territory on the Pacific coast. Within all American commonwealths, old, new, or prospective, Douglas argued that the sovereign people should determine for themselves what their state and local governing priorities ought to be.

In this wise, Douglas's authorship of the Kansas-Nebraska Act early in 1854 was entirely consistent with his already established priorities. He believed that those two prospective territories lay athwart the most practicable railroad routes to the Pacific and that they should be organized and populated by white settlers for that reason. He professed to believe that the provision of the Compromise of 1850 that allowed the citizens of Utah and New Mexico themselves, and not Congress, to determine the status of slavery within their borders established a precedent that solved the problem of slavery in future new territories. Accordingly, he incorporated the same stipulation in the new legislation for Kansas and Nebraska. However, this provision for "popular sovereignty" conflicted with Section 8 of the Missouri Compromise, which forbade the introduction of slavery north of latitude 36° 30' and west of Missouri in the Louisiana Purchase, within which area both Kansas and Nebraska lay. Thus to secure the Southern congressional votes necessary for the bill's passage without altering the anticipated result of the legislation, Douglas acquiesced in a stipulation eventually repealing Section 8 of the Missouri Act. Douglas was undoubtedly sincere in his belief that slavery could never flourish in wintry Kansas or Nebraska, and that the demand for Western development trumped slavery as a significant national issue; indeed, as Harry V. Jaffa puts it, Douglas felt that popular sovereignty "was in fact the best constitutional instrument for giving effect to the overwhelming northern free-soil condemnation of slavery in the territories."[5]

The Kansas-Nebraska Act became law under these terms in May 1854; but Douglas totally underestimated how great an uproar would result from it, and in that underestimation he began to reveal political vulnerability. Nationally, the Kansas-Nebraska Act led to a reconfiguration of the political party system, with the Whig party eventually being replaced by the sectional and antislavery Republican party and with the unity of the Democratic party seriously threatened, and to a resurgence of the slavery issue that would only progressively worsen

---

5. Harry V. Jaffa, *Crisis of the House Divided: An Interpretation of the Issues of the Lincoln-Douglas Debates* (Chicago: University of Chicago Press, 1982 [1959]), 44–45.

until the outbreak of the Civil War. By the late 1850s, in the words of his biographer, Douglas's zeal for national expansion "may have blinded him to the more urgent requirements of the age."[6] After four years of agitation of the slavery issue subsequent to the passage of the Kansas-Nebraska Act, Abraham Lincoln would credibly assert to Douglas that the latter's disregard notwithstanding, slavery was "*the very thing that everybody does care the most about.*"[7]

To Abraham Lincoln, the Kansas-Nebraska Act with its repeal of the Missouri Compromise raised the possibility of a morally reprehensible institution entering an area of the country where it had never previously existed, and from which, by a solemn national covenant which Douglas himself had eulogized not long before seeing to its overturn, it had been banned. Lincoln was appalled that slavery could be expanding in a nation dedicated to the inalienable rights of human beings. He scoffed at the argument that Kansas and Nebraska were climatically inhospitable to slavery as "a *palliation—a lullaby.*"[8] Indeed, Lincoln's reading of the federal Constitution convinced him that, though that document acknowledged the presence of slavery, the founders of the Republic had also intended that the peculiar institution be put on the route to "ultimate extinction," progress toward which the Kansas-Nebraska Act was not merely impeding but indeed potentially reversing. The Kansas-Nebraska Act brought Lincoln's antislavery sentiments into sharp focus, and, in his own words, "aroused him as he had never been before."[9] So galvanized was he that he reentered politics, still as a Whig, speaking in the fall of 1854 in favor of the Anti-Nebraska congressional candidacy of Richard Yates and successfully running for the Illinois House of Representatives himself. That Lincoln's aversion to the Kansas-Nebraska Act was shared by a great many Illinois voters was manifest in the Anti-Nebraska majority that was returned to the state legislature that November, in response to which Lincoln almost immediately undertook a run for the United States Senate, to replace Douglas's Democratic ally, James Shields. Though that candidacy was unsuccessful, Lincoln's return to politics was established, and his opposition to Stephen Douglas for re-election four years later became a virtual certainty. In that campaign he would run as a member of the new Republican Party.

---

6. Robert W. Johannsen, "Stephen A. Douglas and the American Mission," in Robert W. Johannsen, ed., *The Frontier, the Union and Stephen A. Douglas* (Urbana: University of Illinois Press, 1989), 98.

7. Debate at Alton, Illinois, Oct. 15, 1858, p. 281 (italics in original text).

8. "Speech at Peoria, Illinois," Oct. 16, 1854, in Basler et al., *Collected Works*, 2:262 (italics in original text).

9. "Autobiography Written for John L. Scripps," [c. June 1860], ibid. 4:67.

* * *

Though this was certainly not Stephen Douglas's original intention, the terms of the Kansas-Nebraska Act invited conflict in Kansas in that they essentially promised the control of the territory's government to whatever faction was present in the greatest number when the first elections were held there in March 1855. The turmoil that attended the passage of the act by Congress made such contention even more likely.[10] Though eventually most of the permanent immigrants to Kansas came from nonslaveholding northwestern states such as Illinois, Indiana, and Ohio, settlers and invaders from nearby slaveholding Missouri had the initial advantage in this contest, insuring the election of a proslavery Kansas territorial legislature. Though the Pierce administration recognized that body as the official one for the territory, antislavery Kansans refused to, and they established an extralegal government of their own. For eighteen months thereafter the nation witnessed a scene of fraud, violence, and political turmoil in Kansas as Missouri "border ruffians" and antislavery or "Free State" Kansans in increasing numbers fought it out to determine whether the state that would emerge would harbor slavery or forbid it. The concurrent presidential campaign of 1856 insured that the rivalry between the sections that was manifest in Kansas would attain national partisan significance. The new Republican Party in particular made much of the spectacle of "Bleeding Kansas." It was both influenced by it and profited from it, and quite likely thousands of new Republican votes were cast that year in response to the working out of the Kansas-Nebraska Act and the slavery issue in the new territory.

Though intending to brush the issue of slavery in the territories off the national stage, the United States Supreme Court shortly after the inauguration of James Buchanan in March 1857 only added further heat to the growing crisis. In the most inflammatory section of its decision on the *Dred Scott* case, it held the Missouri Compromise unconstitutional, thereby denying the authority of Congress or by implication any creature of Congress such as a territorial legislature, to forbid the existence of slavery in any United States territory. Republicans, Abraham Lincoln among them, of course attacked the Court's decision for seeming to allow slavery to expand without limitation by any federal or territorial authority. But Senator Douglas stood by the decision, which he said must not be resisted. Though it negated the very principle of popular sovereignty, which had been basic

---

10. To slaveholding Missourians, the legalization of slavery in Kansas Territory, which lay immediately to the west of their state, seemed both inevitable and necessary. Were Kansas to forbid slavery, Missouri would be surrounded on three sides by free states, to any of which Missouri slaves might escape. Furthermore, slaveholding interests were especially powerful in Missouri counties bordering Kansas or on the Missouri River approaching Kansas.

to the Kansas-Nebraska Act and to his dream of territorial expansion, Douglas also argued as early as June 1857 that the principle was unaffected by the decision, that slavery could only exist in a territory with popular support and protection by local police regulations and legislation.[11]

∗ ∗ ∗

Prominent in the background of the Illinois senatorial campaign of 1858 was Stephen Douglas's break with the administration of President James Buchanan over the state constitution for Kansas that was drafted at the territorial capital of Lecompton the previous October, and the chain of events that followed. The convention that drew up the Lecompton Constitution met under the auspices of the territory's proslavery legislature, which, though recognized as legal by the national administration, had notoriously come to represent an electoral and demographic minority in Kansas. Many Free-State voters boycotted the election for delegates to the constitutional convention; many others had previously been systematically excluded from the voting franchise. The delegates chosen were therefore almost unanimously proslavery. The convention prepared a constitution committing Kansas to retain slavery, which could be ratified by the territory's voters only through a device allowing the slaves already in Kansas to remain there. The Lecompton Constitution was thus an instrument prepared by a minority faction that would impose slavery on the Free-State majority in Kansas. "Ratification" of the constitution took place in a territorial referendum on December 21, 1857, in which only a minority voted and which Free-State voters again shunned. In spite of this, President Buchanan pressed for the constitution's approval by Congress, professing to believe that the nation's slavery controversy would end once Kansas became a slave state, and desiring also to placate Southern Democrats in Congress and in his cabinet, who by this time would tolerate nothing less. Buchanan's motive was also partisan; Kansas would produce two more Democratic senators.

Senator Douglas broke ranks with the administration over the Lecompton Constitution on December 9, 1857, in a speech that has been called "probably the most significant in his career."[12] He vowed to his senatorial colleagues that "if this constitution is to be forced down our throats, in violation of the fundamental principle of free government, under a mode of submission that is a mockery and an insult, I will resist it to the last." Significantly, Douglas professed indifference to

---

11. *Kansas, Utah, and the Dred Scott Decision. Remarks of Hon. Stephen A. Douglas, Delivered in the State House at Springfield, Illinois, on the 12th of June, 1857,* [Springfield, Illinois, ? 1857?], 3.

12. Johannsen, *Stephen A. Douglas,* 592.

the way the slavery clause of the constitution would be decided, attacking instead the means of its submission to voters as "a system of trickery and jugglery to defeat the fair expression of the will of the people."[13] Douglas's motivation was probably threefold: he was aggrieved at President Buchanan over having been ignored on patronage decisions, and he probably sincerely believed what he affirmed in his December 9 speech, that the Lecompton Constitution's mode of submission violated the principle of popular sovereignty. But his calculations were also plainly self-serving and political.[14] Looking at his prospects in the campaigns of 1858 and 1860, and remembering how he had misread the political signs before promoting the Kansas-Nebraska Act, Douglas had to take the position that would be most acceptable in Illinois and in the North generally. With his ear characteristically to the ground, he ascertained that the Lecompton Constitution was not popular with his Illinois constituents. And winning the 1858 senatorial campaign in Illinois was simply imperative, if Douglas were to be a credible contender for the presidency in 1860.

But Douglas's break with the Buchanan administration confronted Illinois Republicans with a dilemma. Douglas had been their main enemy since they had established themselves as a party, yet many of them favored his position on the Lecompton Constitution, as Republicans in Congress were already doing. Indeed, the possibility of a limited Republican alliance with Douglas and his supporters was discussed over a period of several months in early 1858. Other Illinois Republicans, including Abraham Lincoln, feared that encouraging Douglas would only weaken the Republican cause. It would eventually become clear to Illinois Republicans that Douglas attacked the Lecompton Constitution for mainly procedural reasons, because of the violence it seemed to do to the principle of popular sovereignty. The outcome of a territorial election on slavery if all sides were properly allowed to vote, he claimed, was immaterial to him, though it must again be acknowledged that Douglas personally felt that overwhelming Northern antislavery opinion in Kansas would prevail in such a canvass. To Republicans, popular sovereignty as Douglas defined it, in any of its guises, was an abomination that could allow slavery to expand into the territories. As Lincoln put it, "In voting together in opposition to a constitution being forced upon the people of Kansas, neither Judge Douglas nor the Republicans, has conceded anything which was ever in dispute between them."[15]

---

13. *Congressional Globe,* 35th Cong., Senate, 1st Sess., Dec. 9, 1857, 18.

14. For discussions of SAD's motives underlying his decision to oppose the Lecompton Constitution, see Don G. Fehrenbacher, *Prelude to Greatness: Lincoln in the 1850's* (Stanford: Stanford University Press, 1962), 55–57; Johannsen, *Stephen A. Douglas,* 582–83.

15. AL to Jediah F. Alexander, May 15, 1858, in Basler et al., *Collected Works,* 2: 446–47.

Further complicating matters was the approval of Douglas's course by eastern Republican politicians such as Senators Henry Wilson and William H. Seward, for whom his stance was described an unexpected "God send."[16] Equally rankling to Illinois Republicans was the cheerleading for Douglas that came from eastern newspapers such as Horace Greeley's *New York Tribune*. Beginning in December the *Tribune*, which had thousands of Illinois readers, praised Douglas almost without stint, urging Republicans to work with him, and it was to continue to support him even through the following spring, favoring his candidacy for reelection to the United States Senate, and expressing regret at Lincoln's nomination to oppose him.[17] Irritating as this East Coast attention to Douglas was to Illinois Republicans, it reveals how dominating was Douglas's national reputation and the real delight of eastern politicos and editors that he might be a Republican recruit. It also reveals the obscurity of Abraham Lincoln outside Illinois on the eve of the 1858 campaign.

Anxiety over Republican defections to Douglas persisted through April and May, when the Little Giant came forth in opposition to the English bill, a compromise on the Lecompton issue that was initiated in the House of Representatives and which undertook to placate both pro-Lecompton and anti-Lecompton partisans. Under the bill's terms, Kansans would acquiesce in admission to the Union under the Lecompton Constitution by voting to accept a land grant from Congress. Though the land grant was made the paramount feature of the bill, its intention to foist the Lecompton Constitution on Kansans was nonetheless obvious. A last-ditch effort to get Kansas out of the national political arena and into the Union as a slave state, the English bill would defer statehood if these terms were rejected, until the territory had a population equal to the minimum required of a congressional district. Republicans in Illinois and in Congress found the bill outrageous, as, after some hesitation, did Douglas. "Where there are inducements [the land grant] on one side, and penalties [the Lecompton Constitution] on the other," he said in the senatorial debate on the English bill, "there is no freedom of election."[18] Douglas and Lincoln were in tacit agreement on the English bill, Lincoln scornfully calling it a mere "contrivance."[19]

---

16. Lyman Trumbull to AL, Jan. 3, 1858, Abraham Lincoln Papers, Library of Congress. This collection is accessible on the Library of Congress Web site and is hereinafter cited as Lincoln Papers.

17. *New York Tribune*, Dec. 21, 29, 1857; May 11, 17, June 24, 1858.

18. *Congressional Globe*, 35th Cong., Senate, 1st Sess., Apr. 29, 1858, p. 1869. Despite SAD's opposition, the English bill passed its congressional test, and its provisions were submitted to a vote in Kansas, where they were defeated resoundingly in August.

19. AL to Josiah M. Lucas, May 10, 1858; AL to Elihu B. Washburne, May 15, 1858; Basler et al., *Collected Works*, 2:445, 447.

Illinois Republican fears of party division or diversion at the hands of eastern journalists or Stephen A. Douglas began to be balanced after the first of the year by a split in the state's Democratic party brought on by the Buchanan administration's insistence upon party regularity after Douglas's bolt over the Lecompton Constitution. Thereafter, though Republicans continued to be concerned over the possible loss of their own voters to Douglas or a necessary confederation with their longtime adversary, they exulted at the growing spectacle of a division between Douglas supporters and "National" Democrats, as partisans of the administration were known, a split they were only too glad to encourage. The administration's strategy became apparent late in January when rumors began to circulate that federal contractors and officeholders, postmasters in particular, who were Douglas loyalists, would find their positions in jeopardy.[20] Removals began at the top soon after.

In fact, National Democrat and Republican leaders were not formally plotting together, and Republicans denied the charge that they were, though the objective of both groups, the defeat of Stephen A. Douglas in his Senate reelection campaign, was obviously the same.[21] But they were definitely in touch with one another. Abraham Lincoln was perfectly aware of these contacts and in at least two instances was a party to them, helping thus to create the arresting spectacle of Illinois Republicans trading advice and encouragement with pro-Lecompton Democrats, for the sake of electoral advantage.[22] At approximately the same time, Illinois Republicans and Douglas Democrats stood on the same side, if not necessarily united, in efforts to defeat the Lecompton Constitution and the English bill, which the National Democrats favored. Senator Douglas found himself embattled by adversaries from both his own and the opposing party in a campaign that it was imperative that he dominate.

* * *

On April 21, 1858, the Democrats of Illinois met in their state convention in Springfield. The gathering was organized by Douglas's partisans, whereupon the National

---

20. *Chicago Tribune*, Jan. 27, 1858; Thomas H. Harris to Charles H. Lanphier, Jan. 21, Feb. 9, 1858, Charles H. Lanphier Papers, Abraham Lincoln Presidential Library, Springfield, Illinois.

21. *Chicago Tribune*, June 8, June 19, 1858. In spite of the denial, the *Tribune* gave very full coverage to the National Democratic convention. See ibid., June 10, June 11, 1858.

22. Edward L. Baker to Trumbull, May 1, 1858; William Herndon to Trumbull, June 24, July 9, 1858; Gustave Koerner to Trumbull, June 29, 1858; all in Lyman Trumbull Papers (microfilm edition), Library of Congress; John Wentworth to AL, June 6, 1858; Joseph T. Eccles to AL, Aug. 4, 1858; both in Lincoln Papers; A. Sherman to Ozias Hatch, September 27, 1858, Ozias Hatch Papers, Abraham Lincoln Presidential Library, Springfield, Illinois.

Democrats withdrew and called for their own statewide meeting, which convened on June 9. One week after the National Democrats met, Illinois Republicans came together for only their second state convention since the memorable one that formally organized their party two years before. In all three cases the formal business involved the creation of a platform of party principles, and the nomination of candidates for the two statewide offices to be filled that year, those of the state treasurer and superintendent of public instruction. The Republicans, however, went further still. According to the *Chicago Tribune,* ninety-five Republican county conventions had already resolved before their party's state conclave that Abraham Lincoln should be Stephen A. Douglas's successor in the United States Senate, and accordingly at the state convention the Republican delegates resolved on June 16 that "Abraham Lincoln is our first and only choice for United States Senator to fill the vacancy about to be created by the retirement of Hon. Stephen A. Douglas," in effect precommitting Republican legislators to vote for Lincoln and no other, when the matter of choosing a Senator from Illinois would come before the General Assembly in the coming winter.[23] Stephen A. Douglas was later to say that "probably this was the first time that such a thing was ever done."[24]

Doubtless the *Tribune* spoke for the convention when it asserted that the latter's essential nomination of Lincoln was a rebuke to Eastern politicians and editors, such as Horace Greeley, for urging Illinois Republican collaboration with Douglas after his stand on the Lecompton Constitution. "It is the natural and expected remonstrance against outside intermeddling," said the *Tribune.* "It is the answer of Republican Illinois to the managers and wire-pullers who would have taken her under their own control."[25] Even more directly the resolution was a rebuke to Douglas personally, as a Democrat with whom Republicans could not cooperate, and it brought almost to an end further talk of a Republican alliance with him. And the resolution can be considered a response to Democrats who, hoping to divide Republican strength in the convention and the fall election, had claimed that Chicago's popular former Democratic but now Republican mayor "Long John" Wentworth also had senatorial ambitions.[26] Lincoln's nomination put a stop to such speculations. That Douglas would be the senatorial choice of the Democratic caucus in the forthcoming state legislative session was already a foregone conclusion. Hence the bipartisan lineup for Illinois's 1858 senatorial contest was known by the middle of June rather than during the General As-

---

23. *Chicago Tribune,* June 14, June 18, 1858.
24. See SAD's speech in the Charleston debate, p. 159.
25. *Chicago Tribune,* June 18, June 19, 1858.
26. *Chicago Times,* May 19, May 25, June 8, June 22, 1858; AL to Trumbull, June 23, 1858, in Basler et al., *Collected Works,* 2:472.

sembly's session, as would be customary in that time before the Seventeenth Amendment, when senators were chosen by state legislatures. An unprecedented popular election campaign for the senatorial seat held by Douglas therefore lay in prospect; it would dominate the races for seats in the state House and Senate that were already scheduled.

On the evening of his nomination, Abraham Lincoln delivered his "House Divided" speech, which inaugurated the campaign. Senator Douglas would constantly refer throughout the canvass to that speech's declaration that the Union could not remain half slave and half free and to its attack on the *Dred Scott* decision as the harbinger of a movement to make slavery national. Douglas returned to Chicago from Washington on July 9, and on the evening of his arrival he replied to Lincoln's earlier speech, asserting that Lincoln preached a war between the sections and resistance to the *Dred Scott* decision. Lincoln responded the next night, claiming that the founding fathers' intention to place slavery on the road to ultimate extinction was blockaded by the Kansas-Nebraska Act and the *Dred Scott* decision, and that the Declaration of Independence's promise of life, liberty, and the pursuit of happiness applied to all human beings, not just whites. With this triad of speeches, the bipartisan senatorial campaign was launched, with many of its major talking points now on the table. Douglas spoke four more times in July, with major addresses at Bloomington on July 16 and Springfield the next day, and lesser ones at Clinton and Monticello on July 27 and 29. Lincoln was in Douglas's audience at Bloomington, and he replied to Douglas the next day after Douglas's speech at Springfield. He followed him also to Clinton and Monticello. Douglas traveled by a flag-bedecked special train, to which was hitched at Joliet a flatcar carrying a brass cannon called "Popular Sovereignty," which thereafter loudly signaled the approach of Douglas's entourage at every speaking location. Lincoln called the spectacle "a triumphal entry into, and march through the country," and he expressed disgust at such campaign tactics.[27]

Lincoln's own apparently ad hoc tactic of following his adversary and speaking in response to him was not uncommon in the Illinois politics of the time; it allowed him to reply to Douglas when Douglas's remarks were most fresh; however, it was to draw critical attention almost immediately from both Republicans and Democrats. As early as July 17 Gustave Koerner counseled Lincoln against the sort of campaign pageantry the Douglas forces were using, but he also revealed the extremely informal character of Lincoln's early operation by allowing the obvious, that "perhaps the Central Committee had better meet to agree upon a general plan of campaign."[28] Shortly after, Lincoln was urged to take the offensive

---

27. AL to Gustave P. Koerner, July 15, 1858, in Basler et al., *Collected Works*, 2:502.
28. Gustave Koerner to AL, July 17, 1858, Lincoln Papers.

against Douglas, that the latter might be placed in a position to have to reply to Lincoln, and a Republican editor emphasized the futility of Lincoln's following Douglas, merely to "take the leavings" of Douglas's audience. Instead, he urged Lincoln to challenge Douglas to debate, "giving a fair opportunity to all to hear both sides."[29] Democratic notice of Lincoln's campaign tactics was also early; and eventually the *Chicago Times* accused Lincoln of "hanging at the outskirts of Douglas's meetings, begging the people to turn out to hear him." That newspaper also suggested that to insure himself an audience, Lincoln should follow one of the two circuses that was currently traveling through the state.[30]

The Republican *Chicago Press and Tribune* seems to have been the first to publicly suggest a series of joint encounters. "Let Mr. Douglas and Mr. Lincoln agree to canvass the State together, in the usual western style," it urged on July 22.[31] Two days later, Lincoln approached Douglas with regard to "an arrangement for you and myself to divide time, and address the same audiences during the present canvass." Within a week they were in agreement that a series of seven debates should take place between them at central points within each congressional district in which they had not previously made major speeches. Douglas, as the challenged party, was also able to insist that Lincoln only meet him "at the times specified," to which Lincoln acquiesced.[32] Thereafter, until the first scheduled debate at Ottawa on August 21, Douglas spoke at a number of points in central Illinois. Resuming his speaking schedule after August 11, Lincoln followed a day behind Douglas at a series of engagements along the Illinois River.

The advantage of scheduled joint encounters would probably be greatest for Lincoln; more Republicans would be likely to turn out for a speech by the renowned Douglas than would Democrats just to hear his challenger. The agreed-upon debates could insure that at least in seven instances, Lincoln could reach adherents of both parties, as well as the undecided voters for whose favor both contestants were angling.

* * *

The Lincoln-Douglas Debates were conducted for the most part in the central area of Illinois, between the latitudes of St. Louis and Rock Island, where political

---

29. John Mather to AL, July 19, 1858, and W. J. Usrey to AL, July 19, 1858, Lincoln Papers. The quotations are from the Usrey letter.

30. *Chicago Times*, July 21, July 30, 1858. The quotation is from the July 30 issue.

31. *Chicago Press and Tribune*, July 22, 1858. On July 1, the *Chicago Democratic Press* combined with the *Tribune* to establish a new paper with elements of both former names in its new title.

32. AL to SAD, July 24, July 29, July 31, 1858, Basler et al., *Collected Works*, 2:522, 528–30, 531; SAD to AL, July 24, July 30, ibid., 528–29, 531–32.

allegiances were most divided and hard to identify. Southern-born or Southern-descended Illinoisans living south of that line would generally vote Democratic and in Douglas's favor; those of Yankee and mid-Atlantic origin who predominated in the North would incline to vote Republican. The farthest out points in the debates were Freeport and Jonesboro, respectively far to the north and south of these boundaries. Otherwise, neither Lincoln nor Douglas devoted much attention during the rest of the campaign, in which each gave dozens of speeches in addition to those during the debates, to areas where little support for them could be expected. "We ought not to waste our ammunition, where we can accomplish nothing," wrote Gustave Koerner to Lincoln.[33] None of the debates were exactly discrete units; questions raised in one might be answered in the next, or not answered at all; some arguments persisted throughout the series; some were advanced, then dropped, then revived later; some questions were merely red herrings.

Some northern congressional districts were quite radical; one, the Ottawa district, sent Owen Lovejoy, an avowed abolitionist, to Congress. But neither Lincoln nor Douglas was after the already converted; they were angling for swing voters, prominently former old-line Whigs, abandoned by their old party, which had collapsed after the Kansas-Nebraska Act. Many of these had been first attracted to the nativist Know-Nothing movement, which by 1858 was fast fading in Illinois. Such voters tended to be anti-abolitionist and racist; indeed the immense antiblack racism of the vast majority of nineteenth-century Americans, in Illinois and elsewhere, has to be taken simply as a given. But at the same time the majority of Lincoln's and Douglas's listeners were doubtless basically antislavery and opposed to the extension of slavery into the territories. Both candidates walked a tightrope in appealing to this constituency. To Douglas, in spite of the *Dred Scott* decision's determination to the contrary, slavery was an issue that could be dealt with only in response to local conditions and priorities in an expanding democracy, a position he famously took at Freeport and reiterated during the debates. And the status of African Americans, free or slave, and for whom Douglas had obvious scorn, he insisted must be determined by the white majority, and by no means in accordance with the doctrines of the Declaration of Independence. To Lincoln slavery was a morally reprehensible institution that must not be allowed to expand outside the states where it already existed; the rights of all Americans, white or black, to life, liberty, and the pursuit of happiness were beyond question and not to be amended by local priorities. Obviously, enslaved African Americans were presently deprived of those fundamental rights, but to Lincoln their eventual attainment of them was a necessary national goal.

---

33. Koerner to AL, July 17, 1858, Lincoln Papers.

However, Lincoln did display a persistent, at least partly politically inspired agnosticism regarding the equality of whites and blacks in other respects, and he made it clear at Charleston that he opposed the granting to Negroes of such civil rights as those to vote, hold political office, or sit on juries. Lincoln publicly and privately labored to distinguish his belief that "the negro is included in the word 'men' used in the Declaration of Independence" from his contention that "it does not follow that social and political equality between whites and blacks, must be incorporated, because slavery must not." "The declaration does not so require," he wrote in a letter containing his clearest statement on the matter.[34]

Each candidate appealed to voter anxieties by undertaking to demonize the other as an impossible extremist and thus not attractive to the moderate constituency that was being courted by both. Witness Lincoln's effort to identify Douglas with a reputed aggressive slave power by accusing him, Presidents Pierce and Buchanan, and Chief Justice Taney of conspiring through the Kansas-Nebraska Act and the *Dred Scott* decision to nationalize the institution of slavery. The conclusion of such a tactic would be a Supreme Court decision allowing slavery into any and all of the states, he asserted. In fact, though Douglas dismissed the charge out of hand, there was indeed a case in New York courts, *Lemmon v. The People*, in which that possibility seemed to be threatened. Lincoln also strove to show that Douglas, in spite of being the architect of popular sovereignty, had worked to deny Kansas voters a referendum on slavery in 1856. Douglas, in several different ways, undertook to stigmatize Lincoln as a candidate too radical on the slavery and race issues for an Illinois electorate. In the Ottawa debate he took Lincoln by surprise by charging that he supported and helped to create some strongly worded quasi-abolitionist resolutions, of which Lincoln in fact knew nothing, and which had been adopted at an early Republican meeting in northern Illinois in 1854. And early in the first four debates, Douglas accused Lincoln and Illinois Republican Senator Lyman Trumbull of conspiring to bring both the old Whig and Democratic parties in Illinois within the ambit of abolitionism. Douglas further attacked the "House Divided" speech as a piece of impossible radicalism, twisting Lincoln's meaning to insist that Lincoln called for a uniformity of state and local institutions, and that the policies he favored would lead to racial amalgamation. In fact, Douglas repeatedly accused Lincoln of favoring "negro equality."

By mutual agreement between Lincoln and Douglas, the organization of the debates was more formal than that which usually characterized such political meetings. Each contestant spoke for an hour and a half, with one of them opening for an hour, the other responding for an hour and a half, and the first speaker then allowed a half-hour rejoinder. As the one challenged, Douglas took four

---

34. AL to James N. Brown, Oct. 18, 1858, in Basler et al., *Collected Works*, 3:327–28.

openings and allowed Lincoln three. It was generally thought that the speaker who opened and closed had a peculiar advantage in his ability both to set the terms of the debate and to respond to his adversary on the spot. Neither candidate spoke from a prepared text; the issues of the debates were so well in mind and both were such practiced campaigners that neither really needed one. There was some repetition of content from one debate to the next, especially by Douglas, and fragments survive of preparatory notes that Lincoln wrote out in advance of at least two of the debates.[35] Both speakers also came armed with documents that they either read during their speeches or had inserted into newspaper versions of the debates.

* * *

The senatorial campaign concluded on November 2 with enough Democrats elected to the Illinois General Assembly to insure Douglas's return to the Senate when the legislature convened in January. Though the actual number of popular votes cast was slightly in Lincoln's favor, the outcome reflected a legislative apportionment that did not reflect population changes in Illinois since 1850. Furthermore, the partisan sentiments of thirteen holdover senators helped to make Douglas's reelection a certainty. Nonetheless, the *Press and Tribune* rightly observed that Lincoln had "created for himself a national reputation that is both envied and deserved," an assessment that was vindicated by invitations for him to speak in Ohio, Kansas, New York, and New England in 1859 and 1860, and by his nomination for the presidency at the Chicago Republican national convention in May 1860.[36] Douglas's victory of course was strictly a local one, and his final political triumph. With Douglas's support of the *Dred Scott* decision in mind, along with his prescription for its circumvention as rendered at Freeport and elsewhere, Lincoln affirmed that "Douglas had the ingenuity to be supported in the late contest both as the best means to break down, and to uphold the slave interest." Prophetically, he wrote that "no ingenuity can keep those antagonistic elements in harmony long. Another explosion will soon come."[37] When that explosion came, when the Democratic Party sundered in 1860, Douglas's 1858 victory over Lincoln was revealed as indeed pyrrhic and short term, and the vic-

---

35. "Fragment: Notes for Speeches" [c. August 21, 1858], "Fragment: Notes for Speeches" [c. Sept. 15, 1858], "Notes for the Debate at Jonesboro, Illinois," September 15, 1858, "Fragment: Notes for Speeches" [Oct. 1, 1858], in Basler et al., *Collected Works*, 2:547–53, 3:97–101, 101, 205.

36. *Chicago Press and Tribune*, Nov. 10, 1858.

37. AL to Henry Asbury, Nov. 19, 1858, in Basler et al., *Collected Works*, 3:339. See also AL to Anson S. Miller, November 19, 1858, AL to Charles H. Ray, Nov. 20, 1858, AL to B. Clarke Lundy, Nov. 26, 1858, ibid., 340, 341, 342.

tory of Lincoln and the antislavery forces behind him was rendered inevitable in the presidential election that followed.

THE TEXT OF THIS EDITION

The text of this edition differs substantially from that of all previous editions. All but one of the many editions of the Lincoln-Douglas debates are based directly or indirectly on the scrapbook of newspaper clippings that Abraham Lincoln prepared shortly after the close of the 1858 campaign. An edition offered in 1993 introduced another text of the debates, also based on the contemporary newspaper accounts, but whereas Lincoln had employed texts clipped from the paper politically friendly to each speaker (the Republican *Chicago Press and Tribune* for his own speeches, the Democratic *Chicago Times* for Douglas), this edition reversed the process and employed the accounts printed by the opposition paper.[38] Thus all previous editions of the debates confine themselves to a one set of partisan newspaper texts or another. Both speakers and reporters readily acknowledged that the resulting newspaper accounts were imperfect, due not only to partisanship but to the adverse conditions that prevailed for hearing and taking down and rapidly transcribing what was said. The new text presented in this edition is a critical or fusion text, reaching across the political aisle and drawing on both papers' accounts of a given speech for evidence of what was actually said. The aim is to provide a fuller and more accurate version of the words and arguments put forward in the debates.

The primary text in this edition, as in Lincoln's scrapbook, is that printed by the Chicago newspaper politically friendly to the speaker. At each point where the wording of the primary text has been altered, the mark ° appears in the text and an explanatory note can be found in the back of the book by in the section titled "Textual Annotation." Readers interested in the rationale for a critical approach to the text and the editorial procedures employed in this edition may consult the "Textual Introduction."

---

38. Harold Holzer, ed., *The Lincoln-Douglas Debates: The First Complete, Unexpurgated Text* (New York: Harper-Collins, 1993). This edition is valuable for making available texts of the debates that were reported at the time and that have not previously been reprinted. While giving priority to texts of the speeches that are demonstrably less accurate and complete, this edition has the virtue of being interlaced with a generous sampling of alternate readings from the opposing paper.

TEXTUAL INTRODUCTION

To study Abraham Lincoln then, we must examine his words,
and not only the words that he wrote but also those that
he uttered, insofar as they are known.

—Don E. Fehrenbacher, *Lincoln in Text and Context*

FROM PLATFORM TO PRINT

After his senatorial campaign against Stephen A. Douglas in 1858, Abraham Lincoln compiled a scrapbook of the principal speeches of the contest, the highlight of which was the series of seven "joint debates." For his own speeches, he included the texts printed in the *Chicago Press and Tribune;* for Douglas's speeches, the texts published in the *Chicago Times.*[1] "This," he explained to a prospective publisher, "would represent each of us, as reported by his own friends, and thus be mutual, and fair."[2] The first few proposals to publish the contents of his scrapbook came to naught, but Lincoln's wish to see them in print eventually bore fruit. The printing of the speeches was finally undertaken by the Ohio Republican Party, and the resulting volume, printed directly from his scrapbook, appeared just in time for the Republican presidential nominating convention in May 1860. This text was the basis of all subsequent editions of Lincoln-Douglas debates for more than ninety years, until it was superseded by that published in the *Collected Works of Abraham Lincoln* in 1953. By this time, Lincoln's debates scrapbook, which had been lost sight of, had reappeared, and the editors of the *Collected Works* performed their own careful rendition, which has since become the standard text. The upshot of this brief publishing history of the debates is that Lincoln's

---

1. This general rule needs to be qualified, for AL actually used texts for some of the non-debate speeches from other newspapers. For the seven joint debates, he used the *Press and Tribune* for all but one (Charleston) of his own speeches.

2. AL to William A. Ross, Mar. 26, 1859, Roy P. Basler et al., eds., *The Collected Works of Abraham Lincoln* (New Brunswick: Rutgers University Press, 1953), 3:373; quoted in David C. Mearns, ed., "Introduction," *The Illinois Political Campaign of 1858: A Facsimile of the Printer's Copy of His Debates with Stephen A. Douglas as Edited and Prepared for the Press by Abraham Lincoln* (Washington, D.C.: Library of Congress, n.d.), 6 (hereinafter cited as Debates Scrapbook).

scrapbook has been the ultimate source for all but one of the published texts of these famous debates.[3]

As the first editor of the debates, Lincoln did more than merely cut out clippings of the speeches and paste them into his scrapbook. This is made clear in the first debate at Ottawa, where he inserted a sizeable clipping from an earlier speech, accompanied by a handwritten explanatory note: "This extract from Mr. Lincoln's Peoria Speech of 1854, was read by him in the Ottawa debate, but was not reported fully or accurately, in either the *Times* or *Press and Tribune*. It is inserted now as necessary to a complete report of the debate."[4] In so doing, he augmented the *Press and Tribune*'s printed account by nearly five hundred words. And he made other changes in his own speeches. In sending his scrapbook to Ohio to be set in type, he told the committee in charge of publication, "It would be an unwarrantable liberty for us to change a word or a letter of [Douglas's speeches], and the changes I have made in mine, you perceive, are verbal only, and very few in number."[5]

The circumstance of being the editor as well as one of the speakers made Lincoln keenly aware of the need to keep his changes to a minimum, lest he be perceived as giving himself an unfair advantage. Predictably, this is what Douglas charged as soon as he saw the printed book. "I feel it my duty to protest against the unfairness of this publication," he wrote the publishers, Follett, Foster & Company of Columbus, Ohio. "Upon the slight examination of your publication which I have been able to make, I find that Mr. Lincoln's speeches have been revised, corrected and improved since their publication in the newspapers of Illinois."[6] The unfairness of Lincoln's editing was not the only issue, for Douglas's letter shows that he, like his opponent, was very much aware of the problematic character of the newspaper texts. "The original reports as published in the *Chicago Times,* although intended to be fair and just, were necessarily imperfect, and in some respects erroneous. The speeches were all delivered in the open air to immense crowds of people, and in some instances in stormy and boisterous weather, when it was impossible for the reporters to hear distinctly and report literally."[7] Here, it should be noted, he was referring to the shortcomings of the reports of his own speeches by his own reporter.

---

3. The exception is Harold Holzer, ed., *The Lincoln-Douglas Debates: The First Complete, Unexpurgated Text* (New York: Harper-Collins, 1993). This edition utilizes the texts of the speeches printed in the *opposing,* or unfriendly, newspaper.

4. Debates Scrapbook, 97.

5. AL to George M. Parsons and Others, Dec. 19, 1859, in Basler et al., *Collected Works,* 3:510; quoted in Debates Scrapbook, 9.

6. SAD to Follett, Foster & Co., June 9, 1860, quoted in Debates Scrapbook, 17.

7. Ibid.

The principals in the debates were not the only ones aware of the difficulties that stood in the way of producing accurate reports. Horace White, one of the reporters for Lincoln's paper, the *Press and Tribune*, described the unfavorable conditions under which the reporters worked: "The debates were all held in the open air, on rude platforms hastily put together, shaky, and overcrowded with people. The reporters' tables were liable to be jostled and their manuscript agitated by the wind. Some gaps were certain to occur in the reporters' notes and these, when occurring in Mr. Douglas's speeches, would certainly be straightened out by his own reporters, who would feel no such responsibility for the rough places in Mr. Lincoln's."[8]

White's remark touches on another difficulty with the texts of the debates, namely, the fidelity of the reporting. The shorthand reporters who provided copy on the speeches for the *Times,* James Sheridan and Henry Binmore, were employed by Douglas himself, something that admittedly gave Lincoln pause. He told a prospective publisher:

> Judge Douglas would have the right to correct typographical errors in his, if he desired; but I think the necessity, in his case, would be less than in mine; because he had two hired reporters travelling with him, and probably revised their manuscripts before they went to press; while I had no reporter of my own, but depended on a very excellent one sent by the Press & Tribune; but who never wanted to show me his notes or manuscripts; so that the first I saw of my speeches, after delivering them, was in the Press & Tribune precisely as they now stand.[9]

The *Press and Tribune* reporter Lincoln referred to was not Horace White, who did not write shorthand, but rather Robert R. Hitt, a talented young man who had acquired an excellent reputation as a court reporter. Because he kept a journal at the time and would later testify about the reporting of the debates, we know that Hitt regarded both of Douglas's reporters as very capable. James Sheridan was an experienced reporter for the *Philadelphia Press* and had been sent out to Illinois by his editor, John Forney, expressly to bolster Sen. Douglas's efforts to win reelection. Henry Binmore, who actively sought a position on the senator's staff, had frequently worked with Hitt, who admired his stenographic abilities but looked askance at his slovenly dress, egotistical behavior, and unconventional lifestyle. Lincoln's statement quoted above shows that he clearly had

---

8. William H. Herndon and Jesse W. Weik, *Herndon's Lincoln,* ed. Douglas L. Wilson and Rodney O. Davis (Urbana: University of Illinois Press, 2006 [1889]), 388.

9. AL to William A. Ross, Mar. 26, 1859, in Basler et al., *Collected Works,* 3:373; quoted in Debates Scrapbook, 7.

misgivings about Douglas's reporters, especially Binmore, who was responsible for taking Lincoln's own speeches for the *Times*. Lincoln's supporters protested loudly that the *Times* reporting mangled Lincoln's speeches, and Lincoln himself referred in the course of the debates to the issue of whether he had been "fairly reported." It is probably not coincidental that he once, in a rare display of anger, referred to Binmore from the platform as Douglas's "hireling."[10]

Nonetheless, Horace White later discounted the charge, made so heatedly at the time, that the *Chicago Times* reports of Lincoln's speeches "were purposely mutilated in order to give his competitor a more scholarly appearance before the public," insisting instead that Douglas's reporters simply "took more pains with Mr. Douglas's speeches than with those of his opponent. That was their business. It was what they were paid for, and what they were expected to do."[11] While others were not convinced that the serious deficiencies that plagued these reports had occurred so innocently, there is little disagreement that reports of Lincoln's speeches in the *Chicago Times* were often noticeably deficient. An indirect implication of White's testimony, of course, is that his own paper's reports of Douglas's speeches were also, for the same reasons, less than sterling.

But the accuracy of the shorthand reporting was not the only consideration. The journalism of that age was notoriously partisan, and newspaper reports were likely to be heavily biased, with little pretense to objectivity. Even if the reporters turned in reasonably accurate transcriptions of what was said by the speakers, it was widely assumed that their highly partisan editors would not hesitate to doctor the copy by striking things out, putting things in, and making other alterations. In fact, careful examination of the printed reports of the debates reveals numerous instances of what looks like deliberate distortion, although it is usually impossible to specify whether it originated with the reporters in the field, during the transcription process, or at the editorial desk. Lincoln, as we have seen, suspected that, in the case of the *Times* reports, there might have been another meddling intermediary.

What all of this indicates is that the primary sources for understanding what transpired in these celebrated debates—the purportedly verbatim accounts published by the two Chicago newspapers—are all, in some degree, deficient, being neither accurate nor complete nor free from distortion. And yet, for all their shortcomings, these newspaper accounts are obviously very important historical documents. They are, and will continue to be, the indispensable primary sources for determining what was said in the debates. For all their faults, they are the accounts that were read at the time by tens of thousands of readers, both in Illinois

---

10. For "hireling," see the Quincy debate, p. 249.

11. Herndon and Weik, *Herndon's Lincoln*, 388.

and across the nation. Published in book form in 1860 with very little alteration, Lincoln's selections from those same accounts have constituted the reading text for the debates for 150 years. Nonetheless, we must come to grips with the fact that close comparison confirms that they are, as the speakers themselves testified, demonstrably inaccurate and incomplete.

Lincoln, as we have seen, attempted in his scrapbook to improve upon these newspaper accounts. First, he selected as the texts for each speaker those reported by his "friends." He also included supplementary material that he said had been left out of those newspaper reports. And, finally, he made some handwritten alterations in the texts of his own speeches, which he described as "verbal only, and very few in number." In one sense, Lincoln understated the magnitude of these changes, for a count of those made in the debates proper reveals no fewer than thirty-three alterations. But this number is deceptive, for a large proportion of Lincoln's alterations were taken from the corresponding passage in the "unfriendly" paper, the *Chicago Times*.[12] In other words, Lincoln not only consulted the opposition paper but took advantage of the fact that, in some instances, it reported his own speeches more accurately, or more to his liking, than his own. And it should be added that Lincoln's relatively modest venture in this regard by no means exhausted the possibilities.

Some of the most important features of the editorial approach to the text in the present edition are extensions of Lincoln's practice. All are aimed at presenting as faithfully as possible, and in a readable format, what was uttered by the speakers on the platform as part of the debates. Unexceptional as this may sound, such an approach is in distinct contrast to all other editorial treatments of the debates. Whereas these editions have aimed at a text that was faithful to the reports of one newspaper or the other, this edition aims at a text that is faithful to the utterances of the speakers, regardless of source. The first is a documentary, the latter, a critical approach. Neither is necessarily superior to the other, and both have legitimate aims and uses.[13]

The editors have opted for a critical approach here mainly because what they wish to recapture and present are not so much the reports themselves but, as nearly as possible, the words and arguments of the speakers. These were largely (though not exclusively) extemporaneous utterances, which were essentially sounds, variously recorded by the stenographers and later transcribed into words, phrases,

---

12. Setting aside, for the moment, changes that involve adding material (1), correcting typographical errors therein (2), and correcting other strictly typographical errors (2), Lincoln made twenty-eight substantive changes to the texts of his speeches. Twenty of these, or 71 percent, are either the same as or are confirmed by the opposition text.

13. It should be noted that some *documentary* editions are also *critical* in that they take note of textual variants.

and sentences. A critical approach is thus appropriate because it offers a means of dealing with the discrepancies and inconsistencies in the reporting, which constitutes the pool of evidence for what was said.

CONFRONTING THE IMPERFECTIONS

In the speech that launched the 1858 senatorial campaign and became a principal source of comment and contention in the debates that followed, the famous "House Divided" speech, Abraham Lincoln began by saying "If we could first know *where* we are, and *whither* we are tending, we could then better judge *what* to do, and *how* to do it." [14] Good advice for dealing with almost any problem, Lincoln's remark aptly applies to the task of editing the debates, for it is important at the outset to have a general sense of the character of the texts to be considered before taking up the editorial questions of what needs to be done and how to do it.

It is nearly impossible to determine with any precision what was said on the platform so as to gauge the relative accuracy of the two newspaper reports. As Lincoln's example shows, his own paper let him down badly in neglecting to report in full the section he said he read from his Peoria speech. But this incident nonetheless offers a rare means of comparison, by means of which one can get a sense of how closely, at least in this instance, the "verbatim" account of the friendly *Press and Tribune* followed Lincoln's utterance. A portion of the text of the clipping that Lincoln says he read is on the left; the *Press and Tribune's* report of this passage is on the right.

When southern people tell us they are no more responsible for the origin of slavery, than we; I acknowledge the fact.	When Southern people tell us they are no more responsible for slavery than we are, I acknowledge the fact.
When it is said that the institution exists, and that it is very difficult to get rid of it, in any satisfactory way, I can understand and appreciate the saying.	When they say that it is an existing institution, and there is no way to get rid of it,
I surely will not blame them for not doing what I should not know how to do myself.	I assure them I shall not blame them for not knowing what to do.

---

14. "'A House Divided': Speech at Springfield, Illinois," June 16, 1858, in Basler et al., *Collected Works,* 2:461. Emphasis in the original.

If all earthly power were given me, I should not know what to do, as to the existing institution.	If all earthly power were given me, I would not know what to do with it.
My first impulse would be to free all the slaves, and send them to Liberia,— to their own native land.	My first impulse would be to free them all, and send them to Liberia, their own native land,
But a moment's reflection would convince me, that whatever of high hope, (as I think there is) there may be in this, in the long run, its sudden execution is impossible.	but a moment's reflection would convince me that whatever of high hope there might be in this, its execution would be impossible.

The *Press and Tribune's* report of this 362–word passage totals 315 words, or 87 percent. As one can see from this excerpt, the loss is almost entirely slippage— dropping phrases, combining sentences, and generally condensing the wordage. There is no substantial loss of meaning, but there is, of course, a diminution of Lincoln's voice, his own distinctive way of putting things. For example, there is the loss of some careful qualifications that are the trademark of Lincoln's discourse, such as when he says of the institution of slavery that it is "very difficult to get rid of it, in any satisfactory way." Here his deliberate, lawyer-like qualification, which is part and parcel of his moderate political stance, gets left out. Or when he says that he will not blame the Southern people for not doing "what I should not know how to do myself," this does not quite get through, the report saying simply "I shall not blame them for not knowing what to do." The substance here—that Lincoln does not himself know how to deal with the problem—is nonetheless accurately reflected in the passage as a whole.

The pattern seems reasonably clear: the reporter starts out taking Lincoln's utterances just about word for word but cannot quite keep it up, though he gets most of the key phrases. When the speaker pauses to begin a new sentence, the reporter tends to catch up and again reports pretty accurately, until he has to begin condensing. Of course, we are here gauging the performance of a very able reporter, Robert Hitt, diligently trying to make an accurate report of the speech of his own candidate. Judging by comparison with the reports of Douglas's own stenographer, James Sheridan, Hitt's reports of the speeches of Douglas are usually quite adequate, but more subject to paraphrase and condensation than Sheridan's.

The coverage of Lincoln's remarks by the opposition paper, the *Times,* is a different matter. Here the responsibility fell to Henry Binmore, and his performance in the first debate, especially his coverage of Lincoln's reading from his

Peoria speech, while not actually typical, is nonetheless indicative. At the point in the *Times* account where Lincoln began reading, there is a bracketed note:

> [Mr. L here read, for seven minutes, from a speech delivered by him at Peoria, October, 1854—the intention of which was to show that he did not entertain the idea of the social equality of the negro, &c.]

Following this is a passage in which phrases and approximations from the Peoria passage are mixed in with fragments of what Lincoln is reported in the *Press and Tribune* as saying after he finished reading.[15] After two paragraphs of this largely incoherent mixture comes a paragraph that purports to be quoting from Lincoln's reading of the Peoria passage. It is given here (in the left-hand column) side-by-side with the comparable parts of Lincoln's reading text as given in his debates scrapbook.

"Again, when they remind us," I am reading still, "that they are no more responsible for the existence of slavery than we are, I acknowledge their truth; but all this, to my judgment, furnishes no more excuse for permitting slavery to go into our own free territory, than it would for reviving the African slave trade by law. The law which forbid the bringing of slaves from Africa, and that which has so long forbid the taking of slaves to Nebraska, can hardly be distinguished on any moral principle. I deny that they can be distinguished at all. The repeal of the former could find as many excuses as that of the latter."

When southern people tell us they are no more responsible for the origin of slavery, than we, I acknowledge the fact.

But all this; to my judgment, furnishes no more excuse for permitting slavery to go into our own free territory, than it would for reviving the African slave trade by law. The law which forbids the bringing of slaves *from* Africa; and that which has so long forbid the taking them *to* Nebraska, can hardly be distinguished on any moral principle; and the repeal of the former could find quite as plausible excuses as that of the latter.

The *Times* account here first fused two of Lincoln's sentences nearly four hundred words apart ("When southern people . . ." "When they remind . . .") and then coupled this amalgamation to the final paragraph read to the crowd. While it is difficult to assign responsibility for the shortcomings of this report of what we can be sure Lincoln said, it is probably significant that Binmore's partner, James

---

15. AL put his stamp of approval on this passage by clipping it and including it in a scrapbook he made up for James N. Brown, dated Oct. 18, 1858, to lay out his true position on "negro equality." See the facsimile of the scrapbook, *Abraham Lincoln His Book: A Facsimile Reproduction of the Original*, ed. J. McCan Davis (New York: McClure, 1903), item no. 6; Basler et al., *Collected Works*, 3:326–27.

Sheridan, is reported to have jokingly acknowledged to Hitt what was widely claimed at the time by Republican partisans—that Binmore "mutilated" Lincoln's speeches.[16] Nonetheless, the relative accuracy with which the final paragraph is reported is perhaps revealing. To be sure, it reports an extraneous sentence that does not appear in Lincoln's original—"I deny that they can be distinguished at all"—but we cannot be entirely sure that Lincoln did not make such an interjection at Ottawa. Whatever factors contributed to notable deficiencies that often characterize the *Chicago Times*'s account of Lincoln's speeches, the stenographic ability of the reporter in the field was probably not one of them.

In general, the quality of the reporting, judged by the text of the speaker's remarks that appeared in his own paper, was probably not too different from that observed in the *Press and Tribune*'s transcription of the passage from Lincoln's Peoria speech—not perfect, but reasonably faithful to the language and meaning. But as both speakers and reporters were aware, there were also "rough places" imposed by the conditions under which the debates took place, and definite limits to the fidelity with which such speeches could be taken down in shorthand, hurriedly transcribed, and rushed into print. To this difficulty, one must add, not surprisingly, the bias of the newspaper and reporting team. Especially when the speaker appears to be making effective points and gaining ground with his audience, the accounts in both opposing papers tend to report less fully and show signs of deliberately taking the sting out of the opponent's rhetoric. To find and rectify as many of the significant deficiencies as possible constitutes for this edition the principal goal of the editorial effort.

A passage from Lincoln's speech in the Ottawa debate perhaps illustrates the need for and operation of a critical text. Here it is clear that the of account of the *Press and Tribune*, the primary text, gets the chronology wrong by having Lincoln say that he said something at Springfield and that Douglas then answered him at Springfield; as Douglas spoke first at Springfield, this cannot be right. But this, as we shall see, is only the beginning of the difficulties.

> As an illustration, the next time I met him, which was at Springfield, I used this expression, that I claimed no right under the Constitution, nor had I any inclination, to enter into the Slave States and interfere with the institutions of slavery. He says upon that: Lincoln will not enter into the Slave States, but will go to the banks of the Ohio, on this side, and shoot over! [Laughter.] He runs on, step by step, in the horse-chestnut plan of argument, until in the Springfield speech, he says, "Unless he shall be successful in firing his batteries until he shall have extinguished slavery in all the States, the Union shall be dissolved."

---

16. Reported without direct attribution many years later by Robert Hitt. See Walter B. Stevens, *A Reporter's Lincoln,* ed. Michael Burlingame (Lincoln: University of Nebraska Press, 1994), 78.

What Lincoln had said about claiming "no right," he had said not at Springfield but at Chicago, and what Douglas first said in reply came at Bloomington. Turning to the *Times,* we see that whereas the *Press and Tribune*'s quotation of Lincoln's remark is approximate, the *Times'* is almost letter perfect, and that it also gives the correct location of Douglas's first response. The last part of the passage, which deals with Douglas's second response, is a different story. Here it is the *Times* giving the wrong location (Clinton) and the *Press and Tribune* getting it right. Moreover, the *Times* gives only an abbreviated version of Douglas's second response, while the *Press and Tribune* renders it with considerable fidelity. Here is the *Times* version:

> As an illustration, I had incidentally said that I claimed "no right, and there ought to be no inclination in the people of the free States, to enter into the slave States and interfere with the question of slavery at all." The Judge thereupon, at Bloomington, where I heard him make a speech, said that I had said that I would not go into the slave States, but that I said I will go on the bank of the Ohio and shoot over among them. Well, he runs on step by step in the race, until he gets on at Clinton to using this form of speech, and says that "unless he shall be successful in firing his batteries, the Union cannot stand."

By using the sound parts of each account and correcting the final quotation, we can come much closer to Lincoln's remarks at Ottawa (material from *Times* shown by underlining):

> As an illustration, <u>I had incidentally said,</u> I used this expression, that I claimed "no right, <u>and there ought to be no inclination in the people of the free States, to enter into the slave States and interfere with the question of slavery at all."</u> <u>The Judge thereupon, at Bloomington, where I heard him make a speech, said that I had said that I would not go</u> into the Slave States, but will go to the banks of the Ohio, on this side, and shoot over! [Laughter.] He runs on, step by step, in the horse-chestnut plan of argument, until in the Springfield speech, he says, "unless he shall play his batteries successfully, so as to abolish slavery in every one of the states, that the Union shall be dissolved."

In summary: the primary text, *Press and Tribune,* gets the chronology wrong; in so doing, it has Lincoln saying in Springfield what he had actually said in Chicago; it gives an approximation of his quotation from his own speech; it loses sight of the location (Bloomington) of Douglas's first response. The *Times,* on the other hand, gets all these things right. The *Times* then follows with a less-than-adequate account of Douglas's second response, which it mistakenly locates at Clinton, while the *Press and Tribune* accurately reports what he said and where he said it (Springfield). Only a critical process and a fusion text can put these self-correcting pieces back together.

Because a critical approach is necessarily dependent on judgments rather than certainties, it seems important to follow Lincoln's example in exercising a certain degree of restraint. For this reason, the editors have attempted to confine alteration of the primary text mainly to words that are reported in the opposing paper and to matters that, in some degree, affect meaning. This is, admittedly, not a perfect process and therefore cannot yield a perfect result. What it can provide is some measure of correction and supplementation for speeches that were, in Lincoln's words, "not reported fully or accurately."

EDITORIAL METHOD

To select elements from opposing newspaper accounts and combine them into a fusion text calls for a process that operates by rules rather than whim. What follows is an attempt to describe and illustrate the rules that governed the fashioning of the text of this edition.

1. The primary text for each speech, as in Lincoln's scrapbook, is that appearing in the speaker's newspaper—*Chicago Times* for Douglas and *Chicago Press and Tribune* for Lincoln.

It has been argued by at least one serious editor that it is more appropriate to adopt the opposing paper's text as primary on the theory that it is likely to have been more straightforward and less subject to editorial enhancement.[17] Unfortunately, there is little or no concrete evidence to support such a theory, and it runs into immediate difficulty in accounting for the widely divergent reports of some of Lincoln's speeches. Douglas had little to complain of in the Republican paper's accounts of his speeches, and was said to have complimented the reporter of the opposition paper, Robert Hitt, on his reporting.[18] But as has been noted, Lincoln's supporters cried "foul" more than once at the way their champion's arguments were twisted in the *Chicago Times'* accounts and his eloquence, so ringingly apparent in the *Press and Tribune,* was made to disappear.[19] The theory that these protested accounts are actually the more reliable would seem to require a highly disputable assumption—that Lincoln's well-known dexterity with words and arguments often deserted him on the platform but, through the intervention

17. See Holzer, *Lincoln-Douglas Debates.* As noted previously, the Holzer edition is liberally supplemented with alternative readings from the opposing paper.

18. See Charles S. West, "The Lincoln-Douglas Debates," *The Phonographic Magazine,* Nov. 15 and Dec. 1, 1896, 361.

19. See accusatory articles in the *Chicago Press and Tribune* for Aug. 24, 26, Oct. 11 (two articles), Oct. 13, 16, 19, 1858; in the *Chicago Times* for Aug. 25 (two articles), Aug. 27, Sept. 26, Oct. 12 (two articles), Oct. 16, 21, 1858.

of an equally gifted editor who could perform at lightning speed, was regularly restored in the pages of the *Press and Tribune*.

This is not to deny that editorial intervention occurred; indeed, comparative study of the newspaper texts suggests that intervention from some quarter must have occurred in many instances. And in some cases problems apparently arose from a lack of editorial intervention. Robert Hitt, in later years, called attention to the boast of the *Times's* editor, James Sheahan, who said of the Ottawa debate that "Lincoln's speech was printed verbatim, just as it came from the reporter." Hitt pointed to a single sentence from the *Times* coverage:

> I will remind him also of a piece of Illinois of the time, when the respected party to which the Judge belongs was displeased with a decision of the Supreme Court of Illinois, because they had decided that the governor could not remove a Secretary of State, and he will not deny that he went in for overslaughing that Court, by appointing five new judges, and it ended in his getting his name of Judge in that very way, thus breaking down the Supreme Court, and when he tells me about how a man who shall be appointed on such a principle, by being questioned, I say Judge, you know you have tried it, and when he seeks that the court will be prostituted below contempt.

Identifying this as "an unrevised shorthand report," Hitt says that "the newspaper that would instruct its telegraph editor and proofreader to follow" such a report "with that kind of fidelity in this day and generation [1892] would hurt itself more than the orator it aimed to disgrace."[20]

There are many such run-on sentences in the printed reports, and Hitt's identification of them as raw transcriptions, without benefit of editorial refinement, sheds considerable light on their status and what they represent. It would seem to further confirm what Horace White is quoted as saying above about less time being taken with the opponent's speeches. But whether the reverse was true, that speeches were substantially beefed up by reporters or editors after the fact, is another question. Time was always of the essence in the race to get the speeches transcribed, set up in type, and printed. And while there was probably time for an editor, in reading copy, to strike things out and make small changes, it seems far less likely that there was much time for serious revision or reconstruction. Word count, which shows that opposition accounts averaged 92 percent of those of the speaker's paper, tends to support White's claim.

---

20. Stevens, *A Reporter's Lincoln*, 73.

2. The authority of the primary text is understood as applying only to its words and does not extend to paragraphing, parenthesizing, or to such textual "accidentals" as spelling, punctuation, capitalization, hyphenation, or italicization.

The speakers were not responsible for paragraphing or the lack thereof in the newspaper accounts, which is why long stretches of the debates are printed with scarcely any paragraphing. In this edition, the paragraphing for all speeches is established editorially on the basis of content.

Punctuation and parentheses in the newspaper text judged to be misleading or inappropriate are routinely modified.

Because of a similar lack of authority and inconsistency—and because the principal aim here is to recapture the words, not their orthography—spelling, capitalization, and hyphenation are regularized.

Typographical errors are silently corrected, as are incidental matters of agreement, such as singular and plural, noun and verb.

Italicization in the newspaper accounts, where judged to be an indication of the speaker's emphasis, is retained.[21]

Quotation marks judged to have been used for the same purpose are also retained, but quotation marks misapplied to material not actually quoted are not included.

Material incorporated into the primary text from the opposing paper is treated in the same way.

EXAMPLE:

At Charleston, the *Press and Tribune* account of Lincoln's argument about Douglas's position since the passage of the Kansas-Nebraska bill in 1854 is obscured by the inadequacies of punctuation:

> He promised that it would finish it all up immediately, and he has never made a speech since until he got into a quarrel with the President, about the Lecompton Constitution, in which he has not declared that we are *just at the end* of the slavery agitation.

Emended version:

> He promised that it would finish it all up immediately, and he has never made a speech since—until he got into a quarrel with the President about the Lecomp-

---

21. At least one of the reporters (Horace White) testified that he added such emphasis to the copy for this purpose, but there is no guarantee that editors who were not present might have added italicization as well.

ton Constitution—in which he has not declared that we are *just at the end* of the slavery agitation.

3. Where there is reason to believe that the primary text lacks something of significance, a remedy, wherever possible, is applied.

Whenever it seems likely that something of significance uttered by the speaker is lacking from the primary account, the omitted material, where known, is included in the text. It is important to note that the key here is *significance,* for no attempt has been made to consider, much less include, the multitude of variants that do not affect meaning.

In almost every case, evidence of omitted material comes from the text of the opposing newspaper. The editorial question then becomes whether to include the material found in the opposing text that is lacking in the primary. The principal test governing the decision of whether or not to include is this: given the tendency in these situations of the reporters to conserve effort and editors to conserve space, is it likely that the opposing paper had a selfish reason to include the material in question?

EXAMPLES:

a. Here is Douglas at Ottawa, first as reported by his own paper, then by the opposition.

Times:

> While the Whig and Democratic parties differed in regard to a bank, the tariff, distribution, the specie circular and the sub treasury, they agreed on the great slavery question which now agitates the Union.

Press and Tribune (underlining added):

> While the Whig and the Democratic parties differed in regard to a Bank, <u>and in regard to</u> a Tariff, <u>and in regard to</u> Distribution, <u>and in regard to</u> the Species Circular, and <u>in regard to</u> the Sub-Treasury, they agreed on the great question that now agitates the Union, known as the Slavery question.

The main difference here is the repetitive material, which is certainly common to oral presentation. If we ask which is more likely to have been Douglas's mode of reiteration, the opposing paper's repetition of "in regard to" may well appear more likely, inasmuch as the *Tribune's* reporter would have no reason to add this verbiage, while the copy editors at the *Times* could have saved space by dispensing with it. But if we confine changes to those that bear on meaning, these phrases do not qualify, and thus they are not included in the present edition.

b. At Alton, Lincoln sought to use some words and ideas of the great Whig leader, Henry Clay, to confirm his own position with respect to the Declaration of Independence. After reading from one of Clay's letters, Lincoln is reported by his own paper and the *Times* in approximately the same way, except for the additional phrases in the *Times* shown here by underlining:

> The principle upon which I have insisted <u>from the Declaration of Independence, as applicable to this discussion and</u> this canvass, is in relation to laying the foundations of new societies. I have never sought to apply these principles to the old states <u>where slavery exists</u> for the purpose of abolishing slavery in those states. It is nothing but a miserable perversion of what I <u>have</u> said, to assume that I have <u>brought forth the Declaration of Independence to ask that</u> Missouri, or any other slave state, shall emancipate her slaves.

While it is difficult to say why Lincoln's paper would exclude such germane phrases, it is equally difficult to imagine that the *Times* would take the time and trouble to make them up. Because this material definitely affects meaning and does not seem to reflect bias on the part of the opposition, it is accepted and merged into the primary text.

c. Abbreviated reporting or condensation is not confined in the newspaper accounts to the opposition paper. Here is what seems to be a clear example in Lincoln's paper's reporting of his own speech at Alton.

Press and Tribune:

> I have expressed that as my wish.

Times:

> I have expressed that as my wish, and I have no disposition to shrink from it, but I have a disposition to be not misrepresented about it. I have a disposition to not have it believed by any honest man that I desire to go to war with Missouri. Not at all!

If one were to hazard a reason why Lincoln's paper would leave this much out of a speech by its own candidate, the answer might have something to do with the difference between Lincoln's live audience at Alton, which contained a substantial representation of Missourians, and the reading audience of the *Press and Tribune,* which did not. Whatever the reason, substantive material appearing in the opposition paper, as in this example, has been merged with the primary text.

d. In his own paper, Lincoln found this sentence in his Freeport opening speech:

> I then distinctly intimated to him that I would answer the rest of his inter-rogatories.

In his scrapbook, he added to this sentence: "on condition only that he should agree to answer as many for me." That he did not do it from memory or make it up can be seen by consulting the corresponding sentence in the *Times:*

> I then distinctly intimated to him that I would answer the other of his inter-rogatories upon the terms that he would answer as many for me.

As already noted, a large proportion of Lincoln's handwritten changes in his scrap-book were taken, like this one, from the opposing newspaper account, though not all were, and a few appear to have been after-the-fact revisions. Because the latter are not able to be confirmed, they are noted but not adopted in the text of this edition.

4. Where there is reason to believe that the primary text is not accurate as to what was actually said, a remedy, wherever possible, is applied.

As with material that appears to have been omitted, inaccuracies are also usually corrected from the opposing paper.

EXAMPLES:

a. When obvious gaps or other problems with continuity appear in the primary text, a surprising number of solutions are found simply by consulting the op-position text. Here a glitch in the *Times* text of Douglas's opening speech at Al-ton is easily remedied by supplementation from the opposing paper (shown by underlining).

> I had as much right to judge for myself how I should vote as he had <u>as to</u> how he should recommend.

b. Lincoln's own paper, the *Press and Tribune,* reports him as saying:

> Let us understand this. I am here to prove that we are right and they are wrong.

The *Times* has:

> Now, let us understand here that I have not been trying to prove that we are right and he wrong.

The context, including Lincoln's tone and noncontentious mode of approach, indicates that the *Times* has it right, and the *Press and Tribune* has slipped up. This, incidentally, is confirmed by Lincoln's scrapbook, where he struck out "here" and substituted "not just here, trying."

c. As might be expected, there are a number of aural errors in the debates reporting, instances where the reporter has misheard his own speaker. For example, at Alton, the *Times* reports Douglas as saying (underlining added):

> Mr. Lincoln <u>makes</u> out that line of policy, and appeals to the moral sense <u>of</u> justice and to the Christian feeling of the community to sustain him.

While this is intelligible, it does not look or feel quite right, and these misgivings are confirmed by the text of the opposition paper, which has:

> This is the line of policy that he marks out, and appeals to the moral sense and the justice and the Christian feeling of the North to sustain him.

From this we see that the *Times* text will be more accurate if it is emended, as it is in this edition to read (underlining added):

> Mr. Lincoln <u>marks</u> out that line of policy, and appeals to the moral sense <u>and</u> justice and to the Christian feeling of the community to sustain him.

5. In cases where the speakers read from printed material, the exact or likeliest source text, where known, is substituted for the reported text.

Both speakers in the debates frequently read printed matter from the platform. Very often the reporters recorded what was read stenographically, which is almost never perfectly verbatim, nor does it retain the punctuating, paragraphing, and so forth, of the original. For this reason, texts read aloud from the platform, where either the exact or likeliest source is known, are given as they appear in the printed original. The sources substituted for the newspaper texts are cited in the notes.

This aspect of the reporting can be quite surprising. When the speaker says he is reading from a certain text, one's expectation would be that his own paper, having immediate access to the speaker's copy, would report the printed text, while the opposing paper would more likely report the reading stenographically. But this is not always the case. In the Quincy debate, for example, Lincoln reads from his own remarks at Ottawa, which the opposing paper reports quite accurately from a printed copy while his own paper gives an imperfect stenographic report.

Where the speakers are reading from their own remarks or those of their opponent, it is sometimes difficult to determine which account they are reading from. For example, in the Galesburg debate, Douglas read some remarks Lincoln had made in the previous debate at Charleston. Did he read from the account of his own paper or Lincoln's? The same question arises in the next debate at Quincy, where Lincoln, in answer, read what Douglas had read from his Charleston speech at Galesburg. This causes one to consider how Lincoln must have felt when he came to construct his scrapbook and discovered that he was committed, by his own scheme, to using somewhat inaccurate versions of things he had read, when the opposing paper had printed nearly letter-perfect versions of the same passage in its pages.[22]

Where no source for material read from the platform has been located, the primary text is followed.

6. Printed matter that is referred to by the speakers but not read aloud from the platform is not included in the text of the speeches proper, but appears in the notes.

Both speakers refer to printed matter that was not actually read from the platform but nonetheless appeared in one or more of the newspapers as though it had been. In such cases, the text of the matter referred to but not read appears in this edition not in the speech proper, but in the notes.

EXAMPLE:

In Douglas's opening speech at Ottawa, he said of some Republican resolutions, "I now hold them in my hands and will read a part of them, and cause the others to be printed." He then read only one of three, the one numbered "2," of which he said: "Here is the most important and material resolution of this Abolition platform." The *Times* printed all three resolutions, not indicating which was the "most important and most material one," whereas the *Tribune* printed only "2," apparently never having been furnished the first and third resolutions. This is an example of one text being heard and another being offered to the readers. In this case, readers of the *Times* had no way of knowing that Douglas read only resolution number "2" and that this is what he meant when he said that the Republicans in the crowd have "cheered every one of those propositions." In this edition, only what the speaker read from the platform is given in the text, the unread resolutions being given in the annotation.

---

22. For example, in the Quincy debate, see p. 216.

7. Crowd reactions are described in generic, nonpartisan terms.

A striking feature of the newspaper reporting of the debates is the presence of colorful descriptions of the crowd's reactions. But most of these are blatantly partisan, more akin to cheerleading than reporting, and not to be considered reliable as a gauge of the impression the speaker has made on the crowd. In general, the opposing paper's report of the other speaker says very little about crowd response. By the same token, negative or unfavorable responses are rarely reported by the speaker's own paper, which is a further consequence of partisan reporting. There is even reason to believe that some of the partisan interjections reported by the *Times* came from one of Douglas's hired reporters, who, when he was not reporting Lincoln's speeches, was said to have been acting as a cheerleader for Douglas.[23]

This kind of obvious bias caused the publishers of the first edition of the debates (not Abraham Lincoln, as has been charged) to eliminate all of the crowd responses except those to which the speakers responded.[24] But because these partisan reports are part of the historical record, to say nothing of the color they add to the encounter, modern editors of the newspaper accounts have quite properly included them. Here, where the attempt is to look past the partisanship to what actually occurred, reports that seem to reflect significant crowd reactions (as opposed to those of individuals) are noted in brackets and are recorded in generic language ("cheers," "laughter," "applause"). Where both accounts offer general crowd reactions—one, for example, reporting laughter and the other applause—an attempt is made to include both ("Laughter, applause"). Some reports that appear prejudicial actually coincide with their counterparts in the opposing paper, and these are included.

8. Interjections reported as coming from the audience are only included in the text where the speaker responds.

Interjections from the individual members of the audience were apparently frequent, but the reporting of them seems to have been highly inconsistent and almost always partisan. Here, only those interjections that evoke a response from the speaker are included.

---

23. See the Quincy debate, p. 249
24. See Follett, Foster & Co. to SAD, June 16, 1860: "Remarks by the crowd, which were not responded to, and the reporter's insertions of 'cheers,' 'great applause,' and so forth, which received no answer or comment from the speaker, were, by our direction omitted, as well from Mr. Lincoln's speeches as yours, as we thought their perpetuation in book form would be in bad taste, and were in no manner pertinent to or a part of the speech." Quoted in Debates Scrapbook, 18.

EXAMPLE:

> *Voice:* Well, you are a fool.
> *Lincoln:* Well, that may be, and I guess there are two of us that are that way.

9. A few conjectural readings are offered by the editors where a word is clearly missing or where the word reported in neither the primary text nor the opposition paper fits the context. The conjectural reading is always acknowledged in the textual notes.

EXAMPLES:

a. Insertion of a missing word. In the following examples, both from AL's speech at Alton, the underlined word has been inserted by the editors:

> If you will get everybody else to stop talking about it, I assure <u>you</u> I will quit before they have half done so.

> There is no place to talk about <u>it</u> as being a wrong, although you say yourself it is a wrong.

b. Substitution of a word.

> . . . notwithstanding I had said this, he goes on and <u>insinuates</u> or draws out from my speech this tendency of mine to set the states at war with one another . . .

In this example from Lincoln's speech at Ottawa, the editors have substituted the conjectural word "insinuates" for the word in the *Press and Tribune* text, "eliminates," which seems a clear error.

THE DEBATES

OTTAWA

INTRODUCTION

Senator Douglas selected as sites for the Lincoln-Douglas Debates "one prominent point in each congressional district in the state," save in those districts surrounding Chicago and Springfield, where each candidate had already given major
speeches. He designated Ottawa, in the Third Congressional District, to be the
location of his first meeting with Lincoln, on August 21.

Ottawa, Illinois, located eighty miles southwest of Chicago at the junction
of the Fox and Illinois rivers, was in 1858 a town of about seven thousand citizens. Situated also on the Illinois and Michigan Canal and the Chicago and
Rock Island Railroad, the town had unusual transportation advantages, which
had contributed to its recent growth. Although LaSalle County, of which Ottawa was the seat, had delivered heavy Anti-Nebraska and Republican electoral
majorities since the 1854 election, the town of Ottawa (where a number of Irish
laborers on the canal continued to live after its completion in 1848) remained
resolutely Democratic throughout the 1850s. Ottawa voters never supported their
outspokenly antislavery Republican congressman Owen Lovejoy in an election,
though he had garnered 57 percent of LaSalle County's votes in 1856 and would
carry the county decisively again in 1858. All of this suggests that the crowd that
probably doubled Ottawa's population on August 21 to hear Lincoln and Douglas
may therefore have been fairly evenly divided along partisan lines, representing
the dominant opinions of both Ottawa and its nearby environs.

On the day of the debate, that excited multitude assembled in the public
square after a morning of informal but enthusiastic partisan parades and demonstrations that raised so much dust from Ottawa's unpaved streets that to an

observer "the town resembled a vast smoke house."[1] The heat was of the dreadful sort that is almost invariably produced in Illinois in late August, and was enervating to speakers and listeners alike—the latter being "unprotected by shade trees and unprovided with seats," as another observer noted.[2] The debate, scheduled to begin at 2:00 PM, was delayed a half hour while portions of the throng were sometimes forcibly removed from the speaking platform, which they had occupied, leaving little room for the platform party. Others had climbed onto the wooden awning that gave the platform a little shade, in such numbers that it collapsed, apparently causing no major injuries but contributing further to the delay.

Douglas led off, and he almost immediately put Lincoln on the defensive with a series of radical resolutions that he claimed to constitute the Illinois Republican platform as adopted at Springfield in October 1854, and he demanded to know if Lincoln "stood pledged" to support that platform. After attacking Lincoln's "House Divided" speech and his opposition to the *Dred Scott* decision, Douglas asserted that Lincoln and the Republicans favored the total equality of blacks and whites. And he introduced a countertheme that he would repeat throughout the debates, that African Americans were inferior to whites, that the United States had been established "on the white basis," and that the status of blacks in America was a matter for states and territories to decide. Though he had come prepared with some arguments with which to confront Douglas, Lincoln was obliged to defer them and to respond instead to the senator by denying any connection with the radical 1854 platform with which Douglas had challenged him and caught him off guard. To counter further Douglas's charges of extremism, he read a lengthy portion of his speech delivered at Peoria in October 1854, in which he made clear his hatred of slavery and his conviction that African Americans were entitled to the natural rights enumerated in the Declaration of Independence, but protested that he had no desire to promote the political and social equality of blacks and whites. Recurring then to his prepared positions, Lincoln reiterated the conspiracy theory first enunciated in his "House Divided" speech. He said that though the aim of the Founding Fathers had been to put slavery "in the course of ultimate extinction," Senator Douglas, Presidents Pierce and Buchanan, and Chief Justice Taney all schemed to nationalize slavery, via the Kansas-Nebraska Act, the *Dred Scott* decision, and "the next Dred Scott decision," wherein the Supreme Court would decide that no state could exclude slavery, as it had already ruled that neither Congress nor a territorial legislature could do so.[3]

---

1. *Chicago Press and Tribune,* Aug. 23, 1858.

2. *New York Evening Post,* Aug. 27, 1858.

3. For some of the arguments AL had prepared for the Ottawa debate, see "Fragment: Notes for Speeches," Roy P. Basler et al., eds., *The Collected Works of Abraham Lincoln* (New Brunswick: Rutgers University Press, 1953), 2:547–53.

In his rejoinder Douglas accused Lincoln of talking about everything but the radical platform of 1854 with which he had originally confronted him, and he challenged Lincoln to answer whether he endorsed it. And addressing Lincoln's charge that he was party to a conspiracy to nationalize slavery, Douglas branded it "an infamous lie." Douglas ended the debate by reiterating his insistence on the sovereign right of each state to decide the slavery question as well as other domestic questions for itself, thus denying Lincoln's doctrine of "uniformity between the different states," which Douglas professed to see in the "House Divided" speech.

The Ottawa debate, and the six that followed, attracted wide journalistic attention. They were covered by reporters and correspondents from the major Illinois newspapers in Chicago and Springfield, from Republican and Democratic papers in St. Louis, and by representatives from the press of Philadelphia and New York. Efforts made by the Democratic *Chicago Times* and the Republican *Chicago Press and Tribune* to provide verbatim transcriptions of the debates were somewhat unprecedented (given the shortage of reporters able to take shorthand) and controversial. The reporting of speeches by the intensely partisan newspapers of the mid-nineteenth century was simply expected to be biased; objectivity would not be a criterion for journalists for another half century or more. However, a higher standard of fairness, or at least accuracy, might be anticipated for transcriptions that purported to be literal. Nonetheless, a *Press and Tribune* commentator covering an earlier speech by Douglas at Beardstown, Illinois, had suggested that the *Times's* stenographic reporters had been hired "specially for their genius in exaggeration,"[4] and beginning at Ottawa, each of these papers accused the other of garbling its opponent's speeches, and enhancing those of its favorite.

Although Douglas may have seized the initiative at the beginning of the debates, it was established within two days of the Ottawa meeting that Lincoln had no responsibility for the radical platform that Douglas had read and with which he had created his initial advantage. It was discovered by Robert R. Hitt, the stenographic reporter for the *Press and Tribune,* that those resolutions had been adopted at a congressional district Republican meeting in northern Illinois in September 1854, rather than in the Springfield Republican gathering of that year, as Douglas had alleged. Indeed, the Springfield meeting's resolutions, with which Lincoln likewise had nothing to do, were far more moderate by comparison. Democratic newspapers only grudgingly admitted these facts, while Republicans capitalized on them, emphasizing Douglas's unfairness and misrepresentation of Lincoln and Republicans at the least, and his complicity in the use of forged documents at the most. Lincoln and his Republican journalistic allies would persist with these charges for the rest of the campaign.

---

4. *Chicago Press and Tribune,* Aug. 16, 1858.

A Note on the Use of the Word "nigger"

The word "nigger" was commonly used in Illinois at the time of the Lincoln-Douglas debates, and while its use by whites was recognized as a departure from more polite forms of address, it did not evoke widespread public disapproval. As used by whites, the term always expressed condescension toward blacks, often disrespect, and sometimes outright contempt. Significantly, the word was not used frequently in the debates, both candidates choosing to say "negro" or "negroes" most of the time. This underlines for us that both speakers resorted to it as a way of expressing an attitude or emphasizing a point. In the Ottawa debate, the word is used three times—twice by Lincoln and once by Douglas. Lincoln's uses of the word are, in both cases, ironic, part of a verbal strategy to show that Douglas's representation of his position is a mere caricature. In the first instance, he says Douglas "draws out from my speech this tendency of mine to set the states at war with one another, to make all the institutions uniform, and set the niggers and white people to marrying together." In the second, he ridicules the charge that making slavery national would entail war between the sections. "There is no danger that the people of Kentucky will shoulder their muskets and, with a young nigger stuck on every bayonet, march into Illinois and force them upon us." Douglas's use of the word is closer to contempt, for he characterizes Lincoln's position on natural rights as "preaching up this same doctrine of the Declaration of Independence that niggers were equal to white men."

The reporting of this emotionally charged word in the debates presents a difficulty, even though the reports of both papers reflect that the word was used relatively little. In accounts that totaled some 130,000 words, its reported uses by the debaters (as opposed to its occurrence in quoted material) totaled eight in the *Press and Tribune* and only two in the *Times*.[5] But the latter, Douglas's paper, reported no instances of Douglas using the word, which strains credulity, given what other papers and witnesses reported.[6] Lincoln's paper, by contrast, reported three uses of the word by its own candidate and five by Douglas, which constitutes a more plausible distribution. Inasmuch as reporting the word in

---

5. Two occurrences of the word in each paper appear in quoted material.

6. See Michael Burlingame's forthcoming biography, citing the *Quincy Whig*, Aug. 26, 1858. For Robert Hitt's testimony, see the article "The Lincoln Scrapbooks," in Walter B. Stevens, *A Reporter's Lincoln*, ed. Michael Burlingame (Lincoln: University of Nebraska Press, 1994), 85.

Douglas's speeches was apparently editorially forbidden in the *Times,* the more even-handed reporting of the *Press and Tribune* is followed in all but one case.[7]

---

7. This is the Quincy debate, where the *Times* account has Lincoln say: "Mr. Douglas will insist that I want a nigger wife; but never can he be brought to understand but every man must have a negro slave or a negro wife." Though the *Press and Tribune* does not report this usage of the word, it is plausible in its consistency with what he is reported to have said earlier in the same context, and by the way the *Times* account discriminates between his use of the words "nigger wife" in the first part of the sentence but "negro wife" later on.

DOUGLAS'S OPENING SPEECH

Ladies and gentlemen: I appear before you today for the purpose of discussing the leading political topics which now agitate the public mind. By an arrangement between Mr. Lincoln and myself, we are present here today for the purpose of having a joint discussion as the representatives of the two great political parties of the state and Union, upon the principles in issue between these parties, and this vast concourse of people shows the deep feeling which pervades the public mind in regard to the questions dividing us.

Prior to 1854, this country was divided into two great political parties, known as the Whig and Democratic parties. Both were national and patriotic, advocating principles that were universal in their application. An old line Whig could proclaim his principles in Louisiana and Massachusetts alike. Whig principles had no boundary sectional line. They were not limited by the Ohio river, nor by the Potomac, nor by the line of the free and slave states, but applied and were proclaimed wherever the Constitution ruled or the American flag waved over the American soil. *[Cheers]* So it was, and so it is with the Democratic party, which, from the days of Jefferson until this period, has proven itself to be the historic party of this nation. While the Whig and Democratic parties differed in regard to a bank, the tariff, distribution, the specie circular, and the sub-treasury,[1] they agreed on the great slavery question which now agitates the Union. I say that the Whig party and the Democratic party agreed on this slavery question, while they differed on those matters of expediency to which I have referred.

The Whig party and the Democratic party jointly adopted the compromise measures of 1850 as the basis of a proper and just solution of this slavery question in all its forms. Clay was the great leader, with Webster on his right and Cass on his left, and sustained by the patriots in the Whig and Democratic ranks who had devised and enacted the compromise measures of 1850. In 1851, the Whig party and the Democratic party united in Illinois in adopting resolutions endorsing and approving the principles of the compromise measures of 1850, as the proper adjustments of that question. In 1852, when the Whig party assembled in convention at Baltimore for the purpose of nominating a candidate for the Presidency, the first thing it did was to declare the compromise measures of 1850, in substance and in principle, a suitable adjustment of that question. *[Applause]*

---

1. Historically, Whigs and Democrats had disagreed over the need for a national bank, the wisdom of a protective tariff, the distribution to the states of the surplus from the sale of public lands, the purchase of public lands with specie only, and the depositing of federal receipts in a subtreasury rather than in banks.

My friends, silence will be more acceptable to me in the discussion of these questions than applause. I desire to address myself to your judgment, your understanding, and your consciences, and not your passions or your enthusiasm.

When the Democratic convention assembled in Baltimore in the same year for the purpose of nominating a Democratic candidate for the Presidency, it also adopted the compromise measures of 1850 as the basis of Democratic action. Thus you see that up to 1853–54, the Whig party and the Democratic party both stood on the same platform with regard to the slavery question. That platform was the right of the people of each state, and each territory, to decide their local and domestic institutions for themselves, subject only to the federal Constitution.

During the session of Congress of 1853–54, I introduced into the Senate of the United States a bill to organize the territories of Kansas and Nebraska on that principle, which had been adopted in the compromise measures of 1850, approved by the Whig party and the Democratic party in Illinois in 1851, and endorsed by the Whig party and the Democratic party in national convention in 1852. In order that there might be no misunderstanding in relation to the principle involved in the Kansas and Nebraska bill, I put forth the true intent and meaning of the act in these words: "'It being the true intent and meaning of this act not to legislate slavery into any Territory or State, nor to exclude it therefrom, but to leave the people thereof perfectly free to form and regulate their domestic institutions in their own way, subject only to the federal Constitution."[2] Thus, you see, that up to 1854, when the Kansas and Nebraska bill was brought into Congress for the purpose of carrying out the principles which both parties had up to that time endorsed and approved, there had been no division in this country in regard to that principle except the opposition of the abolitionists. In the House of Representatives of the Illinois legislature, upon a resolution asserting that principle,[3] every Whig and every Democrat in the House voted in the affirmative, and only four men voted against it, and those four men were old line abolitionists. *[Cheers]*

In 1854, Mr. Abraham Lincoln and Mr. Trumbull entered into an arrange-

---

2. *U.S. Statutes at Large* 10, 283.

3. This resolution, adopted on Jan. 22, 1851, reads as follows:

> *Resolved,* That our liberty and independence are based upon the right of the people to form for themselves such a government as they may choose; that this great principle; the birthright of freemen, the gift of Heaven, secured to us by the blood of our ancestors, ought to be extended to future generations, and no limitation ought to be extended to this power in the organization of any territory of the U.S. of either territorial government or state constitution, provided the government so established shall be Republican, and in conformity with the Constitution of the United States.

The resolution was introduced by AL's friend and brother-in-law, Ninian W. Edwards. *Illinois House Journal,* 1851, 128.

ment, one with the other, and each with his respective friends, to dissolve the old Whig party on the one hand, and to dissolve the old Democratic party on the other, and to connect the members of both into an abolition party under the name and disguise of a Republican party. *[Laughter, cheers]* The terms of the arrangement between Mr. Lincoln and Mr. Trumbull have been published to the world by Mr. Lincoln's special friend, James H. Matheny, Esq., and they were that Lincoln should have Shields' place in the U. S. Senate, which was then about to become vacant, and that Trumbull should have my seat when my term expired.[4] *[Laughter]* Lincoln went to work to abolitionize the old Whig party all over the state, pretending that he was then as good a Whig as ever *[Laughter]*, and Trumbull went to work in his part of the state, preaching abolitionism in its milder and lighter form, and trying to abolitionize the Democratic party and bring old Democrats handcuffed and bound hand and foot into the abolition camp. *[Cheers]*

In pursuance of the arrangement, the parties met at Springfield in October, 1854, and proclaimed their new platform. Lincoln was to bring into the abolition camp the old line Whigs and transfer them over to Giddings, Chase, Fred° Douglass, and Parson Lovejoy and Farnsworth,° who were ready to receive them and christen them in the new faith. *[Laughter, cheers]* They laid down on that occasion a platform for their new Republican party, which was to be constructed out of the old Whig party and the old Democratic party, by abolitionizing both and transferring them to abolitionism.° I have the resolutions of their state convention then held, which was the first mass state convention ever held in Illinois by the Black Republican party, and I now hold them in my hands and will read a part of them, and cause the others to be printed. Here is the most important and material resolution of this abolition platform.[5]

---

4. Shortly before the presidential election of 1856, AL's friend James H. Matheny, while briefly a Know-Nothing and politically estranged from AL, was reported to have delivered the speech to which SAD refers. An extract from the speech was read by SAD in the Jonesboro and Charleston debates, pp. 92 and 158.

5. Almost immediately these resolutions, represented by SAD as the 1854 Republican Party's state platform passed in Springfield, were identified by Robert R. Hitt, the stenographic reporter for the *Chicago Press and Tribune,* as resolutions passed at a district convention at Aurora, Illinois, in September of the same year. *Press and Tribune,* Aug. 24, 1858. See note 11, p. 11. See also Walter B. Stevens, *A Reporter's Lincoln,* ed. Michael Burlingame (Lincoln: University of Nebraska Press, 1998), 80–81.

SAD apparently read from a text of the Aurora resolutions published in the *Illinois State Register* (Springfield), Oct. 16, 1854. A slightly different text is in the *Aurora Guardian,* September 28, 1854. Though the actual resolutions passed in the October 5 meeting at Springfield seem not to have been published locally at the time, they were published elsewhere in the state. See *Illinois Weekly Gazette* (Lacon), Oct. 11, 1854, *Freeport Journal,* Oct. 12, 1854, *Ottawa Republican,* Oct. 14, 1854, *Morgan Journal* (Jacksonville), Oct. 19, 1854.

Resolved, That the times imperatively demand the re-organization of parties, and repudiating all previous party attachments, names and predilections, we unite ourselves together in defense of the liberty and constitution of the country, and will hereafter co-operate as the republican party, pledged to the accomplishment of the following purposes: to bring the administration of the government back to the control of first principles; to restore Nebraska and Kansas to the position of free territories; that, as the constitution of the United States, vests in the states, and not in Congress, the power to legislate for the extradition of fugitives from labor, to repeal and entirely abrogate the fugitive slave law; to restrict slavery to those states in which it exists; to prohibit the admission of any more slave states into the Union; to abolish slavery in the District of Columbia; to exclude slavery from all the territories over which the general government has exclusive jurisdiction; and to resist the acquirement of any more territories, unless the practice of slavery therein forever shall have been prohibited. ° *[Cheers throughout]*

Now, gentlemen, you Black Republicans have cheered every one of those propositions *[Cheers],* and yet I venture to say that you cannot get Mr. Lincoln to come out and say that he is now in favor of each one of them. *[Laughter, applause]* That these propositions, one and all, constitute the platform of the Black Republican party of this day, I have no doubt, and when you were not aware for what purpose I was reading them, you Black Republicans cheered them as good Black Republican doctrines. *[Cheers]* My object in reading these resolutions was to put the question to Abraham Lincoln this day, whether he now stands, and will stand, by each article in that creed and carry it out. *[Cheers]*

I desire to know whether Mr. Lincoln today stands, as he did in 1854, in favor of the unconditional repeal of the Fugitive Slave Law. I desire him to answer whether he stands pledged today, as he did in 1854, against the admission of any more slave states into the Union, even if the people want them. I want to know whether he stands pledged against the admission of a new state into the Union with such a constitution as the people of that state may see fit to make. *[Cheers]* I want to know whether he stands today pledged to the abolition of slavery in the District of Columbia. I desire him to answer whether he stands pledged to the prohibition of the slave trade between the different states. I desire to know whether he stands pledged to prohibit slavery in all the territories of the United States, North as well as South of the Missouri Compromise line. I desire him to answer whether he is opposed to the acquisition of any more territory unless slavery is first prohibited therein. I want his answer to these questions. Your affirmative cheers in favor of this abolition platform is not satisfactory. I ask Abraham Lincoln to answer these questions, in order that when I trot him down to lower Egypt, I may put the same questions to him. *[Applause]*

My principles are the same everywhere. *[Cheers]* I can proclaim them alike in the North, the South, the East, and the West. My principles will apply wherever the Constitution prevails and the American flag waves. *[Applause]* I desire to know whether Mr. Lincoln's principles will bear transplanting from Ottawa to Jonesboro. I put these questions to him today distinctly, and ask an answer, for I quote from the platform of the Republican party, made by himself and others at the time that party was formed, and the bargain made by Lincoln to dissolve and kill the old Whig party, and transfer its members, bound hand and foot, to the abolition party, under the direction of Giddings and Fred Douglass. ° *[Cheers]*

In the remarks I have made on this platform, and the position of Mr. Lincoln upon it, I mean nothing personally disrespectful or unkind to that gentleman. I have known him for nearly twenty-five years. There were many points of sympathy between us when we first got acquainted. We were both comparatively boys, and both struggling with poverty in a strange land. I was a school teacher in the town of Winchester, and he a flourishing grocery keeper[6] in the town of Salem. *[Laughter]* He was more successful in his occupation than I was in mine, and hence more fortunate in this world's goods. Lincoln is one of those peculiar men who perform with admirable skill everything which they undertake. I made as good a school teacher as I could, and when a cabinet maker, I made a good bedstead and tables, although my old boss said I succeeded better with bureaus and secretaries than anything else. *[Laughter]* But I believe that Lincoln was always more successful in business than I, for his business enabled him to get into the legislature. I met him there, however, and had a sympathy with him, because of the up-hill struggle we both had in life. *[Cheers]* He was then just as good at telling an anecdote as now. He could beat any of the boys wrestling or running a foot race, in pitching quoits or tossing a copper, could win° more liquor than all the boys of the town put° together.[7] *[Laughter]* And the dignity and impartiality with which he presided at a horse race or fist fight excited the admiration and won the praise of everybody that was present and participated. *[Laughter]* I sympathized with him, because he was struggling with difficulties, and so was I. Mr. Lincoln served with me in the legislature to 1836, when we both retired, and he subsided, or became submerged,[8] and he was lost sight of as a public man for some years.

In 1846, when Wilmot introduced his celebrated proviso, and the abolition

---

6. In mid-nineteenth-century American usage a "grocery" was a dramshop, a place where intoxicants were sold by the drink.

7. "Pitching quoits or tossing a copper": contests involving the throwing of rings around or near a peg stuck in the ground, or the tossing of pennies into a ring or near a line drawn on the ground.

8. Both AL and SAD had been members of the Illinois House of Representatives, but SAD served only in the regular session of the Tenth Illinois General Assembly (1836–37), after which he resigned to become register of the Springfield, Illinois, land office. AL served in the Ninth through the Twelfth Illinois General Assemblies (1834–41).

tornado swept over the country, Lincoln again turned up as a member of Congress from the Sangamon district.[9] I was then in the Senate of the United States and was glad to welcome my old friend and companion. Whilst in Congress, he distinguished himself by his opposition to the Mexican War, taking the side of the common enemy against his own country.[10] *[Cheers, groans]* And when he returned home, he found that the indignation of the people followed him everywhere, and he was again submerged or obliged to retire into private life, forgotten by his former friends. He came up again in 1854, just in time to make this abolition or Black Republican platform, in company with Giddings, Lovejoy, Chase, and Fred Douglass for the Republican party to stand upon.[11] *[Laughter]*

Trumbull, too, was one of our own contemporaries. He was born and raised in old Connecticut, was bred a Federalist, but removing to Georgia, turned nullifier when nullification was popular. And as soon as he disposed of his clocks and wound up his business, migrated to Illinois, *[Laughter]* turned politician and lawyer here, and made his appearance in 1841 as a member of the legislature. He became noted as the author of the scheme to repudiate a large portion of the state debt of Illinois, which, if successful, would have brought infamy and disgrace upon the fair escutcheon of our glorious state.[12] The odium attached to that measure consigned him to oblivion for a time. I helped to do it. I walked into a public meeting in the hall of the House of Representatives and replied to his repudiating speeches, and resolutions were carried over his head denouncing repudiation, and asserting the moral and legal obligation of Illinois to pay every dollar of the debt she owed and every bond that bore her seal. *[Cheers]* Trumbull's malignity has followed me since I thus defeated his infamous scheme.

These two men, having formed this combination to abolitionize the old

---

9. SAD served in the U.S. House of Representatives from 1843 to 1847, and in the U.S. Senate from 1847 until his death in 1861. AL's sole congressional term was from 1847 to 1849.

10. Though AL made no bones about his opposition to the Mexican War during his congressional term, he praised the bravery of American troops and voted for supplies and veterans' benefits for those troops.

11. AL was so aroused by the Kansas-Nebraska Act that he began speaking against it in the fall of 1854, most notably at Springfield on Oct. 4, and at Peoria on Oct. 16. At the time of the Springfield speech, certain leaders of a newly organizing Republican Party attempted unsuccessfully to recruit AL to their central committee, and it was after the Springfield speech that these organizers, without AL's participation, drew up a set of resolutions, which SAD misidentified with a set of resolutions drawn up by a Republican district convention at Aurora. See note 5, p. 8.

12. Lyman Trumbull did not favor the repudiation of Illinois's internal improvement liability during his single term in the Illinois House of Representatives (1840–41). He supported an early version of a bill providing for the payment of interest on that debt, though he voted against the passage of the final version. See *Illinois House Journal* (1841), 118–19, 511.

Whig party and the old Democratic party and put themselves into the Senate of the United States in pursuance of their bargain, are now carrying out that arrangement. Matheny states that Trumbull broke faith, that the bargain was that Lincoln should be the senator in Shields' place and Trumbull was to wait for mine. *[Laughter, cheers]* And the story goes that Trumbull cheated Lincoln. Having control of four or five abolitionized Democrats who were holding over in the Senate, he would not let them vote for Lincoln, and which obliged the rest of the abolitionists to support him in order to secure an abolition Senator. There are a number of authorities for the truth of this beside Matheny, and I suppose that even Mr. Lincoln will not deny it. *[Laughter, applause]*

Mr. Lincoln demands that he shall have the place intended for Trumbull, as Trumbull cheated him and got his, and Trumbull is stumping the state traducing me for the purpose of securing that position for Lincoln, in order to quiet him. It was in consequence of this arrangement that the Republican convention was empanelled to instruct for Lincoln and nobody else, and it was on this account that they passed resolutions that he was their first, their last, and their only choice. Archy Williams was nowhere, Browning was nobody, Wentworth was not to be considered, Judd was not to be considered.° They had no man in the Republican party for the place except Lincoln, for the reason that he demanded that they should carry out the arrangement.

Having formed this new party for the benefit of deserters from Whiggery, and deserters from Democracy, and having laid down the abolition platform which I have read, Lincoln now takes his stand and proclaims his abolition doctrines. Let me read a part of them. In his speech at Springfield to the convention which nominated him for the Senate, he said:[13]

> In my opinion the slavery agitation° will not cease, until a crisis shall have been reached and passed. "A house divided against itself cannot stand." I believe this Government *cannot endure permanently half slave and half free.* I do not expect the Union to be dissolved—I do not expect the house to fall—*but I do expect it will cease to be divided.* It will become all one thing, or all the other. Either the opponents of slavery, *will arrest the further spread of it,* and place it where the public mind shall rest in the belief *that it is in the course of ultimate extinction;* or its advocates *will push it forward, till it shall become alike lawful in all the States,* old as well as new—North as well as South.° *[Cheers]*

I am delighted to hear you Black Republicans say "good." *[Laughter, cheers]*

---

13. What follows is an excerpt from AL's "House Divided" speech to the Illinois Republican state convention on June 16, 1858. For the full text of that speech, see Roy P. Basler et al., eds., *The Collected Works of Abraham Lincoln* (New Brunswick: Rutgers University Press, 1953), 2: 461–69.

I have no doubt that doctrine expresses your sentiments, and I will prove to you now, if you will listen to me, that it is revolutionary and destructive of the existence of this government. *[Cheers]* Mr. Lincoln, in the extract from which I have read, says that this government cannot endure permanently in the same condition in which it was made by its framers—divided into free and slave states. He says that it has existed for about eighty° years thus divided, and yet he tells you that it cannot endure permanently on the same principles and in the same relative condition in which our fathers made it. Why can it not exist divided into free and slave states? Washington, as the President of the convention,° Franklin, Madison, Hamilton, Jay, and the great men of that day made this government divided into free states and slave states, and left each state perfectly free to do as it pleased on the subject of slavery. Why can it not exist on the same principles on which our fathers made it? They knew when they framed the Constitution that, in a country as wide and broad as this, with such a variety of climate, produc-tion, and interest, the people necessarily required different laws and institutions in different localities. They knew that the laws and regulations which would suit the granite hills of New Hampshire would be unsuited to the rice plantations of South Carolina. They therefore provided that each state should retain its own legislature and its own sovereignty, with the full and complete power to do as it pleased within its own limits, in all that was local and not national. *[Applause]*

One of the reserved rights of the states, was the right to regulate the relations between master and servant on the slavery question. At the time the Constitu-tion was formed, there were thirteen states in the Union, twelve of which were slaveholding states and one a free state.[14] Suppose this doctrine of uniformity preached by Mr. Lincoln—that the states should all be free or all be slave—had prevailed. And what would have been the result? Of course, the twelve slavehold-ing states would have overruled the one free state, and slavery would have been fastened by a constitutional provision on every inch of the American republic, instead of being left as our fathers wisely left it, to each state to decide for itself. *[Cheers]* Here I assert that uniformity in the local laws and institutions of the different states is neither possible or desirable. If uniformity had been adopted when the government was established, it must inevitably have been the unifor-mity of slavery everywhere, or else the uniformity of negro citizenship and negro equality everywhere.

We are told by Lincoln that he is utterly opposed to the Dred Scott deci-sion and will not submit to it for the reason that he says it deprives the negro of

---

14. Slavery had been abolished outright in Vermont, Massachusetts, and New Hampshire, and provisions had been made for its gradual extinction in Pennsylvania, Rhode Island, and Connecticut, by the time of the federal Constitutional Convention in 1787.

the rights and privileges of citizenship. *[Laughter, applause]* That is the first and main reason which he assigns for his warfare on the Supreme Court of the United States and its decision. I ask you, are you in favor of conferring upon the negro the rights and privileges of citizenship? *[Cries of "no"]* Do you desire to strike out of our state's constitution that clause which keeps slaves and free negroes out of the state, and allow the free negroes to flow in, and cover your prairies with black settlements? Do you desire to turn this beautiful state into a free negro colony *[Cries of "no"],* in order that when Missouri abolishes slavery, she can send one hundred thousand emancipated slaves into Illinois to become citizens and voters on an equality with yourselves? *[Cries of "never," "no"]* If you desire negro citizenship, if you desire to allow them to come into the state and settle with the white man, if you desire them to vote on an equality with yourselves, and to make them eligible to office, to serve on juries, and to judge your rights, then support Mr. Lincoln and the Black Republican party, who are in favor of the citizenship of the negro. *[Cries of "never"]* For one, I am opposed to negro citizenship in any and every form. *[Cheers]* I believe this government was made on the white basis. I believe it was made by white men, for the benefit of white men and their posterity for ever, and I am in favor of confining citizenship to white men, men of European birth and descent, instead of conferring it upon negroes, Indians, and other inferior races. *[Cheers]*

Mr. Lincoln, following the example and lead of all the little abolition orators who go around and lecture in the basements of schools and churches, reads from the Declaration of Independence that all men were created equal, and then asks how can you deprive a negro of that equality which God and the Declaration of Independence awards to him. He and they maintain that negro equality is guaranteed by the laws of God, and that it is asserted in the Declaration of Independence. If they think so, of course they have a right to say so, and so vote. I do not question Mr. Lincoln's conscientious belief that the negro was made his equal, and hence is his brother. *[Laughter]* But for my own part, I do not regard the negro as my equal, and positively deny that he is my brother or any kin to me whatever. *[Cheers]* Lincoln has evidently learned by heart Parson Lovejoy's catechism. *[Laughter, applause]* He can repeat it as well as Farnsworth, and he could receive baptism° from Father Giddings and Fred Douglass for his abolitionism. *[Laughter]* He holds that the negro was born his equal and yours, and that he was endowed with equality by the Almighty, and that no human law can deprive him of these rights, which were guaranteed to him by the Supreme Ruler of the universe.

Now, I do not believe that the Almighty ever intended the negro to be the equal of the white man. *[Cries of "never"]* If he did, he has been a long time demonstrating the fact. *[Laughter]* For six thousand years° the negro has been a race upon the earth, and during that whole six thousand years,° in all latitudes and climates, wherever he has wandered or been taken, he has been inferior to the race which he has there met. He belongs to an inferior race and must always occupy an inferior position. *[Cheers]*

I do not hold that because the negro is our inferior that therefore he ought to be a slave. By no means can such a conclusion be drawn from what I have said. On the contrary, I hold that humanity and Christianity both require that the negro shall have and enjoy every right, every privilege, and every immunity consistent with the safety of the society in which he lives. On that point, I presume, there can be no diversity of opinion. You and I are bound to extend to our inferior and dependent being every right, every privilege, every facility and immunity consistent with the public good.

The question then arises: what rights and privileges are consistent with the public good? This is a question which each state and each territory must decide for itself. Illinois has decided it for herself. We have provided that the negro shall not be a slave, and we have also provided that he shall not be a citizen, but protect him in his civil rights, in his life, his person, and his property, only depriving him of all political rights whatsoever, and refusing to put him on an equality with the white man.[15] That policy of Illinois is satisfactory to the Democratic party and to me, and if it were to the Republicans, there would then be no question upon the subject. But the Republicans say that he ought to be made a citizen, and when he becomes a citizen, he becomes your equal, with all your rights and privileges. They assert the Dred Scott decision to be monstrous because it denies that the negro is or can be a citizen under the Constitution. Now, I hold that Illinois had a right to abolish and prohibit slavery as she did, and I hold that Kentucky has the same right to continue and protect slavery that Illinois had to abolish it. I hold that New York had as much right to abolish slavery as Virginia has to continue it, and that each and every state of this Union is a sovereign power, with the right to do as it pleases upon this question of slavery, and upon all its domestic institutions.

Slavery is not the only question which comes up in this controversy. There is a far more important one to you, and that is: what shall be done with the free negro? We have settled the slavery question as far as we are concerned. We have prohibited it in Illinois forever. In doing so, I think we have done wisely, and there is no man in the state who would be more strenuous in his opposition to the introduction of slavery than I would. *[Cheers]* But when we settled it for ourselves, we exhausted all our power over that subject. We have done our whole duty, and can do no more. We must leave each and every other state to decide for itself the same question. In relation to the policy to be pursued towards the free negroes,

15. For Illinois's antebellum policy concerning African Americans, see "Illinois and the rights of blacks" in the glossary, p. 326.

we have said that they shall not vote, whilst Maine, on the other hand, has said that they shall vote. Maine is a sovereign state, and has the power to regulate the qualifications of voters within her limits. I would never consent to confer the right of voting and of citizenship upon a negro, but still I am not going to quarrel with Maine for differing from me in opinion. Let Maine take care of her own negroes and fix the qualifications of her own voters to suit herself, without interfering with Illinois, and Illinois will not interfere with Maine.

So with the State of New York. She allows the negro to vote, provided he owns two hundred and fifty dollars' worth of property, but not otherwise. While I would not make any distinction whatever between a negro who held property and one who did not, yet if the sovereign state of New York chooses to make that distinction, it is her business and not mine, and I will not quarrel with her for it. She can do as she pleases on this question, if she minds her own business, and we will do the same thing.[16]

Now, my friends if we will only act conscientiously and rigidly upon this great principle of popular sovereignty which guarantees to each state and territory the right to do as it pleases on all things local and domestic instead of Congress interfering, we will continue at peace one with another. Why should Illinois be at war with Missouri, or Kentucky with Ohio, or Virginia with New York, merely because their institutions differ? Our fathers intended that our institutions should differ. They knew that the North and the South, having different climates, productions and interests, required different institutions. This doctrine of Mr. Lincoln's of uniformity among the institutions of the different states is a new doctrine, never dreamed of by Washington, Madison, or the framers of this government. Mr. Lincoln and the Republican party set themselves up as wiser than these men who made this government, which has flourished for seventy years under the principle of popular sovereignty, recognizing the right of each state to do as it pleased.

Under that principle, we have grown from a nation of three or four millions to a nation of about thirty millions of people. We have crossed the Allegheny mountains and filled up the whole Northwest, turning the prairie into a garden, and building up churches and schools, thus spreading civilization and Christianity where before there was nothing but savage barbarism. Under that principle we have become, from a feeble nation, the most powerful on the face of the earth. If we only adhere to that principle, we can go forward increasing in territory, in power, in strength and in glory until the republic of America shall

---

16. For a brief survey of the peculiar status of African American suffrage in New York, see Leon F. Litwack, *North of Slavery* (Chicago: University of Chicago Press, 1961), 80–84, 87–91.

be the North Star that shall guide the friends of freedom throughout the civilized world. *[Cheers, applause]*

And why can we not adhere to the great principle of self-government, upon which our institutions were originally based? I believe that this new doctrine preached by Mr. Lincoln and his party will dissolve the Union, if it succeeds. They are trying to array all the Northern states in one body against the South, to excite a sectional war between the free states and the slave states, in order that the one or the other may be driven to the wall.

I am told that my time is out. Mr. Lincoln will now address you for an hour and a half, and I will then occupy an half hour in replying to him. *[Cheers]*

LINCOLN'S REPLY

My fellow citizens: When a man hears himself somewhat misrepresented, it provokes him—at least, I find it so with myself. But when the misrepresentation becomes very gross and palpable, it is more apt to amuse him. *[Laughter]* The first thing I see fit to notice is the fact that Judge Douglas alleges, after running through the history of the old Democratic and the old Whig parties, that Judge Trumbull and myself made an arrangement in 1854, by which I was to have the place of Gen. Shields in the United States Senate, and Judge Trumbull was to have the place of Judge Douglas. Now all I have to say upon that subject is that I think no man, not even Judge Douglas, can prove it, *because it is not true.* *[Cheers]* I have no doubt he is *conscientious* in saying it. *[Laughter]*

As to those resolutions that he took such a length of time to read, as being the platform of the Republican party in 1854,[17] I say I never had anything to do with them, and I think Trumbull never had. *[Laughter]* Judge Douglas cannot show that either one of us ever did have anything to do with them. I believe *this* is true about those resolutions. There was a call for a convention to form a Republican party at Springfield, and I think that my friend Mr. Lovejoy, who is here upon this stand, had a hand in it. I think this is true, and I think, if he will remember accurately, he will be able to recollect that he tried to get me into it, and I would not go in. *[Cheers, laughter]* I believe it is also true that I went away from Springfield when the convention was in session to attend court in Tazewell County. It is true they did place my name, though without authority, upon the committee, and afterwards wrote me to attend the meeting of the committee, but

---

17. At this point the following is inserted in the *Chicago Press and Tribune* text of this debate: "These resolutions are a deliberate forgery by Mr. Douglas. None such were passed by the Springfield Convention nor any like them.—Ed. Press And Tribune." See also note 5, p. 8.

I refused to do so, and I never had anything to do with that organization. This is the plain truth about all that matter of the resolutions.

Now, about this story that Judge Douglas tells of Trumbull bargaining to sell out the old Democratic party, and Lincoln agreeing to sell out the old Whig party, I have the means of *knowing* about that. *[Laughter]* Judge Douglas cannot have, and I know there is no substance to it whatever. *[Applause]* Yet I have no doubt he is *conscientious*[18] about it. *[Laughter]* I know that after Mr. Lovejoy got into the legislature that winter, he complained of me that I had told all the old Whigs in his district that the old Whig party was good enough for them, and some of them voted against him because I told them so.

Now I have no means of totally disproving such charges as this which the Judge makes. A man cannot prove a negative, but he has a right to claim that when a man makes an affirmative charge, he must offer some proof to show the truth of what he says. I certainly cannot introduce testimony to show the negative about things, but I have a right to claim that if a man says he *knows* a thing, then he must show *how* he knows it. I always have a right to claim this, and it is not satisfactory to me that he may be *conscientious* on the subject. *[Cheers, laughter]*

Now gentlemen, I hate to waste my time on such things, but in regard to that general abolition tilt that Judge Douglas makes, when he says that I was engaged at the time in selling out and abolitionizing the old Whig party, I hope you will permit me to read a part of a printed speech that I made then at Peoria, which will show altogether a different view of the position I took in the contest of 1854.[19]

Voice: Put on your specs.

Lincoln: Yes sir, I am obliged to do so. I am no longer a young man.

> This is the *repeal* of the Missouri Compromise. The foregoing history may not be precisely accurate in every particular; but I am sure it is sufficiently so, for all the uses I shall attempt to make of it, and in it, we have before us, the chief materials° enabling us to correctly judge whether the repeal of the Missouri Compromise is right or wrong.

---

18. AL's mocking use of the adjective "conscientious" derives from his ire at SAD's earlier condescending assertions that AL was "conscientious" in his advocacy of sectional warfare or the political and social equality of blacks and whites—charges that SAD fabricated as the logical conclusions of positions AL took in his "House Divided" speech and his Chicago speech of July 10. See SAD's July 17 Springfield speech in *Illinois State Register,* July 19, 1858, and AL's two speeches, in Basler et al., *Collected Works,* 2:461–69, 490–94. See also "Fragment: Notes for Speeches," [c. August 21, 1858], in Basler et al., *Collected Works,* 2:548.

19. For the full text of this speech, see "Speech at Peoria, Illinois," Oct. 16, 1854, in Basler et al., *Collected Works,* 2:247–83.

I think, and shall try to show, that it is wrong; wrong in its direct effect, letting slavery into Kansas and Nebraska—and wrong in its prospective principle, allowing it to spread to every other part of the wide world, where men can be found inclined to take it.

This *declared* indifference, but as I must think, covert *real* zeal for the spread of slavery, I can not but hate. I hate it because of the monstrous injustice of slavery itself. I hate it because it deprives our republican example of its just influence in the world—enables the enemies of free institutions, with plausibility, to taunt us as hypocrites—causes the real friends of freedom to doubt our sincerity, and especially because it forces so many really good men amongst ourselves into an open war with the very fundamental principles of civil liberty—criticising the Declaration of Independence, and insisting that there is no right principle of action but *self-interest.*

Before proceeding, let me say I think I have no prejudice against the Southern people. They are just what we would be in their situation. If slavery did not now exist amongst them, they would not introduce it. If it did now exist amongst us, we should not instantly give it up. This I believe of the masses north and south. Doubtless there are individuals, on both sides, who would not hold slaves under any circumstances; and others who would gladly introduce slavery anew, if it were out of existence. We know that some southern men do free their slaves, go north, and become tip-top abolitionists; while some northern ones go south, and become most cruel slave-masters.

When southern people tell us they are no more responsible for the origin of slavery, than we; I acknowledge the fact. When it is said that the institution exists, and that it is very difficult to get rid of it, in any satisfactory way, I can understand and appreciate the saying. I surely will not blame them for not doing what I should not know how to do myself. If all earthly power were given me, I should not know what to do, as to the existing institution. My first impulse would be to free all the slaves, and send them to Liberia,—to their own native land. But a moment's reflection would convince me, that whatever of high hope, (as I think there is) there may be in this, in the long run, its sudden execution is impossible. If they were all landed there in a day, they would all perish in the next ten days; and there are not surplus shipping and surplus money enough in the world to carry them there in many times ten days. What then? Free them all, and keep them among us as underlings? Is it quite certain that this betters their condition? I think I would not hold one in slavery, at any rate; yet the point is not clear enough to me to denounce people upon. What° next? Free them, and make them politically and socially, our equals?

Let the Judge note this. I now am among men who have some abolition tendencies.

Free them, and make them politically and socially, our equals?° My own feelings will not admit of this; and if mine would, we well know that those of the great mass of white people will not. Whether this feeling accords with justice and sound judgment, is not the sole question, if indeed, it is any part of it. A universal feeling, whether well or ill-founded, can not be safely disregarded. We can not, then, make them equals. It does seem to me that systems of gradual emancipation might be adopted; but for their tardiness in this, I will not undertake to judge our brethren of the south.

When they remind us of their constitutional rights, I acknowledge them, not grudgingly, but fully, and fairly; and I would give them any legislation for the reclaiming of their fugitives, which should not, in its stringency, be more likely to carry a free man into slavery, than our ordinary criminal laws are to hang an innocent one.

But all this; to my judgment, furnishes no more excuse for permitting slavery to go into our own free territory, than it would for reviving the African slave trade by law. The law which forbids the bringing of slaves *from* Africa; and that which has so long forbid the taking them *to* Nebraska, can hardly be distinguished on any moral principle; and the repeal of the former could find quite as plausible excuses as that of the latter. °

I have reason to know that Judge Douglas *knows* that I said this. I think he has the answer here to one of the questions he put to me. I do not mean to allow him to catechize me unless he pays back for it in kind. I will not answer questions one after another unless he reciprocates, but as he made this inquiry and I have answered it before, he has got it without my getting anything in return. He has got my answer on the Fugitive Slave Law.

Now gentlemen, I don't want to read at any greater length, but this is the true complexion of all I have ever said in regard to the institution of slavery and the black race. This is the whole of it, and anything that argues me into his idea of perfect social and political equality with the negro is but a specious and fantastic arrangement of words, by which a man can prove a horse chestnut to be a chestnut horse. *[Laughter, applause]* I will say here, while upon this subject, that I have no purpose directly or indirectly to interfere with the institution of slavery in the states where it exists. I believe I have no lawful right to do so, and I have no inclination to do so. I have no purpose to introduce political and social equality between the white and the black races. There is a physical difference between the two, which in my judgment will probably forever forbid their living together upon the footing of perfect equality, and inasmuch as it becomes a necessity that there must be a difference, I, as well as Judge Douglas, am in favor of the race to which I belong having the superior position. I have never said anything to the contrary, but I hold that notwithstanding all this, there is no reason in the world why the negro is not entitled to all the natural rights enumerated in the Declaration of Independence—the right to life, liberty, and the pursuit of happiness. *[Cheers, applause]* I hold that he is as much entitled to these as the white man. I agree with Judge Douglas he is not my equal in many respects—certainly not in color, perhaps not in moral or intellectual endowment. But in the right to eat the bread, without leave of anybody else, which his own hand earns, *he is my equal and the equal of Judge Douglas, and the equal of every living man. [Applause]*

Now I pass on to consider one or two more of these little follies. The Judge is woefully at fault about his early friend Lincoln being a "grocery keeper." *[Laughter]* I don't know as it would be a great sin if I had been, but he is mistaken. Lincoln never kept a grocery anywhere in the world. *[Laughter]* It is true that Lincoln did work the latter part of one winter in a little still house up at the head of a hollow. *[Laughter]* And so I think my friend, the Judge, is equally at fault when he charges me, at the time when I was in Congress, of having opposed our soldiers who were fighting in the Mexican War. The Judge did not make his charge very distinctly, but I can tell you what he can prove by referring to the record. You remember I was an old Whig, and whenever the Democratic party tried to get me to vote that the war had been righteously begun by the President, I would not do it. But whenever they asked for any money, or land warrants, or anything to pay the soldiers there, during all that time, I gave the same votes that Judge Douglas did. *[Applause]* You can think as you please as to whether that was consistent. Such is the truth; and the Judge has the right to make all he can out of it. But when he, by a general charge, conveys the idea that I withheld supplies from the soldiers who were fighting in the Mexican War, or did anything else to hinder the soldiers, he is, to say the least, grossly and altogether mistaken, as a consultation of the records will prove to him.

As I have not used up so much of my time as I had supposed, I will dwell a little longer upon one or two of these minor topics upon which the Judge has spoken. He has read from my speech in Springfield in which I say that "a house divided against itself cannot stand." Does the Judge say it *can* stand? *[Laughter]* I don't know whether he does or not. The Judge does not seem to be attending to me just now, but I would like to know if it is his opinion that a house divided against itself *can stand.* If he does, then there is a question of veracity, not between him and me, but between the Judge and an authority of somewhat higher character. *[Laughter, applause]*

Now, my friends, I ask your attention to this matter for the purpose of saying something seriously. I know that the Judge may readily enough agree with me that the maxim which was put forth by the Savior is true, but he may allege that I misapply it. And the Judge has a right to urge that, in my application, I do misapply it, and then I have a right to show that I do *not* misapply it. When he undertakes to say that because I think this nation, so far as the question of slavery is concerned, will all become one thing or all the other, I am in favor of bringing about a dead uniformity in the various states, in all their institutions, he argues erroneously. The great variety of the local institutions in the states—

springing from differences in the soil, differences in the face of the country, and in the climate—are bonds of union. They do not make a house divided against itself, but they make a house united. If they produce, in one section of the country, what is called for by the wants of another section, and this other section can supply the wants of the first, they are not matters of discord but bonds of union, true bonds of union.

But can this question of slavery be considered as among *these* varieties in the institutions of the country? I leave it to you to say whether, in the history of our government, this institution of slavery has not always failed to be a bond of union, and, on the contrary, been an apple of discord and an element of division in the house. *[Cheers, applause]* I ask you to consider whether—so long as the moral constitution of men's minds shall continue to be the same, after this generation and assemblage shall sink into the grave, and another race shall arise, with the same moral and intellectual development we have—whether, if that institution is standing in the same irritating position in which it now is, it will not continue an element of division? *[Cheers]* If so, then I have a right to say that in regard to this question, the Union is a house divided against itself.

And when the Judge reminds me that I have often said to him that the institution of slavery has existed for eighty years in some states, and yet it does not exist in some others, I agree to the fact, and I account for it by looking at the position in which our fathers originally placed it—restricting it from the new territories where it had not gone, and legislating to cut off its source by the abrogation of the slave trade, thus putting the seal of legislation *against its spread.* The public mind *did* rest in the belief that it was in the course of ultimate extinction. *[Cheers, applause]*

But lately, I think—and in this I charge nothing on the Judge's motives—lately, I think, that he and those acting with him have placed that institution on a new basis, which looks to the *perpetuity and nationalization of slavery. [Cheers]* And while it is placed upon this new basis, I say, and I have said, that I believe we shall not have peace upon the question until the opponents of slavery arrest the further spread of it, and place it where the public mind shall rest in the belief that it is in the course of ultimate extinction; or, on the other hand, that its advocates will push it forward until it shall become alike lawful in all the states, old as well as new, North as well as South. Now, I believe if we could arrest the spread, and place it where Washington and Jefferson and Madison placed it, it *would be* in the course of ultimate extinction, and the public mind *would,* as for eighty years past, believe that it was in the course of ultimate extinction. The crisis would be passed and the institution might be let alone for a hundred years, if it should live so long, in the states where it exists, yet it would be going out of existence in the way best for both the black and the white races. *[Cheers]*

Voice: Then do you repudiate popular sovereignty?

Lincoln: Well, then, let us talk about popular sovereignty. *[Laughter]* What is popular sovereignty? Is it the right of the people to have slavery or not have it, as they see fit, in the territories? I will state—and I have an able man to watch me—my understanding is that popular sovereignty, as now applied to the question of slavery, does allow the people of a territory to have slavery if they want to, but does not allow them *not* to have it if they *do not* want it. *[Applause, laughter]* I do not mean that if this vast concourse of people were in a territory of the United States, any one of them would be obliged to have a slave if he did not want one. But I do say that as I understand the Dred Scott decision, if any one man wants slaves, all the rest have no way of keeping that one man from holding them.

Voice: Well, you are a fool.

Lincoln: Well, that may be, and I guess there are two of us that are that way.°

When I made my speech at Springfield, of which the Judge complains, and from which he quotes, I really was not thinking of the things which he ascribes to me at all. I had no thought in the world that I was doing anything to bring about a war between the free and slave states. I had no thought in the world that I was doing anything to bring about a political and social equality of the black and white races. It never occurred to me that I was doing anything or favoring anything to reduce to a dead uniformity all the local institutions of the various states. But I must say, in all fairness to him, if he thinks I am doing something which leads to these bad results, it is none the better that I did not mean it. It is just as fatal to the country, if I have any influence in producing it, whether I intend it or not.

But can it be true that placing this institution upon the original basis— the basis upon which our fathers placed it—can have any tendency to set the Northern and the Southern states at war with one another, or that it can have any tendency to make the people of Vermont raise sugar cane, because they raise it in Louisiana, or that it can compel the people of Illinois to cut pine logs on the Grand Prairie, where they will not grow, because they cut pine logs in Maine, where they do grow. *[Laughter]* The Judge says this is a new principle started in regard to this question. Does the Judge claim that he is working on the plan of the founders of government? I think he says in some of his speeches—indeed I have one here now—that he saw evidence of a policy to allow slavery to be South of a certain line, while North of it, it should be excluded, and he saw an indisposition on the part of the country to stand upon that policy, and there-fore he set about studying the subject upon *original principles* and upon *original principles* he got up the Nebraska bill.[20] I am fighting it upon these "original

---

20. AL may refer to SAD's earliest speech in the Senate in defense of the Kansas-Nebraska Act. *Congressional Globe,* 33rd Cong., 1st Sess., Senate, Jan. 30, 1854, 1:277–80.

principles"—fighting it in the Jeffersonian, Washingtonian, and Madisonian fashion. *[Laughter, applause]*

Now my friends I wish you to attend for a little while to one or two other things in that Springfield speech. My main object was to show, so far as my humble ability was capable of showing to the people of this country, what I believed was the truth—that there was a *tendency,* if not a conspiracy, among those who have engineered the slavery question for the last four or five years, to make slavery perpetual and universal in this nation. Having made that speech principally for that object, after arranging the evidences that I thought tended to prove my proposition, I concluded with this bit of comment:[21]

> We cannot absolutely *know* that these exact adaptations are the result of pre-concert. But when we see a lot of framed timbers, different portions of which we know have been gotten out at different times and places and by different workmen—Stephen, Franklin, Roger and James, for instance[22]—and when we see these timbers joined together, and see they exactly make the frame of a house or a mill, all the tenons and mortices exactly fitting, and all the lengths and proportions of the different pieces exactly adapted to their respective places, and not a piece too many or too few—not omitting even the scaffolding—or, if a single piece be lacking, we see the place in the frame exactly fitted and prepared yet to bring each piece in—in *such* a case we feel it impossible to not *believe* that Stephen and Franklin and Roger and James all understood one another from the beginning, and all worked upon a common *plan* or *draft* drawn up before the first lick was struck.° *[Cheers]*

When my friend, Judge Douglas, came to Chicago, on the 9th of July, this speech having been delivered on the 16th of June, he made an harangue there in which he took hold of this speech of mine, showing that he had carefully read it. And while he paid no attention to *this* matter at all, but complimented me as being a "kind, amiable and intelligent gentleman," notwithstanding I had said this, he goes on and insinuates° or draws out from my speech this tendency of mine to set the states at war with one another, to make all the institutions uniform, and set the niggers and white people to marrying together.[23] *[Laughter]* Then, as

---

21. What follows is from AL's "House Divided" speech, in Basler et al., *Collected Works,* 2:465–66.

22. Stephen A. Douglas, Franklin Pierce, Roger B. Taney, and James Buchanan.

23. In his July 9 address in Chicago, SAD claimed that AL, in his "House Divided" speech, espoused a policy that would lead to intersectional violence and, ultimately, intersectional uniformity. And he construed AL's observation that the *Dred Scott* decision denied the right of Negroes to American citizenship to be a call for racial equality, which he identified with the inevitable amalgamation of the black and white races. While SAD does not speak of it in the Chicago address, Democrats had long taunted their antislavery opponents with insinuations that a sexual motive underlay their efforts in behalf of blacks.

the Judge had complimented me with these pleasant titles—I must confess to my weakness—I was a little "taken" *[Laughter],* for it came from a great man, and one that the world acknowledges as a great man. I do not speak that in mockery.° I was not very much accustomed to flattery, and it came the sweeter to me. I was rather like the hoosier, with the gingerbread, when he said he reckoned he loved it better than any other man, and got less of it. *[Laughter]*

As the Judge had so flattered me, I could not make up my mind that he meant to deal unfairly with me, so I went to work to show him that he misunderstood the whole scope of my speech, and that I really never intended to set the people at war with one another. As an illustration, I had incidentally said,° I used this expression, that I claimed "no right, and there ought to be no inclination in the people of the free States, to enter into the slave States and interfere with the question of slavery at all."[24] The Judge thereupon, at Bloomington, where I heard him make a speech, said that I had said that I would not go° into the Slave States, but will go to the banks of the Ohio, on this side, and shoot over![25] *[Laughter]* He runs on, step by step, in the horse-chestnut plan of argument, until in the Springfield speech, he says, "unless he shall play his batteries successfully, so as to abolish slavery in every one of the states, that the Union shall be dissolved."°[26]

Now I don't think that was exactly the way to treat a kind, amiable, intelligent gentleman. *[Laughter]* I know if I had asked the Judge to show when or where it was I had said that—if I didn't succeed in firing into the slave states until slavery should be extinguished, the Union should be dissolved—he could not have shown it. I understand what he would do. He would say, "I don't mean to quote from you, but this was the *result* of what you say." But I have the right to ask, and I do ask now: Did you not put it in such a form that an ordinary reader or listener would take it as an expression *from me? [Laughter]*

In a speech at Springfield, on the night of the 17th, I thought I might as well attend to my own business a little, and I recalled his attention as well as I could to this charge of conspiracy to nationalize slavery. I called his attention to the fact

---

See for example, *New York Tribune,* July 4, 1857, for a sharp exchange between Horace Greeley's *Tribune* and a Douglas paper on the use of the term "nigger" and the issue of racial intermarriage. See "Negro equality" in the glossary, pp. 328–29.

24. From AL's "Speech at Chicago," July 10, 1858, in Basler et al., *Collected Works,* 2:492.

25. At Bloomington, SAD is reported as saying, "Well, I never did suppose that he ever dreamed of entering Kentucky to make war upon her institutions. Their mode of making war is not to enter into those States where slavery exists, and there interfere, and render themselves responsible for the consequences. Oh no! They stand on this side of the Ohio river and shoot across." "Speech of Senator Douglas. Delivered at Bloomington, Ill., July 16, 1858," in Debates Scrapbook, 57.

26. From SAD'S July 17 speech at Springfield, published in *Illinois State Register,* July 19. 1858.

that he had carefully read the speech, and, in the language of the lawyers, as he had twice read the speech and still had put in no plea or answer, I took a default on him.[27] I insisted that I had a right then to renew that charge of conspiracy. Ten days afterwards, I met the Judge at Clinton—that is to say, I was on the ground, but not in the discussion—and heard him make a speech. Then he comes in with his plea to this charge, for the first time, and his plea when put in, as well as I can recollect it, amounted to this: that he never had any talk with Judge Taney or the President of the United States with regard to the Dred Scott decision before it was made, and that∘ I, Lincoln, ought to know that the man who makes a charge without knowing it to be true, falsifies as much as he who knowingly tells a falsehood; and lastly, that he would pronounce the whole thing a falsehood. But he would make no personal application of the charge of falsehood—not because of any regard for the "kind, amiable, intelligent gentleman"—but because of his own personal self-respect.[28] *[Laughter]*

I have understood since then—but *[turning to Judge Douglas]* will not hold the Judge to it if he is not willing—that he has broken through the "self-respect" and has got to saying the thing *out.* The Judge nods to me that this is so. *[Laughter]* It is fortunate for me that I can keep as good-humored as I do, when the Judge acknowledges that he has been trying to make a question of veracity with me. I know the Judge is a great man, while I am only a small man, but *I feel that I have got him. [Cheers]* I demur to that plea.[29] I waive all objections that it was not filed till after default was taken, and demur to it upon the merits. What if Judge Douglas never did talk with Chief Justice Taney and the President before the Dred Scott decision was made? Does it follow that he could not have had as perfect an understanding without talking, as with it? I am not disposed to stand upon my legal advantage. I am disposed to take his denial as being like an answer in chancery, that he neither had any knowledge, information, or belief in the existence of such a conspiracy.[30] I am disposed to take his answer as being as broad as though he had put it in those words. And now, I ask, even if he has done so, have not I a right to *prove it on him,* and to offer the evidence of more than two witnesses, by whom to prove it? And if the evidence proves the existence of the conspiracy, does his broad answer denying all knowledge, information, or belief,

---

27. In legal parlance, to "take a default" is to win a judgment by reason of an adversary's failure to appear or to plead.

28. SAD spoke at Clinton on July 27. His speech there is reported in the *Times,* July 30, 1858.

29. In law, to demur is to take exception to an opponent's plea.

30. An answer in chancery is a defendant's response to a bill of complaint filed in a court of chancery. It may deny some or all of the allegations in the complaint, or otherwise explain the actions of the defendant.

disturb the fact? It can only show that he was *used* by conspirators and was not a *leader* of them. *[Cheers]*

Now in regard to his reminding me of the moral rule that persons who tell what they do not know to be true, falsify as much as those who knowingly tell falsehoods. I remember the rule, and it must be borne in mind that in what I have read to you, I do not say that I *know* such a conspiracy to exist. To that, I reply *I believe it.* If the Judge says that I do *not* believe it, then *he* says what *he* does not know, and falls within his own rule, that he who asserts a thing which he does not know to be true, falsifies as much as he who knowingly tells a falsehood.

As to his statement that if it were not for his self-respect he would call the whole thing a falsehood, or, in plain words, to call somebody a liar about it.° I want to call your attention to a little discussion on that branch of the case, and the evidence which brought my mind to the conclusion which I expressed as my *belief.* If, in arraying that evidence, I had stated anything which was false or erroneous, it needed but that Judge Douglas should point it out, and I would have taken it back with all the kindness in the world. I do not deal in that way. If I have brought forward anything not a fact, if he will point it out, it will not even ruffle me to take it back. But if he will not point out anything erroneous in the evidence, is it not rather for him to show, by a comparison of the evidence that I have *reasoned* falsely, than to call the "kind, amiable, intelligent gentleman," a liar? *[Cheers, laughter]* If I have reasoned to a false conclusion, it is the vocation of an able debater to show by argument that I have wandered to an erroneous conclusion.

I want to ask your attention to a portion of the Nebraska bill, which Judge Douglas has quoted:

> It being the true intent and meaning of this act not to legislate slavery into any Territory or State, nor to exclude it therefrom, but to leave the people thereof perfectly free to form and regulate their domestic institutions in their own way, subject only to the Constitution of the United States.°

Thereupon Judge Douglas and others began to argue in favor of "popular sovereignty"—the right of the people to have slaves if they wanted them, and to exclude slavery if they did not want them. "But," said, in substance, a senator from Ohio, Mr. Chase, I believe, "we more than suspect that you do not mean to allow the people to exclude slavery if they wish to, and if you do mean it, accept an amendment which I propose expressly authorizing the people to exclude slavery." I believe I have the amendment here before me, which was offered, and under which the people of the territory, through their proper representatives, might if they saw fit, prohibit the existence of slavery therein. And now I state it as a *fact,* to be taken back if there is any mistake about it, that Judge Douglas and those acting with him *voted that amendment down. [Applause]* I now think that those men who voted it down had a *real reason* for doing so. They know what that reason was. It looks to us, since we have seen the Dred Scott decision pronounced—holding that "under the Constitution" the people cannot exclude slavery—I say it looks to outsiders, poor, simple, "amiable, intelligent gentlemen" *[Laughter]*, as though the niche was left as a place to put that Dred Scott decision in—*[Laughter, cheers]* a niche which would have been spoiled by adopting the amendment. And now, I say again, if *this* was not the reason, it will avail the Judge much more to calmly and good-humoredly point out to these people what that *other* reason was for voting the amendment down, than, swelling himself up, to vociferate that he may be provoked to call somebody a liar. *[Applause]*

Again, there is in that same quotation from the Nebraska bill this clause— "It being the true intent and meaning of this bill not to legislate slavery into any Territory or *State.*" I have always been puzzled to know what business the word "state" had in that connection. Judge Douglas knows. *He put it there.* He knows what he put it there for. We outsiders cannot say what he put it there for. The law they were passing was not about states, and was not making provisions for states. What was it placed there for? After seeing the Dred Scott decision, which holds that the people cannot exclude slavery from a *territory,* if another Dred Scott decision shall come, holding that they cannot exclude it from a *state,* we shall discover that when the word was originally put there, it was in view of something which was to come in due time.[31] We shall see that it was the *other half* of something. *[Applause]* I now say again, if there is any different reason for putting it there, Judge Douglas, in a good-humored way, without calling anybody a liar, *can tell what the reason was. [Cheers]*

When the Judge spoke at Clinton, he came very near making a charge of falsehood against me. He used, as I found it printed in a newspaper, which I remember was very nearly like the real speech, the following language: "I did not answer this charge before for this reason: I did not suppose there was a man in America whose heart was so corrupt as for an instant to believe such a charge could be true." And then the Judge, after I have dropped a part of the quotation, added that he "had ∘ too much respect for Mr. Lincoln to suppose he is serious in making the charge." ∘ [32]

I confess this is rather a curious view, that out of respect for me he should consider I was making what I deemed rather a grave charge in fun. *[Laughter]* I confess it strikes me rather strangely, but I let it pass. As the Judge did not for a moment believe that there was a man in America whose heart was so "corrupt"

---

31. See "another Dred Scott decision" in the glossary. p. 319.
32. *Chicago Times,* July 30, 1858.

as to make such a charge, and as he places me among the "men in America" who have hearts base enough to make such a charge, I hope he will excuse me if I hunt out another charge very like this. And if it should turn out that in hunting I should find that other, and it should turn out to be Judge Douglas himself who made it, I hope he will reconsider this question of the deep corruption of heart he has thought fit to ascribe to me. *[Applause, laughter]*

In Judge Douglas' speech of March 22d, 1858, which I hold in my hand, he says:[33]

> In this connection there is another topic to which I desire to allude. I seldom refer to the course of newspapers, or notice the articles which they publish in regard to myself; but the course of the *Washington Union* has been so extraordinary, for the last two or three months, that I think it well enough to make some allusion to it. It has read me out of the Democratic party every other day, at least, for two or three months, and keeps reading me out, and, as if it had not succeeded, still continues to read me out, using such terms as "traitor," "renegade," "deserter," and other kind and polite epithets of that nature. Sir, I have no vindication to make of my democracy against the *Washington Union*, or any other newspapers. I am willing to allow my history and action for the last twenty years to speak for themselves as to my political principles, and my fidelity to political obligations. The *Washington Union* has a personal grievance. When its editor[34] was nominated for Public Printer I declined to vote for him, and stated that at some time I might give my reasons for doing so. Since I declined to give that vote, this scurrilous abuse, these vindictive and constant attacks have been repeated almost daily on me. Will my friend from Michigan read the article to which I allude.°

This is a speech made on the 22d March, 1858, and this part begins on page 21. I tell you the place so that you may read it for yourselves.° You must excuse me from reading the entire article of the *Washington Union,* as Mr. Stuart read it for Mr. Douglas. The Judge goes on and sums up, as I think correctly:

> Mr. President, you here find several distinct propositions advanced boldly by the Washington Union editorially and apparently *authoritatively,* and every man who questions any of them is denounced as an Abolitionist, a Free-Soiler, a fanatic. The propositions are, first, that the primary object of all government at its original institution is the protection of person and property; second, that the Constitution of the United States declares that the citizens of each State shall be entitled to all the privileges and immunities of citizens in the several

---

33. AL read from a pamphlet version of SAD's speech, printed for public distribution, *Speech of Senator Douglas, of Illinois, against the Admission of Kansas under the Lecompton Constitution* (Washington, D.C.: Lemuel Towers, 1858), 21, 23, 24.

34. The editor of the *Washington Union* was Cornelius Wendell.

States; and that, therefore, thirdly, all State laws, whether organic or otherwise, which prohibit the citizens of one State from settling in another with their slave property, and especially declaring it forfeited, are direct violations of the original intention of the Government and Constitution of the United States; and fourth, that the emancipation of the slaves of the northern States was a gross outrage on the rights of property, inasmuch as it was involuntarily done on the part of the owner.

Remember that this article was published in the Union on the 17th of November, and on the 18th appeared the first article giving the adhesion of the Union to the Lecompton Constitution. It was in these words:

> KANSAS AND HER CONSTITUTION.—The vexed question is settled. The problem is solved. The dread point of danger is passed. All serious trouble to Kansas affairs is over and gone.—

and a column, nearly, of the same sort. Then, when you come to look into the Lecompton constitution, you find the same doctrine incorporated in it which was put forth editorially in the *Union*. What is it?

> Article 7. *Section* 1. The right of property is before and higher than any constitutional sanction; and the right of the owner of a slave to such slave and its increase is the same and as inviolable as the right of the owner of any property whatever.

Then in the schedule is a provision that the constitution may be amended after 1864 by a two-thirds vote, "But no alteration shall be made to affect the right of property in the ownership of slaves."

It will be seen by these clauses in the Lecompton Constitution, that they are identical in spirit with this *authoritative* article in the *Washington Union* of the day previous to its indorsement of this constitution, and every man is branded as a Free-Soiler and Abolitionist, who does not subscribe to them.°

I pass over some portions of the speech, and I hope that any one who feels interested in this matter will read the entire section of the speech, and see whether I do the Judge injustice. He proceeds:

> When I saw that article in the Union of the 17th of November, followed by the glorification of the Lecompton constitution on the 18th of November, and this clause in the constitution asserting the doctrine that no State has a right to prohibit slavery within its limits, I saw that there was a *fatal blow* being struck at the sovereignty of the States of this Union, a death blow to State rights, subversive of the Democratic platform and of the principles upon which the Democratic party have ever stood, and upon which I trust they will ever stand.°

I stop the quotation there, again, requesting that it may all be read. I have read all of the portion I desire to comment upon.

What is this charge that the Judge thinks I must have a very corrupt heart to make? It was a purpose on the part of certain high functionaries to make it impossible for the people of one state to prohibit the people of any other state from entering it with their *property*, so-called, and making it a slave state. In other words, it was a charge implying a design to make the institution of slavery national. And now I ask your attention to what Judge Douglas has himself done here. I know he made that part of the speech as a reason why he had refused to vote for a certain man for public printer, but when we get at it, the charge itself is the very one I made against him, that he thinks I am so corrupt for uttering.

Now whom does he make that charge against? Does he make it against that newspaper editor merely? No, he says it is identical in spirit with the Lecompton Constitution, and so the framers of that constitution are brought in with the editor of the newspaper in that "fatal blow being struck." He did not call it a "conspiracy." In his language, it is a "fatal blow being struck." And if the words carry the meaning better when changed from a "conspiracy" into a "fatal blow being struck," I will change *my* expression and call it "fatal blow being struck." *[Cheers, laughter]* We see the charge made not merely against the editor of the *Union* but all the framers of the Lecompton Constitution. And not only so, but the article was an *authoritative* article. By whose authority? Is there any question but he means it was by the authority of the President, and his cabinet—the administration?

Is there any sort of question but he means to make that charge? Then there are the editors of the *Union*, the framers of the Lecompton Constitution, the President of the United States and his cabinet, and all the supporters of the Lecompton Constitution in Congress and out of Congress, who are all involved in this "fatal blow being struck." I commend to Judge Douglas' consideration the question of *how corrupt a man's heart must be to make such a charge. [Cheers]*

Now my friends, I have but one branch of the subject, in the little time I have left, to which to call your attention, and as I shall come to a close at the end of that branch, it is probable that I shall not occupy quite all the time allotted to me. Although on these questions I would like to talk twice as long as I have, I could not enter upon another head and discuss it properly without running over my time. I ask the attention of the people here assembled and elsewhere to the course that Judge Douglas is pursuing every day, as bearing upon this question of making slavery national. Not going back to the records but taking the speeches he makes, the speeches he made yesterday and day before and makes constantly all over the country. I ask your attention to them.

In the first place what is necessary to make the institution national? Not war. There is no danger that the people of Kentucky will shoulder their muskets and, with a young nigger stuck on every bayonet, march into Illinois and force them upon us. There is no danger of our going over there and making war upon them. Then what is necessary for the nationalization of slavery? It is simply the next Dred Scott decision.[35] It is merely for the Supreme Court to decide that no *state,* under the Constitution, can exclude it, just as they have already decided that, under the Constitution, neither Congress nor the territorial legislature can do it. When that is decided and acquiesced in, the whole thing is done.

This being true, and this being the way, as I think, that slavery is to be made national, let us consider what Judge Douglas is doing every day to that end. In the first place, let us see what influence he is exerting on public sentiment. In this and like communities, public sentiment is everything. With public sentiment, nothing can fail; without it nothing can succeed. Consequently he who moulds public sentiment goes deeper than he who enacts statutes or pronounces decisions. He makes statutes and decisions possible or impossible to be executed. This must be borne in mind, as also the additional fact that Judge Douglas is a man of vast influence. So great that it is enough for many men to profess to believe anything, when they once find out that Judge Douglas professes to believe it. Consider, also, the attitude he occupies at the head of a large party—a party which he claims has a majority of all the votes in the country.

This being borne in mind, what does the Judge do in regard to the Dred Scott decision?° This man sticks to a decision which forbids the people of a territory from excluding slavery, and he does so, not because he says it is right in itself—he does not give any opinion on that—but because it has been *decided by the court.* And being decided by the court, he, as a good citizen, and you, as good citizens,° are bound to take it in your political action as *law*—not that he judges at all of its merits, but because a decision of the court is to him a "*Thus saith the Lord.*" [Applause] He places it on that ground alone, and you will bear in mind that thus committing himself unreservedly to this decision *commits him to the next one* just as firmly as to this. He did not commit himself on account of the merit or demerit of the decision, but it is a "*Thus saith the Lord.*" The next decision, as much as this, will be a "*Thus saith the Lord.*"

There is nothing that can divert or turn him away from this decision. It is nothing that I point out to him that his great prototype, Gen. Jackson, did not believe in the great binding force of Supreme Court° decisions. It is nothing to him that Jefferson did not so believe. I have said that I have often heard him approve of Jackson's course in disregarding the decision of the Supreme Court pronouncing a national bank constitutional.[36] He says, I did not hear him say so. He

---

35. See "another Dred Scott decision" in the glossary, p. 319.

36. In *McCulloch v. Maryland* (1819) the Supreme Court had upheld the power of Congress under the Constitution to charter the Bank of the United States. In the message

denies the accuracy of my recollection. I say he ought to know better than I, but I will make no question about this thing, though it still seems to me that I heard him say it twenty times. *[Applause, laughter]* I will tell him, though, that he now claims to stand on the Cincinnati platform, which affirms that Congress *cannot* charter a national bank, in the teeth of that old standing decision that Congress *can* charter a bank. *[Applause]*

And I remind him of another piece of history on the question of respect for judicial decisions, and it is a piece of Illinois history, belonging to a time when the large party to which Judge Douglas belonged were displeased with a decision of the Supreme Court of Illinois, because they had decided that a Governor could not remove a Secretary of State. You will find the whole story in Ford's history of Illinois, and I know that Judge Douglas will not deny that he was then in favor of overslaughing that decision by the mode of adding five new judges, so as to vote down the four old ones. Not only so, but it ended in *the Judge's sitting down on that very bench as one of the five new Judges to break down the four old ones.* *[Cheers, laughter]* It was in this way precisely that he got his title of Judge.[37]

Now, when the Judge tells me that men appointed conditionally to sit as members of a court will have to be catechized beforehand upon some subject, I say, "You know best, Judge; you have tried it." *[Laughter]* When he says a court of this kind will lose the confidence of all men, will be prostituted and disgraced by such a proceeding, I say, "You know best, Judge; you have been through the mill." *[Laughter]* But I cannot shake Judge Douglas' teeth loose from the Dred Scott decision. Like some obstinate animal (I mean no disrespect) that will hang on when he has once got his teeth fixed, you may cut off a leg or you may tear away an arm, still he will not relax his hold. And so I may point out to the Judge, and say that he is bespattered all over, from the beginning of his political life to the present time, with attacks upon judicial decisions. I may cut off limb after limb of his public record, and strive to wrench him from a single dictum of the

---

accompanying his veto of the bill to recharter that institution in 1832, President Jackson famously wrote that he could not assent to the judges' decision; he believed that the bank was unconstitutional and he denied that "the opinion of the judges" had authority over Congress or the president. That position, that the national bank was unconstitutional, remained the Democratic position in that party's Cincinnati Platform in 1856.

37. To forestall an expected decision denying the right of aliens to vote in Illinois, the Democratic General Assembly acted in its 1840–41 session to pack the Whig-dominated state supreme court with five new justices, all of them Democrats. The court was already unpopular with the legislature for having denied the right of Illinois's Democratic governor to remove a Whig secretary of state from office. SAD was indeed one of those new judges, and he had actively promoted the legislation that authorized their appointment. The account that Lincoln cites is in Thomas Ford, *A History of Illinois,* ed. Rodney O. Davis (Urbana: University of Illinois Press, 1995 [1854]), 145–52.

Court, yet I cannot divert him from it. He hangs to the last to the Dred Scott decision. *[Cheers]* These things show there is purpose strong as *death and eternity* for which he adheres to this decision, and for which he will adhere to *all other decisions* of the same Court. *[Applause]*

   Voice: Give us something besides Dred Scott.°

   Lincoln: Yes, no doubt you want to hear something that don't hurt. *[Laughter, applause]*

   Now, having spoken of the Dred Scott decision, one more word and I am done.[38] Henry Clay—my beau ideal of a statesman, the man for whom I fought all my humble life—Henry Clay once said of a class of men who would repress all tendencies to liberty and ultimate emancipation, that they must, if they would do this, go back to the era of our independence and muzzle the cannon which thunders its annual joyous return. They must blow out the moral lights around us. They must penetrate the human soul, and eradicate there the love of liberty. And then, and not till then, could they perpetuate slavery in this country. *[Cheers]* To my thinking, Judge Douglas is, by his example and vast influence, doing that very thing in this community *[Cheers, applause]* when he says that the negro has no share° in the Declaration of Independence. Henry Clay plainly understood the contrary. Judge Douglas is going back to the era of our Revolution and, to the extent of his ability, muzzling the cannon which thunders its annual joyous return. When he invites any people willing to have slavery, to establish it, he is blowing out the moral lights around us. *[Cheers]* When he says he don't care° whether slavery is voted down or voted up, that it is a sacred right of self government, he is, in my judgment, penetrating the human soul and eradicating the light of reason and the love of liberty in this American people. *[Applause]*

   And now I will only say that when, by all these means and appliances, Judge Douglas shall succeed in bringing public sentiment to an exact accordance with his own views, when these vast assemblages shall echo back all these sentiments, when they shall come to repeat his views and to avow his principles, and to say all that he says on these mighty questions, then it needs only the formality of the second Dred Scott decision, which he endorses in advance, to make slavery alike lawful in all the states—old as well as new, North as well as South.

   My friends, that ends the chapter. The Judge can take his half-hour. *[Cheers]*

---

38. In what follows, AL paraphrases the conclusion to Henry Clay's speech to the American Colonization Society on Jan. 20, 1827. See Mary W. M. Hargreaves and James F. Hopkins, eds., *The Papers of Henry Clay* (Lexington: University Press of Kentucky, 1981), 6:94.

DOUGLAS'S REJOINDER

Fellow citizens: I will now occupy the half hour allotted to me in replying to Mr. Lincoln. The first point to which I will call your attention is as to what I said about the organization of the Republican party in 1854 and the platform that was formed on the 5th of October of that year, and I will then put the question to Mr. Lincoln whether or not he approves of each article in that platform. I have told him that I should call for a specific answer to each of these interrogatories.° I did not charge him with being a member of the committee which reported that platform. I charged that that platform was the platform of the Republican party adopted by them. The fact that it was the platform of the Republican party is not denied, but Mr. Lincoln now says, that although his name was on the committee which reported it, that he does not think he was there, but thinks he was in Tazewell, holding court. *[Protests from the crowd]* Gentlemen, I ask your silence, and no interruption. Now, I want to remind Mr. Lincoln that he was at Springfield when that convention was held and those resolutions adopted. *[Protests from the crowd]*

Mr. Glover, chairman of the Republican committee: I hope no Republican will interrupt Mr. Douglas. The masses listened to Mr. Lincoln attentively, and, as respectable men, we ought now to hear Mr. Douglas, and without interruption.

Douglas: The point I am going to remind Mr. Lincoln of is this: that after I had made my speech in 1854, during the fair, he gave me notice that he was going to reply to me the next day. I was sick at the time, but I stayed over in Springfield to hear his reply and to reply to him. On that day, this very convention, the resolutions adopted by which I have read, was to meet in the Senate chambers.[39] He spoke in the hall of the House, and when he got through his speech—my recollection is distinct, and I shall never forget it—Mr. Codding walked in as I took the stand to reply and gave notice that the Republican state convention would meet instantly in the Senate chamber, and called upon the Republicans to retire there and go into this very convention, instead of remaining and listening to me.

Lincoln: Judge, add that I went along with them.

Douglas: Gentlemen, Mr. Lincoln tells me to add that he went along with them to the Senate chamber. I will not add that, because I do not know whether he did or not.

Lincoln: I know he did not.°

---

39. The resolutions in question were published in the *Register,* Oct. 16, 1854. See note 5, p. 8.

Douglas: I do not know whether he knows it or not.[40] That is not the point, and I will yet bring him to his milk° on the question.[41]

In the first place, Mr. Lincoln was selected by the very men who made the Republican organization on that day to reply to me. He spoke for them and for that party, and he was the leader of the party. And on the very day he made his speech in reply to me, preaching up this same doctrine of the Declaration of Independence that niggers were equal to white men,° this Republican party met in convention. *[Cheers]* Another evidence that he was acting in concert with them is to be found in the fact that that convention waited an hour after its time of meeting to hear Lincoln's speech, and Codding, one of their leading men, marched in the moment Lincoln got through and gave notice that they did not want to hear me and would proceed with the business of the convention. *[Cheers]* Still another fact. I have here a newspaper printed at Springfield, Mr. Lincoln's own town, in October, 1854, a few days afterwards, publishing these resolutions, charging Mr. Lincoln with entertaining these sentiments, and trying to prove that they were also the sentiments of Mr. Yates, the candidate for Congress.[42] This has been published on Mr. Lincoln over and over again, and never before has he denied it. *[Cheers]*

But my friends, this denial of his that he did not act on the committee is a miserable quibble to avoid the main issue *[Applause],* which is that this Republican platform declares in favor of the unconditional repeal of the Fugitive Slave Law. Has Lincoln answered whether he endorsed that or not? *[Cries of "no"]* I called his attention to it when I first addressed you and asked him for an answer, and I then predicted that he would not answer. *[Cheers]* How does he answer? Why, that he was not on the committee that wrote the resolutions. *[Laughter]* I then repeated the next proposition contained in the resolutions, which was to restrict slavery in those states in which it exists, and asked him whether he endorsed it. Does he answer yes or no? He says in reply, "I was not on the committee at the time. I was up in Tazewell." The next question I put to him was, whether he was

---

40. This is a confusing passage. Because we can be sure from AL's own testimony and other evidence that he did *not* attend this convention, the *Chicago Press and Tribune* account must be in error in having him say he did, and the *Chicago Times* account must be right in having him say, in his second remark, that he did not. AL's first remark to SAD was probably intended as a dare: "Judge, add that I went along with them," meaning "Why don't you go ahead and say what you are implying?" SAD probably understood that he was being invited into a trap, and thus declined to say what he would like the audience to infer. AL then stated that he *did* know what happened—that he did not join the exit to the Senate chamber—though his own paper, possibly in a misguided editorial attempt to make his two remarks compatible, had him say the opposite.

41. To "bring him to his milk:" to bring AL to a realization of his proper duty or condition, or to subdue him.

42. *Illinois State Register,* Oct. 16, 1854.

in favor of prohibiting the admission of any more slave states into the Union. I put the question to him distinctly, whether, if the people of the territory, when they had sufficient population to make a state, should form their constitution recognizing slavery, he would vote for or against its admission. He is a candidate for the United States° Senate, and it is possible, if he should be elected, that he would have to vote directly on that question. I asked him to answer me and you whether he would vote to admit a state into the Union, with slavery or without it, as its own people might choose. *[Cheers, applause]* He has not answered that, has he?° He did not answer that question. He dodges that question also, under the cover that he was not on the committee at the time, that he was not present when the platform was made. I want to know if he should happen to be in the Senate when a state applied for admission with a constitution acceptable to her own people, he would vote to admit that state, if slavery was one of its institutions. He avoids the answer.

It is true he gives the abolitionists to understand by a hint that he would not vote to admit such a state. And why? Why, he says that a man who would talk about each state having slavery or not as it pleased—mark that—that a man who would talk about each state having slavery° or not, as it pleased, was akin to the man who would muzzle the guns which thundered forth the annual joyous return of the day of our independence. *[Laughter]* He says that that kind of talk is casting a blight on the glory of this country. What is the meaning of that? That he is not in favor of each state having the right to do as it pleases on the slavery question? *[Cheers, applause]* I will put the question to him again and again, and I intend to force it out of him. *[Applause]*

Then again, this platform which was made at Springfield by his own party, when he was its acknowledged head, provides that Republicans will insist on the abolition of slavery in the District of Columbia, and I asked Lincoln specifically whether he agreed with them in that? Did you get an answer? *[Cries of "no"]* He is afraid to answer it. He knows I will trot him down to Egypt. *[Laughter, cheers]* I intend to make him answer there, or I will show the people of Illinois that he does not intend to answer these questions. *[Cheers]* The convention to which I have been alluding goes a little further and pledges itself to exclude slavery from all the territories over which the general government has exclusive jurisdiction, North of 36 degrees 30 minutes as well as South. Now I want to know whether he approves that provision. *[Cheers]* I want him to answer, and when he does, I want to know his opinion on another point, which is, whether he will redeem the pledge of this platform and resist the acquirement° of any more territory unless slavery therein shall be forever prohibited. I want him to answer this last question.

Each of the questions I have put to him are practical questions, questions based upon the fundamental principles of the Black Republican party, and I want to know whether he is the first, last, and only choice of a party with whom he does not agree in principle. *[Applause]* He does not deny but that that principle was unanimously adopted by the Republican party. He does not deny that the whole Republican party is pledged to it. He does not deny that a man who is not faithful to it is faithless to the Republican party, and now I want to know whether that party is unanimously in favor of a man who does not adopt that creed and agree with them in their principles. I want to know whether the man who does not agree with them, and who is afraid to avow his differences and who dodges the issue, is the first, last, and only choice of the Republican party. *[Cheers]*

Voice: How about the conspiracy?

Douglas: Never mind, I will come to that soon enough. *[Cheers]*

But the platform which I have read to you not only lays down these principles, but it adds:[43]

> *Resolved,* That in furtherance of these principles we will use such constitutional and lawful means as shall seem best adapted to their accomplishment, and that we will support no man for office, under the general or state government, who is not positively and fully committed to the support of these principles, and whose personal character and conduct is not a guaranty that he is reliable, and who shall not have abjured old party allegiance and ties.° *[Cheers]*

The Black Republican party stands pledged that they will never support Lincoln until he has pledged himself to that platform *[Cheers]*, but he cannot devise his answer. He has not made up his mind, whether he will or not. *[Laughter]* He talked about everything else he could think of to occupy his hour and a half, and when he could not think of anything more to say, without an excuse for refusing to answer these questions, he sat down long before his time was out. *[Cheers]*

In relation to Mr. Lincoln's charge of conspiracy against me, I have a word to say. In his speech today he quotes a playful part of his speech at Springfield, about Stephen, and James, and Franklin, and Roger, and says that I did not take exception to it. I did not answer it, and he repeats it again. I did not take exception to this figure of his. He has a right to be as playful as he pleases in throwing his arguments together, and I will not object. But I did take objection to his second Springfield speech, in which he stated that he intended his first speech as a charge of corruption or conspiracy against the Supreme Court of the United States, President Pierce, President Buchanan, and myself. That gave the offensive character to the charge. He then said that when he made it, he did not know whether it was true or not, but inasmuch as Judge Douglas had not denied it,

---

43. Ibid. What follows is the third of three sections printed by the *Chicago Times* in SAD's opening speech, although its appearance here is part of the evidence that he did not actually read it to the audience then (see note 5, p. 8).

although he had replied to the other parts of his speech three times, he repeated it as a charge of conspiracy against me, thus charging me with moral turpitude. When he put it in that form, I did say that inasmuch as he repeated the charge simply because I had not denied it, I would deprive him of the opportunity of ever repeating it again, by declaring that it was in all its bearings an infamous lie. *[Cheers]* He says he will repeat it until I answer his folly, and nonsense about Stephen, and Franklin, and Roger, and Bob, and James.

He studied that out, prepared that one sentence with the greatest care, committed it to memory, and put it in his first Springfield speech, and now he carries that speech around and reads that sentence to show how pretty it is. *[Laughter]* His vanity is wounded because I will not go into that beautiful figure of his about the building of a house. *[Laughter]* All I have to say is, that I am not green enough to let him make charges which he acknowledges he does not know to be true, and then take up my time in answering it, when I know it to be false, and nobody else knows it to be true. *[Cheers]*

I have not brought a charge of moral turpitude against him. When he, or any other man, brings one against me, instead of disproving it, I will say that it is a lie, and let him prove it if he can. *[Applause]* I have lived twenty-five years in Illinois. I have served you with all the fidelity and ability which I possess *[Cheers]*, and Mr. Lincoln is at liberty to attack my public action, my votes, and my conduct. But when he dares to attack my moral integrity, by a charge of conspiracy between myself, Chief Justice Taney, and the Supreme Court, and two Presidents of the United States, I will repel it. *[Cheers]*

Mr. Lincoln has not character enough for integrity and truth, merely on his own *ipse dixit,*[44] to arraign President Buchanan, President Pierce, and nine judges of the Supreme Court, not one of whom would be complimented by being put on an equality with him. *[Cheers]* There is an unpardonable presumption in a man, putting himself up before thousands of people and pretending that his *ipse dixit,* without proof, without fact, and without truth, is enough to bring down and destroy the purest and best of living men. *[Cheers]*

Fellow citizens, my time is fast expiring. I must pass on. Mr. Lincoln wants to know why I voted against Mr. Chase's amendment to the Nebraska bill. I will tell him. In the first place, the bill already conferred all the power which Congress had, by giving the people the whole power over the subject. Chase offered a proviso that they might abolish slavery, which by implication would convey the idea that they could prohibit, but could not introduce° that institution. Gen. Cass asked him to modify his amendment, so as to provide that the people might either prohibit or introduce slavery, and thus make it fair and equal. Chase refused to so modify his

44. *Ipse dixit:* an assertion made on authority but not proved.

proviso, and then Gen. Cass and all the rest of us voted it down. *[Cheers]* These facts appear in the journals and debates of Congress, where Mr. Lincoln found the charge, and if he had told the whole truth, there would have been no necessity for me to occupy your time in explaining the matter. *[Laughter, applause]*

Mr. Lincoln wants to know why the word "state," as well as "territory," was put into the Nebraska bill. I will tell him. It was put there to meet just such false arguments as he has been adducing. *[Laughter]* That first, not only the people of the territories should do as they pleased, but that when they come to be admitted as states, they should come into the Union, with or without slavery, as the people determined. I meant to knock in the head this abolition doctrine of Mr. Lincoln's that there shall be no more slave states, even if the people want them. *[Applause]*

And it does not do for him to say, or for any other Black Republican to say, that there is nobody in favor of the doctrine of no more slave states, and that nobody wants to interfere with the right of the people to do as they please. What was the origin of the Missouri difficulty and the Missouri Compromise? The people of Missouri formed a constitution as a slave state and asked admission into the Union, but the free-soil party of the North, being in a majority, refused to admit her because she had slavery as one of her institutions. Hence this first slavery agitation arose upon a state and not upon a territory, and yet Mr. Lincoln does not know why the word "state" was placed in the Kansas-Nebraska bill. *[Laughter, applause]* The whole abolition agitation arose on that doctrine of prohibiting a state from coming in with slavery or not, as it pleased, and that same doctrine is here in this Republican platform of 1854. It has never been repealed. And every Black Republican stands pledged by that platform never to vote for any man who is not in favor of it. Yet Mr. Lincoln does not know that there is a man in the world who is in favor of preventing a state from coming in as it pleases, notwithstanding. The Springfield platform says that they, the Republican party, will not allow a state to come in under such circumstances. He is an ignorant man. ° *[Cheers]*

Now you see that, upon these very points, I am as far from bringing Mr. Lincoln up to the line as I ever was before. He does not want to avow his principles. I do want to avow mine, as clear as sunlight in mid-day. *[Cheers, applause]* Democracy is founded upon the eternal principle of right. ° The plainer these principles are avowed before the people, the stronger will be the support which they will receive. I only wish I had the power to make them so clear that they would shine in the heavens for every man, woman, and child to read. *[Cheers]* The first of those principles that I would proclaim would be in opposition to Mr. Lincoln's doctrine of uniformity between the different states, and I would declare instead the sovereign right of each state to decide the slavery question, as well as all other domestic questions for themselves, without interference from any other state or power whatsoever. *[Cheers]*

When the principle is recognized, you will have peace and harmony and fraternal feeling between all the states of the Union. Until you do recognize that doctrine, there will be sectional warfare agitating and distracting the country. What does Mr. Lincoln propose? He says that the Union cannot exist divided into free and slave states. If it cannot endure thus divided, then he must strive to make them all free or all slave, which will inevitably bring about a dissolution of the Union. *[Cheers]*

Gentlemen, I am told that my time is out and I am obliged to stop. *[Cheers]*

FREEPORT

INTRODUCTION

"What I am saying here I suppose I say to a vast audience as strongly tending to abolitionism as any audience in the State of Illinois," said Abraham Lincoln in his opening speech at Freeport on August 27, 1858. Certainly Lincoln's Freeport audience tended very strongly toward enthusiastic Republicanism, if not necessarily toward abolitionism. The First Congressional District of Illinois, in which Freeport was located, delivered Republican majorities of 70 percent and greater in 1856 and 1858. The voting behavior of Freeport's Stephenson County echoed that of the district; the county and its seat were firmly in the Republican camp. The audience at Freeport, of those at all the debates sites, was doubtless the friendliest to Lincoln, and correspondingly the most hostile to Douglas.

Freeport, 140 miles west of Chicago and near the Wisconsin border, was home to about five thousand citizens in 1858, and of course the town was crowded with an equal or larger number of partisan visitors for the debate. Senator Douglas arrived the evening before and was honored by local Democrats with a torchlight procession of a thousand torches and their bearers, according to Democratic newspapers, or of only seventy-five, according to Republican reporters. Lincoln arrived the next day and rode to the debate site in a Conestoga wagon, "together with about a dozen good, solid, old-fashioned farmers,"[1] whereas Douglas, originally scheduled to be drawn there in an elaborate carriage, decided to walk. All agree that the day of the debate was cloudy and cool, quite the opposite of condi-

---

1. *Freeport Journal,* Sept. 2, 1858, in Edwin Erle Sparks, ed., *The Lincoln-Douglas Debates of 1858, Collections of the Illinois State Historical Library* (Springfield, Ill.: State Historical Library, 1908), 3:197.

tions at Ottawa. As at Ottawa, however, the speakers' platform was occupied early by members of the crowd, leaving scant room for luminaries or reporters. "They have a wretched way in Illinois of leaving the platform unguarded and exposed to the forcible entry of the mob," wrote an exasperated New York reporter.[2] And the throng's unruliness persisted into the debate: as Douglas rose to speak, he was pelted on one shoulder by a melon thrown from the crowd.

Many of Lincoln's supporters had betrayed uneasiness after his initial performance at Ottawa, fearing with justification that he had been put off balance by the radical resolutions that Douglas had unexpectedly challenged him with, and claiming that he had not been aggressive enough, indeed that he had been too defensive. He was therefore the recipient of both general and specific advice on confronting Douglas the second time around. At Lincoln's initiative several Republicans convened in Chicago on August 26 for a strategy session, apparently then delegating Joseph Medill of the *Chicago Press and Tribune* to hand some recommendations in a letter to Lincoln at Freeport the next day. Lincoln was told he should "put a few ugly questions at Douglas" of his own, and that foremost, he should "not act on the *defensive* at all." "Don't refer to your past speeches or positions," Medill continued in his letter, "but reserve that for farther south, but hold Dug up as a traitor & conspirator a proslavery bamboozelling demagogue."[3]

Lincoln had the advantage of opening at Freeport, and it appears that he took some of the Chicago strategists' advice. He began by responding to the questions Douglas had posed to him at Ottawa, offering up answers that were consistent with Republican positions in 1856 and 1858, as opposed to those claimed by radical northern Illinois Republicans in 1854 with which Douglas had earlier tried to identify him. Then he posed questions of his own, some of which were urged in Medill's letter; the most famous is the second one: "Can the people of a United States Territory, in any lawful way . . . exclude slavery from its limits prior to the formation of a State Constitution?" Lincoln also formally denied any responsibility for the resolutions Douglas had read to him at Ottawa, and he renewed his charge of Douglas's involvement in a proslavery conspiracy.

Lincoln's second question had been asked with implicit reference to the *Dred Scott* decision's determination that neither Congress nor a territorial legislature could prohibit slavery in the national territories. The inconsistency between the Kansas-Nebraska Act's doctrine of popular sovereignty and the *Dred Scott* decision had long been noted, and thus Douglas's answer, that slavery could exist in a territory only with popular support and with the protection of local police regulations, was of no particular surprise in Illinois. Douglas had already affirmed this

---

2. *New York Evening Post,* Sept. 2, 1858.

3. Medill to Lincoln, [Aug. 27, 1858], Abraham Lincoln Papers, Library of Congress.

same position on several occasions and would repeat it many times during the debates. It was probably the only one he could have given to an Illinois audience. Yet this "Freeport Doctrine," as Douglas's answer came to be called, seemed to Southerners to be a mere device for him to dodge the *Dred Scott* decision. In the South, Douglas's recent tacit alliance with Republicans against the Lecompton Constitution and the English bill had already reduced his standing. Otherwise Douglas's performance at Freeport is best remembered for the race-baiting in which he indulged, referring derisively to Frederick Douglass's earlier appearance in the town in a carriage driven by a white man.

In Lincoln's rejoinder, despite his effort to embarrass Douglas in his opening speech, the challenger again appeared to be on the defensive, as he had at Ottawa. As he had done before, he distinguished between the sometimes radical Anti-Nebraska resolutions of 1854 with which Douglas had confronted him, and the more moderate Republican platform of 1856, asserting that wide agreement existed on the latter among all Republicans. And he affirmed that all Republicans of whatever stripe had an obligation to pull together to thwart the ambition of Douglas and his allies to nationalize slavery. But what is perhaps most significant about Lincoln's reply to Douglas lies in what he did not say: he did not comment on Douglas's response to his second question. Though he was to do so, sometimes pungently, in subsequent debates, he failed at Freeport to take advantage of an opportunity to go on the offensive against Douglas, and this failure to make capital of Douglas's Freeport Doctrine at the time it was uttered must have insured that, at least to Lincoln's supporters in the Freeport listening audience, this debate ended anticlimactically, certainly with Lincoln no stronger than before.

LINCOLN'S OPENING SPEECH

L adies and gentlemen: On Saturday last, Judge Douglas and myself first met in public discussion. He spoke one hour, I an hour and a half, and he replied for half an hour. The order is now reversed. I am to speak an hour, he an hour and a half, and then I am to reply for half an hour. I propose to devote myself during the first hour to the scope of what was brought within the range of his half hour speech at Ottawa. Of course, there was brought within the scope in that half hour's speech something of his own opening speech. In the course of that opening argument, Judge Douglas proposed to me seven distinct interrogatories. In my speech of an hour and a half, I attended to some other parts of his speech, and incidentally, as I thought, answered one of the interrogatories then. I then distinctly intimated to him that I would answer the rest of his interrogatories, on condition only that he should agree to answer as many for me.° He made no intimation at the time of the proposition, nor did he in his reply allude at all to that suggestion of mine. I do him no injustice in saying that he occupied at least half of his reply in dealing with me as though I had absolutely and unconditionally° *refused* to answer his interrogatories. I now propose that I will answer any of the interrogatories, upon condition that he will answer questions from me not exceeding the same number. *[Applause]* I shall make no objection to the Judge saying "yes" or "no" right now, or, if it suits him, to remain silent. I pause for a moment to see how it will be. Well, I suppose that I may assume that the Judge chooses to remain silent.° *[Laughter]* I now say to you that I will answer his interrogatories, whether he answers mine or not *[Laughter]*, and that after I have done so, I shall propound mine to him. *[Laughter, applause]*[1]

I desire to say that I have no secret pledges in connection with my position in this canvass to any man or set of men.° I have supposed myself, since the organization of the Republican party at Bloomington, in May, 1856, bound as a party man by the platforms of the party, then and since. If, in any interrogatories which I shall answer, I go beyond the scope of what is within these platforms, it will be perceived that no one is responsible but myself.

---

1. At this point, the *Chicago Press and Tribune* account contains a bracketed comment: "Owing to the press of people against the platform, our reporter did not reach the stand until Mr. Lincoln had spoken to this point. The previous remarks were taken by a gentleman in Freeport, who has politely furnished them to us." Since the "previous remarks" printed in the *Press and Tribune* are remarkably close to the text given in the *Chicago Times,* it seems likely that that cooperative gentleman was Henry Binmore, the *Times*'s stenographic reporter assigned to report AL's speeches.

Having said thus much, I will take up the Judge's interrogatories as I find them printed in the *Chicago Times,* and answer them *seriatim.* In order that there may be no mistake about it, I have copied the interrogatories in writing, and also my answers to them. The first one of these interrogatories is in these words:

Question 1. "I desire to know whether Lincoln today stands, as he did in 1854, in favor of the unconditional repeal of the Fugitive Slave Law."

Answer: I do not now, nor ever did, stand in favor of the unconditional repeal of the Fugitive Slave Law. *[Cheers]*

Question 2. "I desire him to answer whether he stands pledged today, as he did in 1854, against the admission of any more slave states into the Union, even if the people want them."

Answer: I do not now, nor ever did, stand pledged against the admission of any more slave states into the Union.

Question 3. "I want to know whether he stands pledged against the admission of a new state into the Union with such a constitution as the people of that state may see fit to make."

Answer: I do not stand pledged against the admission of a new state into the Union, with such a constitution as the people of that state may see fit to make. *[Cheers]*

Question 4. "I want to know whether he stands today pledged to the abolition of slavery in the District of Columbia."

Answer: I do not stand today pledged to the abolition of slavery in the District of Columbia.

Question 5. "I desire him to answer whether he stands pledged to the prohibition of the slave trade between the different states."

Answer: I do not stand pledged to the prohibition of the slave trade between the different states.

Question 6. "I desire to know whether he stands pledged to prohibit slavery in all the territories of the United States, North as well as south of the Missouri Compromise line."

Answer: I am impliedly, if not expressly, pledged to a belief in the *right* and *duty* of Congress to prohibit slavery in all the United States territories. *[Applause]*

Question 7. "I desire him to answer whether he is opposed to the acquisition of any new territory unless slavery is first prohibited therein."

Answer: I am not generally opposed to honest acquisition of territory, and, in any given case, I would or would not oppose such acquisition, accordingly as I might think such acquisition would or would not aggravate° the slavery question among ourselves. *[Cheers]*

Now, my friends, it will be perceived upon an examination of these questions and answers that so far I have only answered that I was not *pledged* to this, that, or the other. The Judge has not framed his interrogatories to ask me anything more than this, and I have answered in strict accordance with the interrogatories, and have answered truly that, I am not *pledged* at all upon any of the points to which I have answered. But I am not disposed to hang upon the exact form of his interrogatory. I am rather disposed to take up at least some of these questions and state what I really think upon them.

As to the first one, in regard to the Fugitive Slave Law, I have never hesitated to say, and I do not now hesitate to say, that I think, under the Constitution of the United States, the people of the Southern states are entitled to a congressional fugitive slave law. Having said that, I have had nothing to say in regard to the existing Fugitive Slave Law, further than that I think it should have been framed so as to be free from some of the objections that pertain to it, without lessening its efficiency. And inasmuch as we are not now in an agitation in regard to an alteration or modification of that law, I would not be the man to introduce it as a new subject of agitation upon the general question of slavery.

In regard to the other question of whether I am pledged to the admission of any more slave states into the Union, I state to you very frankly that I would be exceedingly sorry ever to be put in a position of having to pass upon that question. I should be exceedingly glad to know that there would never be another slave state admitted into the Union. [*Applause*] But I must add that if slavery shall be kept out of the territories during the territorial existence of any one given territory, and then the people shall, having a fair chance and a clear field when they come to adopt the constitution, do such an extraordinary thing as to adopt a slave constitution, uninfluenced by the actual presence of the institution among them, I see no alternative, if we own the country, but to admit them into the Union. [*Applause*]

The third interrogatory is answered by the answer to the second, it being, as I conceive, the same as the second.

The fourth one is in regard to the abolition of slavery in the District of Columbia. In relation to that, I have my mind very distinctly made up. I should be exceedingly glad to see slavery abolished in the District of Columbia. [*Cheers, applause*] I believe that Congress possesses the constitutional power to abolish it. Yet, as a member of Congress, I should not, with my present views, be in favor of *endeavoring* to abolish slavery in the District of Columbia, unless it would be upon these conditions. *First,* that the abolition should be gradual; *second,* that it should be on a vote of the majority of qualified voters in the District; and *third,* that compensation should be made to unwilling owners. With these three conditions, I confess I would be exceedingly glad to see Congress abolish slavery in the

District of Columbia and, in the language of Henry Clay, sweep from our capital that "foul blot"° upon our nation.[2] *[Applause]*

In regard to the fifth interrogatory, I must say here that, as to the question of the abolition of the slave trade between the different states, I can truly answer, as I have, that I am *pledged* to nothing about it. It is a subject to which I have not given that mature consideration that would make me feel authorized to state a position so as to hold myself entirely bound by it. In other words, that question has never been prominently enough before me to induce me to investigate whether we really have the constitutional power to do it. I could investigate it if I had sufficient time and° bring myself to a conclusion upon that subject, but I have not done so, and I say so frankly to you here, and to Judge Douglas. I must say, however, that if I should be of opinion that Congress does possess the constitutional power to abolish the slave trade° among the different states, I should still not be in favor of the exercise of that power unless upon some conservative principle, as I conceive it, akin to what I have said in relation to the abolition of slavery in the District of Columbia.

My answer as to whether I desire that slavery should be prohibited in all the territories of the United States is full and explicit within itself, and cannot be made clearer by any comments of mine. So I suppose, in regard to the question whether I am opposed to the acquisition of any more territory unless slavery is first prohibited therein, my answer is such that I could add nothing by way of illustration, or making myself better understood, than the answer which I have placed in writing.

Now in all this, the Judge has me and he has me on the record. I suppose he had flattered himself that I was really entertaining one set of opinions for one place and another set for another place—that I was afraid to say at one place what I uttered at another. What I am saying here, I suppose I say to a vast audience as strongly tending to abolitionism as any audience in the State of Illinois, and I believe I am saying that which, if it would be offensive° to any persons and render them enemies to myself, would be offensive to persons in this audience.

I now proceed to propound to the Judge the interrogatories, so far as I have framed them. I will bring forward a new installment when I get them ready. *[Laughter]* I will bring them forward now, only reaching to number four.

The first one is: If the people of Kansas shall, by means entirely unobjectionable in all other respects, adopt a state constitution, and ask admission into the

---

2. Though Henry Clay referred to slavery as a "foul blot on the revered state that gave me birth," it is not clear that he used this phrase for slavery in the District of Columbia. See his "Speech before American Colonization Society," Jan. 20, 1827, in Mary W. M. Hargreaves and James F. Hopkins, eds., *The Papers of Henry Clay* (Lexington: University Press of Kentucky, 1981), 6:92.

Union under it, *before* they have the requisite number of inhabitants according to the English bill—some ninety-three thousand—will you vote to admit them? *[Applause]*

Question 2. Can the people of a United States territory, in any lawful way, against the wish of any citizen of the United States, exclude slavery from its limits prior to the formation of a state constitution? *[Applause, cheers]*

Question 3. If the Supreme Court of the United States shall decide° that states can not exclude slavery from their limits, are you in favor of acquiescing in, adopting, and following such decision as a rule of political action? *[Applause]*

Question 4. Are you in favor of acquiring additional territory, in disregard of how such acquisition may affect the nation on the slavery question? *[Cheers]*

As introductory to these interrogatories which Judge Douglas propounded to me at Ottawa, he read a set of resolutions which he said Judge Trumbull and myself had participated in adopting in the first Republican state convention held at Springfield, in October, 1854.[3] He insisted that I and Judge Trumbull, and perhaps, the entire Republican party, were responsible for the doctrines contained in the set of resolutions which he read, and I understand that it was from that set of resolutions that he deduced the interrogatories which he propounded to me, using these resolutions as a sort of authority for propounding those questions to me. Now I say here today that I do not answer his interrogatories because of their springing at all from that set of resolutions which he read. I answered them because Judge Douglas thought fit to ask them. *[Applause]*

I do not now, nor never did, recognize any responsibility upon myself in that set of resolutions. When I replied to him on that occasion, I assured him that I never had anything to do with them. I repeat here today that I never, in any possible form, had anything to do with that set of resolutions. It turns out, I believe, that those resolutions were never passed in any convention held in Springfield. *[Cheers, laughter]* It turns out that they were never passed at any convention or any public meeting that I had any part in. I believe it turns out, in addition to all this, that there was not, in the Fall of 1854, any convention holding a session in Springfield, calling itself a Republican state convention. *[Applause, laughter]* Yet it is true there was a convention, or assemblage of men calling themselves a convention, at Springfield, that did pass *some* resolutions. But so little did I really know of the proceedings of that convention, or what set of resolutions they had passed, though having a general knowledge that there had been such an assemblage of men there, that when Judge Douglas read the resolutions, I really did not know but they had been the resolutions passed then and there. I did not question that they were the resolutions adopted. For I could not bring myself to suppose that

---

3. See "Springfield resolutions controversy" in the glossary, pp. 331–32.

Judge Douglas could say what he did upon this subject without *knowing* that it was true. *[Cheers, laughter]* I contented myself, on that occasion, with denying, as I truly could, all connection with them, not denying or affirming whether they were passed at Springfield.

Now it turns out that he had got hold of some resolutions passed at some convention or public meeting in Kane County. *[Laughter]* I wish to say here that I don't conceive in any fair and just mind this discovery relieves me at all. I had just as much to do with the convention in Kane County as that at Springfield. I am just as much responsible for the resolutions at Kane County as those at Springfield, the amount of the responsibility being exactly nothing in either case. No more than there would be in regard to a set of resolutions passed in the moon. *[Laughter, cheers]*

I allude to this extraordinary matter in this canvass for some further purpose than anything yet advanced. Judge Douglas did not make his statement upon that occasion as matters that he believed to be true, but he stated them roundly as *being true,* in such form as to pledge his veracity for their truth. When the whole matter turns out as it does, and when we consider who Judge Douglas is—that he is a distinguished senator of the United States—that he has served nearly twelve years as such—that his character is not at all limited as an ordinary senator of the United States, but that his name has become of world-wide renown—it is *most extraordinary* that he should so far forget all the suggestions of justice to an adversary, or of prudence to himself, as to venture upon the assertion of that which the slightest investigation would have shown him to be wholly false. *[Cheers, applause]* I can only account for his having done so upon the supposition that the evil genius which has attended him through his life, giving to him an apparent astonishing prosperity, such as to lead very many good men to doubt there being any advantage in virtue over vice *[Cheers, laughter]*, I say I can only account for it on the supposition that that evil genius has at last made up its mind to forsake him. *[Cheers, laughter]*

And I may add that another extraordinary feature of the Judge's conduct in this canvass, made more extraordinary by this incident, is that he is in the habit, in almost all the speeches he makes, of charging falsehood upon his adversaries, myself and others. I now ask whether he is able to find in anything that Judge Trumbull, for instance, has said, or in anything that I have said, a justification at all compared with what we have, in this instance, for that sort of vulgarity. *[Cheers, applause]*

I have been in the habit of charging as a matter of belief on my part, that, in the introduction of the Nebraska bill into Congress, there was a conspiracy to make slavery perpetual and national. I have arrayed, from time to time, the evidence which I think—I have thought—tends to establish and prove the truth of this charge.° I recurred to this charge at Ottawa. I shall not now have time to dwell upon it at very great length, but inasmuch as Judge Douglas, in his reply of half an hour, made some points upon me in relation to it, I propose noticing a few of them.

The Judge insists that, in the first speech I made in which I very distinctly made that charge, he thought for a good while I was in fun! *[Laughter]*—that I was playful, that I was not sincere about it, and that he only grew angry and somewhat excited when he found that I insisted upon it as a matter of earnestness. He says he characterized it as a falsehood as far as I implicated his *moral character* in that transaction. Well, I did not know, till he presented that view, that I had implicated his moral character. He is very much in the habit, when he argues me up into a position I never thought of occupying, of very cozily saying he has no doubt Lincoln is "conscientious" in saying so. He should remember that I did not know but what he was *altogether "conscientious"* in that matter. *[Laughter]* I can conceive it possible for men to conspire to do a good thing, and I really find nothing in Judge Douglas's course or arguments that is contrary to, or inconsistent with, his belief in° a conspiracy to nationalize and spread slavery as being a good and blessed thing. *[Laughter]* And so I hope he will understand that I do not at all question but that in all this matter he is entirely "conscientious." *[Laughter, cheers]*

But to draw your attention to one of the points I made in this case, beginning at the beginning. When the Nebraska bill was introduced, or a short time afterwards, by an amendment, I believe, it was provided—and I am afraid I shall be offensive to the Judge by quoting it again°—that it must be considered "the true intent and meaning of this act not to legislate slavery into any state or territory,° or to exclude it therefrom, but to leave the people thereof perfectly free to form and regulate their own domestic institutions in their own way, subject only to the Constitution of the United States."[4] I have called his attention to the fact that when he and some others began arguing that they were giving an increased degree of liberty to the people in the territories over and above what they formerly had on the question of slavery, a question was raised whether the law was enacted to give such unconditional liberty to the people. And to test the sincerity of this mode of argument, Mr. Chase of Ohio introduced an amendment, in which he made the law, if the amendment were adopted, expressly declare that the people of the territory should have the power to exclude slavery if they saw fit. I have asked attention also to the fact that Judge Douglas and those who acted with him voted that amendment down, notwithstanding it expressed exactly the thing they said was the true intent and meaning of the law. I have called at-

---

4. *U.S. Statutes at Large*, 10, 283.

tention to the fact that, in subsequent times, a decision of the Supreme Court has been made in which it has been declared that a territorial legislature has no constitutional right to exclude slavery.[5] And I have argued and said that, for men who did intend that the people of the territory should have the right to exclude slavery absolutely and unconditionally, the voting down of Chase's amendment is wholly inexplicable. It is a puzzle—a riddle that cannot be understood. °

But I have said that with men who did look forward to such a decision, or who had it in contemplation, that such a decision of the Supreme Court would or might be made, the voting down of that amendment would be perfectly rational and intelligible. It would keep Congress from coming in collision with the decision when it was made. Anybody can conceive that if there was an intention or expectation that such a decision was to follow, it would not be a very desirable party attitude to get into—for the Supreme Court, all or nearly all its members belonging to the same party, to decide one way, when the party in Congress had decided the other way. Hence it would be very rational, for men expecting such a decision, to keep the niche in that law clear for it.

After pointing this out, I tell Judge Douglas that it looks to me as though here was the reason why Chase's amendment was voted down. I tell him that, as he did it and knows why he did it, if it was done for a reason different from this, *he knows what that reason was, and can tell us what it was.* I tell him, also, it will be vastly more satisfactory to the country for him to give some other plausible, intelligible reason *why* it was voted down than to stand upon his dignity and call people liars. *[Cheers]*

Well, on Saturday he did make his answer, and what do you think it was? He says if I had only taken upon myself to tell the whole truth about that amendment of Chase's, no explanation would have been necessary on his part—or words to that effect. Now, I say here, that I am quite unconscious of having suppressed anything material to the case, and I am very frank to admit, if there is any sound reason other than that which appeared to me material, it is quite fair for him to present it. What reason does he propose? That when Chase came forward with his amendment expressly authorizing the people to exclude slavery from the limits of every territory, Gen. Cass proposed to Chase, if he, Chase, would add to his amendment that the people should have the power to *introduce* or exclude it, ° they would let it go. And because Chase would not do that, they voted his amendment down. I believe I fairly state Judge Douglas's answer. ° This is substantially all of his reply. °

Well, it turns out, I believe, upon examination of the record, ° that Gen. Cass took some part in the little running debate upon that amendment, and then ran

---

5. The *Dred Scott* decision.

away *and did not vote on it at all. [Laughter]* Is not that the fact? *[Applause]* So confident, as I think, was Gen. Cass, that there was a snake somewhere about, he chose to run away from the whole thing. This is an inference I draw from the fact that, though he took part in the debate, his name does not appear in the ayes and noes.

But does Judge Douglas's reply amount to a satisfactory answer? *[Cries of both "Yes" and "No"]* There is some little difference of opinion here. *[Laughter]* But I ask attention to a few more views bearing on the question of whether it amounts to a satisfactory answer. The men who were determined that that amendment should not get into the bill and spoil the place where Dred Scott decision was to come in, sought an excuse to get rid of it some way.° One of these ways—one of these excuses—was to ask Chase to add to his proposed amendment a provision that the people might *introduce* slavery if they wanted to. They very well knew Chase would do no such thing, that Mr. Chase was one of the men differing from them on the broad principle of his insisting that freedom was *better* than slavery, a man who would not consent to enact a law, penned with his own hand, by which he was made to recognize slavery on the one hand and liberty on the other as *precisely equal.* And when they insisted on his doing this, they very well knew they insisted on that which he would not for a moment think of doing, and that they were only bluffing him. I believe—I have not, since he made his answer, had a chance to examine the journals or *Congressional Globe,* and therefore speak from memory—I believe the state of the bill at that time, according to parliamentary rules, was such that no member could propose an additional amendment to Chase's amendment. I rather think this is the truth. The Judge shakes his head. Very well. I would like to know, then, *if they wanted Chase's amendment fixed over, why somebody else could not have offered to do it?* If they wanted it amended, why did they not offer the amendment? Why did they stand there taunting and quibbling at Chase? *[Laughter]* Why did they not *put it in themselves?*

But, to put it on the other ground, suppose that there was such an amendment offered, and Chase's was an amendment to an amendment. Until one is disposed of by parliamentary law, you cannot pile another on. Then all these gentlemen had to do was to vote Chase's on, and then in the amended form in which the whole stood, add their own amendment to it. If they wanted it put in that shape, this was all they were obliged to do, and the ayes and noes show that there were 36 who voted it down, against 10 who voted in favor of it. The 36 held entire sway and control. They could, in some form or other, have put that bill in the exact shape they wanted. If there was a rule preventing their amending it at the time, they could pass that and then Chase's amendment being merged, put it in the shape they wanted. They did not choose to do so, but they went into a quibble with Chase to get him to add what they knew he would not add.

And because he would not, they stand upon that flimsy pretext for voting down what they argued was the meaning and intent of their own bill. They left room thereby for this Dred Scott decision, which goes very far to make slavery national throughout the United States.

I pass one or two points I have because my time will very soon expire, but I must be allowed to say that Judge Douglas recurs again, as he did upon one or two other occasions, to° the enormity of Lincoln—an insignificant individual like Lincoln—upon his ipse dixit[6] charging a conspiracy upon a large number of members of Congress, the Supreme Court, and two presidents, to nationalize slavery. I want to say that, in the first place, I have made no charge of this sort upon my *ipse dixit,* or upon my word.° I have only arrayed the evidence tending to prove it, and presented it to the understanding of others, saying what I think it proves, but giving you the means of judging whether it proves it or not. This is precisely what I have done. I have not placed it upon my *ipse dixit* at all.

On this occasion, I wish to recall his attention to a piece of evidence which I brought forward at Ottawa on Saturday, showing that he had made substantially the *same charge* against substantially the *same persons,* excluding his dear self from the category. I ask him to give some attention to the evidence which I brought forward, that he himself had discovered a "fatal blow being struck" against the right of the people to exclude slavery from their limits, which "fatal blow" he assumed was° in evidence in an article in the *Washington Union,* published "by authority."[7] I ask by whose authority? He discovers a similar or identical provision in the Lecompton Constitution. Made by whom? The framers of that constitution. Advocated by whom? By all the members of the party in the nation who advocated the introduction of Kansas into the Union under the Lecompton Constitution.

I have asked his attention to the evidence that he arrayed to prove that such a "fatal blow" was being struck, and to the facts which he brought forward in sup-

---

6. *Ipse dixit:* an assertion made on authority but not proved.

7. AL alludes here, as he did at Ottawa, to a speech given by SAD on Mar. 22, 1858, in which the Senator arraigned the *Washington Union,* a Buchanan mouthpiece, for claiming on the previous Nov. 17 that the emancipation of slaves in Northern states was a violation of constitutional guarantees of the sanctity of property. The next day the *Union* defended the Lecompton Constitution and its assertion of the inviolability of slave property. SAD in his speech argued that state sovereignty was undermined by such a doctrine as the *Union* expressed. AL's claim here is that SAD's attack on the *Union,* and by implication on the administration it supported, was no less "villainous" than AL's claim of a conspiracy among the senator, Presidents Pierce and Buchanan, and Chief Justice Taney to nationalize slavery, and that indeed at that earlier time SAD was making a claim similar to AL's, though excepting himself from the charge. AL read from a pamphlet version of SAD's speech, printed for public distribution, *Speech of Senator Douglas, of Illinois, against the Admission of Kansas under the Lecompton Constitution* (Washington: Lemuel Towers, 1858); the reference to the "fatal blow being struck" is on p. 24.

port of that charge, being identical with the one which he thinks so villainous in me. He pointed it not at a newspaper editor merely, but at the President and his cabinet and the members of Congress advocating the Lecompton Constitution and those framing that instrument. I must again be permitted to remind him that, although my *ipse dixit* may not be as great as his, yet it somewhat reduces the force of his calling my attention to the *enormity* of my making a like charge against him. *[Applause]*

Go on, Judge Douglas.

DOUGLAS'S REPLY

L adies and Gentlemen: The silence with which you have listened to Mr. Lincoln during his hour is creditable to this vast audience, composed of men of various, of all° political parties. Nothing is more honorable to any large mass of people assembled for the purpose of a fair discussion than that kind and respectful attention that is yielded not only to your political friends, but to those who are opposed to you in politics.

I am glad that at last I have brought Mr. Lincoln to the conclusion that he had better define his position on certain political questions to which I called his attention at Ottawa. He there showed no disposition, no inclination to answer them. I did not present idle questions for him to answer merely for my gratification. I laid the foundation for those interrogatories by showing that they constituted the platform of the party whose nominee he is for the Senate. I did not presume that I had the right to catechize him upon every question° as I saw proper, unless I showed that his party, or a majority of it, stood upon the platform and were in favor of the propositions upon which my questions were based. I desired simply to know, inasmuch as he had been nominated as the first, last, and only choice of his party, whether he concurred in the platform which that party had adopted for its government.

In a few moments I will proceed to review the answers which he has given to these interrogatories, but in order to relieve his anxiety I will first respond to those which he has presented to me. Mark you, he has not presented interrogatories which have ever received the sanction of the party with which I am acting, and hence he has no other foundation for them than his own curiosity.

First, he desires to know if the people of Kansas shall form a constitution by means entirely proper and unobjectionable and ask admission into the Union as a state, before they have the requisite population for a member of Congress, whether I will vote for that admission. Well, now, I regret exceedingly that he did not answer that interrogatory himself before he put it to me, in order that we might understand, and not be left to infer, on which side he is. Mr. Trumbull, during the last session of Congress, voted from the beginning to the end against the admission of Oregon, although a free state, because she had not the requisite population for a member of Congress. Mr. Trumbull would not consent, under any circumstances, to let a state, free or slave, come into the Union until it had the requisite population. As Mr. Trumbull is in the field, fighting for Mr. Lincoln, I would like to have Mr. Lincoln answer his own question and tell me whether he is fighting Trumbull on that issue or not. *[Cheers]* But I will answer his question. In reference to Kansas, it is my opinion that as she has population enough to constitute a slave state, she has people enough for a free state. *[Cheers]*

I will not make Kansas an exceptional case to the other states of the Union. *[Cheers]* I hold it to be a sound rule of universal application to require a territory to contain the requisite population for a member of Congress, before it is admitted as a state into the Union. I made that proposition in the Senate in 1856, and I renewed it during the last session in a bill providing that no territory of the United States should form a constitution and apply for admission until it had the requisite population. On another occasion I proposed that neither Kansas, or any other territory, should be admitted until it had the requisite population. Congress did not adopt any of my propositions containing this general rule, but did make an exception of Kansas. I will stand by that exception. *[Cheers, applause]* Either Kansas must come in as a free state, with whatever population she may have, or the rule must be applied to all the other territories alike.[8] *[Cheers]* I therefore answer at once, that it having been decided that Kansas has people enough for a slave state, I hold that she has enough for a free state. *[Cheers, applause]*

I hope Mr. Lincoln is satisfied with my answer. *[Cheers]* And now I would like to get his answer to his own interrogatory—whether or not he will vote to admit Kansas before she has the requisite population. I want to know whether he will vote to admit Oregon before that territory has the requisite population. Mr. Trumbull will not, and the same reason that commits Mr. Trumbull against the admission of Oregon, commits him against Kansas, even if she should apply for admission as a free state. *[Cheers]* If there is any sincerity, any truth in the argument of Mr. Trumbull in the Senate against the admission of Oregon because she had not 93,420 people, although her population was larger than that of Kansas, he stands pledged against the admission of both Oregon and Kansas until they have 93,420 inhabitants. I would like Mr. Lincoln to answer this question. I would like him to take his own medicine. *[Laughter]* If he differs with Mr. Trumbull,

---

8. Though not directly so stated here, both AL and SAD have reference to provisions of the English bill, which would couple Kansas's admission to the Union with a land grant.

let him answer his argument against the admission of Oregon, instead of poking questions at me. *[Cheers]*

The next question propounded to me by Mr. Lincoln is, "Can the people of a territory, in any lawful way, against the wishes of any citizen of the United States, exclude slavery from their limits prior to the formation of a state constitution?" I answer emphatically, as Mr. Lincoln has heard me answer a hundred times from every stump in Illinois, that in my opinion the people of a territory can, by lawful means, exclude slavery from their limits prior to the formation of a state constitution. *[Applause]* Mr. Lincoln knew that I had answered that question over and over again. He heard me argue the Nebraska bill on that principle all over the state in 1854, in 1855, and in 1856, and he has no excuse for pretending to be in doubt as to my position on that question.[9]

It matters not what way the Supreme Court may hereafter decide as to the abstract question whether slavery may or may not go into a territory under the Constitution. The people have the lawful means to introduce it or exclude it as they please, for the reason that slavery cannot exist a day or an hour anywhere, unless it is supported by local police regulations, furnishing remedies and means of enforcing the right to hold slaves.° Those police regulations can only be established by the local legislature, and if the people are opposed to slavery, they will elect representatives to that body who will, by unfriendly legislation, effectually prevent the introduction of it into their midst. If, on the contrary, they are for it, their legislation will favor its extension. Hence, no matter what the decision of the Supreme Court may be on that abstract question, still the right of the people to make a slave territory or a free territory is perfect and complete under the Nebraska bill. I hope Mr. Lincoln deems my answer satisfactory on that point.

In this connection, I will notice the charge which he has introduced in relation to Mr. Chase's amendment. I thought that I had chased that amendment out of Mr. Lincoln's brain at Ottawa *[Laughter]*, but it seems that it still haunts his imagination, and he is not yet satisfied. I had supposed that he would be ashamed to press that question further. He is a lawyer, and has been a member of Congress, and has occupied his time and amused you by telling you about parliamentary proceedings. He ought to have known better than to try to palm off his miserable impositions upon this intelligent audience. *[Cheers]* The Nebraska bill provided "that the legislative power and authority of the said Territory, should extend to all rightful subjects of legislation consistent with the organic act and the Constitution

---

9. SAD's answer to Lincoln's second question is the famous "Freeport Doctrine," long thought to have ruined the senator's chances for the presidency in 1860 by antagonizing Southern Democrats, though it strengthened him in the Illinois senatorial race.

of the United States."[10] It did not make any exception as to slavery, but gave all the power that it was possible for Congress to give, without violating the Constitution, to the territorial legislature, with no exception or limitation on the subject of slavery at all. The language of that bill, which I have quoted, gave the full power and the full authority over the subject of slavery, affirmatively and negatively, to introduce it or exclude it, so far as the Constitution of the United States would permit. What more could Mr. Chase give by his amendment? Nothing. He offered his amendment for the identical purpose for which Mr. Lincoln is using it, to enable demagogues in the country to try and deceive the people. *[Cheers]*

His amendment was to this effect: it provided that the legislature should have the power to exclude slavery. And General Cass suggested, "why not give the power to introduce as well as exclude?" The answer was, they have the power already in the bill to do both. Chase was afraid his amendment would be adopted if he put the alternative proposition and so make it fair both ways, but would not yield. He offered it for the purpose of having it rejected. He offered it, as he has himself avowed over and over again, simply to make capital out of it for the stump. He expected that it would be capital for small politicians in the country, and that they would make an effort to deceive the people with it, and he was not mistaken, for Lincoln is carrying out the plan admirably.

Lincoln knows that the Nebraska bill, without Chase's amendment, gave all the power which the Constitution would permit. Could Congress confer any more? Could Congress go beyond the Constitution of the country? We gave all, a full grant, with no exception in regard to slavery one way or the other. We left that question, as we left all others, to be decided by the people for themselves, just as they pleased. I will not occupy my time on this question. I have argued it before all over Illinois. I have argued it in this beautiful city of Freeport. I have argued it in the North, the South, the East and the West, avowing the same sentiments and the same principles. I have not been afraid to avow my sentiments up here for fear I would be trotted down into Egypt. *[Cheers, laughter]*

The third question which Mr. Lincoln presented is: If the Supreme Court of the United States shall decide that a state of this Union cannot exclude slavery from its own limits, will I submit to it? I am amazed that Lincoln should ask such a question.

Voice: A school boy knows better.

---

10. SAD quotes, slightly inaccurately, from sect. 24 of the Kansas-Nebraska Act: "That the legislative power of the Territory shall extend to the rightful subjects of legislation consistent with the Constitution of the United States and the provisions of this act." Senate Bill SB 22, 33rd Cong., 1st Sess., 25.

Douglas: Yes, a school boy does know better. Mr. Lincoln's object is to cast an imputation upon the Supreme Court. He knows that there never was but one man in America, claiming any degree of intelligence or decency, who ever for a moment pretended such a thing. It is true that the *Washington Union,* in an article published on the 17th of last °December,[11] did put forth that doctrine, and I denounced the article on the floor of the Senate, in a speech which Mr. Lincoln now pretends was against the President. The *Union* had claimed that slavery had a right to go into the free states, and that any provision in the constitution or laws of the free states to the contrary was° null and void. I denounced it in the Senate, as I said before, and I was the first man who did. Lincoln's friends—Trumbull and Seward and Hale and Wilson—and the whole Black Republican side of the Senate were silent. They left it to me to denounce it. *[Cheers]* And what was the reply made to me on that occasion? Mr. Toombs, of Georgia, got up and undertook to lecture me on the ground that I ought not to have deemed the article worthy of notice, and ought not to have replied to it; that there was not one man, woman or child South of the Potomac, in any slave state, who did not repudiate any such pretension.[12]

Mr. Lincoln knows that that reply was made on the spot, and yet now he asks this question. He might as well ask me, suppose Mr. Lincoln should steal a horse, would I sanction it. *[Laughter]* And it would be as genteel in me to ask him, in the event he stole a horse, what ought to be done with him. He casts an imputation upon the Supreme Court of the United States by supposing that they would violate the Constitution of the United States. I tell him that such a thing is not possible. *[Cheers]* It would be an act of moral treason that no man on the bench could ever descend to. Mr. Lincoln himself would never, in his partisan feelings, so far forget what was right as to be guilty of such an act.

The fourth question of Mr. Lincoln is, are you in favor of acquiring additional territory in disregard as to how such acquisition may affect the Union on the slavery question? This question is very ingeniously and cunningly put. The Black Republican creed lays it down expressly that under no circumstances shall we acquire any more territory, unless slavery is first prohibited in the country. I ask Mr. Lincoln whether he is in favor of that proposition. *[Addressing Lincoln]* Are you opposed to the acquisition of any more territory, under any circumstances, unless slavery is prohibited in it? That he does not like to answer. When I ask him whether he stands up to that article in the platform of his party, he turns, yankee-

---

11. SAD presumably misspoke, as the actual date was November 17.

12. The *Washington Union* article in question was published on Nov. 17, 1857. For SAD's denunciation of it and Toombs's response, see *Congressional Globe, Appendix,* 35th Cong., 1st Sess., Mar. 22, 1858, 194–202.

fashion, and without answering it, asks me whether I am in favor of acquiring territory without regard to how it may affect the Union on the slavery question. I answer that whenever it becomes necessary, in our growth and progress to acquire more territory, that I am in favor of it, without reference to the question of slavery. And when we have acquired it, I will leave the people free to do as they please, either to make it slave or free territory, as they prefer. *[Applause]* It is idle to tell me or you that we have territory enough. Our fathers supposed that we had enough when our territory extended to the Mississippi River, but a few year's growth and expansion satisfied them that we needed more, and the Louisiana territory, from the West bank° of the Mississippi, to the British possessions, was acquired. Then we acquired Oregon, then California and New Mexico. We have enough now for the present, but this is a young and growing nation. It swarms as often as a hive of bees, and as new swarms are turned out each year, there must be hives in which they can gather and make their honey.

In less than fifteen years, if the same progress that has distinguished this country for the last fifteen years continues, every foot of vacant land between this and the Pacific Ocean, owned by the United States, will be occupied. Will you not continue to increase at the end of fifteen years as well as now? I tell you "increase, and multiply, and expand" is the law of this nation's existence. You cannot limit this great republic by mere boundary lines, saying, "Thus far shalt thou go, and no further." Any one of you gentlemen might as well say to a son twelve years old that he is big enough, and must not grow any larger, and in order to prevent his growth put a hoop around him to keep him to his present size. What would be the result? Either the hoop must burst and be rent asunder, or the child must die. *[Laughter]* So it would be with this great nation. With our natural increase, growing with rapidity unknown in any other part of the globe, with the tide of emigration that is fleeing from despotism in the old world to seek a refuge in our own, there is a constant torrent pouring into this country that requires more land, more territory upon which to settle. And just as fast as our interests and our destiny require additional territory in the North, in the South, or on the islands of the ocean, I am for it, and when we acquire it will leave the people, according to the Nebraska bill, free to do as they please on the subject of slavery and every other question. *[Cheers]*

I trust now that Mr. Lincoln will deem himself answered on his four points. He racked his brain so much in devising these four questions that he exhausted himself, and had not strength enough to invent the others. *[Laughter]* As soon as he is able to hold a council with his advisers—Lovejoy, Farnsworth, and Fred Douglass—he will frame and propound others.

Voices: "Good, good."°

Douglas: You Black Republicans who say "good," I have no doubt think that they are all good men. I have reason to recollect that some people in this country think that Fred Douglass is a very good man. The last time I came here to make a speech, while talking from the stand to you people of Freeport, as I am doing to day, I saw a carriage, and a magnificent one it was, drive up and take a position on the outside of the crowd, a beautiful young lady was sitting on the box seat, whilst Fred Douglass and her mother reclined inside, and the owner of the carriage acted as driver. *[Laughter, cheers]* I saw this in your own town.[13]

Voice: What of it?

Douglas: What of it!° All I have to say of it is this—that if you Black Republicans think that the negro ought to be on a social equality with your wives and daughters and ride in a carriage with your wife, whilst you drive the team, you have perfect right to do so. *[Cheers]* I am told that one of Fred Douglass's kinsmen, another rich black negro, is now traveling in this part of the state making speeches for his friend Lincoln as the champion of black men.[14]

Voice: What have you got to say against it?

Douglas: All I have to say on that subject is that those of you who believe that the nigger° is your equal and ought to be on an equality with you socially, politically, and legally, have a right to entertain those opinions, and of course will vote for Mr. Lincoln. *[Cheers]*

I have a word to say on Mr. Lincoln's answer to the interrogatories contained in my speech at Ottawa, and which he has pretended to reply to here today. Mr. Lincoln makes a great parade of the fact that I quoted a platform as having been adopted by the Black Republican party at Springfield in 1854, which, it turns out, was adopted at another place. Mr. Lincoln loses sight of the thing itself in his ecstasies over the mistake I made in stating the place where it was done. He thinks that that platform was not adopted on the right "spot."[15]

When I put the direct questions to Mr. Lincoln to ascertain whether he now stands pledged to that creed—to the unconditional repeal of the Fugitive

---

13. Frederick Douglass and SAD spoke in Freeport on the same day, Oct. 27, 1854. Local tradition has it that Frederick Douglass was the guest of Dexter A. Knowlton, a Freeport merchant, landowner, and Free-Soil activist. *Freeport Journal,* Oct. 26, 1854; *History of Stephenson County 1970* (Freeport: County of Stephenson, 1972), 41.

14. SAD may refer to H. Ford Douglas, a Chicago-based black abolitionist orator and editor. An escapee from slavery when young, Douglas was a proponent of black emigration to Central America, believing that African American rights would not be recognized in the United States until slavery was abolished. H. Ford Douglas was reported as speaking in Illinois in the fall of 1858. See *Peoria Transcript,* Oct. 22, 1858, and *Galesburg Democrat,* Oct. 23, 1858.

15. The platform in question was adopted at a Republican district convention at Aurora, Illinois, in Sept. 1854.

Slave Law; a refusal to admit any more slave states into the Union, even if the people want them; a determination to apply the Wilmot Proviso not only to all the territory we now have, but all that we may hereafter acquire—he refused to answer, and his followers say, in excuse, that the resolutions upon which I based my interrogatories were not adopted at the *"right spot." [Laughter, applause]* Lincoln and his political friends are great on *"spots." [Laughter]* In Congress, as representative of this state, he declared the Mexican War to be unjust and infamous, and would not support it, or acknowledge his own country to be right in the contest, because he said that American blood was not shed on American soil in the *"right spot."* And now he cannot answer the questions I put to him at Ottawa because the resolutions I read were not adopted at the *"right spot."*[16] It may be possible that I was led into an error as to the *spot* on which the resolutions I then read were proclaimed, but I was not, and am not in error, as to the fact of their forming the basis of the creed of the Republican party when that party first organized. *[Cheers]*

I will state to you the evidence I had, and upon which I relied for my statement that the resolutions in question were adopted at Springfield on the 5th of October, 1854. Although I was aware that such resolutions had been passed in this district, and nearly all the Northern congressional districts and county conventions, I had not noticed whether or not they had been adopted by any state convention. In 1856, a debate arose in Congress between Major Thomas L. Harris, of the Springfield district, and Mr. Norton, of the Joliet district, on political matters connected with our state, in the course of which Major Harris quoted those resolutions as having been passed by the first Republican state convention that ever assembled in Illinois. I knew that Major Harris was remarkable for his accuracy, that he was a very conscientious and sincere man, and I also noticed that Norton did not question the accuracy of this statement.[17] I therefore took it for granted that it was so, and the other day, when I concluded to use the resolutions at Ottawa, I wrote to Charles H. Lanphier, editor of the *State Register,* at Springfield, calling his attention to them, telling him that I had been informed that Major Harris was lying sick at Springfield, and desiring him to call upon him and ascertain all the facts concerning the resolutions, the time, and the place where they were adopted. In reply, Mr. Lanphier sent me two copies of his paper, which I have here. The first is a copy of the *State Register,* published at Springfield, Mr. Lincoln's own town, on the 16th of October, 1854, only eleven days after the adjournment of the convention, from which I desire to read the following:

---

16. See "spot resolutions" in the glossary, p. 331.

17. For the exchange between Harris and Jesse O. Norton on Aug. 9, 1856, see *Congressional Globe, Appendix,* 34th Cong., 1st Sess., 1274.

During the late discussions in this city, Lincoln made a speech, to which Judge Douglas replied. In Lincoln's speech he took the broad ground that, according to the Declaration of Independence, the whites and blacks are equal. From this he drew the conclusion, which he several times repeated, that the white man had no right to pass laws for the government of the black man without the nigger's consent. This speech of Lincoln's was heard and applauded by all the abolitionists assembled in Springfield. So soon as Mr. Lincoln was done speaking Mr. Codding arose and requested all the delegates to the black republican convention to withdraw into the senate chamber. They did so, and after long deliberation they laid down the following abolition platform as the platform on which they stood—We call the particular attention of all our readers to it.°

Then follows the identical platform, word for word, which I read at Ottawa. [Cheers] Now, that was published in Mr. Lincoln's own town, eleven days after the convention was held, and it has remained on record up to *this day,* never contradicted.

When I quoted the resolutions at Ottawa and questioned Mr. Lincoln in relation to them, he said that his name was on the committee that reported them, but he did not serve, nor did he think he served, because he was, or thought he was, in Tazewell County at the time the convention was in session. He did not deny that the resolutions were passed by the Springfield convention. He did not know better, and evidently thought that they were, but afterwards his friends declared that they had discovered that they varied in some respects from the resolutions passed by that convention. I have shown you that I had good evidence for believing that the resolutions had been passed at Springfield. Mr. Lincoln ought to have known better, but not a word is said about his ignorance on the subject, whilst I, notwithstanding the circumstances, am accused of forgery.

Now, I will show you that if I have made a mistake as to the place where these resolutions were adopted—and when I get down to Springfield I will investigate the matter and see whether or not I have—that the principles they enunciate were adopted as the Black Republican platform in the various counties and congressional districts throughout the North end of the state in 1854. This platform was adopted in nearly every county that gave a Black Republican majority for the legislature in that year, and here is a man [pointing to Cyrenius B. Denio] who knows as well as any living man that it was the creed of the Black Republican party at that time. I would be willing to call Denio as a witness, or any other honest man belonging to that party. I will now read the resolutions adopted at the Rockford Convention on the 30th of August, 1854, which nominated Washburne for Congress. You elected him on the following platform:[18]

18. SAD's source for the following resolutions is undoubtedly a newspaper account, but which one is not clear. Some reports of the Rockford convention show slight variations from this version. See, for example, *Free West* (Chicago), Sept. 7, 1854.

Resolved, That the continued and increasing aggressions of slavery in our country are destructive of the best rights of a free people, and that such aggressions cannot be successfully resisted without the united political action of all good men.

Voices: All right.
Douglas: You say that is all right. Now for the next. °

Resolved, That the citizens of the United States hold in their hands peaceful, constitutional, and efficient remedy against the encroachments of the slave power, the ballot box, and, if that remedy is boldly and wisely applied, the principles of liberty and eternal justice will be established. *[Cheers]*
Resolved, That we accept this issue forced upon us by the slave power, and, in defense of freedom, will co-operate and be known as Republicans, pledged to the accomplishment of the following purposes:

> To bring the Administration of the Government back to the control of first principles; to restore Kansas and Nebraska to the position of free Territories; to repeal and entirely abrogate the fugitive slave law.

Voice: That's all right.
Douglas: That's all right, you say. Mr. Lincoln tells you he is not for it, and yet it is all right. Here is the next purpose to which you Black Republicans are pledged by this platform.
Voices: White Republicans! White! White!
Douglas: Wait until I read it. The next is°

> To restrict slavery to those States in which it exists; to prohibit the admission of any more slave States into the Union.

Voices: Good. Good.
Douglas: You answer by a loud voice that is all right. Now for the next.°

> To exclude slavery from all the territories over which the general government has exclusive jurisdiction, and to resist the acquisition of any more territories unless the introduction of slavery therein forever shall have been prohibited.

Well, you think that is a very good platform, do you not? *[Cries of approval, cheers]* If you do, if you approve it now, and think it is all right, you will not join with those men who say that I libel you by calling these your principles, will you? *[Laughter, cheers]* Now, Mr. Lincoln complains. Mr. Lincoln charges that I did you and him injustice by saying that this was the platform of your party. *[Laughter]* I am told that Washburne made a speech in Galena last night in which he abused me awfully for bringing to light this platform on which he was elected to Congress. He thought that you had forgotten it, as he and Mr. Lincoln desire to. *[Laughter]* He did not deny but that you had adopted it, and that he had subscribed to and was pledged to it, but he did not think it was fair to call it up and remind the people that it was their platform. But I am glad to find that you are more honest in your abolitionism than your leaders, by avowing that it is your platform, and right in your opinion. *[Laughter, cheers]* Now I will read another resolution:°

> *Resolved,* That in furtherance of these principles we will use such constitutional and lawful means as shall seem best adapted to their accomplishment, and that we will support no man for office under the General or State Government who is not positively committed to the support of these principles and whose personal character and conduct is not a guaranty that he is reliable and shall abjure all party allegiance and ties.
>
> *Resolved,* That we cordially invite persons of all former political parties whatever in favor of the object expressed in the above resolutions to unite with us in carrying them into effect.°

In the adoption of that platform, you not only declared that you would resist the admission of any more slave states, and work for the repeal of the Fugitive Slave Law, but you pledged yourselves not to vote for any man for state or federal offices who was not committed to these principles.

Voice: Exactly so.

Douglas: Yes, you say exactly.° You were thus committed. Similar resolutions to those were adopted in your county convention here, and now with your admissions that they are your platform and embody your sentiments now as they did then, what do you think of Mr. Lincoln, your candidate for the U. S. Senate, who is attempting to dodge the responsibility of this platform because it was not adopted in the right spot. *[Laughter, cheers]* I thought that it was adopted in Springfield, but it turns out it was not, that it was adopted at Rockford and in the various counties which comprise this congressional district. When I get into the next district, I will show that the same platform was adopted there, and so on through the state, until I nail the responsibility of it upon the back of the Black Republican party throughout the state.

Voices: White! White Republicans!°

Voice: Couldn't you modify and call it brown? *[Laughter]*

Douglas: Not a bit. I thought that you were becoming a little brown when your members in Congress voted for the Crittenden-Montgomery bill, but since you have backed out from that position and gone back to abolitionism, you are black and not brown. *[Laughter, cheers]*

Gentlemen, I have shown you what your platform was in 1854. You still adhere to it. The same platform was adopted by nearly all the counties where the Black Republican party had a majority in 1854. I wish now to call your attention to the action of your representatives in the legislature when they assembled together at Springfield. In the first place you must remember that this was the organization of a new party. It is so declared in the resolutions themselves, which say that you are going to dissolve all old party ties and call the new party Republican. The old Whig party was to have its throat cut from ear to ear, and the Democratic party was to be annihilated and blotted out of existence, whilst in lieu of these parties the Black Republican party was to be organized on this abolition platform. You know who the chief leaders were in breaking up and destroying these two great parties. Lincoln on the one hand and Trumbull on the other—being disappointed politicians *[Laughter]*, and having retired or been driven to obscurity by an outraged constituency because of their political sins—formed a scheme to abolitionize the two parties and lead the old line Whigs and old line Democrats captive, bound hand and foot, into the abolition camp. Giddings, Chase, Fred Douglass and Lovejoy were here to christen them whenever they were brought in. *[Laughter]* Lincoln went to work to dissolve the old line Whig party. Clay was dead, and although the sod was not yet green on his grave, this man undertook to bring into disrepute those great compromise measures of 1850, with which Clay and Webster were identified.

Up to 1854, the old Whig party and the Democratic party had stood on a common platform so far as this slavery question was concerned. You Whigs and we Democrats differed about the bank, the tariff, distribution, the specie circular and the sub-treasury, but we agreed on this slavery question and the true mode of preserving the peace and harmony of the Union. The compromise measures of 1850 were introduced by Clay, were defended by Webster, and supported by Cass, and were approved by Fillmore, and sanctioned by the national men of both parties. They constituted a common plank upon which both Whigs and Democrats stood. In 1852 the Whig party in its last national convention at Baltimore endorsed and approved these measures of Clay, and so did the national convention of the Democratic party held that same year. Thus the old line Whigs and the old line Democrats stood pledged to the great principle of self-government, which guarantees to the people of each territory the right to decide the slavery question for themselves, as laid down in the compromise measures of 1850, and carried out in the Kansas-Nebraska bill.° In 1854, after the death of Clay and Webster, Mr. Lincoln, on the part of the Whigs, undertook to abolitionize the Whig party, by dissolving it, transferring the members into the abolition camp and making them train under Giddings, Fred Douglass, Lovejoy, Chase, Farnsworth, and other abolition leaders. Trumbull undertook to dissolve the Democratic party by taking old Democrats into the abolition camp. Mr. Lincoln was aided in his efforts by many leading Whigs throughout the state, your member of Congress, Mr. Washburne, being one of the most active. Trumbull was aided by many renegades from the

Democratic party, among whom were John Wentworth *[Laughter]*, Tom Turner, and others with whom you are familiar.

Thomas J. Turner (from the platform): I drew these resolutions.°

Douglas: Yes, and Turner says that he drew these resolutions. *[Cheers from both sides]* That is right, give Turner cheers for drawing the resolutions, if you approve them. If he drew those resolutions, he will not deny that they are the creed of the Black Republican party.

Turner: They are our creed exactly. *[Cheers]*

Douglas: Turner says they are his—that is the Black Republican creed—exactly.° And yet Lincoln denies that he stands on them. *[Laughter]* Mr. Turner says that the creed of the Black Republican party is the admission of no more slave states, and yet Mr. Lincoln declares that he would not like to be placed in a position where he would have to vote for them. All I have to say to friend Lincoln is that I do not think there is much danger of his being placed in a position where he will have to vote on the admission of a slave state.° *[Laughter]* As Mr. Lincoln would be very sorry to be placed in such an embarrassing position as to be obliged to vote on the admission of any more slave states, I propose, out of mere kindness, to relieve him from any such necessity. *[Laughter, cheers]*

When the bargain between Lincoln and Trumbull was completed for abolitionizing the Whig and Democratic parties, they "spread" over the state, Lincoln still pretending to be an old line Whig in order to "rope in" the Whigs, and Trumbull pretending to be as good a Democrat as he ever was in order to coax the Democrats over into the abolition ranks. They played the part that "decoy ducks" play down on the Potomac River. In that part of the country they make artificial ducks and put them on the water in places where the wild ducks are to be found for the purpose of decoying them. Well, Lincoln and Trumbull played the part of these "decoy ducks" and deceived enough old line Whigs and old line Democrats to elect a Black Republican legislature. When that legislature met, the first thing it did was to elect as Speaker of the House the very man who is now boasting that he wrote the abolition platform on which Lincoln will not stand. *[Cheers]* I want to know of Mr. Turner whether or not, when he was elected, he was a good embodiment of Republican principles?

Turner: I hope I was then and am now.

Douglas: He answers that he hopes he was then and is now. *[Applause, cheers]* He wrote that Black Republican platform and is satisfied with it now. *[Cheers]* I admire and acknowledge Turner's honesty. Every man of you know that what he says about these resolutions being the platform of the Black Republican party is true, and you also know that each one of these men who are shuffling and trying to deny it are only trying to cheat the people out of their votes for the purpose of deceiving them still more after the election. *[Cheers]*

I propose to trace this thing a little further, in order that you can see what additional evidence there is to fasten this revolutionary platform upon the Black Republican party. When the legislature assembled, there was a United States Senator to elect in the place of Gen. Shields, and before they proceeded to ballot, Lovejoy insisted on laying down certain principles by which to govern the party. It has been published to the world and satisfactorily proven that there was, at the time the alliance was made between Trumbull and Lincoln to abolitionize the two parties, an agreement that Lincoln should take Shields's place in the United States Senate, and Trumbull should have mine so soon as they could conveniently get rid of me. *[Laughter]* When Lincoln was beaten for Shields's place in a manner I will refer to in a few minutes, he felt very sore and restive. His friends grumbled, and some of them came out and charged that the most infamous treachery had been practiced against him; that the bargain was that Lincoln was to have had Shields's place, and Trumbull was to have waited for mine, but that Trumbull having the control of a few abolitionized Democrats, he prevented them from voting for Lincoln, thus keeping him within a few votes of an election until he succeeded in forcing the party to drop him and elect Trumbull. Well, Trumbull having cheated Lincoln, his friends made a fuss, and in order to keep them and Lincoln quiet, the party were obliged to come forward, in advance, at the last state election, and make a pledge that they would go for Lincoln and nobody else. Lincoln could not be silenced in any other way.[19]

Now, there are a great many Black Republicans of you who do not know this thing was done. *[Cries of "White Republicans"]* I wish to remind you that while Mr. Lincoln was speaking there was not a Democrat vulgar and black-guard enough to interrupt him. *[Applause, cheers]* But I know that the shoe is pinching you. I am clinching Lincoln now, and you are scared to death for the result. *[Cheers]* I have seen this thing before. I have seen men make appointments for joint discussions, and the moment their man has been heard, try to interrupt and prevent a fair hearing of the other side. I have seen your mobs before, and defy your wrath. *[Applause, cheers]* My friends, do not cheer, for I need my whole time. The object of the opposition is to occupy my attention in order to prevent me from giving the whole evidence and nailing this double dealing on the Black Republican party.

As I have before said, Lovejoy demanded a declaration of principles on the part of the Black Republicans of the legislature before going into an election for

19. SAD alludes to charges concerning AL's failed 1855 Senate candidacy that were made by AL's friend James A. Matheny in a speech in 1856. Parts of the speech appeared in the *Chicago Times*, June 25, 1858, and were read by SAD at Jonesboro (pp. 91–93) and Charleston (pp. 158–59).

United States Senator. He offered the following preamble and resolutions which I hold in my hand. I will read the resolutions and hand the preamble to the reporters, that they may publish the whole.°

> *Resolved by the House of Representatives, the Senate concurring therein,* That our senators in Congress be instructed, and our representatives requested, to introduce, if not otherwise introduced, and to vote for a bill to restore such prohibition to the aforesaid territories, and also to extend a similar prohibition to all territory which now belongs to the United States, or which may hereafter come under their jurisdiction.
>
> *Resolved,* That our senators in congress be instructed, and our representatives requested, to vote against the admission of any state into the Union, the constitution of which does not prohibit slavery, whether the territory out of which such state may have been formed shall have been acquired by conquest, treaty, purchase, or from original territory of the United States.
>
> *Resolved,* That our senators in congress be instructed and our representatives requested to introduce and vote for a bill to repeal an act entitled "An act respecting fugitives from justice and persons escaping from the service of their masters,"[20] and failing in that, for such a modification of it as shall secure the right of *habeas corpus* and trial by jury before the regularly constituted authorities of the state, to all persons claimed as owing service or labor.[21]

Voices: Good, Good.

Douglas: Yes, you say "good, good," and I have no doubt you think so. Those resolutions were introduced by Mr. Lovejoy immediately preceding the election

---

20. The reference is to the Fugitive Slave Law of 1850.

21. The text SAD read is from *Journal of the House of Representatives of the Nineteenth General Assembly of the State of Illinois* (Springfield: Lanphier & Walker, 1855), Feb. 6, 1855, 283–84, 306–9. The preamble was apparently not read but handed to the reporters, though neither paper printed it. It reads as follows:

> Whereas, human slavery is a violation of the principles of natural and revealed rights; and whereas, the fathers of the Revolution, fully imbued with the spirit of these principles, declared freedom to be the inalienable birthright of all men; and whereas, the preamble to the Constitution of the United States avers that that instrument was ordained to establish justice, and secure the blessings of liberty to ourselves and our posterity; and whereas, in furtherance of the above principles, slavery was forever prohibited in the old northwest territory, and more recently in all that territory lying west and north of the State of Missouri, by the act of the federal government; and whereas, the repeal of the prohibition last referred to, was contrary to the wishes of the people of Illinois, a violation of an implied compact, long deemed and held sacred by the citizens of the United States, and a wide departure from the uniform action of the general government in relation to the extension of slavery; therefore,

of senator. They declared first, that the Wilmot Proviso[22] must be applied to all territory North of 36 degrees, 30 minutes. Secondly, that it must be applied to all territory South of 36 degrees, 30 minutes. Thirdly, that it must be applied to all the territory now owned by the United States, and finally, that it must be applied to all territory hereafter to be acquired by the United States. The next resolution declares that no more slave states shall be admitted into this Union under any circumstances whatever, no matter whether they are formed out of territory now owned by us or that we may hereafter acquire, by treaty, by Congress, or in any manner whatever.

Voice: That is right.

Douglas: You say that is right. We will see in a moment.

The next resolution demands the unconditional repeal of the Fugitive Slave Law, although its unconditional repeal would leave no provision for carrying out that clause of the Constitution of the United States which guarantees the surrender of fugitives. If they could not get an unconditional repeal, they demanded that that law should be so modified as to make it as nearly useless as possible. Now I want to show you who voted for these resolutions. When the vote was taken on the first resolution it was decided in the affirmative—yeas 41, nays 32, and here are the votes, which I will hand to the reporter to copy.°

You will find that this is a strict party vote, between Democrats, on the one hand, and the Black Republicans, on the other.

Voices: White, white.

Douglas: I know your name, and always call things by their right name.

The point I wish to call your attention to, is this: that these resolutions were adopted on the 7th day of February, and that on the 8th they went into an election for a U.S. Senator, and on that day every man who voted for these resolutions, with but two exceptions, voted for Lincoln for the U.S. Senate.

Voice: Give us their names.

Douglas: I will read the names over to you if you want them, but I believe your object is to occupy my time.

On the next resolution, the vote stood—yeas 33, nays 40, and on the third resolution—yeas 25,° nays 47. I wish to impress it upon you, that every man who voted for those resolutions, with but two exceptions, voted on the next day for Lincoln, for U.S. Senator. Bear in mind that the members who thus voted for Lincoln were elected to the legislature, pledged to vote for no man for office under the state or federal government who was not committed to this Black Republican platform. *[Cries of "white, white" and cheers]* They were all so pledged. Mr. Turner,

---

22. See glossary, pp. 333–34.

who stands by me, and who then represented you, and who says that he wrote those resolutions, voted for Lincoln, when he was pledged not to do so unless Lincoln was committed in favor of those resolutions. I now ask Mr. Turner, did you violate your pledge in voting for Mr. Lincoln, or did he commit himself to your platform before you cast your vote for him?°

Not only is the name of Turner here, but there are names from the adjoining counties.° I could go through the whole list of names here and show you that all the Black Republicans in the legislature, who voted for Mr. Lincoln, with two exceptions,° had voted on the day previous for these resolutions. For instance, here are the names of Sargent and Little of Jo Daviess and Carroll; Thomas J. Turner, of Stephenson; Lawrence, of Boone and McHenry; Swan, of Lake; Pinckney, of Ogle county, and Lyman, of Winnebago. Thus you see every member from your congressional district voted for Mr. Lincoln, and they were pledged not to vote for him unless he was committed to the doctrine of no more slave states, the prohibition of slavery in the territories, and the repeal of the Fugitive Slave Law. Mr. Lincoln tells you today that he is not pledged to any such doctrine. Either Mr. Lincoln was then committed to those propositions, or Mr. Turner violated his pledges to you when he voted for him. Either Lincoln was pledged to each one of those propositions, or else every Black Republican representative from this congressional district violated his pledge of honor to his constituents by voting for him.

I ask you which horn of the dilemma will you take? Will you hold Lincoln up to the platform of his party, or will you accuse every representative you had in the legislature of violating his pledge of honor to his constituents? There is no escape for you. Either Mr. Lincoln was committed to those propositions, or your members violated their faith. Take either horn of the dilemma you choose. There is no dodging the question.

I want Lincoln's answer. He says he was not pledged to repeal the Fugitive Slave Law, that he does not quite like to do it. He will not introduce a law to repeal it, but thinks there ought to be some law. He does not tell what it ought to be. Upon the whole, he is altogether undecided, and don't know what to think or to do. That is the substance of his answer upon the repeal of the Fugitive Slave Law. I put the question to him distinctly, whether he endorsed that part of the Black Republican platform which calls for the entire abrogation and repeal of the Fugitive Slave Law. He answers no, that he does not endorse that, but he does not tell what he is for, or what he will vote for. His answer is, in fact, no answer at all. Why cannot he speak out and say what he is for and what he will do? In regard to there being no more slave states, he is not pledged to that. He would not like, he says, to be put in a position where he would have to vote one way or another upon that question. I pray you do not put him in a position that would embarrass him so much. *[Laughter]* Gentlemen, if he goes to the Senate, he may be put in that position, and then which way will he vote? Will he vote for or against the admission of a slave state?°

Voice: How will you vote?

Douglas: I will vote for the admission of just such a state as, by the form of their constitution, the people show they want. If they want slavery, they shall have it. If they prohibit slavery, it shall be prohibited. They can form their institutions to please themselves, subject only to the Constitution, and I for one stand ready to receive them into the Union. *[Cheers]* Why cannot your Black Republican candidates talk out as plain as that when they are questioned? *[Cheers]* I do not want to cheat any man out of his vote. No man is deceived in regard to my principles, if I have the power to express myself in terms explicit enough to convey my ideas.

Mr. Lincoln made a speech when he was nominated for the U.S. Senate which covers all these abolition platforms. He there lays down a proposition so broad in its abolitionism as to cover the whole ground.°

> In my opinion, it (the slavery agitation)° will not cease, until a crisis shall have been reached and passed. "A house divided against itself cannot stand." I believe this government cannot endure permanently half slave and half free. I do not expect the house to fall°—but I do expect it will cease to be divided. It will become all one thing, or all the other. Either the opponents of Slavery, will arrest the further spread of it, and place it where the public mind shall rest in the belief that it is in the course of ultimate extinction; or its advocates will push it forward, till it shall become alike lawful in all the States, old as well as new—North as well as South.[23]

There you find that Mr. Lincoln lays down the doctrine that this Union cannot endure divided as our fathers made it, with free and slave states. He says they must all become one thing, or all the other, that they must be all free or all slave, or else the Union cannot continue to exist. It being his opinion that to admit any more slave states, to continue to divide the Union into free and slave states, will dissolve it. I want to know of Mr. Lincoln whether he will vote for the admission of another slave state. He tells you the Union cannot exist unless the states are all free or all slave; he tells you that he is opposed to making them all slave, and hence he is for making them all free, in order that the Union may exist. And yet he will not say that he will not vote against the admission of another slave state, knowing that the Union must be dissolved if he votes for it. *[Laughter]*

I ask you if that is fair dealing? The true intent and inevitable conclusion to be drawn from his first Springfield speech is, that he is opposed to the admission

---

23. SAD quotes an excerpt from AL's "House Divided" speech of June 16, 1858. See Roy P. Basler et al., eds., *The Collected Works of Abraham Lincoln* (New Brunswick: Rutgers University Press, 1953), 2: 461–62.

of any more slave states under any circumstance. If he is so opposed, why not say so? If he believes this Union cannot endure divided into free and slave states, that they must all become free in order to save the Union, he is bound, as an honest man, to vote against any more slave states. If he believes it, he is bound to do it. Show me that it is my duty in order to save the Union to do a particular act, and I will do it, if the Constitution does not prohibit it. *[Applause]* I am not for the dissolution of the Union under any circumstances. *[Applause]* I will pursue no course of conduct that will give just cause for the dissolution of the Union. The hope of the friends of freedom throughout the world rests upon the perpetuity of this Union. The down-trodden and oppressed people who are suffering under European despotism all look with hope and anxiety to the American Union as the only resting place and permanent home of freedom and self-government.

Mr. Lincoln says that he believes that this Union cannot continue to endure with slave states in it, and yet he will not tell you distinctly whether he will vote for or against the admission of any more slave states, but says he would not like to be put to the test. *[Laughter]* I do not think he will be put to the test. *[Laughter]* I do not think that the people of Illinois desire a man to represent them who would not like to be put to the test on the performance of a high constitutional duty. *[Cheers]* I will retire in shame from the Senate of the United States when I am not willing to be put to the test in the performance of my duty. *[Applause]* I have been put to severe tests. I have stood by my principles in fair weather and in foul, in the sunshine and in the rain. I have defended the great principles of self-government here among you, when Northern sentiment ran in a torrent against me. And I have defended that same great principle when Southern sentiment came down like an avalanche upon me. I was not afraid of any test they put to me. I knew I was right. I knew my principles were sound. I knew that the people would see in the end that I had done right, and I knew that the God of Heaven would smile upon me if I was faithful in the performance of my duty. *[Cheers]*

Mr. Lincoln makes a charge of corruption against the Supreme Court of the United States, and two presidents of the United States, and attempts to bolster it up by saying that I did the same against the *Washington Union*. Suppose I did make that charge of corruption against the *Washington Union*, when it was true. Does that justify him in making a false charge against me and others? That is the question I would put. He says that at the time the Nebraska bill was introduced, and before it was passed, there was a conspiracy between the Judges of the Supreme Court, President Pierce, President Buchanan, and myself, by that bill and the decision of the Court, to break down the barrier and establish slavery all over the Union. Does he not know that that charge is historically false as against President Buchanan? He knows that Mr. Buchanan was at that time in England, representing this country with distinguished ability at the Court of St. James, that he was there for a long time before and did not return for a year or more after. He knows that to be true, and that fact proves his charge to be false as against Mr. Buchanan. *[Cheers]* Then again, I wish to call his attention to the fact that, at the time the Nebraska bill was passed, the Dred Scott case was not before the Supreme Court at all. It was not upon the docket of the Supreme Court; it had not been brought there, and the judges in all probability, knew nothing of it. Thus the history of the country proves the charge to be false as against them. As to President Pierce, his high character as a man of integrity and honor is enough to vindicate him from such a charge *[Laughter, applause]*, and as to myself, I pronounce the charge an infamous lie, whenever and wherever made, and by whomsoever made.

I am willing that Mr. Lincoln should go and rake up every public act of mine, every measure I have introduced, report I have made, speech delivered, and criticize them. But when he charges upon me a corrupt conspiracy for the purpose of perverting the institutions of the country, I brand it as it deserves. I say the history of the country proves it to be false, and that it could not have been possible at the time. But now he tries to protect himself in this charge, because I made a charge against the *Washington Union*. My speech in the Senate against the *Washington Union* was made because it advocated a revolutionary doctrine, by declaring that the free states had not the right to prohibit slavery within their own limits. Because I made that charge against the *Washington Union*, Mr. Lincoln says it was a charge against Mr. Buchanan. Suppose it was. Is Mr. Lincoln the peculiar defender of Mr. Buchanan? Is he so interested in the federal administration, and so bound to it, that he must jump to the rescue and defend it from every attack that I may make against it? *[Laughter, cheers]* I understand the whole thing. The *Washington Union*, under that most corrupt of all men, Cornelius Wendell, is advocating Mr. Lincoln's claim to the Senate. Wendell was the printer of the Black Republican House of Representatives. He was a candidate before the present Democratic House, but was ignominiously kicked out, and then he took the money which he had made out of the public printing by means of the Black Republicans, bought the *Washington Union*, and is now publishing it in the name of the Democratic party, and advocating Mr. Lincoln's election to the Senate. Mr. Lincoln therefore considers any attack upon Wendell and his corrupt gang as a personal attack upon him. *[Cheers, laughter]* This only proves what I have charged, that there is an alliance between Lincoln and his supporters and the federal officeholders of this state, and presidential aspirants out of it, to break me down at home. *[Cheers]*

Mr. Lincoln feels bound to come in to the rescue of the *Washington Union*. In that speech which I delivered in answer to the *Washington Union*, I made it distinctly against the *Union*, and against the *Union* alone.[24] I did not choose to go beyond that. If I have occasion to attack the President's conduct, I will do it in language that will not be misunderstood. When I differed with the President, I spoke out so that you all heard me. *[Cheers]* That question passed away. It resulted in the triumph of my principle by allowing the people to do as they please, and there is an end of the controversy. *[Cheers]* Whenever the great principle of self-government—the right of the people to make their own constitution, and come into the Union with slavery or without it, as they see proper—shall again arise, you will find me standing firm in defense of that principle, and fighting whoever fights it. *[Cheers]* If Mr. Buchanan stands, as I doubt not he will, by the recommendation contained in his message—that hereafter all state constitutions ought to be submitted to the people before the admission of the state into the Union—he will find me standing by him firmly, shoulder to shoulder, in carrying it out. I know Mr. Lincoln's object. He wants to divide the Democratic party, in order that he may defeat me and get to the Senate.

LINCOLN'S REJOINDER

My friends, it will readily occur to you that I cannot in half an hour notice all the things that so able a man as Judge Douglas can say in an hour and a half, and I hope, therefore, if there be anything that he has said upon which you would like to hear something from me, but which I omit to comment upon, you will bear in mind that it would be expecting an impossibility for me to go over his whole ground. I can but take up some of the points that he has dwelt upon, and employ my half-hour specially on them.

The first thing I have to say to you is a word in regard to Judge Douglas's declaration about the "vulgarity and blackguardism" in the audience—that no such thing, as he says, was shown by any Democrat while I was speaking. Now, I only wish, by way of reply on this subject, to say that while *I* was speaking *I* used no "vulgarity or blackguardism" towards any Democrat. *[Laughter, applause]*

Now, my friends, I come to all this long portion of the Judge's speech—perhaps half of it—which he has devoted to the various resolutions and platforms that have been adopted in the different counties in the different congressional districts, and in the Illinois legislature, which he supposes are at variance with the positions I have assumed before you today. It is true that many of these resolutions are at variance with the positions I have here assumed. All I have to ask is that we talk reasonably and rationally about it. I happen to know, the Judge's opinion to the contrary notwithstanding, that I have never tried to conceal my opinions,

---

24. See note 7, p. 55.

nor tried to deceive any one in reference to them. He may go and examine all the members who voted for me for United States Senator in 1855, after the election of 1854. They were pledged to certain things here at home and were determined to have pledges from me, and if he will find any of these persons who will tell him anything inconsistent with what I say now, I will resign, or rather retire from the race, and give him no more trouble. *[Applause]*

The plain truth is this. At the introduction of the Nebraska policy, we believed there was a new era being introduced in the history of the republic, which tended to the spread and perpetuation of slavery. But in our opposition to that measure we did not agree with one another in everything. The people in the North end of the state were for stronger measures of opposition than we of the central and Southern portions of the state, but we were all opposed to the Nebraska doctrine. We had that one feeling and that one sentiment in common. You at the North end met in your conventions and passed your resolutions. We in the middle of the state and further South did not hold such conventions and pass the same resolutions, although we had, in general, a common view and a common sentiment. So that these meetings which the Judge has alluded to, and the resolutions he has read from, were local and did not spread over the whole state. We at last met together in 1856, from all parts of the state, and we agreed upon a common platform. You who held more extreme notions either yielded those notions, or if not wholly yielding them, agreed to yield them practically, for the sake of embodying the opposition to the measures which the opposite party were pushing forward at that time. We met you then, and if there was anything yielded, it was for practical purposes. We agreed then upon a platform for the party throughout the entire State of Illinois, and now we are all bound as a party *to that platform.*[25] And I say here to you, if any one expects of me, in the case of my election, that I will do anything not signified by our Republican platform and my answers here today, I tell you very frankly that person will be deceived. I do not ask for the vote of any one who supposes that I have secret purposes or pledges that I dare not speak out.

Cannot the Judge be satisfied? If he fears, in the unfortunate case of my election *[Laughter]*, that my going to Washington will enable me to advocate sentiments contrary to those which I expressed when you voted for and elected me, I assure him that his fears are wholly needless and groundless. Is the Judge really afraid of any such thing? *[Laughter]* I'll tell you what he is afraid of. *He is afraid we'll all pull together. [Applause, laughter]* This is what alarms him more

---

25. The founding convention of the Illinois Republican Party was held in Bloomington on May 29, 1856. It drew up a platform that was more moderate than some of those that were propounded in 1854, but which was satisfactory to all factions.

than anything else. *[Laughter]* For my part, I do hope that all of us, entertaining a common sentiment in opposition to what appears to us a design to nationalize and perpetuate slavery, will waive minor differences on questions which either belong to the dead past or the distant future, and all pull together in this struggle. What are your sentiments? *[Cries of "We will, we will," cheers]* If it be true, that on the ground which I occupy—ground which I occupy as frankly and boldly as Judge Douglas does his—my views, though partly coinciding with yours, are not as perfectly in accordance with your feelings as his are, I do say to you in all candor, go for him and not for me. I hope to deal in all things fairly with Judge Douglas and with the people of the state in this contest. And if I should never be elected to any office, I trust I may go down with no stain of falsehood upon my reputation, notwithstanding the hard opinions Judge Douglas chooses to entertain of me. *[Laughter]*

The Judge has again addressed himself to the abolition tendencies of a speech of mine made at Springfield in June last. I have so often tried to answer what he is always saying on that melancholy theme that I almost turn with disgust from the discussion, from the repetition of an answer to it. I trust that nearly all of this intelligent audience have read that speech. If you have, I may venture to leave it to you to inspect it closely, and see whether it contains any of those "bugaboos" which frighten Judge Douglas. *[Laughter]*

But there is one particular branch of this discussion to which I wish to ask the attention of this audience, more especially than to others, and which I have some apprehension of omitting; but still another smaller one occurs to me, and it is this:° the Judge complains that I did not fully answer his questions. If I have the sense to comprehend and answer those questions, I have done so fairly. If it can be pointed out to me how I can more fully and fairly answer him, I aver I have not the sense to see how it is to be done. He says I do not declare I would, in any event, vote for the admission of a slave state into the Union. When he shall see my speech in print,° if I have been fairly reported,[26] he will see that I did give an explicit answer to his interrogatories. I did not merely say that I would dislike to be put to the test, but I said clearly, if I were put to the test, and a territory from which slavery had been excluded should present herself with a state constitution sanctioning slavery—a most extraordinary thing and wholly unlikely ever to happen—I did not see how I could avoid voting for her admission. I said that in very plain language.° But he refuses to understand that I said so, and he wants

---

26. The *Times'* version of Lincoln's speech at Ottawa was attacked by the *Press and Tribune* as an unfairly mutilated and distorted reporting of what Lincoln actually said. *Chicago Press and Tribune,* Aug. 24, 26–27, 1858; *Chicago Times,* Aug. 25, 27, 1858.

this audience to understand that I did not say so. Yet it will be so reported in the printed speech that he cannot help seeing it.

He says if I should vote for the admission of a slave state, I would be voting for a dissolution of the Union, because I hold that the Union can not permanently exist half slave and half free. I repeat that I do not believe this government *can* endure permanently half slave and half free, yet I do not admit, nor does it at all follow, that the admission of a single slave state will permanently fix the character and establish this as a universal slave nation. The Judge is very happy indeed at working up these quibbles. *[Laughter, cheers]*

Before leaving the subject of answering questions, I aver as my confident belief, when you come to see our speeches in print, that you will find every question which he has asked me more fairly and boldly and fully answered than he has answered those which I put to him. Is not that so? *[Cries of "Yes, yes"]* The two speeches may be placed side by side, and I will venture to leave it to impartial judges whether his questions have not been more directly and circumstantially answered than mine.

And now, then, there is one subject to which I wish to call your attention.° Judge Douglas says he made a charge upon the editor of the *Washington Union, alone,* of entertaining a purpose to rob the states of their power to exclude slavery from their limits. I undertake to say, and I make the direct issue, that he did *not* make his charge against the editor of the *Union* alone. *[Applause]* I will undertake to prove by the record here that he made that charge against more and higher dignitaries than the editor of the *Washington Union.* I am quite aware that he was shirking and dodging around the form in which he put it, but I can make it manifest that he leveled his "fatal blow" against more persons than this Washington editor. Will he dodge it now by alleging that I am trying to defend Mr. Buchanan against the charge? Not at all. Am I not making the same charge myself? *[Laughter, applause]* I am trying to show that you, Judge Douglas, are a witness on my side. *[Laughter]* I am not defending Buchanan, and I will tell Judge Douglas that in my opinion, when he made that charge, he had an eye farther North than he has° today. He was then fighting against people who called *him* a Black Republican and an abolitionist. It is mixed all through his speech, and it is tolerably manifest that his eye was a great deal farther North than it is today. *[Cheers, laughter]*

The Judge says that though he made this charge, Toombs got up and declared there was not a man in the United States (I don't know that I give the Judge's exact language),° except the editor of the *Union,* who was in favor of the doctrines put forth in that article. And thereupon, I understand that the Judge withdrew the charge merely because Mr. Toombs got up and made a speech.° Although he had taken extracts from the newspaper, and then from the Lecompton Constitution, to show the existence of a conspiracy to bring about a "fatal blow," by which the states were to be deprived of the right of excluding slavery, it all went to pot as soon as Toombs got up and told him it was not true. *[Laughter]* It reminds me of the story that John Phoenix, the California railroad surveyor, tells.[27] He says when° they started out from the Plaza to the Mission of Dolores, they had two ways of determining distances. One was by a chain and pins taken over the ground; the other was by a "go-it-ometer"—an invention of his own—a three-legged instrument, with which he computed a series of triangles between the points.

    Voice: Turn this way.

    Lincoln: Well then, I shan't be this way!°

    At night he said when they had done their day's work, why,° he turned to the chain-man to ascertain what distance they had come, and found that by some mistake he had merely dragged the chain over the ground and stuck no pins. So he turned to the man with the go-it-ometer to see the number of paces marked, and found that it indicated four and a half miles, which he knew must be about nine or ten times as far as they had come. About that time, he being much perplexed, a drayman came by and he asked him° how far it was to the plaza. The drayman replied it was just half a mile, and the surveyor put it down in his book—just as Judge Douglas says, after he had made his calculations and computations, he took Toombs's statement. *[Laughter]* I have no doubt that after Judge Douglas had made his charge, he was as easily satisfied about its truth as the surveyor was of the drayman's statement of the distance to the plaza. *[Laughter]*

    There is another thing I believe is true about that editor of the *Union* that Douglas opposed. I believe it turned out that after all the opposition to him, that the Democratic party elected him. I think that the man that° put forth all that matter which Douglas deemed a "fatal blow" at state sovereignty was elected by the Democrats as Public Printer.

    Well, now my friends, as I have got less time than I thought I had, I will ask your attention to a speech of Judge Douglas' made in 1858, on the 22d of March,° beginning about the middle of page 21, and reading to the bottom of page 24,° and you will find the evidence on which I say that he did not make his charge against the editor of the *Union* alone.[28] I cannot stop to read it, but I will give it to the reporters.° After he had quoted the article from the editor of the *Union,* he then said:° "Mr. President, you here find several distinct propositions advanced boldly,

---

    27. AL refers to the Western humorist John Phoenix [George Horatio Derby]. See his *Phoenixiana; or, Sketches and Burlesques* (New York: Appleton, 1856), 20. The Mission of Dolores is in San Francisco.

    28. See note 7, p. 55.

and apparently *authoritatively."*° By whose authority, Judge Douglas? *[Cheers, laughter]* Again, he says in another place, "It will be seen by these clauses in the Lecompton constitution, that they are identical in spirit with this *authoritative* article in the *Washington Union* of the day previous to its indorsement of this constitution, and every man is branded as a Free-Soiler and Abolitionist, who does not subscribe to them."° By *whose authority? [Cheers]* Who do you mean to say authorized the publication of these articles? He knows that the Washington *Union* is considered the organ of the administration. *I* demand of Judge Douglas *by whose authority* he meant to say those articles were published, if not by the authority of the President of the United States and his cabinet? I defy him to show whom he referred to, if not to these high functionaries in the federal government. More than this, he says the articles in that paper and the provisions of the Lecompton Constitution are "identical," and being identical, he argues that the authors are cooperating and conspiring together. He does not use the word "conspiring," but what other construction can you put upon it? I ask you to read it yourselves.° He winds up with this:

> When I saw that article in the Union of the 17th of November, followed by the glorification of the Lecompton constitution on the 18th of November, and this clause in the constitution asserting the doctrine that no State has a right to prohibit slavery within its limits, I saw that there was a *fatal blow* being struck at the sovereignty of the States of this Union, a death blow to State rights, subversive of the Democratic platform and of the principles upon which the Democratic party have ever stood, and upon which I trust they will ever stand.°

I ask him if all this fuss was made over the editor of this newspaper. *[Laughter]* It would be a terribly "*fatal* blow," indeed, which a single man could strike, when no president, no cabinet officer, no member of Congress was giving strength and efficiency to the movement. Out of respect to Judge Douglas's good sense, I must believe he didn't manufacture his idea of the "fatal" character of that blow out of such a miserable scapegrace as he represents that editor to be.

I repeat here that if any man shall take these pages in his speech and carefully read them, he shall see that while Judge Douglas does not use the term "conspiracy," he uses the term, "the fatal blow being struck," and he certainly means that, to make that "fatal blow" which he sees being struck, it is by those who have the power to carry it into execution unless he resists it. And when he says it is "authoritative," it leaves in no doubt who he means gives the authority, and we find it is distinctly announced. I would appeal to this audience, aye, to twelve Democrats—Douglas Democrats, on oath—to answer faithfully to the proposition that he made it not against the editor of the *Union* alone, but against the President, against the cabinet, against the framers of the Lecompton Constitution, and against all its advocates, in and out of Congress. No man can examine these pages and fail to see that such was the fact.°

But the Judge's eye is farther South now. *[Laughter, cheers]* Then, it was very peculiarly and decidedly North. His hope rested on the idea of visiting the great "Black Republican" party, and making it the tail of his new kite. *[Laughter]* He knows he was then expecting from day to day to turn Republican and place himself at the head of° our organization. He has found that these despised "Black Republicans" estimate him by a standard which he has taught them none too well. Hence he is crawling back into his old camp, and you will find him eventually installed in full fellowship among those whom he was then battling, and with whom he now pretends to be at such fearful variance. *[Applause, cries of "Go on, go on"]*

I cannot, gentlemen, my time has expired.

JONESBORO

INTRODUCTION

Almost three weeks, more than four hundred miles, and profound local political and ideological differences separated the scene of the Freeport debate on August 27, 1858, from that of the third meeting in the series at Jonesboro on September 15. During the interim, both candidates campaigned across central Illinois, where it seemed certain that the contest would be decided. Douglas traveled farther into the heavily Democratic southern part of the state, undertaking to mobilize the faithful there, but for Lincoln such a foray would have been expensive and profitless. His Jonesboro speech was the only one Lincoln made south of St. Louis.

Jonesboro, "an ancient village in the heart of Egypt,"[1] is in the longest-settled and poorest portion of Illinois, and its Union County is the second county north of the southern tip of the state, where the Ohio River joins the Mississippi. The area is as far south as southern Virginia. At the time of the debate the town had only lately been connected with the rest of the world by the newly constructed Illinois Central Railroad, two miles distant. Hostile both to blacks and to Republicans, the surrounding Ninth Congressional District had given less than four percent of its vote to Republican John C. Fremont in the 1856 presidential election, and no Republican candidate ran for the Illinois General Assembly to represent Union County in 1858. Senator Douglas had boasted that he would "bring [Lincoln] to his milk"[2] in Egypt, as southern Illinois was popularly known; that he would make Lincoln repeat to a Negrophobic southern Illinois audience his previously

---

1. *New York Evening Post,* Sept. 22, 1858.
2. To "bring Lincoln to his milk": to bring him to a realization of his proper duty or condition, or to subdue him.

stated doctrine that under the Declaration of Independence, whites and blacks are equal. Yet though Lincoln had very few political friends in Jonesboro, the potential Democratic support there for Douglas was also pared down. The senator's opposition to the Lecompton Constitution had divided the Democratic Party in Illinois, and John Dougherty, the best-known pro-Lecompton leader in the state, was also the most prominent Democrat in Union County and a candidate for the office of state treasurer.

The break in the summer heat that had given speakers and listeners a little relief at Freeport was only temporary; the dog days had returned in September and continued to prevail at Jonesboro. They doubtless contributed to the overall listlessness that seems to have characterized the preliminaries there. Jonesboro was a mere village with fewer than nine hundred inhabitants; its overnight accommodations were limited and primitive; and the state fair at nearby Centralia seems to have attracted as much local attention as the debate between Lincoln and Douglas. Lincoln was greeted by no welcoming procession at all when he arrived at Jonesboro the day before the debate, and the Douglas reception the next day was meager and unenthusiastic. Without the accompaniment of political fanfare, Lincoln was able to spend a quiet evening on the porch of the hotel at Jonesboro, admiring the astronomical spectacle of Donati's two-tailed comet. In the absence of an animated local contingent of supporters, Douglas brought several carloads of campaign enthusiasts with him from Cairo, Illinois, south of Jonesboro, along with his signature noisy brass cannon towed on a flatcar. Estimates of the crowd that heard the debaters on the September 15 range from twelve hundred to fifteen hundred listeners, the smallest audience in the series. Neither Lincoln nor Douglas had much to lose or gain locally from the Jonesboro debate, but both were very conscious of the much wider reading public that was paying close attention to the proceedings there.

In Douglas's opening, the senator asserted that though the Democratic Party was still a national party, the party of Lincoln and Trumbull which had succeeded the Whigs was merely sectional and without internal unity. Though retreating from his earlier position on a set of radical resolutions as constituting the state Republican platform in 1854, Douglas claimed that such radical principles could never be promoted outside strongly antislavery northern Illinois, nor could the name "Republican" be used everywhere in the state, whereas the principles and name of the Democratic party were valid in all places. He attacked Lincoln's "House Divided" speech once again, maintaining that the Union should remain peacefully divided on the slavery issue, and he insisted again that the rights of black people in America were matters of state concern, and not defined by the Declaration of Independence.

Lincoln's response found the challenger in more of an attack mode than previously; indeed, for the remainder of the series Lincoln was more likely than before to advance new charges of his own, and less likely merely to respond to Douglas's allegations. He claimed that Douglas, in promoting the Kansas-Nebraska Act, had radically redirected the situation of slavery from where the nation's founders had placed it, in the course of ultimate extinction. He complained again of Douglas holding him responsible for radical resolutions passed by others earlier in the decade, and showed that several Illinois Democrats had supported comparably radical positions on slavery. And though he had been silent on the Freeport Doctrine at the previous debate, Lincoln assailed it at Jonesboro, asserting its incompatibility with the *Dred Scott* decision and insisting that Douglas as a senator had a sworn obligation to support that decision which guaranteed the right to hold slaves in the territories, instead of suggesting a means to circumvent it, as he had done at Freeport. Lincoln went further and maintained that under the *Dred Scott* decision, Congress was obligated to give federal legislative support to the security of slave property, and he posed another crucial question to Douglas: Would the Senator support such legislation as a member of Congress?

In his rejoinder, and in spite of Lincoln's attack, Douglas reiterated the Freeport Doctrine, that even under the *Dred Scott* decision, slaveholding was a barren right without a supportive population and protective local legislation. And he answered Lincoln's question by saying that it was a fundamental article of the Democratic Party's creed that Congress should not interfere with slavery in the states or territories, implying thus that he would never support such legislation. This position, which Douglas would reiterate explicitly over the next two years, would haunt him at the Democratic national convention in Charleston in 1860. That convention broke up over the opposition of Douglas and his partisans to the party's support for a national slave code for the territories.

DOUGLAS'S OPENING SPEECH

Ladies and gentlemen: I appear before you today in pursuance of a previous notice, and have made arrangements with Mr. Lincoln to divide
time and discuss with him the leading political topics that now agitate
the country.

Prior to 1854 this country was divided into two great political parties, known as
Whig and Democratic. These parties differed from each other on certain questions
which were then deemed to be important to the best interests of the republic. Whigs
and Democrats differed about a bank, the tariff, distribution, the specie circular,
and the sub-treasury. On those issues, we went before the country and discussed
the principles, objects, and measures of the two great parties. Each of the parties
could proclaim its principles in Louisiana as well as in Massachusetts, in Kentucky
as well as in Illinois. Since that period, a great revolution has taken place in the
formation of parties, by which they now seem to be divided by a geographical line,
a large party in the North being arrayed under the abolition or Republican banner
in hostility to the Southern states, Southern people, and Southern institutions.

It becomes important for us to inquire how this transformation of parties
has occurred, made from those of national principles to geographical factions.
You remember that in 1850, when° this country was agitated from its center to
its circumference about this slavery question, it became necessary for the leaders of the great Whig party and the leaders of the great Democratic party to
postpone, for the time being, their particular disputes and unite first to save the
Union before they should quarrel as to the mode in which it was to be governed.
During the Congress of 1849–50, Henry Clay was the leader of the Union men,
supported by Cass and Webster and leaders of the Democracy and the leaders
of the Whigs, in opposition to Northern abolitionists or Southern disunionists.
That great contest of 1850 resulted in the establishment of the compromise measures of that year, which measures rested on the great principle that the people
of each state and each territory of this Union ought to be permitted to regulate
their own domestic institutions in their own way, subject to no other limitation
than that which the federal Constitution imposes.[1]

---

1. SAD rests this characterization of the Compromise of 1850 on one of its provisions that
allowed Utah and New Mexico territories in the Mexican Cession to organize without reference to slavery in their enabling acts. He had earlier argued that this provision represented a
new general basis for the organization of territories "by withdrawing the question of slavery
from the halls of Congress and the political arena," where it had been located by such earlier
measures as the Northwest Ordinance and the Missouri Compromise. *Senate Reports,* 33rd
Cong., 1st Sess., 1854, XV, 1–4, cited in Johannsen, 406, 914.

I now wish to ask you whether that principle was right or wrong which guaranteed to every state and every community the right to form and regulate their domestic institutions to suit themselves. These measures were adopted, as I have previously said, by the joint action of the Union Whigs and Union Democrats, in opposition to Northern abolitionists and Southern disunionists. In 1852, when the Whig party assembled at Baltimore, in national convention for the last time, they adopted the principle of the compromise measures of 1850 as their rule of party action in the future. One month thereafter, the Democrats assembled at the same place to nominate a candidate for the Presidency and declared the same great principle as the rule of action by which the Democracy would be governed. The presidential election of 1852 was fought on that basis. It is true that the Whigs claimed special merit for the adoption of those measures, because they asserted that their great Clay originated them, their God-like Webster defended them, and their Fillmore signed the bill making them the law of the land. But on the other hand the Democrats claimed special credit for the Democracy upon the ground that we gave twice as many votes in both houses of Congress for the passage of these measures as the Whig party. Thus you see that in the presidential election of 1852, the Whigs were pledged by their platform and their candidate to the principle of the compromise measures of 1850, and the Democracy were likewise pledged by our principles, our platform, and our candidate to the same line of policy, to preserve peace and quiet between the different sections of this Union.

Since that period, the Whig party has been transformed into a sectional party, under the name of the Republican party, whilst the Democratic party continues the same national party it was at that day. All sectional men, all men of abolition sentiments and principles, no matter whether they were old abolitionists or had been Whigs or Democrats, rally under the sectional Republican banner, and consequently all national men, all Union-loving men—whether Whigs, Democrats, or by whatever name they have been known—ought to rally under the stars and stripes in defense of the Constitution, as our fathers made it, and of the Union as it has existed under the Constitution.

How has this departure from the faith of the Democracy and the faith of the Whig party been accomplished? In 1854, certain restless, ambitious, and disappointed politicians throughout the land took advantage of the temporary excitement created by the Nebraska bill to try and dissolve the old Whig party and the old Democratic party, to abolitionize their members and lead them, bound hand and foot, captives into the abolition camp. In the State of New York, a convention was held by some of these men and a platform adopted, every plank of which was black as night, each one relating to the nigger,° and not one referring to the interests of the white man. That example was followed throughout the Northern states, the effect being made to combine all the free states in hostile array against the slave states. The men who thus thought that they could build up a great sectional party and, through its organization, control the political destinies of this country, based all their hopes on the single fact that the North was the stronger division of the nation, and hence, if the North could be combined against the South, a sure victory awaited their efforts.

I am doing no more than justice to the truth of history when I say that, in this state, Abraham Lincoln, on behalf of the Whigs, and Lyman Trumbull, on behalf of the Democrats, were the leaders who undertook to perform this grand scheme of abolitionizing the two parties to which they belonged. It is true according to the evidence and the history of the transaction, that° they had a private arrangement as to what should be the political destiny of each of the contracting parties before they went into the operation. The arrangement was that Mr. Lincoln was to take the old line Whigs with him, claiming that he was still as good a Whig as ever, over to the abolitionists, and Mr. Trumbull was to run for Congress in the Belleville district, and, claiming to be a good Democrat, coax the old Democrats into the abolition camp. And then,° by the joint efforts of the abolitionized Whigs, the abolitionized Democrats, and the old line abolition and Free-Soil party of this state, they should secure a majority in the legislature. Lincoln was then to be made United States Senator in Shields's place, Trumbull remaining in Congress until I should be accommodating enough to die or resign, and give him a chance to follow Lincoln. *[Laughter, applause]* That was a very nice little bargain so far as Lincoln and Trumbull were concerned, if it had been carried out in good faith, and friend Lincoln had attained to senatorial dignity according to the contract.

They went into the contest in every part of the state, calling upon all disappointed politicians to join in the crusade against the Democracy, and appealed to the prevailing sentiments and prejudices in all the Northern counties of the state. In three congressional districts in the North end of the state they adopted, as the platform of this new party thus formed by Lincoln and Trumbull in connection° with the abolitionists, all of those principles which aimed at a warfare on the part of the North against the South. They declared in that platform that the Wilmot Proviso was to be applied to all the territories of the United States, North as well as South of 36 degrees, 30 minutes, and not only to all the territory we then had, but all that we might hereafter acquire; that hereafter no more slave states should be admitted into this Union, even if the people of such states desired slavery; that the Fugitive Slave Law should be absolutely and unconditionally repealed; that slavery should be abolished in the District of Columbia; that the slave trade should be abolished between the different states, and, in fact, every article in their creed related to this slavery question, and pointed to a Northern geographical party in hostility to the Southern states of this Union.

Such were their principles in Northern Illinois. A little further South they became bleached and grew paler just in proportion as public sentiment moderated and changed in this direction. They were Republicans or abolitionists in the North, anti-Nebraska men down about Springfield, and in this neighborhood they contented themselves with talking about the inexpediency of the repeal of the Missouri Compromise. *[Laughter]* In the extreme Northern counties they brought out men to canvass the state whose complexion suited their political creed, and hence Fred Douglass, the negro, was to be found there, following General Cass, and attempting to speak on behalf of Lincoln, Trumbull, and abolitionism against that illustrious senator. *[Laughter]* Why, they brought Fred Douglass to Freeport when I was addressing a meeting there in a carriage driven by the white owner, the negro sitting inside with the white lady and her daughter. *[Mixed reaction]* When I got through canvassing the Northern counties that year and progressed as far South as Springfield, I was met and opposed in discussion by Lincoln, Lovejoy, Trumbull, and Sidney Breese, who were on one side. *[Laughter]* Father Giddings, the high priest of abolitionism, had just been there, and Chase came about the time I left.

Voice: Why didn't you shoot him?

Douglas: I did take a running shot at them, but as I was single-handed against the white, black, and mixed drove, I had to use a shot° gun and fire into the crowd, instead of taking them off singly with a rifle. *[Laughter, cheers]* Trumbull had for his lieutenants, in aiding him to abolitionize the Democracy, such men as John Wentworth, of Chicago, Gov. Reynolds, of Belleville, Sidney Breese, of Carlyle, and John Dougherty, of Union *[Applause, cheers]*, each of whom modified his opinions to suit the particular locality he was in. Dougherty, for instance, would not go much further than to talk about the inexpediency of the Nebraska bill, whilst his allies at Chicago advocated negro citizenship and negro equality, putting the white man and the negro on the same basis under the law.

Now these men, four years ago, were engaged in a conspiracy to break down the Democracy. Today they are again acting together for the same purpose![2] They do not hoist the same flag; they do not own the same principles, or profess the same faith, but conceal their union for the sake of policy. In the Northern counties, you find that all the conventions are called in the name of the Black Republican party; at Springfield, they dare not call a Republican convention, but

2. Though Trumbull, Wentworth, Reynolds, Breese, and Dougherty had as a common objective the defeat of SAD in 1858, the last three considered themselves loyal pro-Administration Democrats, whereas the first two were opposed to much of what the Buchanan administration stood for. The two groups could hardly be considered "allies."

invite all the enemies of the Democracy to unite, and when they get down into Egypt, Trumbull issues notices calling upon the *"Free Democracy"* to assemble and hear him speak. *[Laughter]* I have one of the handbills calling a Trumbull meeting at Waterloo the other day, which I received there, which is in the following language:

> A meeting of the Free Democracy will take place in Waterloo on Monday, Sept. 13th inst. whereat Hon. Lyman Trumbull, Hon. Jehu Baker and others will address the people upon the different political topics of the day. Members of all parties are cordially invited to be present, and hear and determine for themselves. Signed: "The Monroe Free Democrats." °

What is that name of "Free Democrats" put forth for, unless to deceive the people, and make them believe that Trumbull and his followers are not the same party as that which raises the black flag of abolitionism in the Northern part of this state and makes war upon the Democratic party throughout the state? When I put that question to them at Waterloo on Saturday last, one of them rose and stated that they had changed their name for political effect in order to get votes. There was a candid admission. Their object in changing their party organization and principles in different localities was avowed to be an attempt to cheat and deceive some portion of the people until after the election. Why cannot a political party that is conscious of the rectitude of its purposes and soundness of its principles declare them everywhere alike? I would disdain to hold any political principles that I could not avow in the same terms in Kentucky that I declared in Illinois, in Charleston as well as in Chicago, in New Orleans as well as in New York. *[Cheers]* So long as we live under a constitution common to all the states, our political faith ought to be as broad, as liberal, and just as that Constitution itself, and should be proclaimed alike in every portion of the Union. But it is apparent that our opponents find it necessary, for partisan effect, to change their colors in different counties in order to catch the popular breeze, and hope, with these discordant materials combined together, to secure a majority in the legislature for the purpose of putting down the Democratic party.

This combination did succeed in 1854 so far as to elect a majority of their confederates to the legislature, and the first important act which they performed was to elect a senator in the place of the eminent and gallant Senator Shields. His term expired in the United States Senate at that time, and he had to be crushed by the abolition coalition for the simple reason that he would not join in their conspiracy to wage war against one-half of the Union. That was the only objection to Gen. Shields. He had served the people of the state with ability in the legislature; he had served you with fidelity and ability as auditor; he had performed his duties to the satisfaction of the whole country at head of the Land Department at Washington; he had covered the state and the Union with immortal glory on the bloody fields of Mexico in defense of the honor of our flag, and yet he had to be stricken down by this unholy combination. And for what cause? Merely because he would not join a combination of one-half of the states to make war upon the other half, after having poured out his heart's blood for all the states in the Union.

Trumbull was put in his place by abolitionism. How did Trumbull get there? Before the abolitionists would consent to go into an election for United States Senator, they required all the members of this new combination to show their hands upon this question of abolitionism. Lovejoy, one of their high priests, brought in resolutions defining the abolition creed, and required them to commit themselves on it by their votes—yea or nay. In that creed, as laid down by Lovejoy, they declared first, that the Wilmot Proviso must be put on all the territories of the United States, North as well as South of 36 degrees, 30 minutes, and that no more territory should ever be acquired unless slavery was first° prohibited therein. Second, that no more states should ever be received into the Union unless slavery was first prohibited by constitutional provision in such states. Third, that the Fugitive Slave Law must be immediately repealed, or, failing in that, then such amendments were to be made to it as would render it useless and inefficient for the objects for which it was passed, and so forth. The next day, after these resolutions were offered, they were voted upon—part of them carried, and the others defeated—the same men who voted for them, with only two exceptions, voting soon after for Abraham Lincoln as their candidate for the United States Senate.[3]

He came within one or two votes of being elected, but he could not quite get the number required, for the simple reason that his friend Trumbull, who was a party to the bargain by which Lincoln was to take Shields's place, controlled a few abolitionized Democrats in the legislature and would not allow them all to vote for him, thus wronging Lincoln by permitting him on each ballot to be almost elected, but not quite, until he forced them to drop Lincoln and elect him, Trumbull, in order to unite the party. *[Laughter]* Thus you find that although the legislature was carried that year by the bargain between Trumbull, Lincoln, and the abolitionists, and the union of these discordant elements in one harmonious party, yet Trumbull violated his pledge and played a yankee trick[4] on Lincoln when they came to divide the spoils. *[Laughter, applause]*

Perhaps you would like a little evidence on this point. If you would, I will call Col. James H. Matheny, of Springfield, to the stand, Mr. Lincoln's especial confidential friend for the last twenty years, and see what he will say upon the

---

3. *Illinois House Journal*, 1855, 283–84, 306–9.
4. "Yankee trick": an advantage gained by misrepresentation.

subject of this bargain. Matheny is now the Black Republican or abolition candidate for Congress in the Springfield district against the gallant Col. Harris and is making speeches all over that part of the state against me and in favor of Lincoln, in concert with Trumbull. He ought to be a good witness, and I will read an extract from a speech which he made in 1856, when he was mad because his friend Lincoln had been cheated. It is one of numerous speeches of the same tenor that were made about that time, exposing this bargain between Lincoln, Trumbull, and the abolitionists. Matheny then said

> that two years ago this fall° "the whigs, abolitionists, know-nothings and renegade democrats, made a solemn compact for the purpose of carrying the State against the Democracy" on this plan: 1st. That they would all combine and elect Mr. Trumbull to Congress, and thereby carry his district for the Legislature, in order to throw all the strength that could be obtained into that body against the Democrats. 2d. That when the Legislature should meet, the officers of that body, such as speaker, clerks, doorkeepers, etc., would be given to the abolitionists; and, 3d. That the whigs were to have the United States Senator. That accordingly, in good faith, Trumbull was elected to Congress, and his district carried for the Legislature; and when it convened, the abolitionists got all the officers of that body; and thus far the "bond" was fairly executed. The whigs, on their part, demanded the election of Abraham Lincoln to the United States Senate, that the bond might be fulfilled, the other parties to the contract having already secured to themselves all that was called for. But, said Mr. Matheny, "in the most perfidious manner they *refused* to elect Mr. Lincoln, and the mean, low-lived, sneaking Trumbull succeeded by *pledging all that was required by any party* in thrusting Lincoln aside and foisting himself, an excrescence from the rotten bowels of the Democracy, into the United States Senate; and thus it has ever been, that an *honest* man makes a bad bargain when he conspires or contracts with rogues."[5] *[Laughter]*

Matheny thought that his friend Lincoln made a bad bargain when he conspired and contracted with such rogues as Trumbull and his abolition associates in that campaign. *[Cheers, laughter]* Lincoln was shoved off the track, and he and his friends all at once began to mope, became sour and mad *[Laughter]* and disposed to tell, but dare not. *[Laughter]* And this they stood for a long time until the abolitionists coaxed and flattered him back by their assurances that he should certainly be a senator in Douglas's place. *[Laughter]* In that way, the abolitionists have been enabled to hold Lincoln to the alliance up to this time, and

5. SAD reads from an article in the *Chicago Times,* June 24, 1858, crediting and quoting from a Petersburg, Illinois, newspaper, the *Menard Index,* which "brings forth from its files the following extract from a report of a speech delivered by Mr. M just before the [1856] Presidential election."

now they have brought him into a fight against me, and he is to see if he is again to be cheated by them. Lincoln this time, though, required more of them than a promise, and holds their bond, if not security, that Lovejoy shall not cheat him as Trumbull did. *[Laughter]*

When the Republican convention assembled at Springfield in June last for the purpose of nominating state officers only, the abolitionists could not get Lincoln and his friends into it until they would pledge themselves that Lincoln should be their candidate for the Senate. And you will find, in proof of this, that that convention passed a resolution unanimously declaring that Abraham Lincoln was the "first, last and only choice" of the Republicans for United States Senator. He was not willing to have it understood that he was merely their first choice, or their last choice, but their *only* choice. The Black Republican party had nobody else. Browning was nowhere, Gov. Bissell was of no account. Archie Williams was not to be taken into consideration. John Wentworth was not worth mentioning. John M. Palmer was to be discarded, ° and their party presented the extraordinary spectacle of having but one—the first, last, and only—choice for the Senate. *[Laughter]*

Suppose Lincoln should die, what a horrible condition the Republican party would be in. *[Laughter]* They would have nobody left. They have no other choice, and it was necessary for them to put themselves before the world in this ludicrous, ridiculous attitude of having no other choice in order to quiet Lincoln's suspicions and assure him that he was not to be cheated by Lovejoy and the trickery by which Trumbull out generaled him. Well, gentlemen, I think they will have a nice time of it before they get through. I do not intend to give them any chance to cheat Lincoln at all this time. *[Cheers, laughter]* I intend to relieve him and them from all anxiety upon that subject and spare them the mortification of more exposures of contracts violated, and the pledged honor of rogues forfeited. *[Applause]*

But I wish to invite your attention to the chief points at issue between Mr. Lincoln and myself in this discussion. Mr. Lincoln, knowing that he was to be the candidate of his party on account of the arrangement of which I have already spoken, knowing that he was to receive the nomination of the convention for the United States Senate, had his speech, accepting the nomination, all written and committed to memory, ready to be delivered the moment the nomination was announced. Accordingly, when it was made he was in readiness, and delivered his speech, a portion of which I will read, in order that I may state his political principles fairly, by repeating them in his own language. °

> We are now far into the fifth year, since a policy was initiated with the avowed object, and confident promise, of putting an end to slavery agitation. Under the operation of that policy, that agitation has only not ceased, but has constantly augmented. In my opinion, it will not cease, until a crisis shall have been reached

and passed. "A house divided against itself cannot stand." I believe this government cannot endure permanently half slave and half free. I do not expect the
Union to be dissolved—I do not expect the house to fall—but I do expect it
will cease to be divided. It will become all one thing, or all the other. Either the
opponents of slavery, will arrest the further spread of it, and place it where the
public mind shall rest in the belief that it is in the course of ultimate extinction;
or its advocates will put it forward, till it shall become alike lawful in all the
States, old as well as new—North as well as South.[6]

There you have Mr. Lincoln's first and main proposition, upon which he
bases his claims, stated in his own language. He tells you that this republic cannot
endure permanently divided into slave and free states, as our fathers made it. He
says that they must all become free or all become slave, that they must all be one
thing or all be the other, or this government cannot last. Why can it not last, if
we will execute the government in the same spirit and upon the same principles
upon which it is founded? Lincoln, by his proposition, says to the South: "If you
desire to maintain your institutions as they are now, you must not be satisfied
with minding your own business, but you must invade Illinois and all the other
Northern states, establish slavery in them and make it universal." And in the same
language he says to the North: "You must not be content with regulating your
own affairs and minding your own business, but if you desire to maintain your
freedom, you must invade the Southern states, abolish slavery there and everywhere, in order to have the states all one thing or all the other." I say that this is
the inevitable and irresistible result of Mr. Lincoln's argument, inviting a warfare
between the North and the South, to be carried on with ruthless vengeance until
the one section or the other shall be driven to the wall and become the victim of
the rapacity of the other.

What good would follow such a system of warfare? Suppose the North should
succeed in conquering the South. How much would she be the gainer? Or suppose the South should conquer the North. Could the Union be preserved in that
way? Is this sectional warfare to be waged between Northern states and Southern
states until they all shall become uniform in their local and domestic institutions,
merely because Mr. Lincoln says that a house divided against itself cannot stand,
and pretends that this scriptural quotation, this language of our Lord and Master,
is applicable to the American Union and the American Constitution?

Washington and his compeers in the convention that framed the Constitution made this government divided into free and slave states. It was composed
then of thirteen sovereign and independent states, each having sovereign author-

---

6. SAD quotes from the beginning of AL's "House Divided" speech of June 16, 1858, in
Basler et al., *Collected Works,* 2:461–62.

ity over its local and domestic institutions, and all bound together by the federal Constitution. Mr. Lincoln likens that bond of the federal Constitution joining free and slave states together to a house divided against itself and says that it is contrary to the law of God and cannot stand. Where° did he learn, and by what authority does he proclaim, that this government made by our fathers° is contrary to the law of God, and cannot stand? It has stood thus divided into free and slave states from its organization up to this day.

During that period we have increased from four millions to thirty millions of people. We have extended our territory from the Mississippi to the Pacific Ocean. We have acquired the Floridas and Texas and other territory sufficient to double our geographical extent. We have increased in population, in wealth, and in naval and military° power beyond any example on earth. We have risen from a weak and feeble power to become the terror and admiration of the civilized world. And all this has been done under a constitution which Mr. Lincoln, in substance, says is in violation of the law of God, and under a Union divided into free and slave states, which Mr. Lincoln thinks, because of such division, cannot stand.

Surely Mr. Lincoln is a wiser man than those who framed the government. Washington did not believe, nor did his compatriots, that the local laws and domestic institutions that were well adapted to the Green Mountains of Vermont were suited to the rice plantations of South Carolina. They did not believe at that day that, in a republic so broad and expanded as this, containing such a variety of climate, soil, and interest, that uniformity in the local laws and domestic institutions was either desirable or possible. They believed then, as our experience has proven to us now, that each locality, having different interests, a different climate and different surroundings, required different local laws, local policy, and local institutions, adapted to the wants of that locality. Thus our government was formed on the principle of diversity in the local institutions and laws, and not on that of uniformity.

As my time flies, I can only glance at these points and not present them as fully as I would wish, because I desire to bring all the points in controversy between the two parties before you in order to have Mr. Lincoln's reply. He makes war on the decision of the Supreme Court in the case known as the Dred Scott case. I wish to say to you, fellow-citizens, that I have no war to make on that decision, or any other ever rendered by the Supreme Court. I am content to take that decision as it stands, delivered by the highest judicial tribunal on earth, a tribunal established by the Constitution of the United States for that purpose, and hence that decision becomes the law of the land, binding on you, on me, and on every other good citizen, whether we like it or not. Hence I do not choose to go into an argument to prove, before this audience, whether or not Chief Justice Taney understood the law better than Abraham Lincoln. *[Laughter]*

Mr. Lincoln objects to that decision, first and mainly, because it deprives the negro of the rights of citizenship. I am as much opposed to his reason for that objection as I am to the objection itself. I hold that a negro is not, and never ought to be, a citizen of the United States. *[Applause, cheers]* I hold that this government was made on the white basis, by white men, for the benefit of white men and their posterity forever, and should be administered by white men and none others. I do not believe that the Almighty made the negro capable of self-government. I am aware that all the abolition lecturers that you find traveling about through the country are in the habit of reading the Declaration of Independence to prove that all men were created equal and endowed by their creator with certain inalienable rights, among which are life, liberty, and the pursuit of happiness. Mr. Lincoln is very much in the habit of following in the track of Lovejoy in this particular, by reading that part of the Declaration of Independence to prove that the negro was endowed by the Almighty with the inalienable right of equality with white men.

Now I say to you, my fellow citizens, that in my opinion, the signers of the Declaration had no reference to the negro whatever when they declared all men to be created equal. They desired to express by that phrase, white men, men of European birth and European descent, and had no reference either to the negro, the savage Indians, the Fejee, the Malay, or any other inferior and degraded race, when they spoke of the equality of men. One great evidence that such was their understanding is to be found in the fact that, at that time, every one of the thirteen colonies was a slaveholding colony, every signer of the Declaration represented a slaveholding constituency, and we know that no one of them emancipated his slaves, much less offered citizenship to them when they signed the Declaration. And yet, if they had intended to declare that the negro was the equal of the white man, and entitled by divine right to an equality with him, they were bound, as honest men, that day and hour to have put their negroes on an equality with themselves. *[Cheers]* Instead of doing so, with uplifted eyes to heaven, they implored the divine blessing upon them, during the seven-years' bloody war they had to fight to maintain that Declaration, never dreaming that they were violating divine law by still holding the negroes in bondage and depriving them of equality.

My friends, I am in favor of preserving this government as our fathers made it. It does not follow by any means that because a negro is not your equal or mine that hence he must necessarily be a slave. On the contrary, it does follow that we ought to extend to the negro every right, every privilege, every immunity which he is capable of enjoying, consistent with the good of society. When you ask me what these rights are, what their nature and extent is, I tell you that that is a question which each state of this Union must decide for itself. Illinois has already decided the question. We have decided that the negro must not be a slave within our limits, but we have also decided that the negro shall not be a citizen within our limits, that he shall not vote, hold office, or exercise any political rights. I maintain that Illinois, as a sovereign state, has a right thus to fix her policy with reference to the relation between the white man and the negro. But while we had that right to decide the question for ourselves, we must recognize the same right in Kentucky and in every other state to make the same decision, or a different one. Having decided our own policy with reference to the black race, we must leave Kentucky and Missouri and every other state perfectly free to make just such a decision as they see proper on that question.[7]

Kentucky has decided that question for herself. She has said that within her limits a negro shall not exercise any political rights, and she has also said that a portion of the negroes under the laws of that state shall be slaves. She had as much right to adopt that as her policy as we had to adopt the contrary for our policy. New York has decided that in that state, a negro may vote if he has $250 worth of property, and if he owns that much, he may vote upon an equality with the white man. I, for one, am utterly opposed to negro suffrage anywhere and under any circumstances. Yet, inasmuch as the Supreme Court have decided in the celebrated Dred Scott case that a state has a right to confer the privilege of voting upon free negroes, I am not going to make war upon New York because she has adopted a policy repugnant to my feelings. But New York must mind her own business, and keep her negro suffrage to herself and not attempt to force it upon us. *[Applause]*

In the State of Maine they have decided that a negro may vote and hold office on an equality with a white man. I had occasion to say to the senators from Maine, in a discussion last session, that if they thought that the white people within the limits of their state were no better than negroes, I would not quarrel with them for it, but they must not say that my white constituents of Illinois were no better than negroes, or we would be sure to quarrel. *[Laughter, cheers]*

The Dred Scott decision covers the whole question, and declares that each state has the right to settle this question of suffrage for itself, and all questions as to the relations between the white man and the negro. Judge Taney expressly lays down the doctrine. I receive it as law, and I say that while those states are adopting regulations on that subject, disgusting and abhorrent according to my views, I will not make war on them if they will mind their own business and let us alone. *[Cheers]*

I now come back to the question, why cannot this Union exist forever divided into free and slave states, as our fathers made it? It can thus exist if each state will carry out the principles upon which our institutions were founded, to

---

7. For Illinois's antebellum policy concerning African Americans, see "Illinois and the rights of blacks" in the glossary, pp. 325–26.

wit: the right of each state to do as it pleases, without meddling with its neighbors. Just act upon that great principle, and this Union will not only live forever,
but it will extend and expand until it covers the whole continent, and make this
confederacy one grand ocean-bound republic. We must bear in mind that we
are yet a young nation growing with a rapidity unequalled in the history of the
world, that our natural° increase is great, and that the emigration from the old
world is increasing, requiring us to expand and acquire new territory from time
to time in order to give our people land to live upon. If we live upon the principle of state rights and state sovereignty, each state regulating its own affairs and
minding its own business, we can go on and extend indefinitely, just as fast and
as far as we need the territory.

The time may come, indeed has now come, when our interests would be
advanced by the acquisition of the island of Cuba. *[Applause]* When we get Cuba
we must take it as we find it, leaving the people to decide the question of slavery
for themselves, without interference on the part of the federal government, or
of any state of this Union. So, when it becomes necessary to acquire any portion
of Mexico or Canada, or of this continent or the adjoining islands, we must take
them as we find them, leaving the people free to do as they please, to have slavery
or not, as they choose. I never have inquired, and never will inquire, whether a
new state applying for admission has slavery or not for one of her institutions.
If the constitution that is presented be the act and deed of the people and em-
bodies their will, and they have the requisite population, I will admit them with
slavery or without it, just as the people shall determine. *[Cheers]* My objection
to the Lecompton Constitution did not consist in the fact that it made Kansas
a slave state. I would have been as much opposed to its admission under such a
constitution as a free state as I was opposed to its admission under it as a slave
state. I hold that that was a question which that people had a right to decide for
themselves, and that no power on earth ought to have interfered with that decision. In my opinion, the Lecompton Constitution was not the act and deed of the
people of Kansas, and did not embody their will, and the recent election in that
territory, at which it was voted down by nearly ten to one, shows conclusively
that I was right in saying, when the constitution was presented, that it was not
the act and deed of the people and did not embody their will.[8]

If we wish to preserve our institutions in their purity, and transmit them
unimpaired to our latest posterity, we must preserve with religious good faith that
great principle of self-government which guarantees to each and every state, old
and new, the right to make just such constitutions as they desire, and come into

---

8. Under the provisions of the English bill, the Lecompton Constitution was submitted to
a vote in Kansas on August 2, when it was rejected by 11,812 to 1,926.

the Union with their own constitution and not one palmed upon them. *[Cheers]* Whenever you sanction the doctrine that Congress may crowd a constitution down the throats of an unwilling people against their consent, you will subvert the great fundamental principle upon which all our free institutions rest.

I say that our institutions rest on that great principle.° In the future I have no fear that the attempt will ever be made. President Buchanan declared in his annual message that hereafter the rule adopted in the Minnesota case, requiring a constitution to be submitted to the people, should be followed in all future cases. And if he stands by the recommendation, there will be no division in the Democratic party on that principle in the future. Hence, the great mission of the Democracy is to unite the fraternal feeling of the whole country, restore peace and quiet by teaching each state to mind its own business, and regulate its own domestic affairs, and all to unite carrying out the Constitution as our fathers made it, and thus to preserve the Union and render it perpetual in all time to come. Why should we not act as our fathers who made the government? There was no sectional strife in Washington's army. They were all brethren of a common confederacy. They fought under a common flag that they might bestow upon their posterity a common destiny, and to this end they poured out their blood in common streams and shared in some instances a common grave. I am told my time is out.° *[Cheers]*

LINCOLN'S REPLY

Ladies and gentlemen: There is very much in the principles that Judge Douglas has here enunciated that I most cordially approve, and over which I shall have no controversy with him. In so far as he has insisted that all the states have the right to do exactly as they please about all their domestic relations, including that of slavery, I agree entirely with him. He places me wrong in spite of all I can tell him, though I repeat it again and again, insisting that I have no difference with him upon this subject. I have made a great many speeches, some of which have been printed, and it will be utterly impossible for him to find anything that I have ever put in print contrary to what I now say upon this subject. I hold myself under constitutional obligations to allow the people in all the states without interference, direct or indirect, to do exactly as they please, and I deny that I have any inclinations to interfere with them, even if there were no such constitutional obligations. I can only say again that I am placed improperly—altogether improperly in spite of all I can say—when it is insisted that I entertain any other view or purposes in regard to that matter.

While I am upon this subject, I will make some answers briefly to certain propositions that Judge Douglas has put. He says, "Why can't this Union endure permanently, half slave and half free?" I have said that I supposed it could not, and I will try, before this new audience, to give briefly some of the reasons for entertaining that opinion. Another form of his question is, "Why can't we let it stand as our fathers placed it?" That is the exact difficulty between us. I say that Judge Douglas and his friends have changed the policy° from the position in which our fathers originally placed it. I say, in the way our fathers originally left the slavery question, the institution was in the course of ultimate extinction, and the public mind rested in the belief that it *was* in the course of ultimate extinction. I say when this government was first established, it was the policy of its founders to prohibit the spread of slavery into the new territories of the United States, where it had not existed. But Judge Douglas and his friends have broken up that policy and placed it upon a new basis by which it is to become national and perpetual. All I have asked or desired anywhere is that it should be placed back again upon the basis that the fathers of our government originally placed it upon. I have no doubt that it would become extinct, for all time to come, if we but re-adopted the policy of the fathers by restricting it to the limits it had already covered, restricting it from the new territories.

I do not wish to dwell at great length on this branch of the subject at this time, but allow me to repeat one thing that I have stated before. Brooks, the man who assaulted Senator Sumner on the floor of the Senate, and who was complimented with dinners and silver pitchers and gold-headed canes and a good many other things for that feat, in one of his speeches declared that when this government was originally established, nobody expected that the institution of slavery would last until this day.[9] That was but the opinion of one man, but it was such an opinion as we can never get from Judge Douglas or anybody in favor of slavery in the North at all. You *can* sometimes get it from a Southern man. He said at the same time that the framers of our government did not have the knowledge that experience has taught us, that experience and the invention of the cotton-gin have taught us that the perpetuation of slavery is a necessity. He insisted, therefore, upon its being changed from the basis upon which the fathers of the government left it to the basis of its perpetuation and nationalization. I insist that this is the difference between Judge Douglas and myself—that Judge Douglas is helping that change along. I insist upon this government being placed where our fathers originally placed it.

I remember Judge Douglas once said that he saw the evidence, on the statute books of Congress, of a policy in the origin of government to divide slavery and freedom by a geographical line, that he saw an indisposition to maintain that

---

9. AL refers to Congressman Preston Brooks's speech as reported in *Congressional Globe, Appendix,* 33rd Cong., 1st Sess., Mar. 15, 1854, 372.

policy, and therefore he set about studying up a way to settle the institution on the right basis—the basis which he thought it ought to have been placed upon at first. And in that speech he confesses that he seeks to place it, not upon the basis that the fathers placed it upon, but upon one gotten up on "original principles." When he asks me why we cannot get along with it in the attitude where our fathers placed it, he had better clear up the evidence that he has himself changed it from that basis, that he has himself been chiefly instrumental in changing the policy of the fathers. *[Applause]* Any one who will read his speech of the 22d of last March, will see that he there makes an open confession, showing that he set about fixing the institution upon an altogether different set of principles.[10] I think I have fully answered him when he asks me why we cannot let it alone upon the basis where our fathers left it, by showing that he has himself changed the whole policy of the government in that regard.

Now, fellow citizens, in regard to this matter about a contract that was made between Judge Trumbull and myself, and all that long portion of Judge Douglas's speech on this subject, I wish simply to say what I have said to him before, that he cannot know whether it is true or not, and I *do know* that there is not a word of truth in it. And I have told him so before. *[Applause]*

Voice: We all knew it was a lie.°

Lincoln: I don't want any harsh language indulged in, but I do not know how to deal with this persistent insisting on a story that I know to be utterly without truth. It used to be a fashion amongst men that when a charge was made, some sort of proof was brought forward to establish it, and if no proof was found to exist, the charge was dropped. I don't know how to meet this kind of an argument. I don't want to have a fight with Judge Douglas, and I have no way of making an argument up into the consistency of a corn cob and stopping his mouth with it. *[Laughter, applause]* All I can do is, good-humoredly to say that from the beginning to the end of all that story about a bargain between Judge Trumbull and myself, *there is not a word of truth in it. [Applause]* I can only ask him to show some sort of evidence of the truth of his story. He brings forward here and reads from what he contends is a speech by James H. Matheny charging such a bargain between Trumbull and myself.[11] My own opinion is that Matheny did do some such immoral thing as to tell a story that he knew nothing about. I believe he did. I contradicted it instantly, and it has been contradicted by Judge Trumbull, while nobody has produced any proof, because there is none. Now whether the

---

10. AL quotes from this speech at Ottawa using a pamphlet version, *Speech of Senator Douglas, of Illinois, against the Admission of Kansas under the Lecompton Constitution* (Washington: Lemuel Towers, 1858).

11. See note 5, p. 92.

speech which the Judge brings forward here is really the one Matheny made, I do not know, and I hope the Judge will pardon me for doubting the genuineness of this document, since his production of those Springfield resolutions at Ottawa.[12] *[Laughter, cheers]* I do not wish to dwell at any great length upon this matter. I can say nothing when a long story like this is told except it is not true, and demand that he who insists upon it shall produce some proof. That is all any man can do, and I leave it in that way, for I know of no other way of dealing with it.

The Judge has gone over a long account of the old Whig and Democratic parties, and it connects itself with this charge against Trumbull and myself. He says that they agreed upon a compromise in regard to the slavery question in 1850, that in a national Democratic convention resolutions were passed to abide by that compromise as a finality upon the slavery question. He also says that the Whig party, in national convention, agreed to abide by and regard as a finality, the Compromise of 1850. I understand the Judge to be altogether right about that. I understand that part of the history of the country as stated by him to be correct. I recollect that I, as a member of that party, acquiesced in that compromise. I recollect in the presidential election which followed, when we had General Scott up for the presidency, Judge Douglas was around berating us Whigs as abolitionists, precisely as he does today—not a bit of difference. I have often heard him. We could do nothing when the old Whig party was alive that was not abolitionism, but it has got an extremely good name since it has passed away. *[Laughter]*

When that compromise was made, it did not repeal the old Missouri Compromise. It left a region of United States territory half as large as the present territory of the United States, North of the line of 36 degrees, 30 minutes, in which slavery was prohibited by act of Congress. This compromise did not repeal that one. It did not affect or propose to repeal it. But at last it became Judge Douglas's duty, as he thought (and I find no fault with him) as Chairman of the Committee on Territories, to bring in a bill for the organization of a territorial government, first of one, then of two territories North of that line. When he did so, it ended in his inserting a provision substantially repealing the Missouri Compromise. That was because the Compromise of 1850 *had not* repealed it. And now I ask why he could not have let that compromise alone? We were quiet from the agitation of the slavery question. We were making no fuss about it. All had acquiesced in the compromise measures of 1850. We never had been seriously disturbed by any abolition agitation before that period. When he came to form governments for the territories north of the line of 36 degrees, 30 minutes, why could he not have let that matter stand as it was standing? *[Applause]* Was it necessary to the organization of a territory?

---

12. See note 5 of the Ottawa debate, p. 8, and "Springfield resolutions controversy" in the glossary, pp. 331–32.

Not at all. Iowa lay north of the line and had been organized as a territory and had come into the Union as a state without disturbing that Compromise. There was no sort of necessity for destroying it to organize these territories.

But gentlemen, it would take up all my time to meet all the little quibbling arguments of Judge Douglas to show that the Missouri Compromise was repealed by the Compromise of 1850. My own opinion is that a careful investigation of all the arguments to sustain the position that that Compromise was virtually repealed by the Compromise of 1850 would show that they are the merest fallacies. I have the report that Judge Douglas first brought into Congress at the time of the introduction of the Nebraska bill, which in its original form *did not* repeal the Missouri Compromise, and he there expressly stated that he had forborne to do so *because it had not been done by the Compromise of* 1850. I close this part of the discussion on my part by asking him the question again, "Why, when we had peace under the Missouri Compromise, could you not have let it alone?"

In complaining of what I said in my speech at Springfield in which he says I accepted my nomination for the senatorship—where by the way he is at fault, for if he will examine it he will find no acceptance in it—he again quotes that portion in which I said that "a house divided against itself cannot stand." Let me say a word in regard to that matter. He tries to persuade us that there must be a variety in the different institutions of the states of the Union, that that variety necessarily proceeds from the variety of soil, climate, of the face of the country and the differences in the natural features of the states. I agree to all that. Have these very matters ever produced any difficulty amongst us? Not at all. Have we ever had any quarrel over the fact that they have laws in Louisiana designed to regulate the commerce that springs from the production of sugar? Or because we have a different class relative to the production of flour in this state? Have they produced any differences? Not at all. They are the very cement of this Union. They don't make the house a house divided against itself. They are the props that hold up the house and sustain the Union.

But has it been so with this element of slavery? Have we not always had quarrels and difficulties over it? And when will we cease to have quarrels over it? Like causes produce like effects. It is worth while to observe that we have generally had comparative peace upon the slavery question and that there has been no cause for alarm until it was excited by the effort to spread it into new territory. Whenever it has been limited to its present bounds and there has been no effort to spread it, there has been peace. All the trouble and convulsion has proceeded from efforts to spread it over more territory. It was thus at the date of the Missouri Compromise. It was so again with the annexation of Texas, so with the territory acquired by the Mexican War, and it is so now. Whenever there has been an effort to spread it, there has been agitation and resistance.

Now I appeal to this audience, very few of whom are my political friends, as national men, whether we have reason to expect that the agitation in regard to this subject will cease, while the causes that tend to reproduce agitation are actively at work? Will not the same causes that produced agitation in 1820 when the Missouri Compromise was formed, that which produced the agitation upon the annexation of Texas and at other times, work out the same results always? Do you think that the nature of man will be changed, that the same causes that produced agitation at one time will not have the same effect at another?

This has been the result, so far as my observation of the slavery question and my reading in history extends. What right have we then to hope that the trouble will cease—that the agitation will come to an end—until it shall either be placed back where it originally stood and where the fathers originally placed it, or on the other hand, until it shall entirely master all opposition. This is the view I entertain, and this is the reason I entertained it, as expressed in the extract which° Judge Douglas has read from my Springfield speech. Upon that subject I suppose that I have dwelt about as long as I ought, measuring and dividing my time as I best can.°

Now, my friends, there is one other thing that I feel myself under some sort of obligation to mention. Judge Douglas has here today—in a very rambling way, I was about saying—spoken of the platforms for which he seeks to hold me, and those who act with me,° responsible. He says, "Why can't you come out and make an open avowal of principles in all places alike?" and he reads from an advertisement that he says was used to notify the people of a speech to be made by Judge Trumbull at Waterloo. In commenting on it, he desires to know why° we cannot speak frankly and manfully, as he and his friends do! How, I ask, do his friends speak out their own sentiments? A convention of his party in this state met on the 21st of April, at Springfield, and passed a set of resolutions which they proclaim to the country as their platform. This does constitute their platform, and it is because Judge Douglas claims it is his platform—that these are his principles and purposes—that he has a right to declare he speaks his sentiments "frankly and manfully." On the 9th of June, Col. John Dougherty, Gov. Reynolds, and others calling themselves National Democrats met in Springfield and adopted a set of resolutions which are as easily understood, as plain and as definite in stating to the country and to the world what they believed in and would stand upon, as Judge Douglas's platform.[13] Now, what is the reason that Judge Douglas is not willing that Col. Dougherty and Gov. Reynolds should stand upon their own written and printed platform, as well as he upon his? Why must he look farther than their platform, when he claims himself to stand by his platform?

---

13. See "National Democrats" in the glossary, p. 328.

Again, in reference to our platform. On the 16th of June, the Republicans had their convention and published their platform, which is as clear and distinct as Judge Douglas's. In it they spoke their principles as plainly and as definitely to the world. What is the reason that Judge Douglas is not willing I should stand upon that platform? Why must he go around hunting for someone who is supporting me, or has supported me at some time in his life, and who has said something at some time contrary to that platform? Does the Judge regard that rule as a good one? If it turns out that the rule is a good one for me—that I am responsible for any and every opinion that any man has expressed who is my friend—then it is a good rule for him. I ask, is it not as good a rule for him as it is for me? In my opinion, it is not a good rule for either of us. Do you think differently, Judge?

Douglas: I do not.

Lincoln: Judge Douglas says he does not think differently. I am glad of it. Then can he tell me why he is looking up resolutions of five or six years ago, and insisting that they were my platform, notwithstanding my protest that they are not, and never were my platform, and my pointing out the platform of the state convention which he delights to say nominated me for the Senate. I cannot see what he means by parading these resolutions, if it is not to hold me responsible for them in some way. If he says to me here that he does not hold the rule to be good, one way or the other, I do not comprehend how he could answer me more fully, if he answered me at greater length. I will therefore put in as my answer to the resolutions that he has hunted up against me, what I, as a lawyer, would call a good plea to a bad declaration. *[Laughter]* I understand that it is a maxim of law that a poor plea may be a good plea to a bad declaration.[14] I think that the opinions the Judge brings from those who support me, yet differ from me, is a bad declaration against me; but if I can bring the same things against him, I am putting in a good plea to that kind of declaration, and now I propose to try it.

At Freeport Judge Douglas occupied a large part of his time in producing resolutions and documents of various sorts, as I understood, to make me somehow responsible for them, and I propose now doing a little of the same sort of thing for him. In 1850 a very clever gentleman by the name of Thompson Campbell, a personal friend of Judge Douglas and myself, a political friend of Judge Douglas and opponent of mine, was a candidate for Congress in the Galena district. He was interrogated as to his views on this same slavery question. I have here before me the interrogatories and Campbell's answers to them.[15] I will read them:

---

14. In law, a declaration is the statement in which a plaintiff presents his claim in an action. A plea is an allegation made by a party to a lawsuit in support of his claim or defense.

15. AL's source text has not been identified.

First. Will you, if elected, vote for and cordially support a bill prohibiting slavery in the territories of the United States?

Second. Will you vote for and support a bill abolishing slavery in the District of Columbia?

That is one and two. Now I read the answers to one and two: "To the first and second interrogations, I answer unequivocally in the affirmative." °

Third. Will you oppose the admission of any slave states which may be formed out of Texas or the territories?

Fourth. Will you vote for and advocate the repeal of the Fugitive Slave Law passed at the recent session of Congress?

Fifth. Will you advocate and vote for the election of a speaker of the House of Representatives who shall be willing to organize the committees of the House so as to give the free states their just influence in the business of legislation?

Sixth. What are your views not only as to the constitutional right of Congress to prohibit the slave trade between the states, but also as to the expediency of exercising that right immediately?

I read the answers, leaving out the first ones that I have read: °

To the third interrogatory I reply, that I am opposed to the admission of any more slave states into the Union, that may be formed out of Texas or any other territory.

To the fourth and fifth interrogatories, I unhesitatingly answer in the affirmative.

To the sixth interrogatory I reply, that so long as the slave states continue to treat slaves as articles of commerce, the Constitution confers power on Congress to pass laws regulating that peculiar COMMERCE, and that the protection of human rights imperatively demands the interposition of every constitutional means to prevent this most inhuman and iniquitous traffic. T. Campbell.

I want to say here that Thompson Campbell was elected to Congress on that platform as the Democratic candidate in the Galena district. He was elected to Congress over a very good man named° Martin P. Sweet.

Douglas: Give me the date of the letter.

Lincoln: The time Campbell ran was in 1850. I have not the exact date here. It was some time in 1850 that these interrogatories were put and the answer given. Campbell was elected to Congress, and served out his term. I think a second election came up before he served out his term, and he was not re-elected. Whether defeated or not nominated, I do not know.° At the end of his term of election upon this platform,° his very good friend, Judge Douglas, got him a high office from President Pierce, and sent him off to California. Is not that the fact? Just at the end of his term in Congress, it appears that our mutual friend, Judge Douglas, got our mutual friend, Campbell, a good office, and sent him to California upon it. And not only so, but on the 27th of last month, when Judge Douglas and myself spoke at Freeport in joint discussion, there was his same friend Campbell, come all the way from California to help the Judge beat me. And there was poor Martin P. Sweet sneaking about—I take back that ugly word, [to the reporters] you must not put that in°—standing on the platform trying to help poor me to be elected.[16] [Laughter] That is true of one of Judge Douglas's friends.

So again, in that same race of 1850, there was a congressional convention assembled at Joliet, and it nominated R. S. Molony, for Congress, and unanimously adopted the following resolutions:

> Resolved, That we are uncompromisingly opposed to the extension of slavery; and while we would not make such opposition a ground of interference with the interest of the States where it exists, yet we moderately but firmly insist that it is the duty of Congress to oppose its extension into Territory now free, by all means compatible with the obligations of the Constitution, and with good faith to our sister States; that these principles were recognized by the Ordinance of 1787, which received the sanction of Thomas Jefferson, who is acknowledged by all to be the great oracle and expounder of our faith.°

Subsequently those same interrogatories were propounded to Dr. Molony which had been addressed to Campbell, as above, with the exception of the sixth respecting the interstate slave trade, to which Dr. Molony, the Democratic nominee for Congress, replied as follows: °

> I received the within interrogatories this day, and, as you will see by the La-Salle Democrat and Ottawa Free Trader, I took at Peru on the 5th, and at Ottawa on the 7th, the affirmative side of interrogatories 1st and 2d, and in relation to the admission of any more slave States from free Territory, my position, taken at those meetings, as correctly reported in said papers, was emphatically and distinctly opposed to it. In relation to the admission of any more slave States, from Texas, whether I shall go against it or not, will depend upon the opinion that I may hereafter form of the true meaning and nature of the Resolutions of Annexation. If, by said resolutions, the honor and good faith of the nation is pledged to admit more slave States from Texas, when she (Texas) may apply for the admission of such States, then I should, if in Congress, vote for their admission. But if not so pledged and bound by sacred contract, then a bill for the admission of more slave States from Texas would never receive my vote.°
>
> To your 4th interrogatory, I answer most decidedly in the affirmative, and for reasons set forth in my reported remarks at Ottawa last Monday.

---

16. AL's letter to Sweet the next day indicates he had said something about Sweet he regretted. See AL to Martin Sweet, Sept. 16, 1858, in Basler et al., Collected Works, 3:144.

To your 5th interrogatory I also reply in the affirmative *most cordially*, and that I will use my utmost exertions to secure the nomination and election of a man who will accomplish the objects of said interrogatories.

I most cordially approve of the resolutions adopted at the union meeting held at Princeton on the 27th September ult.Yours, &c., R. S. Molony.[17]

All I have to say in regard to Dr. Molony is that he was the regularly nominated Democratic candidate for Congress in his district, was elected at that time, at the end of his term was appointed to a land office at Danville. I never heard anything of Judge Douglas's instrumentality in this. He held office a considerable time, and when we were at Freeport the other day, there were handbills scattered about notifying the public that after our debate was over, R. S. Molony would make a Democratic speech in favor of Judge Douglas. That is all I know of my own personal knowledge. It is added here to this resolution, and truly I believe that:

> Among those who participated in the Joliet Convention, and who supported its nominee, with his platform as laid down in the resolution of the Convention and his reply as above given, we call at random the following names, all of which are recognized at this day as leading Democrats:[18]Cook County—E. B. Williams, Charles McDonell, Arno Voss, Thomas Hoyne, Isaac Cook,[19]

I reckon we ought to except Ike° Cook. *[Laughter]*

> F. C. Sherman.
> Will—Joel A. Matteson, S. W. Bowen.
> Kane—B. F. Hall, G. W. Renwick, A. M. Herrington, Elijah Wilcox.
> McHenry—W. M. Jackson, Enos W. Smith, Neil Donnelly.
> La Salle—John Hise, William Reddick.

William Reddick! Another one of Judge Douglas's friends that stood on the stand with him at Ottawa, at the time the Judge says my knees trembled so that I had to be carried away. *[Laughter]* The names are all here:

> DuPage—Nathan Allen.
> DeKalb—Z. B. Mayo.

Here is another set of resolutions which I think are apposite to the matter in hand, which, according to the custom that Judge Douglas has established, I

---

17. The Joliet resolutions and Molony's response are printed in the *Chicago Democrat*, Oct. 11, 1850, which may have been AL's source text.

18. In the list of names that follows, AL's intention is to embarrass SAD by identifying leading Democrats who had supported Molony's antislavery positions in 1850, but who in 1858 were supporting SAD.

19. Isaac Cook had recently been reappointed postmaster in Chicago as a result of his opposition to SAD's position on the Lecompton Constitution.

believe that I will adopt, in handing to the reporter without reading.° On the 28th of February of the same year, a Democratic district convention was held at Naperville to nominate a candidate for circuit judge. Among the delegates were Bowen and Kelly, of Will; Captain Naper, H. H. Cody, Nathan Allen, of DuPage; W. M. Jackson, J. M. Strode, P. W. Platt and Enos W. Smith, of McHenry; J. Horseman and others, of Winnebago. Col. Strode presided over the convention. The following resolutions were unanimously adopted: the first on motion of P. W. Platt, the second on motion of William M. Jackson.

> *Resolved,* That this Convention is in favor of the Wilmot Proviso, both in *Principle* and *Practice,* and that we know of no good reason why any *person* should oppose the largest latitude in *Free Soil, Free Territory* and *Free Speech.*
> *Resolved,* That in the opinion of this Convention the time has arrived when *all men should be free,* whites as well as others.[20]

There is some portion of this that I will hand to the reporter to save time. There is only one other thing that I wish to comment upon.°

Douglas: What is the date of those resolutions?

Lincoln: I understand it was in 1850, but I do not *know* it. I do not state a thing and say I know it, when I do not. But I have the highest belief that this is so. I was not present at these conventions and do not know them to be true. It is not impossible that there is some error in it.° I know of no way to arrive at the conclusion that there is an error in it. I mean to put a case no stronger than the truth will allow.

But what I was going to comment upon is an extract from a newspaper in DeKalb County, and it strikes me as being rather singular, I confess, under the circumstances. There is a Judge Mayo in that county, who is a candidate for the legislature, for the purpose, if he secures his election, of helping to re-elect Judge Douglas. He is the editor of a newspaper,° and in that paper I find the extract I am going to read. It is part of an editorial article in which he was electioneering as fiercely as he could for Judge Douglas and against me. It was a curious thing, I think, to be in such a paper. I will agree to that, and the Judge may make the most of it:[21]

> Our education has been such, that we have ever been rather *in favor of the equality of the blacks; that is, that they should enjoy all the privileges of the whites where they reside.* We are aware that this is not a very popular doctrine. We have had many a confab with some who are now strong "Republicans," we taking the broad ground of equality and they the opposite ground. We were brought up

---

20. No source located.

21. The following text read by AL is apparently from the *DeKalb County Sentinel* (Sycamore), July 26, 1858. See textual note, p. 305.

in a State where blacks were voters, and we do not know of any inconvenience resulting from it, though perhaps it would not work as well, where the blacks are more numerous. We have no doubt of the right of the whites to guard against such an evil if it is one. Our opinion is, that it would be best for all concerned to have the colored population in a State by themselves,

In this I agree with him.°

but if within the jurisdiction of the U. S. *we say by all means they should have the right to have their Senators and Representatives in Congress, and to vote for President.* With us "Worth makes the man, and want of it the fellow." We have seen many a "nigger" that we thought more of than some white men.°

That is one of Judge Douglas's friends. Now I do not want to leave myself in an attitude where I can be misrepresented, so I will say I do not think the Judge is responsible for this article, but he is quite as responsible for it as I would be if one of my friends had said it. I think that is fair enough. *[Cheers]*

I have here also a set of resolutions which I will give to the reporter,° passed by a Democratic state convention in Judge Douglas's own good old State of Vermont.

Voice from the platform:[22] Your time is half over!°

Lincoln: I now understand that my time is half out.°

At Freeport I answered several interrogatories that had been propounded to me by Judge Douglas at the Ottawa meeting. The Judge has yet not seen fit to find any fault with the position that I took in regard to those seven interrogato-

---

22. The voice announcing AL's time as half over, which is only reported in the *Chicago Times,* probably came from a Lincoln partisan as a warning that he should consider not reading yet another example. It is unlikely that Lincoln took the time to read the Vermont resolutions, which are not in the *Chicago Times,* though they appear in the *Chicago Press and Tribune.* They are:

> *Resolved,* That liberty is a right inherent and inalienable in man, and that herein *all men are equal.*
>
> *Resolved,* That we claim no authority in the Federal Government to abolish slavery in the several States, but we do claim for it constitutional power perpetually to prohibit the introduction of slavery into territory now free, and abolish it wherever, under the jurisdiction of Congress it exists.
>
> *Resolved,* That this power ought immediately to be exercised in prohibiting the introduction and existence of slavery in New Mexico and California, in abolishing slavery and the slave trade in the District of Columbia, on the high seas, and wherever else, under the Constitution, it can be reached.
>
> *Resolved,* That no more slave States should be admitted into the Federal Union.
>
> *Resolved,* That the Government ought to return to its ancient policy, not to extend, nationalize or encourage, but to limit, localize and discourage slavery.

ries, which were certainly broad enough, in all conscience, to cover the entire ground. In my answers, which have been printed, and all have had the opportunity of seeing, I take the ground that those who elect me must expect that I will do nothing which is not in accordance with those answers. I have some right to assert that Judge Douglas has no fault to find with them. But he chooses to still try to thrust me upon different ground without paying any attention to my answers, the obtaining of which from me cost him so much trouble and concern.

At the same time, I propounded four interrogatories to him, claiming it as a right that he should answer as many interrogatories for me as I did for him, and I would reserve myself for a future installment when I got them ready. The Judge, in answering me upon that occasion, put in what I suppose he intends as answers to all four of my interrogatories. The first one of these interrogatories I have before me, and it is in these words:

> Question 1. If the people of Kansas shall, by means entirely unobjectionable in all other respects, adopt a State Constitution, and ask admission into the Union under it, *before* they have the requisite number of inhabitants according to the English Bill—some ninety-three thousand—will you vote to admit them?°

As I read the Judge's answer in the newspaper, and as I remember it as pronounced at the time, he does not give any answer which is equivalent to yes or no, I will or I won't. He answers at very considerable length, rather quarreling with me for asking the question, and insisting that Judge Trumbull had done something that I ought to say something about, and finally getting out such statements as induce me to infer that he means to be understood he will, in that supposed case, vote for the admission of Kansas. I only bring this forward now for the purpose of saying that if he chooses to put a different construction upon his answer, he may do it. But if he does not, I shall from this time forward assume that he will vote for the admission of Kansas in disregard of° the English bill. He has the right to remove any misunderstanding I may have. I only mention it now that I may hereafter assume this to be the true construction of his answer, if he does not now choose to correct me.

The second interrogatory that I propounded to him, was this:

> Question 2. Can the people of a United States Territory, in any lawful way, against the wish of any citizen of the United States, exclude slavery from its limits prior to the formation of a State Constitution?°

To this Judge Douglas answered that they can lawfully exclude slavery from the territory prior to the formation of a constitution. He goes on to tell us how it can be done. As I understand him, he holds that it can be done by the territorial legislature refusing to make any enactments for the protection of slavery in the territory, and especially by adopting unfriendly legislation to it. For the sake of clearness I state it again: that they can exclude slavery from the territory, first, by withholding what he assumes to be an indispensable assistance to it in the way of legislation, and second, by unfriendly legislation. If I rightly understand him, I wish to ask your attention for a while to his position.

In the first place, the Supreme Court of the United States has decided that any congressional prohibition of slavery in the territories is unconstitutional, that they have reached this proposition as a conclusion from their former proposition that the Constitution of the United States expressly recognizes property in slaves, and from that other constitutional provision that no person shall be deprived of property without due process of law. Hence they reach the conclusion that, as the Constitution of the United States expressly recognizes property in slaves, and prohibits any person from being deprived of property without due process of law, to pass an act of Congress by which a man who owned a slave on one side of a line would be deprived of him if he took him on the other side, is depriving him of that property without due process of law. That I understand to be the decision of the Supreme Court. I understand also that Judge Douglas adheres most firmly to that decision, and the difficulty is: How is it possible for any power to exclude slavery from the territory unless in violation of that decision? That is the difficulty.

In the Senate of the United States, in 1856, Judge Trumbull in a speech, substantially if not directly, put the same interrogatory to Judge Douglas, as to whether the people of a territory had the lawful power to exclude slavery prior to the formation of a constitution. Judge Douglas then answered at considerable length, and his answer will be found in the *Congressional Globe,* under date of June 9th, 1856.[23] I am not sure that I have the page, but that is the date.° The Judge said that whether the people could exclude slavery prior to the formation of a constitution or not *was a question to be decided by the Supreme Court.* He put that proposition, as will be seen by the *Congressional Globe,* in a variety of forms, all running to the same thing in substance—that it was a question for the Supreme Court.

I maintain that when he says, after the Supreme Court have decided the question, that the people may yet exclude slavery by any means whatever, he does virtually say that it is *not* a question for the Supreme Court. *[Applause]* He shifts his ground. He shakes his head!° I appeal to you whether he did not say it was a question for the Supreme Court. Has not the Supreme Court decided that question? When he now says the people may exclude slavery, does he not make it a question for the people? Does he not virtually shift his ground and say that it is *not* a question for the Court, but for the people? This is a very simple proposition—a

---

23. *Congressional Globe,* 34th Cong., 1st Sess., Senate, June 9, 1856, 2:1371, 1374.

very plain and naked one. It seems to me that there is no difficulty in deciding it. In a variety of ways he said that it was a question for the Supreme Court. He did not stop then to tell Trumbull ° that whatever the Supreme Court decides the people can, by withholding necessary "police regulations," keep slavery out. He did not make any such answer then. ° I submit to you now, whether the new state of the case has not induced the Judge to sheer away from his original ground. *[Applause]* Would not this be the impression of every fair-minded man?

This is not all with regard to that answer of his. ° I hold that the proposition that slavery cannot enter a new country without police regulations is historically false. It is not true at all. I hold that the history of this country shows that the institution of slavery was originally planted upon this continent *without* these "police regulations" which the Judge now thinks necessary for the actual establishment of it. Not only so, but is there not another fact? How came this Dred Scott decision to be made? It was made upon the case of a negro being taken and actually held in slavery in Minnesota Territory, claiming his freedom because the act of Congress prohibited his being so held there.[24] *Will the Judge pretend that Dred Scott was not held there without police regulations?* There is at least one matter of record as to his having been held in slavery in the territory, not only without police regulations, but in the teeth of congressional legislation supposed to be valid at the time. This shows that there is vigor enough in slavery to plant itself in a new country even against unfriendly legislation. It takes not only law but the *enforcement* of law to keep it out. That is the history of this country upon the subject.

I wish to ask one other question. It being understood that the Constitution of the United States guarantees property in slaves in the territories, if there is any infringement of the right of that property, would not the United States courts, organized for the government of the territory, apply such remedy as might be necessary in that case? It is a maxim held by the courts, that there is no wrong without its remedy, and the courts have a remedy for whatever is acknowledged and treated as a wrong.

Again, I will ask you, my friends, if you were elected members of the legislature, what would be the first thing you would have to do before entering upon your duties? *Swear to support the Constitution of the United States.* Suppose you believe, as Judge Douglas does, that the Constitution of the United States guarantees to your neighbor the right to hold slaves in that territory, that they are his property. How can you clear your oaths unless you give him such legislation as is necessary to enable him to enjoy that property? What do you understand

---

24. Dred Scott was held in slavery in the late 1830s in a portion of Wisconsin Territory originally taken from that portion of Louisiana Territory where slavery had been banned by the Missouri Compromise. Minnesota Territory was not created until 1849.

by supporting the constitution of a state or of the United States? Is it not to give such constitutional helps to the rights established by that constitution as may be practically needed? Can you, if you swear to support the Constitution and believe that the Constitution establishes a right, clear your oath without giving it support? Do you support the Constitution if, knowing or believing there is a right established under it which needs specific legislation, you withhold that legislation? Do you not violate and disregard your oath? I can conceive of nothing plainer in the world. There can be nothing in the words "support the Constitution," if you may run counter to it by refusing support to any right established under the Constitution.

And what I say here will hold with still more force against the Judge's doctrine of "unfriendly legislation." How could you, having sworn to support the Constitution and believing it guaranteed the right to hold slaves in the territories, assist in legislation *intended to defeat that right?* How could you?° That would be violating your own view of the Constitution. Not only so, but if you were to do so, how long would it take the courts to hold your votes unconstitutional and void? Not a moment.

Lastly I would ask, is not Congress itself under obligation to give legislative support to any right that is established under the United States Constitution? I repeat the question—is not Congress itself bound to give legislative support to any right that is established in the United States Constitution? A member of Congress swears to support the Constitution of the United States, and if he sees a right established by that Constitution which needs specific legislative protection, can he clear his oath without giving that protection? Let me ask you why many of us who are opposed to slavery upon principle give our acquiescence to a fugitive slave law? Why do we hold ourselves under obligations to pass such a law, and abide by it when it is passed? Because the Constitution makes provision that the owners of slaves shall have the right to reclaim them. It gives the right to reclaim slaves, and that right is, as Judge Douglas says, a "barren right," unless there is legislation that will enforce it.

The mere declaration "No Person held to Service or Labor in one State, under the Laws thereof, escaping into another, shall, in Consequence of any Law or Regulation therein, be discharged from such Service or Labor, But shall be delivered up on Claim of the Party to whom such Service or Labor may be due"[25] is powerless without specific legislation to enforce it. Now on what ground would a member of Congress who is opposed to slavery in the abstract vote for a fugitive law, as I would deem it my duty to do? Because there is a Constitutional right which needs legislation to enforce it. And although it is distasteful to me, I have sworn to sup-

---

25. U.S. Constitution, Art. IV, Sect. 2.

port the Constitution, and having so sworn, I cannot conceive that I do support it if I withhold° from that right any necessary legislation to make it practical.

And if that is true in regard to a fugitive slave law, is the right to have fugitive slaves reclaimed any better fixed in the Constitution than the right to hold slaves in the territories? For this decision is a just exposition of the Constitution, as Judge Douglas thinks. Is the one right any better than the other? Is there any man who, while a member of Congress, would give support to the one any more than the other? If I wished to refuse to give legislative support to slave property in the territories, if a member of Congress, I could not do it holding the view that the Constitution establishes that right. If I did it at all, it would be because I deny that this decision properly construes the Constitution. But if I acknowledge with Judge Douglas that this decision properly construes the Constitution, I cannot conceive that I would be less than a perjured man if I should refuse in Congress to give such protection to that property as in its nature it needed.

At the end of what I have said here I propose to give the Judge my fifth interrogatory which he may take and answer at his leisure. My fifth interrogatory is this: If the slaveholding citizens of a United States territory should need and demand congressional legislation for the protection of their slave property in such territory, would you, as a member of Congress, vote for or against such legislation?

Douglas: Will you repeat that? I want to answer that question.

Lincoln: If the slaveholding citizens of a United States territory should need and demand congressional legislation for the protection of their slave property in such territory, would you, as a member of Congress, vote for or against such legislation?

I am aware that in some of the speeches Judge Douglas has made he has spoken as if he did not know or think that the Supreme Court had decided that a territorial legislature cannot exclude slavery. Precisely what the Judge would say upon the subject—whether he would say definitely that he does not understand they have so decided, or whether he would say he does understand that the Court have so decided—I do not know. But I know that in his speech at Springfield,[26] he spoke of it as a thing they had not decided yet, and in his answer to me at Freeport, he spoke of it, so far again as I can comprehend it, as a thing that had not yet been decided. Now I hold that if the Judge does entertain that view, I think he is not mistaken in so far as it can be said that the Court has not decided anything save the mere question of jurisdiction. I know the legal arguments that can be made, that after a court has decided that it cannot take jurisdiction of a case, it then has

---

26. The reference is to SAD's speech in Springfield on July 17, 1858, which was printed in *Illinois State Register*, July 19, 1858.

decided all that is before it, and that is the end of it. A plausible argument can be made in favor of that proposition, but I know that Judge Douglas has said in one of his speeches that the court went forward *like honest men as they were* and decided all the points in the case. If any points are really extra judicially decided because not necessarily before them, then this one as to the power of the territorial legislature to exclude slavery is one of them, as also the one that the Missouri Compromise was null and void. They are both extra-judicial, or neither is, according as the Court held that they had no jurisdiction in the case between the parties, because of want of capacity of one party to maintain a suit in that Court.

I want, if I have sufficient time, to show that the Court did *pass its opinion*, but that is the only thing actually done in the case. If they did not decide, they showed what they were ready to decide whenever the matter was before them. What is that opinion? After having argued that Congress had no power to pass a law excluding slavery from a United States territory, they then used language to this effect: that inasmuch as Congress itself could not exercise such a power, it followed as a matter of course that it could not authorize a territorial government to exercise it, for the territorial legislature can do no more than Congress could do. Thus it expressed its opinion emphatically against the power of a territorial legislature to exclude slavery, leaving us in just as little doubt on that point as upon any other point they really decided.

Now, my fellow citizens, I will detain you only a little while longer. My time is very nearly out. I find a report of a speech made by Judge Douglas at Joliet, since we last met at Freeport, published, I believe, in the *Missouri Republican* on the ninth of this month, in which Judge Douglas says:

> You know at Ottawa I read this platform and asked him if he concurred in each and all of the propositions set forth in it. He would not answer these questions. ° At last I said frankly, I want you to answer them, because when I get you up where the color of your principles are a little darker than in Egypt, I intend to trot you down to Jonesboro. The very notice that I was going to take him down to Egypt, made him tremble in the knees, so that he had to be carried from the platform. He laid up seven days, and in the meantime held a consultation with his political physicians. They had Lovejoy and Farnsworth and all the leaders of the Abolition party. They consulted it all over, and at last Lincoln came to the conclusion that he would answer, so he came up to Freeport last Friday. °

Now that statement altogether furnishes a subject for philosophical contemplation. *[Laughter]* I have been treating it in that way, and I have really come to the conclusion that I can explain it in no other way than by believing the Judge is crazy. *[Laughter]* If he was in his right mind, I cannot conceive how he would have risked disgusting the four or five thousand of his own friends who stood there, and knew, as to my having been carried from the platform, that there was not a word of truth in it.

Douglas: Didn't they carry you off?

Lincoln: There!° That question illustrates the character of this man Douglas exactly. He smiles now and says, "Didn't they carry you off?" But he said then, "*He had to be carried off.*" And he said it to convince the country that he had so completely broken me down by his speech that I had to be carried away. Now he seeks to dodge it, and asks, "Didn't they carry you off?" Yes, they did. *But, Judge Douglas, why didn't you tell the truth? [Laughter, cheers]* I would like to know why you didn't tell the truth about it.

Douglas: I did.°

Lincoln: And then again, "He laid up seven days." He puts this in print for the people of the country to read as a serious document. I think if he had been in his sober senses, he would not have risked that barefacedness in the presence of thousands of his own friends, who knew that I made speeches within six of the seven days at Henry, Marshall County; Augusta, Hancock County; and Macomb, McDonough County, including all the necessary travel to meet him again at Freeport at the end of the six days. Now, I say, there is no charitable way to look at that statement, except to conclude that he is actually crazy. *[Laughter]*

There is another thing in that statement that alarmed me very greatly as he states it, that he was going to "trot me down to Egypt." Thereby he would have you to infer that I would not come to Egypt unless he forced me, that I could not be got here, unless he, giant-like, had hauled me down here. *[Laughter]* That statement he makes, too, in the teeth of the knowledge that I had made the stipulation to come down here, *and that he himself had been very reluctant to enter into the stipulation. [Cheers, laughter]* More than all this, Judge Douglas, when he made that statement, must have been crazy, and wholly out of his sober senses, or else he would have known that when he got me down here, that promise, that windy promise of his powers to annihilate me, wouldn't amount to anything. Now, how little do I look like being carried away trembling? Let the Judge go on, and after he is done with his half hour, I want you all, if I can't go home myself, to let me stay and rot here. And if anything happens to the Judge, if I cannot carry him to the hotel and put him to bed, let me stay here and rot. *[Laughter]*

I say, then, there is something *extraordinary* in this statement. I ask you if you know any other living man who would make such a statement? *[Cries of both "no" and "yes"]* I will ask my friend Casey, over there, if he would do such a thing? Would he send that out and have his men take it as the truth? Did the Judge talk of trotting me down to Egypt to scare me to death? Why, I know this people better than he does. I was raised just a little east of here. I am a part of this people. But the Judge was raised further north, and perhaps he has some horrid idea of what this people might be induced to do. *[Laughter, cheers]*

But really I have talked about this matter perhaps longer than I ought, for it is no great thing, and yet the smallest are often the most difficult things to deal with. The Judge has set about seriously trying to make the impression that when we meet at different places, I am literally in his clutches, that I am a poor, helpless, decrepit mouse, and that I can do nothing at all. This is one of the ways he has taken to create that impression. I don't know any other way to meet it, except this. I don't want to quarrel with him, to call him a liar, but when I come square up to him, I don't know what else to call him, if I must tell the truth out. *[Cheers, laughter]* I want to be at peace, and reserve all my fighting powers for necessary occasions. My time, now, is very nearly out, and I give up the trifle that is left to the Judge to let him set my knees trembling again, if he can.

DOUGLAS'S REJOINDER

My friends, while I am very grateful to you for the enthusiasm which you show for me, I will say in all candor that your quietness will be much more agreeable than your applause, inasmuch as you deprive me of some part of my time whenever you cheer.

I will commence where Mr. Lincoln left off, and make a remark upon this serious complaint of his about my speech at Joliet. I did say there in a playful manner that when I put these questions to Mr. Lincoln at Ottawa, he failed to answer, and that he trembled and had to be carried off the stand, and required seven days to get up his reply. *[Laughter]* That he did not walk off from that stand he will not deny. That when the crowd went away from the stand with me, a few persons carried him home on their shoulders and laid him down, he will admit. *[Laughter]* I wish to say to you that whenever I degrade my friends and myself by allowing them to carry me on their backs along through the public streets when I am able to walk, I am willing to be deemed crazy. *[Laughter, applause]* I did not say whether I beat him or he beat me in the argument. It is true I put these questions to him, and I put them not as mere idle questions, but showed that I based them upon the creed of the Black Republican party, as declared by their conventions in that portion of the state which he depends upon to elect him, and desired to know whether he endorsed that creed. He would not answer. When I reminded him that I intended bringing him into Egypt and renewing my questions if he refused to answer, he then consulted and did get up his answers one week after, answers which I may refer to in a few minutes and show you how equivocal they are. My object was to make him avow whether or not he stood by the platform of his party. The resolutions I then read, and upon which I based my questions, had been adopted by his party in the Galena congressional district, and the Chicago and Bloomington congressional districts, composing a large majority of the counties in this state that give Republican or abolition majorities. Mr. Lincoln cannot and will not deny that the doctrines laid down in these resolutions were in substance put forth in Lovejoy's resolutions which were voted for by a majority of his party, some of them, if not all, receiving the support of every man of his party.[27]

Hence, I laid a foundation for my questions to him before I asked him whether that was or was not the platform of his party. He says that he answered my questions. One of them was whether he would vote to admit any more slave states into the Union. The creed of the Republican party as set forth in the resolutions of their various conventions was that they would, under no circumstances, vote to admit another slave state. It was put forth in the Lovejoy resolutions in the legislature; it was put forth and passed in a majority of all the counties of this state which give abolition or Republican majorities, or elect members to the legislature of that school of politics. I had a right to know whether he would vote for or against the admission of another slave state in the event the people wanted it. He first answered that he was not pledged on the subject, and then said:

> In regard to the other question of whether I am pledged to the admission of any more slave states into the Union, I state to you very frankly that I would be exceedingly sorry ever to be put in the position of having to pass on that question. [Laughter] I should be exceedingly glad to know that there would never be another slave State admitted into the Union; but I must add, that if slavery shall be kept out of the Territories during the territorial existence of any one given Territory, and then the people shall, having a fair chance and clear field when they come to adopt a Constitution, do such an extraordinary thing as adopt a Slave Constitution, uninfluenced by the actual presence of the institution among them, I see no alternative, if we own the country, but to admit them into the Union.°

Now analyze that answer. In the first place, he says he would be exceedingly sorry to be put in a position where he would have to vote on the question of the admission of a slave state. Why is he a candidate for the Senate if he would be sorry to be put in that position? I trust the people of Illinois will not put him in a position which he would be so sorry to occupy. The next position he takes is that he would be glad to know that there would never be another slave state, yet, in certain contingencies, he might have to vote for one. What is that contingency? If Congress keeps slavery out by law while it is a territory, and then the people should have a fair chance and should adopt slavery, uninfluenced by the presence of the institution, he supposed he would have to admit the state. Suppose

---

27. See note 3, p. 91.

Congress should not keep slavery out during their territorial existence, then how would he vote when the people applied for admission into the Union with a slave constitution? That he does not answer, and that is the condition of every territory we have now got.

Slavery is not kept out of Kansas by act of Congress, and when I put the question to Mr. Lincoln whether he will vote for the admission with or without slavery, as her people may desire, he will not answer, and you have not got an answer from him. In Nebraska, slavery is not prohibited by act of Congress, but the people are allowed, under the Nebraska bill, to do as they please on the subject. And when I ask him whether he will vote to admit Nebraska with a slave constitution if her people desire it, he will not answer. So with New Mexico, Washington Territory, Arizona, and the four new states to be admitted from Texas. You cannot get an answer from him to these questions. His answer only applies to a given case, to a condition—things which he knows do not exist in any one territory in the Union. He tries to give you to understand that he would allow the people to do as they please, and yet he dodges the question as to every territory in the Union.

I now ask why cannot Mr. Lincoln answer to each of these territories? He has not done it, and he will not do it. The abolitionists up north understand that this answer is made with a view of not committing himself on any one territory now in existence. It is so understood there, and you cannot expect an answer from him on a case that applies to any one territory, or applies to the new states which, by compact, we are pledged to admit out of Texas, when they have the requisite population and desire admission. I submit to you whether he has made a frank answer, so that you can tell how he would vote in any one of these cases. He would be sorry to be put in the position. Why would he be sorry to be put in this position if his duty required him to give the vote? If the people of a territory ought to be permitted to come into the Union as a state, with slavery or without it, as they pleased, why not give the vote admitting them cheerfully? If, in his opinion, they ought not to come in with slavery, even if they wanted to, why not say that he would cheerfully vote against their admission? His intimation is that conscience would not let him vote "No," and he would be sorry to do that which his conscience would compel him to do as a honest man. *[Laughter, cheers]*

In regard to the contract or bargain between Trumbull, the abolitionists, and him, which he denies, I wish to say that the charge can be proved by notorious historical facts. Trumbull, Lovejoy, Giddings, Fred Douglass, Hale, and Banks were traveling the state at that time, making speeches on the same side and in the same cause with him. He contents himself with the simple denial that no such thing occurred. Does he deny that he, and Trumbull, and Breese, and Giddings, and Chase, and Fred Douglass, and Lovejoy, and all those abolitionists and deserters from the Democratic party, did make speeches all over this state in the same common cause? Does he deny that Jim Matheny was then and is now his confidential friend and wire worker?

Lincoln: Yes, sir.°

Douglas: And does he deny that Matheny made the charge of the bargain and fraud in his own language, as I have read it from his printed speech. Matheny spoke of his own personal knowledge of that bargain existing between Lincoln, Trumbull, and the abolitionists. He still remains Lincoln's confidential friend and is now a candidate for Congress, and is canvassing the Springfield district for Lincoln. I assert that I can prove the charge to be true in detail, if I can ever get it where I can summon and compel the attendance of witnesses.

Lincoln: If you will name the witnesses, I will bring them to you.°

Douglas: I have the statement of another man to the same effect as that made by Matheny, which I am not permitted to use yet, but Jim Matheny is a good witness on that point, and the history of the country is conclusive upon it. That Lincoln up to that time had been a Whig, and then undertook to abolitionize the Whigs and bring them into the abolition camp, is beyond denial. That Trumbull up to that time had been a Democrat, and deserted, and undertook to abolitionize the Democracy and take them into the abolition camp, is beyond denial. That they are both now active, leading, distinguished members of this abolition Republican party, in full communion, is a fact that cannot be questioned or denied.

But Lincoln is not willing to be responsible for the creed of his party. He complains because I hold him responsible, and in order to avoid the issue, he attempts to show that individuals in the Democratic party, many years ago, expressed abolition sentiments. It is true that Tom Campbell, when a candidate for Congress in 1850, published the letter which Lincoln read. When I asked Lincoln for the date of that letter, he could not give it. The date of the letter has been suppressed by other speakers who have used it, though I take it for granted that Lincoln did not know the date. If he will take the trouble to examine, he will find that the letter was published only two days before the election, and was never seen until after it, except in one county. Tom Campbell would have been beat to death by the Democratic party if that letter had been made public in his district.

As to Molony, it is true he uttered sentiments of the kind referred to by Mr. Lincoln, and the best Democrats would not vote for him for that reason. I returned from Washington after the passage of the compromise measures in 1850, and when I found Molony running under John Wentworth's tutelage, and on his platform, I denounced him, and declared that he was no Democrat. In a speech at Chicago just before the election of that year, I went before the infuriated people of that city and vindicated the compromise measures of 1850. Remember the City Council had passed resolutions nullifying acts of Congress and instructing the police to withhold their assistance from the execution of the laws. And as I was the only man in the city of Chicago who was responsible for the passage of the compromise measures, I went before the crowd, justified each and every one of those measures, and let it be said to the eternal honor of the people of Chicago, that when they were convinced by my exposition of those measures that they were right and they had done wrong in opposing them, they repealed their nullifying resolutions and declared that they would acquiesce in and support the laws of the land.[28] These facts are well known, and Mr. Lincoln can only get up individual instances, dating back to 1849, '50, which are contradicted by the whole tenor of the Democratic creed.

But Mr. Lincoln does not want to be held responsible for the Black Republican doctrine of no more slave states. Farnsworth is the candidate of his party today in the Chicago district, and he made a speech in the last Congress in which he called upon God to palsy his right arm if he ever voted for the admission of another slave state, whether the people wanted it or not. Lovejoy is making speeches all over the state for Lincoln now, and taking ground against any more slave states. Washburne, the Black Republican candidate for Congress in the Galena district, is making speeches in favor of this same abolition platform declaring no more slave states.

Why are men running for Congress in the Northern districts, and taking that abolition platform for their guide, when Mr. Lincoln does not want to be held to it down here in Egypt and in the center of the state, and objects to it, so as to get votes here? Let me tell Mr. Lincoln that his party in the Northern part of the state hold to that abolition platform, and that if they do not in the South and in the center, they present the extraordinary spectacle of a house divided against itself, and hence cannot stand. *[Cheers]* I now bring down upon him the vengeance of his own scriptural quotation, and give it a more appropriate application than he did, when I say to him that his party, abolition in one end of the state and opposed to it in the other, is a house divided against itself, and cannot stand, and ought not to stand, for it attempts to cheat the American people out of their votes by disguising its sentiments. *[Cheers]*

Mr. Lincoln attempts to cover up and get over his abolitionism by telling you that he was raised a little east of you *[Laughter]*, beyond the Wabash in Indiana, and he thinks that makes a mighty sound and good man of him on all these questions, because he was raised in Indiana.° I do not know that the place where a man is born or raised has much to do with his political principles. The worst

---

28. On Oct. 23, 1850, after the city council of Chicago ordered the police of that city not to enforce the Fugitive Slave Law, SAD addressed a crowd there that evening and defended the law and the other provisions of the Compromise of 1850. The city council reversed its action the next night. See Johannsen, 301–3.

abolitionists I have ever known in Illinois have been men who have sold their slaves in Alabama and Kentucky, and have come here and turned abolitionists, while spending the money got for the negroes they sold. *[Laughter]* And I do not know that an abolitionist from Indiana or Kentucky ought to have any more credit because he was born and raised among slaveholders. I do not know that a native of Kentucky is more excusable because raised among slaves, his father and mother having owned slaves, he comes to Illinois, turns abolitionist, and slanders the graves of his father and mother, and breathes curses upon the institutions under which he was born, and his father and mother bred.

True, I was not born out west here. I was born away down in Yankee land. I was born in a valley in Vermont, with the high mountains around me. I love the old green mountains and valleys of Vermont, where I was born, and where I played in my childhood. I went up to visit them some seven or eight years ago, for the first time for twenty odd years. When I got there they treated me very kindly. They invited me to the commencement of their college, placed me on the seats with their distinguished guests, and conferred upon me the degree of L.L.D. in Latin, the same as they did on Old Hickory, at Cambridge, many years ago. And I give you my word and honor I understood just as much of the Latin as he did.[29] *[Laughter]* When they got through conferring the honorary degree, they called upon me for a speech, and I got up with my heart full and swelling with gratitude for their kindness, and I said to them, "My friends, Vermont is the most glorious spot on the face of this globe for a man to be born in, *provided* he emigrates when he is very young." *[Laughter]*

I emigrated when I was very young. I came out here when I was a boy, and I found my mind liberalized and my opinions enlarged when I got on these broad prairies, with only the heavens to bound my vision, instead of having them circumscribed by the little narrow ridges that surrounded the valley where I was born. But, I discard all flings of the land where a man was born. I wish to be judged by my principles, by those great public measures and constitutional principles upon which the peace, the happiness, and the perpetuity of this republic now rest.

Mr. Lincoln has framed another question, propounded it to me, and desired my answer. As I have said before, I did not put a question to him that I did not first lay a foundation for, by showing that it was a part of the platform of the party whose votes he is now seeking, adopted in a majority of the counties where he now hopes to get a majority, and supported by the candidates of his party now running in those counties. But I will answer his question. It is as follows: "If the slaveholding citizens of a United States territory should need and demand congressional legislation for the protection of their slave property in such territory,

---

29. Middlebury College conferred an honorary degree upon SAD in 1851.

would you, as a member of Congress, vote for or against such legislation?"° I answer him that it is a fundamental article in the Democratic creed that there should be non-interference and non-intervention by Congress with slavery in the states or territories. *[Cheers]* Mr. Lincoln could have found an answer to his question in the Cincinnati platform, if he had desired it. *[Applause]* The Democratic party have always stood by that great principle of non-interference and non-intervention by Congress with slavery in the states and territories alike, and I stand on that platform now. *[Applause, cheers]*

Now I desire to call your attention to the fact that Lincoln did not define his own position in his own question. *[Laughter]* How does he stand on that question? He put the question to me at Freeport whether or not I would vote to admit Kansas into the Union before she had 93,420 inhabitants. I answered him at once that, it having been decided that Kansas had now population enough for a slave state, she had population enough for a free state. *[Cheers]*

I answered the question unequivocally, and then I asked him whether he would vote for or against the admission of Kansas before she had 93,420 inhabitants, and he would not° answer me. Today he has called attention to the fact that, in his opinion, my answer on that question was not quite plain enough, and yet he has not answered it himself. *[Laughter]* He now puts a question in relation to congressional interference in the territories to me. I answer him direct, and yet he has not answered the question himself.

I ask you whether a man has any right, in common decency, to put questions in these public discussions, to his opponent, which he will not answer himself, when they are pressed home to him. I have asked him three times, whether he would vote to admit Kansas whenever the people applied with a constitution of their own making and their own adoption, under circumstances that were fair, just and unexceptionable, but I cannot get an answer from him. Nor will he answer the question which he put to me, and which I have just answered in relation to congressional interference in the territories, by making a slave code there.

It is true° that he goes on to answer the question by arguing that, under the decision of the Supreme Court, it is the duty of a man to vote for a slave code in the territories. He says that it is his duty, under the decision that the Court has made, and if he believes in that decision, he would be a perjured man if he did not give the vote. I want to know whether he is not bound to a decision which is contrary to his opinions just as much as to one in accordance with his opinions. If the decision of the Supreme Court, the tribunal created by the Constitution to decide the question, is final and binding, is he not bound by it just as strongly as if he was for it, instead of against it, originally. Is every man in this land allowed to resist decisions he does not like, and only support those that meet his approval? What are important courts worth unless their decisions are binding on all good citizens? It is the fundamental principle of the judiciary that its decisions are final. It is created for that purpose so that, when you cannot agree among yourselves on a disputed point, you appeal to the judicial tribunal, which steps in and decides for you, and that decision is then binding on every good citizen. It is the law of the land just as much with Mr. Lincoln against it as for it. And yet he says that if that decision is binding, he is a perjured man if he does not vote for a slave code in the different territories of this Union. Well, if you *[turning to Lincoln]* are not going to resist the decision, if you obey it, and do not intend to array mob law against the constituted authorities, then, according to your own statement, you will be a perjured man if you do not vote to establish slavery in these territories.

My doctrine is that, even taking Mr. Lincoln's view that the decision recognizes the right of a man to carry his slaves into the territories of the United States if he pleases, yet after he gets there, he needs affirmative law to make that right of any value. The same doctrine not only applies to slave property, but all other kinds of property. Chief Justice Taney places it upon the ground that slave property is on an equal footing with other property. Suppose one of your merchants should move to Kansas and open a liquor store. He has a right to take groceries and liquors there, but the mode of selling them, and the circumstances under which they shall be sold, and all the remedies must be prescribed by local legislation, and if that is unfriendly, it will drive him out just as effectually as if there was a constitutional provision against the sale of liquor. So the absence of local legislation to encourage and support slave property in a territory excludes it practically just as effectually as if there was a positive constitutional provision against it.[30] Hence, I assert that under the Dred Scott decision, you cannot maintain slavery a day in a territory where there is an unwilling people and unfriendly legislation. If the people are opposed to it, your° right is a° barren, worthless, useless right, and if they are for it, they will support and encourage it.

We come right back, therefore, to the practical question. If the people of a territory want slavery, they will have it, and if they do not want it, you cannot force it on them. And this is the practical question, the great principle upon which our institutions rest. I am willing to take the decision of the Supreme Court as it was pronounced by that august tribunal without stopping to inquire whether I would have decided that way or not. I have had many a decision made against me on questions of law which I did not like, but I was bound by them just as much as if I had had a hand in making them, and approved them. Did you ever see a lawyer who lost his case and liked the decision° or a client who did not think the

---

30. As in this instance, SAD would repeat his Freeport Doctrine several times during these debates.

decision unjust?° They always think the decision unjust when it is given against them. In a government of laws, like ours, we must sustain the Constitution as our fathers made it, and maintain the rights of the states as they are guaranteed under the Constitution; sustain the constitutional authorities as they exist,° and then we will have peace and harmony between the different states and sections of this glorious Union. *[Cheers]*

CHARLESTON

SEPTEMBER 18, 1858

INTRODUCTION

Abraham Lincoln was on familiar ground during his fourth meeting with Stephen Douglas at Charleston, Illinois, on September 18, 1858, just three days after the Jonesboro debate. Lincoln's father was buried nearby; his stepmother still lived in a log cabin in the area; and several stepsiblings and cousins resided in Charleston or in surrounding Coles County. Lincoln had occasionally practiced law in the local courthouse, and he was on close terms with a number of area lawyers and politicians. Charleston was the first debate site to be located in the central region of the state where, after the collapse of the Whig party, partisan divisions were least distinct, and where it was felt that the outcome of the senatorial campaign would be determined. The remaining debates would also be conducted within this region. The first three had been conducted at opposite ends of the state, in districts whose political complexion was very predictable. Coles County had been safely Whig until the passage of the Kansas-Nebraska Act, subsequent to which the formerly Whig local vote had sometimes been divided between Republican and Know-Nothing candidates, allowing Democrats to gain a plurality there. In other instances in the mid-1850s the Republican and Democratic votes had been almost evenly split. All this insured that Coles County's electoral performance was especially uncertain. The county was also intensely Negrophobic; 94.9 percent of its citizens had voted in 1848 to ban African Americans from living in the state.

With a population of about 2,200, Charleston was smaller than most of the other debate sites, yet the county's Democratic and Republican partisans, especially active as they were in an area where political competition was keen, made elaborate preparations for the debate. Both Lincoln and Douglas were escorted the ten miles to Charleston from nearby Mattoon by processions of local political delegations and enthusiasts from both places, and townspeople and visitors from as far distant as Indiana beheld the unusually large and colorful floats and banners that adorned the town's streets. "I have seen and watched these other demonstrations," wrote a relatively dispassionate Eastern witness, "but have failed to notice the hot and fevered flush which has marked this one," while a Chicago correspondent wrote that both Ottawa and Freeport together "would not have made so imposing a display of the etceteras of a great campaign."[1] That same Eastern observer guessed the size of the crowd in attendance at the debate site on the county fairgrounds to be about five thousand, while enthusiastic Illinoisans of both parties claimed as many as twelve thousand to fifteen thousand. Lew Wallace, at this time a young Democratic member of the Indiana senate, was present at Charleston. Much later Wallace, the author of *Ben Hur,* remembered that "the platform for the speakers reminded me of an island barely visible in a restless sea—so great was the gathering."[2]

The Charleston debate is probably most notorious for the five minutes or so that Lincoln devoted to the topic of Negro equality in his opening speech, denying more emphatically than in any other debate, any claim that he favored full equality for blacks. However, the major portion of that speech was given over to a totally different issue, which Lincoln pursued with vigor at Charleston, if nowhere else. His preoccupation there with Douglas's involvement with the Toombs bill[3] in 1856 is best understood as being related to the senator's recent opposition to the Lecompton Constitution, which he claimed to be a device foisted without a true popular vote upon an unwilling electorate in Kansas. If Douglas had indeed blocked the submission to the people of Kansas of the constitution that had earlier been anticipated in the Toombs bill, his opposition to Lecompton's mode of submission could be made to appear to his Democratic followers as hypocritical and inconsistent, and merely expedient. Indeed his very devotion to the doctrine of popular sovereignty could be called into question. More important, the issue of submission was especially crucial to antislavery partisans. It had been obvious since 1857 that Free-State voters were a majority in Kansas and that in a totally free election they would decisively reject a proslavery constitution. Any apparent opposition by Douglas to the submission of an earlier constitution to Kansas voters could be made to discredit him among antislavery voters in Illinois who might otherwise have been attracted to him on account of his opposition to Lecompton. That opposition could be construed as unprincipled, and no guide

---

1. *New York Evening Post,* Sept. 25, 1858; *Chicago Press and Tribune,* Sept. 21, 1858.
2. Lew Wallace, *An Autobiography* (New York: Harper, 1906), I:253.
3. See glossary, pp. 332–33.

to Douglas's future conduct.[4] How seriously Lincoln took the matter of the earlier constitution anticipated in the Toombs bill seems manifest in his devoting almost his entire opening speech at Charleston to it. Though the details of the controversy may seem to have been tedious, that interest appears to have been reciprocated by the audience.

Douglas began his rebuttal by dismissing Lincoln's Toombs bill charge as without merit and as a tactic to divert the audience's attention from the debate's real issues, yet he devoted nonetheless a good bit of care and attention to the dismissal. He then again denied Lincoln's earlier accusation that he was in league with Presidents Pierce and Buchanan and Chief Justice Taney in a conspiracy to nationalize slavery, and renewed some previous charges of his own, one being that the Republican Party was a mere regional party even in Illinois, which because it had such disparate identities from north to south in the state was itself a "house divided." He played to Negrophobic local sympathies by reminding listeners that African American orators, including Frederick Douglass, had supported the Republican cause in northern Illinois. He also asserted that Lincoln's conviction that African Americans were entitled to the natural rights enumerated in the Declaration of Independence indicated that Lincoln was indeed in favor of black citizenship, to which position Douglas, again declaring that the American government was established "on the white basis," emphatically demurred.

Where Douglas obviously struck a nerve in his rebuttal was in a tangential reference to Lincoln's opposition to the Mexican War, suggesting a lack of patriotism on Lincoln's part. Lincoln's demand in his rejoinder that another of the platform party, Orlando Ficklin, defend him against the charge of disloyalty was a dramatic if rather indecisive moment in the debate. Otherwise Lincoln denied favoring black citizenship, and he concluded the meeting by asking whether Senator Douglas, in dismissing Lincoln's original accusation about his action on the Toombs bill, had successfully rebutted that charge.

A Republican newspaper's assertion that Douglas's speech at Charleston was "in the main, a rehash of some of his former speeches," even after being discounted for partisanship, was not wholly off the mark.[5] Aside from variations to accommodate local circumstances, Senator Douglas's speeches tended to emphasize the same points throughout the debates, whereas Lincoln, as is suggested by his opening at Charleston and his speeches at the two previous encounters, tended to pose somewhat different arguments at each debate site. As Lincoln told Hor-

---

4. For a complete discussion of this issue, see David Zarefsky, *Lincoln, Douglas and Slavery: In the Crucible of Public Debate* (Chicago: University of Chicago Press, 1990), 97–103.

5. *The Prairie Beacon* (Paris, Illinois), Sept. 24, 1858.

ace White, the subjects of the debates "kept enlarging and widening in his mind as he went on, and it was much easier to make a new speech than to repeat an old one."[6] Though the debates essentially went into recess for almost three weeks between September 18 and October 7 at Galesburg, this pattern would persist.

6. White quoted in William H. Herndon and Jesse W. Weik, *Herndon's Lincoln,* ed. Douglas L. Wilson and Rodney O. Davis (Urbana: University of Illinois Press, 2006), 392.

LINCOLN'S OPENING SPEECH

L adies and gentlemen: It will be very difficult for an audience so large as this to hear distinctly what a speaker says, and consequently it is important that as profound silence be preserved as possible.

While I was at the hotel today, an elderly gentleman called upon me to know whether I was really in favor of producing a perfect equality between the negroes and white people. *[Laughter]* While I had not proposed to myself on this occasion to say much on that subject, yet as the question was asked me, I thought I would occupy perhaps five minutes in saying something in regard to it. I will say then that I am not, nor ever have been, in favor of bringing about in any way the social and political equality of the white and black races; *[Applause]* that I am not, nor ever have been, in favor of making voters or jurors of negroes, nor of qualifying them to hold office, nor to intermarry with white people. And I will say in addition to this that there is a physical difference between the white and black races which I believe will forever forbid the two races living together on terms of social and political equality. And inasmuch as they cannot so live, while they do remain together there must be the position of superior and inferior, and I as much as any other man am in favor of having the superior position assigned to the white race. I say upon this occasion I do not perceive that because the white man is to have the superior position, the negro should be denied everything. I do not understand that because I do not want a negro woman for a slave, I must necessarily want her for a wife. *[Cheers, laughter]* My understanding is that I can just let her alone. I am now in my fiftieth year, and I certainly never have had a black woman for either a slave or a wife. So it seems to me quite possible for us to get along without making either slaves or wives of negroes.[1]

I will add to this that I have never seen to my knowledge a man, woman, or child who was in favor of producing a perfect equality, social and political, between negroes and white men. I recollect of but one distinguished instance that I ever heard of so frequently as to be entirely satisfied of its correctness, and that is the case of Judge Douglas's old friend, Col. Richard M. Johnson.[2] *[Laughter, cheers]*

---

1. Though never in these debates, SAD elsewhere during the senatorial campaign identified Republican policy, as expressed in AL's "House Divided" speech, with inevitable racial amalgamation. See the Ottawa debate, note 21, p. 24. See also "Negro equality" in the glossary, pp. 328–29.

2. AL alludes to the common-law marriage of Col. Richard M. Johnson, vice-president of the United States under Martin Van Buren, to an African American woman, who was also his slave, and to his two mixed-race daughters.

I will also add to the few remarks I have made, for I am not going to enter at large upon this subject, that I have never had the least apprehension that I or my friends would marry negroes if there was no law to keep them from it. *[Laughter]* But as Judge Douglas and his friends seem to be in great apprehension that they might, if there were no law to keep them from it, *[Laughter]* I give him the most solemn pledge that I will, to the very last, stand by the law of this state which forbids the marrying of white people with negroes. *[Laughter, applause]*

I will add one further word, which is this: that I do not understand there is any place where an alteration of the social and political relations of the negro and the white man can be changed except in the state legislature, not in the Congress of the United States. And as I do not really apprehend the approach of any such thing myself, and as Judge Douglas *seems* to be in constant horror that some such danger is rapidly approaching, *I propose, as the best means to prevent it, that the Judge be kept at home and placed in the state legislature to fight the measure. [Laughter, cheers]* I do not propose dwelling longer at this time on this subject.

When Judge Trumbull, our other senator in Congress, returned to Illinois in the month of August, he made a speech at Chicago in which he made what may be called *a charge* against Judge Douglas, which I understand proved to be very offensive to him. The Judge was at that time out upon one of his speaking tours through the country, and when the news of it reached him, as I am informed, he denounced Judge Trumbull in rather harsh terms for having said what he did in regard to that matter. I was traveling at that time and speaking at the same places with Judge Douglas on subsequent days, and when I heard of what Judge Trumbull had said of Douglas, and what Douglas had said back again, I felt that I was in a position where I could not remain entirely silent in regard to the matter. Consequently, upon two or three occasions I alluded to it, and I alluded to it in no other wise than to say that, in regard to the charge brought by Trumbull against Douglas, I *personally* knew nothing and sought to say nothing about it; that I did personally know Judge Trumbull; that I believed him to be a man of veracity; that I believed him to be a man of capacity sufficient to know very well whether an assertion he was making, as a conclusion drawn from a set of facts, was true or false; and as a conclusion of my own from that, I stated it as my belief, that° if Trumbull should ever be called upon, he would prove everything he had said. I said this upon two or three occasions.

Upon a subsequent occasion, Judge Trumbull spoke again before an audience at Alton and, upon that occasion, not only repeated his charge against Douglas, but arrayed the evidence he relied upon to substantiate it. This speech was published at length, and subsequently, at Jacksonville, Judge Douglas alluded to the matter. In the course of his speech, and near the close of it, he stated in regard to myself what I will now read:[3] "Judge Douglas proceeded to remark that he should not hereafter occupy his time in refuting such charges made by Trumbull, but that Lincoln having endorsed the character of Trumbull for veracity, he should hold him (Lincoln) responsible for the slanders." ∘ I have done simply what I have told you to subject me to this invitation to notice the charge. I now wish to say that it had not originally been my purpose to discuss that matter at all. But inasmuch as it seems to be the wish of Judge Douglas to hold me responsible for it, then for once in my life I will play Gen. Jackson, and to the just extent, *I take the responsibility.*[4] *[Applause, cheers]* I say to the just extent, I take the responsibility. ∘

I wish to say at the beginning that I will hand to the reporters that portion of Judge Trumbull's Alton speech which was devoted to this matter, and also that portion of Judge Douglas's speech made at Jacksonville in answer to it. I shall thereby furnish the readers of this debate with the complete discussion between Trumbull and Douglas. I cannot now read them, for the reason that it would take half of my first hour to do so. I can only make some comments upon them.[5] Trumbull's charge is in the following words:[6] "*Now, the charge is that there was a plot entered into to have a Constitution formed for Kansas, and put in force without giving the people an opportunity to vote upon it, and that Mr. Douglas was in the plot.*" ∘ I will state, without quoting further, for all will have an opportunity of reading it hereafter, that Judge Trumbull brings forward what he regards as sufficient evidence to substantiate this charge.

It will be perceived Judge Trumbull shows that Senator Bigler, upon the floor of the Senate, had declared there had been a conference among the senators, in which conference it was determined to have an enabling act passed for the people of Kansas to form a constitution under, and in this conference it was

---

3. The following is from SAD's Sept. 6 speech at Jacksonville. The texts of Trumbull's speeches of Aug. 7 in Chicago and Aug. 27 at Alton are in the *Chicago Press and Tribune,* Aug. 9 and Aug. 31, 1858. Unidentified newspaper clippings containing extracts from the Alton and Jacksonville speeches are included in the Debates Scrapbook, 142–44, 146.

4. AL repeats a famous remark by Andrew Jackson that had wide currency, uttered on the occasion of his ordering the removal of federal funds from the Bank of the United States in 1833 over the objection of Treasury Secretary William Duane. See Jackson to Duane, June 26, 1833, in John Spencer Bassett, ed., *The Correspondence of Andrew Jackson* (Washington: Carnegie Institute of Washington, 1931), 5:128.

5. Contrary to AL's expectation, neither paper printed the lengthy excerpt from Trumbull's speech that Lincoln says he handed to the reporters. The *Chicago Press and Tribune* inserted at this point, within brackets, the following editorial note: "The extracts handed by Mr. Lincoln to our reporter are too lengthy to appear in this number of the PRESS AND TRIBUNE. Judge Trumbull's speech at Alton has already had a place in our columns, and Senator Douglas' remarks at Jacksonville are faithfully repeated in his portion of this (Charleston) debate."

6. The following is from Trumbull's Alton speech, in Debates Scrapbook, 142.

agreed among them that it was best not to have a provision for submitting the constitution to a vote of the people after it should be formed.[7] He then brings forward what he deems the evidence to prove that there was a bill which went into the hands of Judge Douglas, as Chairman of the Committee on Territories, which contained a provision in it for submitting the constitution that might be made to the vote of the people.° He then brings forward evidence to show, and showing, as he deemed it, that Judge Douglas reported the bill back to the Senate with that clause stricken out. He then shows that there was a new clause inserted into the bill, which would, in its nature, *prevent* a reference of the constitution back for a vote of the people, if, indeed, upon a mere silence in the law, it could be assumed that they had the right to vote upon it. These are the general statements that he has made.

I propose to examine the points in Judge Douglas's speech, in which he attempts to answer that speech of Judge Trumbull's. When you come to examine Judge Douglas's speech, you will find that the first point he makes is:[8] "Suppose it were true that there was such a clause in the bill and that I struck it out, is that proof of a plot to force a constitution upon a people against their will?"° And he argues from that that it does not follow that it was intended to prevent the people having the right to vote upon their constitution.° His striking out such a provision, if there was such a one in the bill, he argues, does not establish the proof that it was stricken out for the purpose of robbing the people of that right. I would say, in the first place, that that would be the *most manifest* reason for it. It is true, as Judge Douglas states, that many territorial bills have passed without having such a provision in them. I believe it is true, though I am not certain, that, in some instances, constitutions framed under such bills have been submitted to a vote of the people, with the law silent on the subject. But it does not appear that they once had their enabling acts framed with an express provision *for* submitting the constitution to be framed to a vote of the people, and then that they were stricken out when Congress did not mean to alter the effect of the law. That there have been bills which never had the provision in, I do not question; but why° was that provision taken out of one that it was in? More especially, does this evidence tend to prove the proposition that Trumbull advanced, when we remember that that provision was stricken out of the bill almost simultaneously with the time that Bigler says there was a conference among certain senators, and in which it was agreed that a bill should be passed leaving that out? Judge Douglas, in answering Trumbull,

---

7. Bigler's remarks are contained in Trumbull's Alton speech, Debates Scrapbook, 143, and more fully in *Congressional Globe,* 35th Cong., 1st Sess., Senate, Dec. 9, 1857, Dec. 21, 1857, 1:21, 113.

8. The following is from SAD's Jacksonville speech, Debates Scrapbook, 146.

omits to attend to the testimony of Bigler, that there was a meeting in which it was agreed they should so frame the bill that there should be no submission of the constitution to a vote of the people. The Judge does not notice this part of it. If you take this as one piece of evidence, and then ascertain that simultaneously Judge Douglas struck out a provision that did require it to be submitted, and put the two together, I think it will make a pretty fair show of proof that Judge Douglas did, as Trumbull says, enter into a plot to put in force a constitution for Kansas, without giving the people any opportunity of voting upon it.

But I must hurry on. The next proposition that Judge Douglas puts is this: "But upon examination, it turns out that the Toombs bill never did contain a clause requiring the constitution to be submitted."[9] This is a mere question of fact, and can be determined by evidence. I only want to ask this question: Why did not Judge Douglas say that those words *were not* stricken out of the Toombs bill, or this bill from which it is alleged the provision was stricken out, a bill which goes by the name of Toombs, because he originally brought it forward? I ask why, if the Judge wanted to make a direct issue with Trumbull, did he not take the exact proposition Trumbull made in his speech and say that it was *not* stricken out? Trumbull has given the exact words that he says were in the Toombs bill, and he alleges that when the bill came back, they were stricken out. Judge Douglas does not say that the words which Trumbull says were stricken out *were not so stricken out,* but he says there was no provision in the Toombs bill to submit the constitution to a vote of the people. We see at once that he is merely making an issue upon the meaning of the words. He has not undertaken to say that Trumbull tells a lie about these words being stricken out, but he is really, when pushed up to it, only taking an issue upon the meaning of the words.

Now then, if there be any issue upon the meaning of the words, or if there be upon the question of fact as to whether these words were stricken out, I have before me what I suppose to be a genuine copy of the Toombs bill, in which it can be shown that the words Trumbull says were in it, *were in fact originally there.* If there be any dispute upon that fact, I have got the documents here to show they were there. If there be any controversy upon the sense of the words—whether these words which were stricken out really constituted a provision for submitting the matter to a vote of the people—as that is a matter of argument, I think I may as well use Trumbull's own argument. Judge Douglas did not meet him at all on that, although he put it down fairly, but passes it off in the manner in which I have stated. Trumbull° says that the proposition is in these words:[10]

---

9. Ibid.

10. Trumbull's Alton speech, Debates Scrapbook, 143. Capitalization reflects that of newspaper clipping.

That the following propositions be and the same are hereby offered to the said Convention of the people of Kansas, when formed, for their free acceptance or rejection, which, if accepted by the Convention and ratified by the people at the election for the adoption of the constitution, shall be obligatory on the United States, and upon the said State of Kansas. °

Now Trumbull alleges that these last words were stricken out of the bill when it came back, and he says this was a provision for submitting the constitution to a vote of the people, and his argument is this:[11] "Would it have been possible to ratify the land propositions 'at the election for the adoption of the constitution,' unless such an election was to be held?" ° [Applause, laughter] That is Trumbull's argument. Now Judge Douglas does not meet the charge at all, but he stands up and says there was no such provision ° in that bill for submitting the constitution to be framed to a vote of the people. Trumbull admits that the language is not a direct provision for submitting it, but it is a provision necessarily implied from another provision. He asks you how it is possible to ratify the land proposition at the election for the adoption of the constitution, *if there was no election to be held for the adoption of the constitution.* And he goes on to show that it is not any less a law because the provision is put in that indirect shape than it would be if it was put directly. But I presume I have said enough to draw attention to this point, and I pass it by also.

Another one of the points that Judge Douglas makes upon Trumbull, and at very great length, is that Trumbull, while the bill was pending, said in a speech in the Senate that he supposed the constitution to be made would have to be submitted to the people. He asks, if Trumbull thought so, what reason there is now for any one to suppose the contrary. He asks, if Trumbull thought so then, what ground is there for anybody thinking otherwise now? Fellow citizens, this much may be said in reply. That bill had been in the hands of a party to which Trumbull did not belong. It had been in the hands of the committee at the head of which Judge Douglas stood. Trumbull perhaps had a printed copy of the original Toombs bill. I have not the evidence on that point, except a sort of inference I draw from the general course of business there. What alterations, or what provisions in the way of altering, were going on in committee, Trumbull had no means of knowing, until the altered bill was reported back. Soon afterwards, when it was reported back, there was a discussion over it, and perhaps Trumbull in reading it hastily in the altered form did not perceive all the bearings of the alterations. He was hastily borne into the debate, and it does not follow that because there was something in it Trumbull did not perceive, that something did not exist.

More than this, is it true that what Trumbull did can have any effect on what

---

11. The following is from ibid.

Douglas did? *[Applause]* Suppose Trumbull had been in the plot with these other men—would that let Douglas out of it? *[Applause, laughter]* Would it exonerate Douglas that Trumbull didn't then perceive he was in the plot? He also asks the question: why didn't Trumbull propose to amend the bill, if he thought it needed any amendment? Why, I believe that everything Judge Trumbull had proposed, particularly in connection with this question of Kansas and Nebraska since he had been on the floor of the Senate, had been promptly voted down by Judge Douglas and his friends. He had no promise that an amendment offered by him to any thing on this subject would receive the slightest consideration. Judge Trumbull did bring to the notice of the Senate at that time the fact that there was no provision for submitting the constitution about to be made for the people of Kansas to a vote of the people. I believe I may venture to say that Judge Douglas made some reply to this speech of Judge Trumbull's, *but he never noticed that part of it at all.* And so the thing passed by. I think, then, the fact that Judge Trumbull offered no amendment, does not throw much blame upon him; and if it did, it does not reach the question of fact *as to what Judge Douglas was doing. [Applause]* I repeat that if Trumbull had himself been in the plot, it would not at all relieve the others who were in it from blame. It would not touch the question at all.° If I should be indicted for murder, and upon the trial it should be discovered that I had been implicated in that murder, but that the prosecuting witness was guilty too, that would not at all touch the question of my crime. It would be no relief to my neck that they discovered this other man who charged the crime upon me to be guilty, too.

Another one of the points Judge Douglas makes upon Judge Trumbull is that when he spoke in Chicago, he made his charge to rest upon the fact that the bill had the provision in it for submitting the constitution to a vote of the people when it went into his (Judge Douglas's) hands, that it was missing when he reported it to the Senate, and that in a public speech he had subsequently said the alterations in the bill were made while it was in committee, and that they were made in consultation between him (Judge Douglas) and Toombs. Let me not be misunderstood as saying specifically that he made these alterations with his own hand, but he said that the alterations in the bill made while it was in the committee were made on consultation between him (Judge Douglas) and Mr. Toombs.°

And Judge Douglas goes on to comment upon the fact of Trumbull's adducing in his Alton speech the proposition that the bill not only came back with that proposition stricken out but with another clause and another provision in it, saying that[12] "until the complete execution of this act no other election shall

---

12. This quotation from the Toombs bill (S. 356) SAD reported to the Senate on June 30, 1856, is cited in both Trumbull's Alton speech (Debates Scrapbook, 144) and SAD's speech at Jacksonville (144, 146).

be held in said Territory"°—which Trumbull argued was not only taking the provision for submitting to a vote of the people out of the bill, but was adding an affirmative one, in that it prevented the people from exercising the right under a bill that was merely silent on the question.

Now in regard to what he says—that Trumbull shifts the issue, that he shifts his ground, and I believe he uses the term, that "it being proven false, he has changed ground"—I call upon all of you, when you come to examine that portion of Trumbull's speech (for it will make a part of mine) to examine whether Trumbull has shifted his ground or not. I say he *did not* shift his ground, but that he brought forward his original charge and the evidence to sustain it yet more fully, but precisely as he originally made it. Then, in addition thereto, he brought in a new piece of evidence. He shifted no ground. He brought no new piece of evidence inconsistent with his former testimony, and he brought a new piece tending, as he thought, and as I think, to prove his proposition. To illustrate: A man brings an accusation against another, and on trial, the man making the charge introduces A and B to prove the accusation. At a second trial he introduces the same witnesses, who tell the same story as before, and a third witness, who tells the same thing, and in addition, gives further testimony corroborative of the charge. So with Trumbull. There was no shifting of ground, nor inconsistency of testimony, between the new piece of evidence and what he originally introduced.

But Judge Douglas says that he himself moved to strike out that last provision of the bill, and that on his motion it was stricken out and a substitution inserted. That, I presume, is the truth. I presume it is truth that that last proposition was stricken out by Judge Douglas. Trumbull has not said it was not. Trumbull has himself said that it was so stricken out. He says I am speaking of the bill as Judge Douglas reported it back. It was amended somewhat in the Senate before it passed, but I am speaking of it as he brought it back.° Now when Judge Douglas parades the fact that the provision was stricken out of the bill when it came back, he asserts nothing contrary to what Trumbull alleges. Trumbull has only said that he originally put it in, not that he did not strike it out. Trumbull says it was not in the bill when it went to the committee. When it came back, it *was* in, and Judge Douglas said the alterations were made by him in consultation with Toombs. Trumbull alleges, therefore, as his conclusion that Judge Douglas put it in. Then if Douglas wants to contradict Trumbull and call him a liar, let him say he did not put it in, and not that he didn't take it out again.

It is said that a bear is sometimes hard enough pushed to drop a cub, and so I presume it was in this case. *[Applause]* I presume the truth is that Douglas put it in and afterwards took it out. *[Laughter, cheers]* That I take it is the truth about it. Judge Trumbull says one thing; Douglas says another thing, and the two don't contradict one another at all. The question is what did he put it in for? In the first place, what did he take the other provision out of the bill for, the provision which Trumbull argued was necessary for submitting the constitution to a vote of the people? What did he take that out for, and having taken it out, what did he put this in for? I say that in the run of things it may have become apparent enough to any one that these were his cubs,° and it is not unlikely forces conspire to render it vastly expedient for Judge Douglas to take that latter clause out again. The question that Trumbull has made is that Judge Douglas put it in, and he don't meet Trumbull at all unless he denies that.

In the close° of Judge Douglas's speech upon this subject, he uses this language towards Judge Trumbull. He says:[13] "He forged his evidence from beginning to end, and by falsifying the record he endeavors to bolster up his false charge."° Well, that is a pretty serious statement. Trumbull "forges his evidence from beginning to end." Now upon my own authority I say that is not true. [Cheers, laughter] What is a forgery? Consider the evidence that Trumbull has brought forward. When you come to read the speech, as you will be able to, examine whether the evidence is "a forgery from beginning to end." He had the bill or document in his hand like that [holding up a paper]. He says that is a copy of the Toombs bill—the amendment offered by Toombs. He says that is a copy of the bill as it was introduced and went into Judge Douglas's hands. Now, does Judge Douglas say that is a forgery? That is one thing Trumbull brought forward. Judge Douglas says he forged it, from beginning to end. That is the beginning, we will say. Does Douglas say that is a forgery? Let him say it today, and we will have a subsequent examination upon this subject. [Applause]

Trumbull then holds up another document like this and says that is an exact copy of the bill as it came back in the amended form out of Judge Douglas's hands. Does Judge Douglas say that is a forgery? Does he say it in his general sweeping charge? Does he say so now? If he does not, then take this Toombs bill and the bill in the amended form and it only needs to compare them to see that the provision is in the one and not in the other. It leaves the inference inevitable that it was taken out. [Applause]

But while I am dealing with this question, let us see what Trumbull's other evidence is, if I have time to do so. One piece of evidence I have already read.° Trumbull says there are in this original Toombs bill these words:[14]

That the following propositions be and the same are hereby offered to the said Convention of the people of Kansas, when formed, for their free acceptance or rejection, which, if accepted by the Convention, and ratified by the people at the

---

13. The following is from SAD's Jacksonville speech, Debates Scrapbook, 146.
14. The following is from Trumbull's Alton speech, Debates Scrapbook, 143. Capitalization reflects that of newspaper clipping.

election for the adoption of the constitution, shall be obligatory on the United States, and upon the said State of Kansas.°

Now, if it is said that this is a forgery, we will open the paper here and see whether it is or not.

Again, Trumbull says, as he goes along, that Mr. Bigler made the following statement in his place in the Senate, December 9, 1857, and then adds, "I read from part 1, *Congressional Globe* of last session, page 21:"°

> I was present when that subject was discussed by Senators, before the bill was introduced, and the question was raised and discussed, whether the Constitution, when formed, should be submitted to a vote of the people. It was held by those most intelligent on the subject, that in view of all the difficulties surrounding that Territory, the danger of any experiment at that time of a popular vote, it would be better there should be no such provision in the Toombs Bill; and it was my understanding, in all the intercourse I had, that the convention would make a Constitution and send it here without submitting it to the popular vote.° [15]

Then Trumbull follows on:[16]

> In speaking of this meeting again on the 21st December, 1857, *Congressional Globe,* same vol. page 113, Senator Bigler said:
>
> > Nothing was farther from my mind than to allude to any social or confidential interview. The meeting was not of that character. Indeed, it was semi official and called to promote the public good. My recollection was clear that I left the conference under the impression that it had been deemed best to adopt measures to admit Kansas as a State through the agency of one popular election, and that for delegates to this convention. This impression was stronger, because I thought the spirit of the bill infringed upon the doctrine of non-intervention, to which I had great aversion: but with the hope of accomplishing a great good, and as no movement had been made in that direction in the territory, I waived this objection, and concluded to support the measure. I have a few items of testimony as to the correctness of these impressions, and with their submission I shall be content. I have before me the bill reported by the Senator from Illinois, on the 7th of March, 1856, providing for the admission of Kansas as a State, the third section of which reads as follows:
> >
> > > That the following propositions be, and the same are hereby offered to the said convention of the people of Kansas, when formed, for their free acceptance or rejection; which if accepted by the conven-

---

15. Trumbull quotes from *Congressional Globe,* 35th Cong., 1st Sess., Senate, Dec. 9, 1857, 21; Debates Scrapbook, 143.

16. Trumbull quotes from *Congressional Globe,* 35th Cong., 1st Sess., Senate, Dec. 21, 1857. 113–14; Debates Scrapbook, 143. Capitalization reflects that of newspaper clipping.

tion, and ratified by the people at the election for the adoption of the Constitution shall be obligatory upon the United States and the said State of Kansas.

The bill read in place by the Senator from Georgia, on the 25th of June, and referred to the Committee on Territories, contained the same section word for word. Both these bills were under consideration at the conference referred to, but, sir, when the Senator from Illinois reported the Toombs bill° to the Senate, with amendments, the next morning, it did not contain that portion of the third section which indicated to the Convention that the Constitution should be approved by the people. The words "AND RATIFIED BY THE PEOPLE AT THE ELECTION FOR THE ADOPTION OF THE CONSTITUTION" had been stricken out.°

Now these things Trumbull says were stated by Bigler upon the floor of the Senate on certain days, and that they are recorded in the *Congressional Globe* on certain pages. Does Judge Douglas say this is a forgery? Does he say there is no such thing in the *Congressional Globe*? What does he mean when he says Judge Trumbull forges his evidence from beginning to end?

So again he says in another place, that Judge Douglas, in his speech Dec. 9, 1857, *Congressional Globe*, part 1, page 15, stated:[17]

That during the last session of Congress I [Mr. Douglas] reported a bill from the Committee on Territories, to authorize the people of Kansas to assemble and form a constitution for themselves. Subsequently the Senator from Georgia [Mr. Toombs] brought forward a substitute for my bill which, AFTER HAVING BEEN MODIFIED BY HIM AND MYSELF IN CONSULTATION, was passed by the Senate.°

Now Trumbull says that is a quotation from a speech of Douglas, and is recorded in the *Congressional Globe*. Is *it* a forgery? Is it there or not? It may not be there, but I want the Judge to take these pieces of evidence, *and distinctly say they are forgeries, if he dare do it. [Applause]* That is what I want him to do.°

Voice: He will.

Lincoln: Well, sir, you had better not commit him. *[Cheers, laughter]* He gives other quotations—another from Judge Douglas. He says:[18]

I will ask the Senator to show me an intimation from any one member of the Senate, in the whole debate on the Toombs Bill, and in the Union from any quarter, that the Constitution was not to be submitted to the people. I will venture to say that on all sides of the chamber it was so understood at the time:—If

---

17. Trumbull quotes from SAD's speech against the Lecompton Constitution, *Congressional Globe*, 35th Cong., 1st Sess., Senate, Dec. 9, 1857, 1:15; Debates Scrapbook, 143–44.

18. Trumbull quotes from *Congressional Globe*, 35th Cong., 1st Sess., Senate, Dec. 9, 1857, 1:21; Debates Scrapbook, 144.

the opponents of the bill had understood it was not, they would have made the point on it; and if they had made it we should certainly have yielded to it, and put in the clause. That is a discovery made since the President found out that it was not safe to take it for granted that that would be done, which ought in fairness to have been done. °

Judge Trumbull says Douglas made that speech and it is recorded. Does Judge Douglas say it is a forgery and was not true? Trumbull says somewhere, and I propose to skip it, but it will be found by any one who will read this debate, that he did distinctly bring it to the notice of those who were engineering the bill, that it lacked that provision and then he goes on to give another quotation from Judge Douglas, where Judge Trumbull uses this language:[19]

> Judge Douglas, however on the same day, and in the same debate, probably recollecting, or being reminded of the fact, that I had objected to the Toombs bill when pending, that it did not provide for a submission of the Constitution to the people, made another statement which is to be found in the same volume of the *Congressional Globe,* page 22, in which he says:
>
>> That the bill was silent on this subject is true, and my attention was called to that about the time it was passed; and I took the fair construction to be, that powers not delegated were reserved, and that of course the Constitution would be submitted to the people. °

Trumbull adds upon that: °

> Whether this statement is consistent with the statement just before made, that had the point been made it would have been yielded to, or that it was a new discovery, you will determine; for if the public records do not convict and condemn him, he may go uncondemned, so far as I am concerned. ° [20]

So I say. I do not know whether Judge Douglas will dispute this, and yet maintain his position that Trumbull's evidence "was forged from beginning to end." I will remark that I have not got these *Congressional Globes* with me. They are large books and difficult to carry about, and if Judge Douglas shall say that on these points where Trumbull has quoted from them, there are no such passages there, I shall not be able to prove they are there upon this occasion, but I will have another chance. Whenever he points out the forgery and says, "I declare that this particular thing which Trumbull has uttered is not to be found where he says it is," then my attention will be drawn to that, and I will arm myself for the

---

19. Trumbull quotes from *Congressional Globe,* 35th Cong., 1st Sess., Senate, Dec. 9, 1857, 1:22; Debates Scrapbook, 144.

20. Trumbull's Alton speech, Debates Scrapbook, 144.

contest, stating now that I have not the slightest doubt on earth that I will find every quotation just where Trumbull says it is.

Then the question is, how can Douglas call that a forgery? How can he make out that it is a forgery? What is a forgery? It is the bringing forward something in writing or in print purporting to be of certain effect when it is altogether untrue. If you come forward with my note for one hundred dollars when I have never given such a note, there is a forgery. If you come forward with a letter purporting to be written from me which I never wrote, there is another forgery. If you produce anything in writing or print saying it is so and so, the document not being genuine, a forgery has been committed. How do you make this a forgery when every piece of the evidence is genuine?

If Judge Douglas does say these documents and quotations are false and forged, he has a full right to do so, but until he does it specifically, we don't know how to get at him. If he does say they are false and forged, I will then look further into it, and I presume I can procure the certificates of the proper officers that they are genuine copies. I have no doubt each of these extracts will be found exactly where Trumbull says it is. Then I leave it to you if Judge Douglas, in making his sweeping charge that Judge Trumbull's evidence is forged from beginning to end, at all meets the case, if that is the way to get at the facts. I repeat again, if he will point out which one is a forgery, I will carefully examine it, and if it proves that any one of them is really a forgery, it will not be me who will hold to it any longer.

I have always wanted to deal with every one I meet candidly and honestly. If I have made any assertion not warranted by facts, and it is pointed out to me, I will withdraw it cheerfully. But I do not choose to see Judge Trumbull calumniated, and the evidence he has brought forward branded in general terms, "a forgery from beginning to end." That is not the legal way of meeting a charge, and I submit to all intelligent persons, both friends of Judge Douglas and of myself, whether it is.

Now coming back—how much time have I left?

Moderator: Three minutes.

Lincoln: The point upon Judge Douglas is this. The bill that went into his hands had the provision in it for a submission of the constitution to the people. And I say its language amounts to an express provision for a submission, and that he took the provision out. He says it was known that the bill was silent in this particular, *but I say: Judge Douglas, it was not silent when you got it. [Applause]* It was vocal with the declaration, when you got it, for a submission of the constitution to the people. And now, my direct question to Judge Douglas is, to answer why, if he deemed the bill silent on this point, he found it necessary to strike out those particular harmless words. If he had found the bill silent and without this provision, he might say what he does now. If he supposed it was implied that the constitution would be submitted to a vote of the people, how could these two lines so encumber the statute as to make it necessary to strike them out? How could he infer that a submission was still implied, after its express provision had been stricken from the bill? I find the bill vocal with the provision, while he silenced it. He took it out, and although he took out the other provision preventing a submission to a vote of the people, I ask: *why did you first put it in?* I ask him whether he took the original provision out, which Trumbull alleges was in the bill? If he admits that he did take it, *I ask him what he did it for?* It looks to us as if he had altered the bill. If it looks differently to him—if he has a different reason for his action from the one we assign him—*he can tell it.* I insist upon knowing why he made the bill silent upon that point, when it was vocal before he put his hands upon it.

I was told, before my last paragraph, that my time was within three minutes of being out. I presume it is expired now. I therefore close. *[Cheers]*

DOUGLAS'S REPLY

Ladies and gentlemen: I had supposed that we assembled here today for the purpose of a joint discussion between Mr. Lincoln and myself upon the political questions that now agitate the whole country. The rule of such discussions is, that the opening speaker shall touch upon all the points he intends to discuss in order that his opponent, in reply, shall have the opportunity of answering them. Let me ask you what questions of public policy relating to the welfare of this state or the Union, has Mr. Lincoln discussed before you? *[Applause]* Gentlemen, allow me to suggest that silence is the best compliment you can pay me. I need my whole time, and your cheering only occupies it. Mr. Lincoln simply contented himself at the outset by saying that he was not in favor of social and political equality between the white man and the negro, and did not desire the law so changed as to make the latter voters or eligible to office. I am glad that I have at last succeeded in getting an answer out of him upon this question of negro citizenship and eligibility to office, for I have been trying to bring him to the point on it ever since this canvass commenced.

I will now call your attention to the question which Mr. Lincoln has occupied his entire time in discussing. He spent his whole hour in retailing a charge made by Senator Trumbull against me. The circumstances out of which that charge was manufactured occurred prior to the last Presidential election, over two years ago. If the charge was true, why did not Trumbull make it in 1856, when I was discussing the questions of that day all over this state with Lincoln and him, and when it was pertinent to the then issue? He was then as silent as the grave on the subject. If that charge was true, the time to have brought it forward was the canvass of 1856, the year when the Toombs bill passed the Senate, when the facts were fresh in the public mind, when the Kansas question was the paramount question of the day, and when such a charge would have had a material bearing on the election. Why did he and Lincoln remain silent then, knowing that such a charge could be made and proven if true? Were they not false to you and false to the country in going through that entire campaign, concealing their knowledge of this enormous conspiracy which, Mr. Trumbull says, he then knew and would not tell? *[Laughter]*

Mr. Lincoln intimates in his speech, a good reason why Mr. Trumbull would not tell, for, he says, that it might be true, as I proved that it was at Jacksonville, that Trumbull was also in the plot, yet that the fact of Trumbull's being in the plot would not in any way relieve me. He illustrates this argument by supposing himself on trial for murder, and says that it would be no extenuating circumstance if, on his trial, another man was found to be a party to his crime. Well, if Trumbull was in the plot, and concealed it in order to escape the odium which would have fallen upon himself, I ask you whether you can believe him now when he turns state's evidence, and avows his own infamy in order to implicate me. *[Cheers]* I am amazed that Mr. Lincoln should now come forward and endorse that charge, occupying his whole hour in reading Mr. Trumbull's speech in support of it. Why, I ask, does not Mr. Lincoln make a speech of his own, instead of taking up his time reading Trumbull's speech at Alton? *[Cheers]* I supposed that Mr. Lincoln was capable of making a public speech on his own account, or I should not have accepted the banter from him for a joint discussion. *[Cheers]*

Voice: Why don't you reply to the charge? °

Douglas: Do not trouble yourselves, I am going to make my speech in my own way, and, I trust, as the Democrats listened patiently and respectfully to Mr. Lincoln, that his friends will not interrupt me when I am answering him.

Now, I propose to first state the charge in Trumbull's own language. ° When Mr. Trumbull returned from the East, the first thing he did when he landed at Chicago was to make a speech wholly devoted to assaults upon my public character and public action. Up to that time, I had never alluded to his course in Congress, or to him directly or indirectly, and hence his assaults upon me were entirely without provocation and without excuse. Since then he has been traveling from one end of the state to the other repeating his vile charge. I propose now to read it in his own language:

> Now, fellow citizens, I make the distinct charge that there was a preconcerted arrangement and plot entered into by the very men who now claim credit for opposing a constitution not submitted to the people to have a constitution formed

and put in force without giving the people any opportunity to pass upon it. This, my friends, is a serious charge, but I charge it to-night, that the very men who traverse the country under banners proclaiming popular sovereignty, by design, concocted a bill on purpose to force a constitution upon that people. °

In answer to someone in the crowd who asked him a question, Trumbull said:[21]

> And you want to satisfy yourself that he was in the plot to force a Constitution upon that people? I will satisfy you.—I will cram the truth down any honest man's throat until he cannot deny it. And to the man who does deny it, I will cram the lie down his throat, till he shall cry enough.
> It is preposterous—it is the most damnable effrontery that man ever put on to conceal a scheme to defraud and cheat the people out of their rights, and then claim credit for it. °

That is the polite language Senator Trumbull applied to me, his colleague, when I was two hundred miles off. Why did he not speak out as boldly in the Senate of the United States, and cram the lie down my throat when I denied the charge, first made by Bigler, and made him take it back? *[Applause]* You all recollect how Bigler assaulted me when I was engaged in a hand-to-hand fight, resisting a scheme to force a constitution on the people of Kansas against their will. He then attacked me with this charge, but I proved its utter falsity, nailed the slander to the counter, and made him take the back track.[22] There is not an honest man in America who read that debate who will pretend that the charge is true. *[Cheers]* Trumbull was then present in the Senate, face to face with me, and why did he not then rise and repeat the charge, and say he would cram the lie down my throat. I tell you that Trumbull then knew it was a lie. He knew that Toombs denied that there ever was a clause in the bill he brought forward calling for and requiring submission of the Kansas constitution to the people.

I will tell you what the facts of the case were. I introduced a bill to authorize the people of Kansas to form a constitution and come into the Union as a state whenever they should have the requisite population for a member of Congress, and Mr. Toombs proposed a substitute, authorizing the people of Kansas, with their then population of only 25,000, to form a constitution and come in at once. The question at issue was, whether we would admit Kansas with a population of 25,000 or make her wait until she had the ratio entitling her to a representative in Congress, which was 93,420. That was the point of dispute in the Committee on Territories, to which both my bill and Mr. Toombs's substitute had been referred.

---

21. Trumbull's Chicago speech, Aug. 7, 1858, *Chicago Press and Tribune,* Aug. 9, 1858.
22. For SAD's reply to Bigler, see *Congressional Globe,* 35th Cong., 1st Sess., Senate, Dec. 9, 1857, 1:21.

I was overruled by a majority of the committee, my proposition rejected, and Mr. Toombs's proposition to admit Kansas then, with her population of 25,000, adopted. Accordingly, a bill to carry out his idea of immediate admission was reported as a substitute for mine, the only points at issue being, as I have already said, the question of population, and the adoption of safeguards against frauds at the election.

Trumbull knew this—the whole Senate knew it—and hence he was silent at that time. He waited until I became engaged in this canvass, and, finding that I was showing up Lincoln's abolitionism and negro equality doctrines, *[Cheers]* that I was driving Lincoln to the wall, and white men would not support his rank abolitionism, he came back from the East and trumped up a system of charges against me, hoping that I would be compelled to occupy my entire time in defending myself, so that I would not be able to show up the enormity of the principles of the abolitionists. Now, the only reason, and the true reason, why Mr. Lincoln has occupied the whole of his first hour in this issue between Trumbull and myself is to conceal from this vast audience the real questions which divide the two great parties. *[Cheers]*

I am not going to allow them to waste much of my time with these personal matters. I have lived in this state twenty-five years, most of that time have been in public life, and my record is open to you all. If that record is not enough to vindicate me from these petty, malicious assaults, I despise ever to be elected to office by slandering my opponents and traducing other men. *[Cheers]* Mr. Lincoln asks you to elect him to the United States Senate today solely because he and Trumbull can slander me. Has he given any other reason? Has he avowed what he was desirous to do in Congress on any one question? He desires to ride into office not upon his own merits, not upon the merits and soundness of his principles, but upon his success in fastening a stale old slander upon me. *[Cheers]*

I wish you to bear in mind that up to the time of the introduction of the Toombs bill, and after its introduction, there had never been an act of Congress for the admission of a new state which contained a clause requiring its constitution to be submitted to the people. The general rule made the law silent on the subject, taking it for granted that the people would demand and compel a popular vote on the ratification of their constitution. Such was the general rule under Washington, Jefferson, Madison, Jackson and Polk, under the Whig presidents and the Democratic presidents from the beginning of the government down, and nobody dreamed that an effort would ever be made to abuse the power thus confided to the people of a territory. For this reason our attention was not called to the fact of whether there was or was not a clause in the Toombs bill compelling submission, but it was taken for granted that the constitution would be submitted to the people whether the law compelled it or not.

Now, I will read from the report made by me as Chairman of the Committee on Territories at the time I reported back the Toombs substitute to the Senate. It contained several things which I had voted against in committee, but had been overruled by a majority of the members, and it was my duty as Chairman of the committee to report the bill back as it was agreed upon by them. The main point upon which I had been overruled was the question of population. In my report accompanying the Toombs bill, I said:[23]

> In the opinion of your committee, whenever a constitution shall be formed in any territory, preparatory to its admission into the Union as a state, justice, the genius of our institutions, the whole theory of our republican system impera-tively demand that the voice of the people shall be fairly expressed, and their will embodied in that fundamental law, without fraud or violence, or intimidation, or any other improper or unlawful influence, and subject to no other restrictions than those imposed by the Constitution of the United States.° [Cheers]

There you find that we took it for granted that the constitution was to be submitted to the people, whether the bill was silent on the subject or not. Sup-pose I had reported it so, following the example of Washington, Adams, Jefferson, Madison, Monroe, Adams, Jackson, Van Buren, Harrison, Tyler, Polk, Taylor, Fillmore, and Pierce, would that fact have been evidence of a conspiracy to force a constitution upon the people of Kansas against their will? [Cries of "No"] If the charge which Mr. Lincoln makes be true against me, it is true against Zachary Taylor, Millard Fillmore, and every Whig president as well as every Democratic president, and against Henry Clay, who, in the Senate or the House, for forty years advocated bills similar to the one I reported, no one of them containing a clause compelling the submission of the constitution to the people. Are Mr. Lincoln and Mr. Trumbull prepared to charge upon all those eminent men, from the beginning of the government down to the present day, that the absence of a provision compelling submission in the various bills passed by them authoriz-ing the people of territories to form state constitutions, is evidence of a corrupt design on their part to force a constitution upon an unwilling people?

I ask you to reflect on these things, for I tell you that there is a conspiracy to carry this election for the Black Republicans by slander, and not by fair means. Mr. Lincoln's speech this day is conclusive evidence of the fact. He has devoted his entire time to an issue between Mr. Trumbull and myself and has not uttered a word about the politics of the day. Are you going to elect Mr. Trumbull's col-league upon an issue between Mr. Trumbull and me? [Laughter, cheers] I thought I was running against Abraham Lincoln, that he claimed to be my opponent, and

---

23. *Senate Reports*, 34th Cong., 1st Sess., No. 198, 7; cited in Robert W. Johannsen, *Stephen A. Douglas* (Urbana: University of Illinois Press, 1997), 525, 926.

challenged me to a discussion of the public questions of the day with him, and was discussing these questions with me. But it turns out that his only hope is to ride into office on Trumbull's back, who will carry him by falsehood. *[Cheers]*

Permit me to pursue this subject a little further. An examination of the record proves that Trumbull's charge—that the Toombs bill originally contained a clause requiring the constitution to be submitted to the people—*is false.* The printed copy of the bill which Mr. Lincoln held up before you, and which he pretends contains such a clause, merely contains a clause requiring a submission of the land grant, and *there is no clause in it requiring a submission of the constitution.*[24] Mr. Lincoln cannot find such a clause in it. My report shows that we took it for granted that the people would require a submission of the constitution, and secure it for themselves. There never was a clause in the Toombs bill requiring the constitution to be submitted. Trumbull knew it at the time, and his speech made on the night of its passage discloses the fact that he knew it was silent on the subject.

Lincoln pretends, and tells you, that Trumbull has not changed his evidence in support of his charge since he made his speech in Chicago. Let us see. The *Chicago Times* took up Trumbull's Chicago speech, compared it with the official records of Congress, and proved that speech to be false in its charge that the original Toombs bill required a submission of the constitution to the people. Trumbull then saw that he was caught—and his falsehood exposed—and he went to Alton, and, under the very walls of the penitentiary, *[Laughter]* made a new speech, in which he predicated his assault upon me on° the allegation that I had caused to be voted into the Toombs bill a clause which prohibited the convention from submitting the constitution to the people, and quoted what he pretended was the clause. Now, has not Mr. Trumbull entirely changed the evidence on which he bases his charge? *[Cheers]* The clause which he quoted in his Alton speech, which he has published and circulated broadcast over the state, as having been put into the Toombs bill by me is in the following words: "And until the complete execution of this act, no other election shall be held in said territory." Trumbull says that the object of that amendment was to prevent the convention from submitting the constitution to a vote of the people.

Now, I will show you that when Trumbull made that statement at Alton, he knew it to be untrue. I read from Trumbull's speech in the Senate on the Toombs bill on the night of its passage. He then said:[25]

---

24. The original Toombs bill did not require popular ratification of the constitution, but it clearly anticipated it. See p. 136.

25. From Trumbull's Senate speech on the admission of Kansas in *Congressional Globe, Appendix*, 34th Cong., 1st Sess., July 2, 1856, 779.

There is nothing said in this bill, so far as I have discovered, about submitting the constitution which is to be framed, to the people for their sanction or rejection. Perhaps the convention would have the right to submit it if it should think proper, but it is certainly not compelled to do so according to the provisions of the bill. °

Thus you see that Trumbull, when the bill was on its passage in the Senate, said that it was silent on the subject of submission, and that there was nothing in the bill one way or the other on it. In his Alton speech, he says that there was a clause in the bill preventing its submission to the people, and that I had it voted in as an amendment. Thus I convict him of falsehood and slander by quoting from him on the passage of the Toombs bill in the Senate of the United States, his own speech, made on the night of July 2, 1856, and reported in the *Congressional Globe* for the 1st session 34th Congress, Vol. 33. What will you think of a man who makes a false charge and falsifies the records to prove it?

I will now show you that the clause which Trumbull says was put in the bill on my motion was never put in at all by me, but was stricken out on my motion and another substituted in its place. I call your attention to the same volume of the *Congressional Globe* to which I have already referred, page 795, where you will find the following in the report of the proceedings of the Senate:[26]

> MR. DOUGLAS—I have an amendment to offer from the committee on territories. On page 8, section 11, strike out the words "until the complete execution of this act no other election shall be held in said territory," and insert the amendment which I hold in my hand. °

You see from this that I moved to strike out the very words that Trumbull says I put in. The Committee on Territories overruled me in committee and put the clause in, but as soon as I got the bill back into the Senate, I moved to strike it out and put another clause in its place. On the same page you will find that my amendment was agreed to *unanimously.* I then offered another amendment, recognizing the right of the people of Kansas under the Toombs bill, to order just such election as they saw proper. You can find it on page 796 of the same volume. I will read it.[27]

> MR. DOUGLAS—I have another amendment to offer from the committee, to follow the amendment which has been adopted. The bill reads now, "and until the complete execution of this act, no other election shall be held in said territory." It has been suggested that it should be modified in this way, "and to avoid conflict in the complete execution of this act, all other elections in said Terri-

26. From SAD's Senate speech, July 2, 1856, ibid., 795.
27. Ibid., 796.

tory are hereby postponed until such time as said convention shall appoint," so that they can appoint the day in the event that there should be a failure to come into the Union. °

The amendment was *unanimously* agreed to, clearly and distinctly recognizing the right of the convention to order just as many elections as they saw proper in the execution of the act. Trumbull concealed in his Alton speech the fact that the clause he quoted had been stricken out in my motion, and the other fact that this other clause was put in the bill on my motion, and made the false charge that I incorporated into the bill a clause preventing submission, in the face of the fact, that on my motion, the bill was so amended before it passed as to recognize in express words the right and duty of submission.

On this record that I have produced before you, I repeat my charge that Trumbull did falsify the public records of the country, in order to make his charge against me. *[Cheers, applause]* And I tell Mr. Abraham Lincoln that if he will examine these records, he will then know that what I state is true. Mr. Lincoln has this day endorsed Mr. Trumbull's veracity after he had my word for it that that veracity was proved to be violated and forfeited by the public records. It will not do for Mr. Lincoln, in parading his calumnies against me, to put Mr. Trumbull between him and the odium and responsibility which justly attaches to such calumnies. I tell him that I am as ready to prosecute° the endorser as the maker of a forged note. *[Cheers, applause]*

I regret the necessity of occupying my time with these petty personal matters. It is unbecoming the dignity of a canvass for an office of the character for which we are candidates. When I commenced the canvass at Chicago, I spoke of Mr. Lincoln in terms of kindness as an old friend. I said that he was a good citizen, of unblemished character, against whom I had nothing to say. I repeated these complimentary remarks about him in my successive speeches, until he became the endorser for these and other slanders against me. If there is anything personally disagreeable, uncourteous or disreputable in these personalities, the sole responsibility rests on Mr. Lincoln, Mr. Trumbull, and their backers.

I will show you another charge made by Mr. Lincoln against me, as an offset to his expression of a° willingness to take back anything that is incorrect and to correct any false statement he may have made. He has several times charged that the Supreme Court, President Pierce, President Buchanan and myself, at the time I introduced the Nebraska bill in January, 1854, at Washington, entered into a conspiracy to have the Dred Scott case decided in such a manner as° to establish slavery all over this country. He charged a conspiracy between us.° I branded this charge as a falsehood, and then he repeated it, asked me to analyze its truth and answer it. I told him, "Mr. Lincoln, I know what you are after. You want to occupy my time in personal matters to prevent me from showing up the revolutionary principles which the abolition party, whose candidate you are, have proclaimed to the world." But he asked me to analyze his proof, and I did so. I called his attention to the fact that at the time the Nebraska bill was introduced, there was no such case as the Dred Scott case pending in the Supreme Court, nor was it brought there for years afterwards, and hence that it was impossible there could have been any such conspiracy between the judges of the Supreme Court and the other parties involved. I proved by the record that the charge was false, and what did he answer? Did he take it back like an honest man and say that he had been mistaken? No, he repeated the charge and said that, although there was no such case pending that year, that there was an understanding between the Democratic owners of Dred Scott and the judges of the Supreme Court and other parties involved that the case should be brought up.

I then demanded to know who these Democratic owners of Dred Scott were. He could not or would not tell; he did not know. In truth, there were no Democratic owners of Dred Scott on the face of the land. *[Laughter]* Dred Scott was owned at that time by the Rev. Dr. Chaffee, an abolition member of Congress from Springfield, Massachusetts, and his wife. *[Laughter, applause]* And Mr. Lincoln ought to have known that Dred Scott was so owned, for the reason that as soon as the decision was announced by the court, Dr. Chaffee and his wife executed a deed emancipating him, and put that deed on record. *[Cheers]* It was a matter of public record, therefore, that at the time the case was taken to the Supreme Court, Dred Scott was owned by an abolition member of Congress, a friend of Lincoln's, and a leading man of his party, while the defense was conducted by abolition lawyers, and thus the abolitionists managed both sides of the case.[28] *[Laughter]* I have exposed these facts to Mr. Lincoln, and yet he will not withdraw his charge of conspiracy. I now submit to you, whether you can place any confidence in a man who continues to make a charge when its utter falsity is proven by the public records?

I will state another fact to show how utterly reckless and unscrupulous this charge against the Supreme Court, President Pierce, President Buchanan and myself is. Lincoln says that President Buchanan was in the conspiracy at Wash-

---

28. Dred Scott's attorneys before the Supreme Court were Montgomery Blair, later to be in AL's cabinet, and George Ticknor Curtis, a Whig who became a Democrat. The defense was conducted by Senator Henry S. Geyer, a Missouri Whig, and Reverdy Johnson, former attorney general of the United States. None could be called abolitionists; indeed, in pursuance of the case, Johnson is said to have declared before the court that the extension of slavery might be the only means of protecting the nation's constitutional freedoms. See Allan Nevins, *The Emergence of Lincoln: Douglas, Buchanan and Party Chaos* (New York: Scribner's, 1950), I:86, citing *New York Tribune*, Dec. 23, 1856.

ington in the winter of 1854, when the Nebraska bill was introduced. The history of this country shows that James Buchanan was at that time representing this country at the court of St. James, Great Britain, with distinguished ability and usefulness, that he had not been in the United States for nearly a year previous, and that he did not return until about three years after. *[Cheers]* Yet Mr. Lincoln keeps repeating this charge of conspiracy against Mr. Buchanan, when the public records prove it to be untrue. Having proved it to be false as far as the Supreme Court and President Buchanan are concerned, I drop it, leaving the public to say whether I, by myself, without their concurrence, could have gone into a conspiracy with them. *[Laughter, cheers]*

My friends, you see that the object clearly is to conduct the canvass on personal matters, and hunt me down with charges that are proven to be false by the public records of the country. I am willing to throw open my whole public and private life to the inspection of any man, or all men who desire to investigate it. Having resided among you twenty-five years, during nearly the whole of which time a public man, exposed to more assaults, perhaps more abuse than any man living of my age, or who ever did live, and having survived it all and still commanded your confidence, I am willing to trust to your knowledge of me and my public conduct without making any more defense against these assaults. *[Cheers, applause]*

Fellow citizens, I came here for the purpose of discussing the leading political topics which now agitate the country. I have no charges to make against Mr. Lincoln, none against Mr. Trumbull, for I was not aware that he was a candidate, *[Laughter]*° and none against any man who is a candidate, except in repelling their assaults upon me. If Mr. Lincoln is a man of bad character, I leave you to find it out. If his votes in the past are not satisfactory, I leave others to ascertain the fact. If his course on the Mexican War was not in accordance with your notions of patriotism and fidelity to our own country as against a public enemy, I leave you to ascertain the fact. I have no assaults to make upon him except to trace his course on the questions that now divide the country and engross so much of the people's attention.

You know that prior to 1854 this country was divided into two great political parties, one the Whig, the other the Democratic. I, as a Democrat for twenty years prior to that time, had been in public discussions in this state as an advocate of Democratic principles, and I can appeal with confidence to every old line Whig within the hearing of my voice to bear testimony that during all that period, I fought you Whigs like a man on every question that separated the two parties. I had the highest respect for Henry Clay as a gallant party leader, as an eminent statesman, and as one of the bright ornaments of this country, but I conscientiously believed that the Democratic party was right on the questions which separated the Democrats from the Whigs. The man does not live who can say that I ever personally assailed Henry Clay or Daniel Webster, or any one of the leaders of that great party, whilst I combated with all my energy the measures they advocated. What did we differ about those days? Did Whigs and Democrats differ about this slavery question? On the contrary, did we not, in 1850, unite to a man in favor of that system of compromise measures which Mr. Clay introduced, Webster defended, Cass supported, and Fillmore approved and made the law of the land by his signature? While we agreed on those compromise measures, we differed about a bank, the tariff, distribution, the specie circular, the sub-treasury, and other questions of that description. Now let me ask you which one of those questions on which Whigs and Democrats then differed now remains to divide two great parties. Every one of those questions which divided Whigs and Demo-crats has passed away. The country has out-grown them; they have passed into history. Hence it is immaterial whether you were right or I was right on the bank, the sub-treasury, and other questions, because they no longer continue living issues. What then has taken the place of those questions about which we once differed? The slavery question has now become the leading and controlling issue. That question on which you and I agreed, on which the Whigs and Democrats united, has now become the leading issue between the national Democracy on the one side, and the Republican or abolition party on the other.

Just recollect for a moment the memorable contest of 1850, when this country was agitated from its center to its circumference by the slavery agitation. All eyes in this nation were then turned to the three great lights that survived the days of the revolution. They looked to Clay, then in retirement at Ashland, and to Web-ster and Cass in the United States Senate. Clay had retired to Ashland, having, as he supposed, performed his mission on earth, and was preparing himself for a better sphere of existence in another world. In that retirement, he heard the discordant, harsh, and grating sounds of sectional strife and disunion, and he aroused and came forth and resumed his seat in the Senate, that great theatre of his great deeds. From the moment that Clay arrived among us, he became the leader of all the Union men, whether Whigs or Democrats. For nine months, we each assembled each day in the council chambers, Clay in the chair, with Cass upon his right hand and Webster upon his left, and the Democrats and Whigs gathered around, forgetting differences, and only animated by one common, patriotic sentiment to devise means and measures by which we could defeat the mad and revolutionary schemes of the Northern abolitionists and Southern dis-unionists. [Cheers, applause]

We did devise those means. Clay brought them forward, Cass advocated them, the Union Democrats and Union Whigs voted for them, Fillmore signed them, and they gave peace and quiet to the country. Those compromise measures of 1850 were founded upon the great fundamental principle that the people of each state and each territory ought to be left free to form and regulate their own domestic institutions in their own way, subject only to the federal Constitution. *[Cheers, applause]* I will ask every old line Democrat and every old line Whig within the hearing of my voice, if I have not truly stated the issues as they then presented themselves to the country. You recollect that the abolitionists raised a howl of indignation and cried for vengeance and the destruction of Democrats and Whigs both, who supported those compromise measures of 1850. When I returned home to Chicago, I found the citizens inflamed and infuriated against the authors of those great measures. Being the only man in that city who was held responsible for affirmative votes on all those measures, I came forward and addressed the assembled inhabitants, defended each and every one of Clay's compromise measures as they passed the Senate and the House and were approved by President Fillmore.

Previous to that time, the City Council had passed resolutions nullifying the act of Congress and instructing the police to withhold all assistance from its execution. But the people of Chicago listened to my defense and like candid, frank, conscientious men, when they became convinced that they had done an injustice to Clay, Webster, Cass, and all of us who had supported those measures, they repealed their nullifying resolutions and declared that the laws should be executed and the supremacy of the Constitution maintained.[29] Let it always be recorded in history, to the immortal honor of the people of Chicago, that they returned to their duty when they found that they were wrong and did justice to those whom they had blamed and abused unjustly.

When the legislature of this state assembled that year, they proceeded to pass resolutions approving the compromise measures of 1850. When the Whig party assembled in 1852 at Baltimore in national convention for the last time, to nominate Scott for the Presidency, they adopted as a part of their platform the compromise measures of 1850 as the cardinal plank upon which every Whig would stand and by which he would regulate his future conduct. When the Democratic party assembled at the same place one month after to nominate Gen. Pierce, we adopted the same platform so far as those compromise measures were concerned, agreeing that we would stand by those glorious measures as a cardinal article in the Democratic faith. Thus you see that in 1852 all the old Whigs and all the old Democrats stood on a common plank, so far as this slavery question was concerned, differing on other questions.

Now, let me ask how is it, that since that time so many of you Whigs have wandered from the true path marked out by Clay and carried out broad and wide by the great Webster? How is it that so many old line Democrats have abandoned

---

29. See the Jonesboro debate, note 28, p. 122.

the old faith of their party and joined with abolitionism and freesoilism to over-turn the platform of the old Democrats, and the platform of the old Whigs? You cannot deny that since 1854, there has been a great revolution on this one ques-tion. How has it been brought about? I answer that no sooner was the sod grown green over the grave of the immortal Clay, no sooner was the rose planted on the tomb of the god-like Webster, than many of the leaders of the Whig party, such as Seward of New York and his followers, led off and attempted to abolition-ize the Whig party, and transfer all your old Whigs bound hand and foot into the abolition camp. Seizing hold of the temporary excitement produced in this country by the introduction of the Nebraska bill, the disappointed politicians in the Democratic party, united with the disappointed politicians in the Whig party, and endeavored to form a new party composed of all the abolitionists, of abolitionized Democrats and abolitionized Whigs, banded together in an aboli-tion platform.

And who led that crusade against national principles in this state? I answer, Abraham Lincoln on behalf of the Whigs, and Lyman Trumbull on behalf of the Democrats, formed a scheme by which they would abolitionize the two great parties in this state on condition that Lincoln should be sent to the United States Senate in place of Gen. Shields, and that Trumbull should go to Congress from the Belleville district, until I would be accommodating enough either to die or resign for his benefit, and then he was to go to the Senate in my place. You all remember that during the year 1854, these two worthy gentlemen, Mr. Lincoln and Mr. Trumbull, one an old line Whig and the other an old line Democrat, were hunting in partnership to elect a legislature against the Democratic party. I canvassed the state that year from the time I returned home until the election came off, and spoke in every county that I could reach during that period. In the Northern part of the state I found Lincoln's ally, in the person of Fred Douglass, the negro, preaching abolition doctrines, while Lincoln was discussing the same principles down here, and Trumbull, a little farther down, was advocating the election of members to the legislature who would act in concert with Lincoln's and Fred Douglass's friends. I witnessed an effort made at Chicago by Lincoln's then associates, and now supporters, to put Fred Douglass, the negro, on the stand at a Democratic meeting to reply to the illustrious Gen. Cass when he was addressing the people there.[30] They had the same negro hunting me down, and

---

30. Cass spoke in support of the Kansas-Nebraska Act in Chicago on October 20, 1854. Douglass was in the audience and was called upon to answer Cass, but he declined. John W. Blassingame, ed., *The Frederick Douglass Papers* (New Haven, Conn.: Yale University Press, 1982), ser. 1, 2:551n.

they now have a negro traversing the Northern counties of the state, and speaking in behalf of Lincoln.[31]

Lincoln knows that when we were at Freeport in joint discussion, there was a distinguished colored friend of his there then who was on the stump for him, *[Laughter]* and who made a speech there the night before we spoke, and another the night after, a short distance from Freeport, in favor of Lincoln, and in order to show how much interest the colored brethren felt in the success of their brother Abe. *[Laughter]* I have with me here, and would read if it would not occupy too much of my time, a speech made by Fred Douglass in Poughkeepsie, New York, a short time since to a large convention, in which he conjures all the friends of negro equality and negro citizenship to rally as one man around Abraham Lincoln, the perfect embodiment of their principles, and by all means to defeat Stephen A. Douglas.[32] *[Laughter]* Thus you find that this Republican party in the Northern part of the state had colored gentlemen for their advocates in 1854, in company with Lincoln and Trumbull, as they have now.

When in October, 1854, I went down to Springfield to attend the state fair, I found the leaders of this party all assembled together under the title of an anti-Nebraska meeting. It was Black Republicans up north, and anti-Nebraska at Springfield. I found Lovejoy, a high priest of abolitionism, and Lincoln, one of the leaders who was towing the old line Whigs into the abolition camp, and Trumbull, Sidney Breese, and Gov. Reynolds, all making speeches against the Democratic party and myself, at the same place and in the same cause. The same men who are now fighting the Democratic party and the regular Democratic nominees in this state were fighting us then. They did not then acknowledge that they had become abolitionists, and many of them deny it now. Breese, Dougherty, and Reynolds were then fighting the Democracy under the title of anti-Nebraska men, and now they are fighting the Democracy under the pretence that they are *simon pure* Democrats, *[Laughter]* saying that they are authorized to have every office-holder in Illinois beheaded who prefers the election of Douglas to that of Lincoln, or the success of the Democratic ticket in preference to the abolition ticket for members of Congress, state officers, members of the legislature, or any office in the state.[33] They canvassed the state against us in 1854, as they are doing

---

31. SAD may refer to H. Ford Douglas, a Chicago-based black abolitionist orator and editor, who was speaking in Illinois in the fall of 1858. See *Peoria Transcript*, Oct. 22, 1858 and *Galesburg Democrat*, Oct. 23, 1858.

32. Douglass spoke at Poughkeepsie on Aug. 2, 1858. See Blassingame, *Douglass Papers*, ser. 1, 3:214–42.

33. Sidney Breese, John Dougherty and John Reynolds hardly belong in this category of abolitionized Whigs and Democrats whom SAD refers to here. They were leaders of the small

now, owning different names and different principles in different localities, but having a common object in view: the defeat of all men holding national principles in opposition to this sectional abolition party.

They carried the legislature in 1854, and when it assembled in Springfield they proceeded to elect a United States Senator, all voting for Lincoln with one or two exceptions, which exceptions prevented them from quite electing him. And why should they not elect him? Had not Trumbull agreed that Lincoln should have Shields's place? Had not the abolitionists agreed to it? Was it not the solemn compact, the condition of which Lincoln agreed to abolitionize the old Whigs that he should be senator? Still, Trumbull having control of a few abolitionized Democrats, would not allow them all to vote for Lincoln on any one ballot, and thus kept him for some time within one or two votes of an election until he wearied∘ Lincoln's friends, and compelled them to drop him and elect Trumbull, in violation of the bargain. [Cheers] I desire to read you a piece of testimony in confirmation of the notoriously public facts which I have stated to you. Col. James H. Matheny, of Springfield, is and for twenty years has been the confidential personal and political friend and manager of Mr. Lincoln. Matheny is this very day the candidate of the Republican or abolition party for Congress against the gallant Major Thomas L. Harris, in the Springfield district, and is making speeches for Lincoln and against me. I will read you the testimony of Matheny about this bargain between Lincoln and Trumbull when they undertook to abolitionize Whigs and Democrats only four years ago. Matheny being mad at Trumbull for having played a Yankee trick on Lincoln, exposed the bargain in a public speech two years ago, and I will read the published report of that speech,[34] the correctness of which Mr. Lincoln will not deny:

> "the whigs, abolitionists, know-nothings and renegade democrats, made a solemn compact for the purpose of carrying the State against the Democracy" on this plan: 1st. That they would all combine and elect Mr. Trumbull to Congress, and thereby carry his district for the Legislature, in order to throw all the strength that could be obtained into that body against the Democrats. 2d. That when the Legislature should meet, the officers of that body, such as speaker, clerks, doorkeepers, etc., would be given to the abolitionists; and, 3d. That the whigs were to have the United States Senator. That accordingly, in good faith, Trumbull was elected to Congress, and his district carried for the Legislature; and when it convened, the abolitionists got all the officers of that body; and thus

---

faction of National Democrats, or "Danites," in Illinois who were loyal to the Buchanan administration and opposed to SAD's position on the Lecompton Constitution. SAD constantly insisted that the National Democrats were in league with the Republicans in Illinois.

34. See the Jonesboro debate, note 5, p. 92.

far the "bond" was fairly executed. The whigs, on their part, demanded the election of Abraham Lincoln to the United States Senate, that the bond might be fulfilled, the other parties to the contract having already secured to themselves all that was called for. But, said Mr. Matheny, "in the most perfidious manner they *refused* to elect Mr. Lincoln, and the mean, low-lived, sneaking Trumbull succeeded by *pledging all that was required by any party* in thrusting Lincoln aside and foisting himself, an excrescence from the rotten bowels of the Democracy, into the United States Senate; and thus it has ever been, that an *honest* man makes a bad bargain when he conspires or contracts with rogues." °

Lincoln's confidential friend, Matheny, thought that Lincoln made a bad bargain when he conspired with such rogues as Trumbull and the abolitionists. *[Laughter]* I would like to know whether Lincoln had as high an opinion of Trumbull's veracity when the latter agreed to support him for the Senate, and then cheated him, as he does now *[Laughter]*, when Trumbull comes forward and makes charges against me. You could not then prove Trumbull an honest man either by Lincoln, by Matheny, or by any of Lincoln's friends. They charged everywhere that Trumbull had cheated them out of the bargain, and Lincoln found, sure enough, that it was a *bad bargain* to contract and conspire with rogues. *[Laughter]*

And now I will explain to you what has been a mystery all over the state and Union, the reason why Lincoln was nominated for the United States Senate by the Black Republican convention. You know it has never been usual for any party or any convention to nominate a candidate for the United States Senator. Probably this was the first time that such a thing was ever done. The Black Republican convention had not been called for that purpose, but to nominate a state ticket, and every man was surprised and many disgusted when Lincoln was nominated. Archie Williams thought he was entitled to it. Browning knew that he deserved it. Wentworth was certain that he would get it. Peck had hopes. Judd felt sure that he was the man, and Palmer had claims and had made arrangements to secure it. But to their utter amazement, Lincoln was nominated by the convention. *[Laughter]* And not only that, but he received the nomination unanimously, by a resolution declaring that Abraham Lincoln was the first, last, and only choice of the Republican party.

How did this occur? Why, because they could not get Lincoln's friends to make another bargain with "rogues" *[Laughter]*, unless the whole party would come up as one man and pledge their honor that they would stand by Lincoln first, last, and all the time, and that he should not be cheated by Lovejoy this time, as he was by Trumbull before. Thus, by passing this resolution, the abolitionists are all for him, Lovejoy and Farnsworth are canvassing for him, Giddings is ready to come here in his behalf, and the negro speakers are already on the stump for him, and he is sure not to be cheated this time. He would not go into the arrangement until he got their bond for it, and Trumbull is compelled now to take the stump, get up false charges against me, and travel all over the state to try and elect Lincoln in order to keep Lincoln's friends quiet about the bargain in which Trumbull cheated them four years ago.

You see, now, why it is that Lincoln and Trumbull are so mighty fond of each other. *[Laughter]* They have entered into a conspiracy to break me down by these assaults on my public character, in order to draw my attention from a fair exposure of the mode in which they attempted to abolitionize the old Whig and the old Democratic parties and lead them captive into the abolition camp. Do you not all remember that Lincoln went around here four years ago making speeches to you, and telling you that you should all go for the abolition ticket, and swearing that he was as good a Whig as he ever was *[Laughter],* and that Trumbull went all over the state making pledges to the old Democrats, and trying to coax them into the abolition camp, swearing by his Maker, with the uplifted hand, that he was still a Democrat, always intended to be, and that never would he desert the Democrat party? *[Laughter]* He got your votes to elect an abolition legislature, which passed abolition resolutions, attempted to pass abolition laws, and sustained abolitionists for office, state and national.

Now, the same game is attempted to be played over again. Then Lincoln and Trumbull made captives of the old Whigs and old Democrats and carried them into the abolition camp where Father Giddings, the high priest of abolitionism, received and christened them in the dark cause just as fast as they were brought in. *[Cheers]* Giddings found the converts so numerous that he had to have assistance, and he sent for John P. Hale, N. P. Banks, Chase, and other abolitionists, and they came on, and with Lovejoy and Fred Douglass, the negro, helped to baptize these new converts just as fast° as Lincoln, Trumbull, Breese, Reynolds, and Dougherty could capture them and bring them within the abolition clutch.[35]

Gentlemen, they are now around making the same kind of speeches. Trumbull was down in Monroe County the other day assailing me and making a speech in favor of Lincoln, and I will show you under what notice his meeting was called. You see these people are Black Republicans or abolitionists up north, while at Springfield today they dare not call their convention "Republican," but are obliged to say it's "a convention of all men opposed to the Democratic party," and in Monroe County and lower Egypt Trumbull advertises their meetings as follows:

> A meeting of the Free Democracy will take place at Waterloo, on Monday, September 13th° inst., whereat Hon. Lyman Trumbull, Hon. Jehu° Baker, and others, will address the people upon the different political topics of the day.

---

35. See note 33, pp. 157–58.

Members of all parties are cordially invited to be present, and hear and determine for themselves.

September 9, 1858.

The Free Democracy.

Did you ever before hear of this new party called the "Free Democracy?" What object have these Black Republicans in changing their name in every county? They have one name in the North, another in the center, and another in the South. When I used to practice law before my distinguished judicial friend, whom I recognize in the crowd before me, if a man was charged with horse stealing and the proof showed that he went by one name in Stephenson county, another in Sangamon, a third in Monroe, and a fourth in Randolph, we thought that the fact of his changing his name so often to avoid detection was pretty strong evidence of his guilt. I would like to know why it is that this great free soil abolition party is not willing to avow the same name in all parts of the state? If this party believes that its course is just, why does it not avow the same principle in the North and in the South, in the East and in the West, wherever the American flag waves over American soil? *[Cheers]*

Voice: The party does not call itself Black Republican in the North.

Douglas: Sir, if you will get a copy of the paper published at Waukegan, fifty miles from Chicago, which advocates the election of Mr. Lincoln and has his name flying at its mast-head, you will find that it declares that "this paper is devoted to the cause of *Black Republicanism.*" *[Cheers, applause]* I had a copy of it and intended to bring it down here into Egypt to let you see what name the party rallied under up in the Northern part of the state, and to convince you that their principles are as different in the two sections of the state as is their name. I am sorry that I have mislaid it and have not got it here. Their principles in the North are jet black, in the center they are in color a decent mulatto, and in lower Egypt they are almost white. *[Laughter]* Why, I admired many of the white sentiments contained in Lincoln's speech at Jonesboro, and could not help but contrast them with the speeches of the same distinguished orator made in the Northern part of the state. Down here he denies that the Black Republican party is opposed to the admission of any more slave states, under any circumstances, and says that they are willing to allow the people of each state when it wants to come into the Union, to do just as it pleases on the question of slavery. In the North, you find Lovejoy, their candidate for Congress in the Bloomington district, Farnsworth, their candidate in the Chicago district, and Washburne, their candidate in the Galena district, all declaring that never will they consent, under any circumstances, to admit another slave state, even if the people want it. Thus, while they avow one set of principles up there, they avow another and entirely different set down here.

And here let me recall to Mr. Lincoln the scriptural quotation which he has applied to the federal government, that a house divided against itself cannot stand, and ask him how does he expect this abolition party to stand, when in one-half of the state it advocates a set of principles which it has repudiated in the other half. *[Laughter, applause]*

I am told that I have but eight minutes more. I would like to talk to you an hour and a half longer, but I will make the best use I can of the remaining eight minutes.

Mr. Lincoln said in his first remarks that he was not in favor of the social and political equality of the negro with the white man. Everywhere up North he has declared that he was not in favor of the social and political equality of the negro, but he would not say whether or not he was opposed to negroes voting and negro citizenship. I want to know whether he is for or against negro citizenship? He declared his utter opposition to the Dred Scott decision, and advanced as a reason that the Court had decided that it was not possible for a negro to be a citizen under the Constitution of the United States.[36] If he is opposed to the Dred Scott decision for that reason, he must be in favor of conferring the right and privilege of citizenship upon the negro! I have been trying to get an answer from him on that point, but have never yet obtained one, and I will show you why. In every speech he made in the North, he quoted the Declaration of Independence to prove that all men were created equal, and insisted that the phrase "all men" included the negro as well as the white man, and that the equality rested upon divine law. Here is what he said on that point:[37]

> I should like to know if taking this old Declaration of Independence, which declares that all men are equal upon principle, and making exceptions to it where will it stop. If one man says it does not mean a negro, why may not another say it does not mean some other man? If that declaration is not the truth, let us get the statute book in which we find it, and bear it out!°

Lincoln maintains there that the Declaration of Independence asserts that the negro is equal to the white man, and that under divine law, and if he believes so, it was rational for him to advocate negro citizenship, which, when allowed, puts the negro on an equality under the law. I say to you in all frankness, gentlemen, that in my opinion a negro is not a citizen, cannot be, and ought not to be,

---

36. SAD alludes to AL's "House Divided" speech in Springfield to the Illinois Republican state convention of June 16, 1858.

37. SAD quotes from AL's Chicago speech of July 10, 1858, as reported either by the *Press and Tribune* (July 12) or the *Times* (July 13), both of which use the word "bear." See Roy P. Basler et al., eds., *The Collected Works of Abraham Lincoln* (New Brunswick: Rutgers University Press, 1953), 2:500–501.

under the Constitution of the United States. I will not even qualify my opinion to meet the declaration of one of the judges of the Supreme Court in the Dred Scott case, that a negro descended from African parents, who was imported into this country as a slave, is not a citizen, and cannot be. I say that this government was established on the white basis. It was made by white men, for the benefit of white men and their posterity forever, and never should be administered by any except white men. [Cheers] I declare that a negro ought not to be a citizen, whether his parents were imported into this country as slaves or not, or whether or not he was born here. It does not depend upon the place a negro's parents were born, or whether they were slaves or not, but upon the fact that he is a negro, belonging to a race incapable of self-government, and for that reason ought not to be on an equality with white men. [Applause]

My friends, I am sorry that I have not time to pursue this argument further, as I might have done but for the fact that Mr. Lincoln compelled me to occupy a portion of my time in repelling those gross slanders and falsehoods that Trumbull has invented against me and put in circulation. In conclusion, let me ask you why should this government be divided by a geographical line, arraying all men North in one great hostile party against all men South? Mr. Lincoln tells you, in his speech at Springfield, that a house divided against itself cannot stand; that this government, divided into free and slave states, cannot endure permanently; that they must either be all free or all slave—all one thing or all the other.[38] Why cannot this government endure divided into free and slave states, as our fathers made it? When this government was established by Washington, Jefferson, Madison, Jay, Hamilton, Franklin, and the other sages and patriots of that day, it was composed of free states and slave states, bound together by one common constitution. We have existed and prospered from that day to this thus divided, and have increased with a rapidity never before equaled in wealth, the extension of territory, and all the elements of power and greatness, until we have become the first nation on the face of the globe. Why can we not thus continue to prosper? We can if we will live up to and execute the government upon those principles upon which our fathers established it. During the whole period of our existence Divine Providence has smiled upon us, and showered upon our nation richer and more abundant blessings than have ever been conferred upon any people on the face of the globe.° [Applause]

---

38. A paraphrase of part of the "House Divided" speech.

LINCOLN'S REJOINDER

It follows as a matter of course that a half-hour answer to a speech of an hour-and-a-half can be but a very hurried one. I shall only be able to touch upon a few of the points suggested by Judge Douglas, and give them a brief attention, while I shall have to totally omit others for the want of time.

Judge Douglas has said to you that he has not been able to get from me an answer to the question whether I am in favor of negro citizenship. So far as I know, the Judge never asked me the question before. *[Applause]* He shall have no occasion to ever ask it again, for I tell him very frankly that I am not in favor of negro citizenship. *[Applause]* This furnishes me an occasion for saying a few words upon the subject. I mentioned in a certain speech of mine,[39] which has been printed, that the Supreme Court had decided that a negro could not possibly be made a citizen, and without saying what was my ground of complaint in regard to that, or whether I had any ground of complaint, Judge Douglas has from that thing manufactured nearly every thing that he ever says about my disposition to produce an equality between the negroes and the white people. *[Laughter, applause]* If any one will read my speech, he will find I mentioned that as one of the points decided in the course of the Supreme Court opinions, but I did not state what objection I had to it. But Judge Douglas tells the people what my objection was when I did not tell them myself. *[Applause, laughter]* Now my own opinion is that the different states have the power to make a negro a citizen under the Constitution of the United States if they choose. The Dred Scott decision decides that they have not that power. If the State of Illinois had that power, I should be opposed to the exercise of it. *[Cheers, applause]* That is all I have to say about it.

Judge Douglas has told you that he heard my speeches North and my speeches South, that he had heard me at Ottawa and at Freeport in the North, and recently at Jonesboro in the South, and there was a very different cast of sentiment in the speeches made at the different points. I will not charge upon Judge Douglas that he willfully misrepresents me, but I call upon every fair-minded man to take these speeches and read them, *and I dare him to point out any difference between my printed speeches North and South.* *[Cheers]*

While I am here perhaps I ought to say a word, if I have the time, in regard to the latter portion of the Judge's speech, which was a sort of declamation in reference to my having said I entertained the belief that this government would not endure, half slave and half free. I have said so, and I did not say it without what seemed to me to be good reasons. It perhaps would require more time than

---

39. The "House Divided" speech.

I have now to set forth these reasons in detail, but let me ask you a few questions. Have we ever had any peace on this slavery question? When are we to have peace upon it if it is kept in the position it now occupies? How are we ever to have peace upon it? That is an important question. To be sure, if we will all stop and allow Judge Douglas and his friends to march on in their present career until they plant the institution all over the nation, here and wherever else our flag waves, and we acquiesce in it, there will be peace.

But let me ask Judge Douglas how he is going to get the people to do that? *[Applause]* They have been wrangling over this question for at least forty years. This was the cause of the agitation resulting in the Missouri Compromise. This produced the trouble at the annexation of Texas, in the acquisition of the territory acquired in the Mexican War. Again, this was the trouble which was quieted by the Compromise of 1850, when it was settled *"forever,"* as both the great political parties declared in their national conventions. That "forever" turned out to be just four years *[Laughter], when Judge Douglas himself re-opened it. [Applause, cheers]*

When is it likely to come to an end? He introduced the Nebraska bill in 1854 to put *another end* to the slavery agitation. He promised that it would finish it all up immediately, and he has never made a speech since—until he got into a quarrel with the President about the Lecompton Constitution—in which he has not declared that we are *just at the end* of the slavery agitation. But in one speech, I think last winter, he did say that he didn't quite see when the end of the slavery agitation would come. *[Laughter, cheers]* Now he tells us again that it is all over, and the people of Kansas have voted down the Lecompton Constitution.

How is it over? That was only one of the attempts at putting an end to the slavery agitation, one of these "final settlements." *[Laughter]* Is Kansas in the Union? Has she formed a constitution that she is likely to come in under? Is not the slavery agitation still an open question in that territory? Has the voting down of that constitution put an end to all the trouble? Is that more likely to settle it than every one of these previous attempts to settle the slavery agitation? Now at this day in the history of the world, we can no more foretell where the end of this slavery agitation will be than we can see the end of the world itself. The Nebraska-Kansas bill was introduced four years and a half ago, and if the agitation ever comes to an end, we may say we are four years and a half nearer the end. So, too, we can say we are four and a half years nearer the end of the world, and we can just as clearly see the end of the world as we can the end of this agitation. *[Applause]* The Kansas settlement did not conclude it. If Kansas should sink today and leave a great vacant space in the earth's surface, this vexed question would still be among us. I say, then, there is no way of putting an end to the slavery agitation amongst us but to put it back upon the basis where our fathers placed it *[Applause]*, no way but to keep it out of our new territories *[Applause]*, to restrict it forever to the old states where it now exists. *[Cheers]* Then the public mind *will* rest in the belief that it is in the course of ultimate extinction. That is one way of putting an end to the slavery agitation. *[Applause]*

The other way is for us to surrender and let Judge Douglas and his friends have their way and plant slavery over all the states, cease speaking of it as in any way a wrong, regard slavery as one of the common matters of property, and speak of negroes as we do of our horses and cattle. But while it drives on in its state of progress as it is now driving, and as it has driven for the last five years, I have ventured the opinion, and I say today, that we will have no end to the slavery agitation until it takes one turn or the other. *[Applause]* I do not mean that when it takes a turn towards ultimate extinction, it will be in a day, nor in a year, nor in two years. I do not suppose that in the most peaceful way ultimate extinction would occur in less than a hundred years at the least. But that it will occur in the best way for both races in God's own good time, I have no doubt. *[Applause]*

But, my friends, I have used up more of my time than I intended on this point. Now, in regard to this matter about Trumbull and myself having made a bargain to sell out the entire Whig and Democratic parties in 1854. Judge Douglas brings forward no evidence to sustain his charge, except the speech Matheny is said to have made in 1856, in which he told a cock-and-bull story of that sort, upon the same moral principle that Judge Douglas tells it here today. *[Applause]* This is the simple truth. I do not care greatly for the story, but this is the truth of it, and I have twice told Judge Douglas to his face that from beginning to end there is not one word of truth in it. *[Applause]* I have called upon him for the proof, and he does not at all meet me as Trumbull met him upon that of which we were just talking, by producing the record. He didn't bring the record, because there was no record for him to bring. *[Cheers, laughter]*

When he asks if I am ready to endorse Trumbull's veracity after he has broken a bargain with me, I reply that if Trumbull *had* broken a bargain with me, I would not be likely to endorse his veracity. *[Laughter, applause]* But I am ready to endorse his veracity because *neither in that thing, nor in any other, in all the years that I have known Lyman Trumbull, have I known him to fail of his word or tell a falsehood large or small. [Cheers]* It is for that reason that I endorse Lyman Trumbull.

Voice:[40] What does Ford's *History* say about him?

Lincoln: Some gentleman asks me what Ford's *History* says about him. My own recollection is that Ford speaks of Trumbull in very disrespectful terms in several portions of his book, *and that he talks a great deal worse of Judge*

---

40. This voice is identified in the *Chicago Press and Tribune* as that of "Mr. James Brown—(Douglas Post Master)."

Douglas.[41] *[Laughter, applause]* I made that answer off-hand by my friend asking me a question, without having referred to Ford's history upon the subject. °
I refer you, sir, to the history for examination. *[Cheers]*

Judge Douglas complains, at considerable length, about a disposition on the part of Trumbull and myself to attack him personally. I want to attend to that suggestion a moment. I don't want to be unjustly accused of dealing illiberally or unfairly with an adversary, either in court, or in a political canvass, or anywhere else. I would despise myself if I supposed myself ready to deal less liberally with an adversary than I was disposed to be treated myself. Judge Douglas, in a general way, revives the old charge against me, without putting it in a direct shape, in reference to the Mexican War. He does not take the responsibility of putting it in a very definite form, but makes a general reference to it. That charge is more than ten years old. He complains of Trumbull and myself, because he says we bring charges against him one or two years old. He knows, too, that in regard to the Mexican War story, the more respectable papers of his own party throughout the state have been compelled to take it back and acknowledge that it was a lie.[42] *[Applause]*

[Here Lincoln laid hold of a member of the platform party, Orlando B. Ficklin, and led him forward]

I do not mean to do anything with Mr. Ficklin except to present his face and tell you that *he personally knows that is a lie.* He was a member of Congress at the only time I was in Congress, and he knows that whenever there was an attempt to procure a vote of mine which would endorse the origin and justice of the war, I refused to give such endorsement, and voted against it. But I never voted against the supplies for the Army, and he knows, as well as Judge Douglas, that whenever a dollar was asked by way of compensation or otherwise, for the benefit of the soldiers, *I gave all the votes that Ficklin or Douglas did, and perhaps more. [Applause]*

Ficklin: My friends, I wish to say this in reference to the matter. Mr. Lincoln and myself are just as good personal friends as Judge Douglas and myself. In reference to this Mexican War, my recollection is that when the Ashmun resolution was offered by Mr. Ashmun of Massachusetts, in which he declared that

---

41. Historian and former governor Thomas Ford was indeed critical of both SAD and Trumbull. See Thomas Ford, *A History of Illinois,* ed. Rodney O. Davis (Urbana: University of Illinois Press, 1995), 150–51, 212–15, 260, 272–75, 277, 280.

42. On June 23, 1858, the *Chicago Times* accused AL of voting, when in Congress, against an appropriation for medical supplies for American troops in Mexico. On June 26 the Democratic *Illinois State Register* of Springfield admitted that the vote in question had been cast by John Henry, AL's immediate predecessor in Congress from their central Illinois district.

the Mexican War was unnecessarily and unconstitutionally commenced by the President, my recollection is that Mr. Lincoln voted for the resolution.

Lincoln: That is the truth. Now you all remember that was a resolution censuring the President for the manner in which the war was *begun.* You know they have charged that I voted against the supplies, by which I starved the soldiers who were out fighting the battles of their country. I say that Ficklin knows it is false. When that charge was brought forward by the *Chicago Times,* the Springfield *Register* reminded the *Times* that the charge really applied to John Henry. And I do know that *John Henry is now making speeches and fiercely battling for Judge Douglas.* [Applause] If the Judge now says that he offers this as a sort of set off to what I said today in reference to Trumbull's charge, then I remind him that he made this charge before I said a word about Trumbull's. He brought this forward at Ottawa, the first time we met face to face, and in the opening speech that Judge Douglas made, he attacked me in regard to a matter ten years old. Isn't he a pretty man to be whining about people making charges against him only *two* years old? [Cheers]

The Judge thinks it is altogether wrong that I should have dwelt upon this charge of Trumbull's at all. I gave the apology for doing so in my opening speech. Perhaps it didn't fix your attention. I said that when Judge Douglas was speaking at places where I spoke on the succeeding day, he used very harsh language about this charge. Two or three time afterwards I said I had confidence in Judge Trumbull's veracity and intelligence, and my own opinion was, from what I knew of the character of Judge Trumbull, that he would vindicate his position, and prove whatever he had stated to be true. This I repeated two or three times; and then I dropped it, without saying anything more on the subject for weeks, perhaps a month. I passed it by without noticing it at all, till I found at Jacksonville, Judge Douglas, in the plentitude of his power, is not willing to answer Trumbull and let me alone, but he comes out there and uses this language:[43] "he should not hereafter occupy his time in refuting such charges made by Trumbull, but that Lincoln, having endorsed the character of Trumbull for veracity, he should hold him (Lincoln) responsible for the slanders." °

What was Lincoln to do? [Laughter] Did he not do right, when he had the fit opportunity of meeting Judge Douglas here, to tell him he was ready for the responsibility? [Cheers] I ask a candid audience whether in doing thus Judge Douglas was not the assailant rather than I? [Cheers] Here I meet him face to face and say I am ready to take the responsibility, so far as it rests upon me.

Having done so, I ask the attention of this audience to the question whether I have succeeded in sustaining the charge, and whether Judge Douglas has at all

---

43. From SAD's speech at Jacksonville, AL's Debates Scrapbook, 146.

succeeded in rebutting it. You all heard me call upon him to say *which of these pieces of evidence was a forgery*. Does he say that what I present here as a copy of the official Toombs bill is a forgery? *[Cries of "No"]* Does he say that what I present as a copy of the bill reported by himself is a forgery? *[Cries of "No"]* Or what is presented as a transcript from the *Globe* of the quotations from Bigler's speech is a forgery? *[Cries of "No"]* Does he say the quotations from his own speech are forgeries? *[Cries of "No"]* Does he say this transcript from Trumbull's speech is a forgery? *[Cries of "No"]* *I would then like to know how it comes about that when each piece of a story is true, the whole story turns out false?* *[Cheers, laughter]* I take it these people have some sense. They see plainly that Judge Douglas is playing cuttlefish *[Laughter]*, a small species of fish that has no mode of defending itself when pursued except by throwing out a black fluid, which makes the water so dark the enemy cannot see it and thus it escapes. *[Laughter]* Ain't the Judge playing the cuttlefish? *[Cheers]*

Now I would ask very special attention to the consideration of Judge Douglas's speech at Jacksonville, and when you shall read his speech of today, I ask you to watch closely and see which of these pieces of testimony, every one of which he says is a forgery, he has shown to be such. *Not one of them has he shown to be a forgery*. Then I ask the original question: if each of the pieces of testimony is true, *how is it possible that the whole is a falsehood?* That is what I want to know. ° *[Cheers]*

In regard to Trumbull's charge that he, Douglas, inserted a provision into the bill to prevent the constitution being submitted to the people, what is his answer? He comes here and reads from the *Congressional Globe* to show that, on his motion, that provision was struck out of the bill. Why, Trumbull has not said it was not stricken out, but Trumbull says he, Douglas, put it in, and it is no answer to the charge to say he afterwards took it out. Both are perhaps true. It was in regard to the thing precisely that I told him he had dropped the cub. *[Laughter]* Trumbull shows you that by his introducing the bill, it was *his cub*. *[Laughter]* It is no answer to that assertion to call Trumbull a liar merely because he did not specially say Douglas struck it out. Suppose that were the case, does it answer Trumbull? I assert that you *[pointing to an individual]* are here today, and you undertake to prove me a liar by showing that you were in Mattoon yesterday. *[Laughter]* I say that you took your hat off your head, and you prove me a liar by putting it on your head. *[Laughter]* That is the whole force of Douglas's argument.

Now, I want to come back to my original question. Trumbull says that Judge Douglas had a bill with a provision in it for submitting a constitution to be made to a vote of the people of Kansas. Does Judge Douglas deny that fact? Does he deny that the provision which Trumbull reads was put in that bill? Then Trumbull says he struck it out. Does he dare to deny that? He does not, and I have the right to repeat the question: *why Judge Douglas took it out?* [Applause] Bigler has said there was a combination of certain senators, among whom he did not include Judge Douglas, by which it was agreed that the Kansas bill should have a clause in it not to have the constitution formed under it submitted to a vote of the people. He did not say that Douglas was among them, but we prove by another source that about the same time Douglas comes into the Senate *with that provision stricken out of the bill.* Although Bigler cannot say they were all working in concert, yet it looks very much as if the thing was agreed upon and done with a mutual understanding after the conference. And while we do not know that it was absolutely so, yet it looks so probable that we have a right to call upon the man who knows the true reasons why it was done *to tell what that true reason was.* [Cheers] When he will not tell what the true reason was, he stands in the attitude of an accused thief who has stolen goods in his possession, and when called to account, refuses to tell where he got them. [Applause] Not only is this the evidence, but when he comes in with the bill having the provision stricken out, he tells us in a speech, not then but since, that these alterations and modifications in the bill *had been made by him, in consultations with Toombs, the originator of the bill.* He tells us the same today. He says there were certain modifications made in the bill in committee that he did not vote for. I ask you to remember while certain amendments were made which he disapproved of but which a majority of the committee voted in, he has himself told us that in this particular the *alterations and modifications were made by him upon consultation with Toombs.* [Cheers] We have his own word that these alterations were made by him and not by the committee.

Now I ask what is the reason Judge Douglas is so chary about coming to the exact question? What is the reason he will not tell you anything about *how* it was made, *by whom* it was made, or that he remembers it being made at all. Why does he stand playing upon the meaning of words, and quibbling around the edges of the evidence? If he can explain all this, but leaves it unexplained, I have a right to infer that Judge Douglas understood it was the purpose of his party, in engineering that bill through, to make a constitution and have Kansas come into the Union with that constitution, *without its being submitted to a vote of the people.* If he will explain his action on this question, by giving a *better reason* for the facts that happened than he has done, it will be satisfactory. But until he does that—until he gives a better or more plausible reason than he has offered against the evidence in the case—*I suggest to him it will not avail him at all that he swells himself up, takes on dignity, and calls people liars.* [Applause, laughter]

Why, sir, there is not a word in Trumbull's speech that depends on Trumbull's veracity at all. He has only arrayed the evidence and told you what follows as a matter of reasoning. There is not a statement in the whole speech that depends on Trumbull's word. If you have ever studied geometry, you remember that by a course of reasoning Euclid proves that all the angles in a triangle are equal to two right angles. Euclid has shown you how to work it out. Now, if you undertake to disprove that proposition, and to show that it is erroneous, would you prove it to be false by calling Euclid a liar? ∘ *[Laughter, cheers]*

They tell me that my time is out, and therefore I close.

GALESBURG

INTRODUCTION

After almost three weeks of practically nonstop campaigning by Lincoln and Douglas across Illinois's central counties following the Charleston debate, the final three joint meetings between the two contestants took place over a nine-day period in October 1858. The two candidates confronted each other in the first of these encounters on October 7 at Galesburg in west-central Illinois, a town called by a St. Louis reporter "the chief seat of the abolitionists of this State."[1] Galesburg and Knox College were founded together twenty years earlier as a colony supporting a college by settlers from New York and New England. Since their founding, the town and the college had had almost a joint Yankee leadership that had indeed acquired a wide reputation for supporting antislavery causes and the Underground Railroad. Politically, Galesburg also had a tradition of favoring the Liberty and Free-Soil parties, and in 1858 it was far more Republican than the rest of surrounding Knox County. However the town had also developed into a major regional railroad hub during the 1850s, and its resultant rapid population growth, from eight hundred in 1850 to almost five thousand in 1858, brought to it a much more diverse citizen body. And Galesburg's new railroad connections also insured that much of the October 7 debate audience consisted of delegations from outlying counties and was thus more bipartisan than a merely local one would be. Senator Douglas was no stranger to Knox County, having served as presiding judge on the local judicial circuit in the 1840s, but Lincoln's previous acquaintance with the area was scant.

---

1. *St. Louis Missouri Republican*, Oct. 11, 1858.

In spite of cold and disagreeable weather, the Galesburg debate was preceded by what was becoming the usual Fourth of July sort of array of partisan floats, bandwagons, military companies, banners, and at least one wagon filled with young women representing the several states. One banner in particular attracted attention, caricaturing the Freeport Doctrine by depicting Douglas unsuccessfully trying to ride two donkeys labeled "Popular Sovereignty" and "Dred Scott." Douglas and Lincoln arrived in Galesburg from opposite directions on the debate day, to be feted at noon meals by partisan hosts, and then at 2:00 PM escorted in two four-horse carriages driven side by side to the debate location, which was an uncovered platform at the east side of the principal building of Knox College. Above the platform on the building's wall hung a long banner proclaiming "Knox College for Lincoln." That college structure, now known as "Old Main," still stands as a well-used office and classroom building which proudly commemorates its status as a debate site. Newspapers of both political persuasions agreed that the Galesburg audience was the largest of the series thus far. "[I]t seemed that everybody gathered—and brought all their relations," said one.[2] The day's wind may have made hearing the speakers especially difficult, and Douglas seems to have compensated by speaking slowly. One listener found that style of speaking especially difficult to listen to. He found Douglas's discourse "disjointed as if he could not be heard if he spoke two words without a pause between," but Lincoln, who made no such effort, "was heard quite as far as Douglas, & yet spoke right along."[3]

Douglas decried in his opening what he claimed to be Lincoln's inconsistency, in asserting at Chicago on July 10 that the dictum in the Declaration of Independence that "all men are created equal" applied to blacks, while declaring later in the Charleston debate that as long as blacks and whites live together, there must be a superior and inferior race. Such inconsistency, Douglas indicated, mirrored the divisions within the Republican Party, whose doctrines differed in Illinois from north to south. Following that, Douglas repeated his contention that the Declaration of Independence applied only to whites and that the United States was a white man's country in which Negroes were entitled only to those privileges which a community could safely bestow.

Lincoln denied Douglas's charge of inconsistency. While acknowledging what he considered the impossibility of a "perfect social and political equality" between the races, Lincoln reaffirmed his conviction that in their rights to life, liberty, and the pursuit of happiness, blacks and whites were equal. This was a difficult and paradoxical position for Lincoln to continue to maintain, and one that could only

---

2. *Chicago Times,* Oct. 12, 1858.

3. Samuel Wright's Journal, 1839–1860, Oct. 11, 1858, Knox College Archives, Galesburg, Illinois.

be plausible at a time, as in 1858, when no clear positive conception or definition of United States citizenship even existed. Lincoln then took new ground, which he would occupy for the remainder of the debate series. Douglas, he said, could see no wrong in slavery, whereas Lincoln and his fellow Republicans contemplated it as a moral, social, and political evil, and they looked forward to its end. Lincoln claimed that Douglas's defense of the *Dred Scott* decision was a means to prepare the public for a new verdict that would nationalize slavery, and in a memorable passage paraphrasing Henry Clay, he accused Douglas of "blowing out the moral lights around us" in his project to bring that about. Referring then to Douglas's charge that he had been responsible for radical resolutions actually passed by others in 1854, Lincoln claimed that a forgery had been committed when those spurious resolutions were published in the Springfield Democratic newspaper, and he demanded the identity of the forger.

Lincoln's hint that Douglas might be a party to forgery brought Douglas to contend in his rejoinder that Lincoln might bring matters to the point of personal difficulties between them. Douglas once again claimed that divisions within the Republican Party insured that Republicans adhered to different sets of principles in northern and southern Illinois. And he chided Lincoln for attacking the United States Supreme Court, denying that one of its decisions would ever impose slavery on the states, and claiming that Lincoln's attacks only served to undermine public confidence in the "highest judicial tribunal on earth." Though he would do so subsequently, Douglas hardly noticed Lincoln's appeal to morality at Galesburg.

Reviving a charge made after the Ottawa debate, Republican newspapers claimed that the *Chicago Times* had garbled Lincoln's Galesburg speech, the Galesburg paper alone citing 180 alleged misquotations and altered meanings, the aim of which was "to blunt the keen edge of Lincoln's wit, to mar the beauty of his most eloquent passages, and make him talk like a booby, a half-witted numbskull."[4] The *Times* replied that it had simply quoted Lincoln as he actually spoke, and in turn accused *Chicago Press and Tribune* editors of rushing the manuscripts of his speech to Chicago to allow them to have time to "*re-write or alter Lincoln's part of the debate at Galesburg.*"[5] Given the hindsight of a century and a half, the allegations of partisan tampering with the debate texts cannot be dismissed. Yet it is also conceivable that the inclement weather at Galesburg contributed to the discrepancies. Years later Horace White, who reported all the debates, said as much,[6] but for partisan intent to be imputed was probably inevitable.

---

4. *Chicago Press and Tribune,* Oct. 11, 1858; *Galesburg Democrat,* Oct. 13, 1858.

5. *Chicago Times,* Oct. 12, 1858. Italics in original.

6. White quoted in William H. Herndon and Jesse W. Weik, *Herndon's Lincoln,* ed. Douglas L. Wilson and Rodney O. Davis (Urbana: University of Illinois Press, 2006), 388.

DOUGLAS'S OPENING SPEECH

Ladies and gentlemen: Four years ago I appeared before the people of Knox County for the purpose of defending my political action upon the compromise measures of 1850 and the passage of the Kansas-Nebraska bill.[1] Those of you before me who were present then will remember that I vindicated myself for supporting those two measures by the fact that they rested upon the great fundamental principle that the people of each state and each territory of this Union have the right, and ought to be permitted to exercise the right, of regulating their own domestic concerns in their own way, subject to no other limitation or restriction than that which the Constitution of the United States imposes upon them. I then called upon the people of Illinois to decide whether that principle of self-government was right or wrong. If it was and is right, then the compromise measures of 1850 were right, and, consequently, the Kansas and Nebraska bill, based upon the same principle, must necessarily have been right. *[Cheers]*

The Kansas and Nebraska bill declared, in so many words, that it was[2] "the true intent and meaning of the act not to legislate slavery into any state or territory, nor to exclude it therefrom, but to leave the people thereof perfectly free to form and regulate their domestic institutions in their own way, subject only to the Constitution of the United States." ° For the last four years I have devoted all my energies, in private and public, to commend that principle to the American people. Whatever else may be said in condemnation or support of my political course, I apprehend that no honest man will doubt the fidelity with which, under all circumstances, I have stood by it.

During the last year a question arose in the Congress of the United States whether or not that principle would be violated by the admission of Kansas into the Union under the Lecompton Constitution. In my opinion, the attempt to force Kansas in under that constitution was a gross violation of the principle enunciated in the compromise measures of 1850 and Kansas and Nebraska bill of 1854, and therefore I led off in the fight against the Lecompton Constitution and conducted it until the effort to carry that constitution through Congress was abandoned. And I can appeal to all men, friends and foes, Democrats and Republicans, Northern men, Southern men, that during the whole of that fight, I carried the banner of popular sovereignty aloft and never allowed it to trail in the dust, or lowered my flag, until victory perched upon our arms. *[Cheers]*

---

1. On Oct. 13, 1854, SAD defended the Kansas-Nebraska Act in a speech at Knoxville, Illinois, near Galesburg. President Jonathan Blanchard of Knox College replied to Douglas there.

2. *U.S. Statutes at Large* 10, 283.

When the Lecompton Constitution was defeated, the question arose in the minds of those who had advocated it what they should next resort to in order to carry out their views. They devised a measure known as the English bill and granted a general amnesty and political pardon to all men who had fought against the Lecompton Constitution, provided they would support that bill. I, for one, did not choose to accept the pardon or to avail myself of the amnesty granted on that condition. The fact that the supporters of Lecompton were willing to forgive all differences of opinion at that time, in the event those who opposed it favored the English bill, was an admission that they did not think that opposition to Lecompton impaired a man's standing in the Democratic party.

Now the question arises, what was that English bill, which certain men are now attempting to make a test of political orthodoxy in this country? It provided, in substance, that the Lecompton Constitution should be sent back to the people of Kansas for their adoption or rejection at an election which was held in August last, and, in case they refused admission under it, that Kansas should be kept out of the Union until she had 93,420 inhabitants.[3] I was in favor of sending the constitution back in order to enable the people to say whether or not it was their act and deed, and embodied their will. But the other proposition, that if they refused to come into the Union under it, they should be kept out until they had double or treble the population they then had, I never would sanction by my vote. The reason why I could not sanction it is to be found in the fact that by the English bill, if the people of Kansas had only agreed to become a slaveholding state under the Lecompton Constitution, they could have done so with 35,000 people. But if they insisted on a being free state, as they had a right to do, then they were to be punished by being kept out of the Union until they had nearly three times that population. I then said in my place in the Senate, as I now say to you, that whenever Kansas has population enough for a slave state, she has population enough for a free state. [Cheers]

I have never yet given a vote, and I never intend to record one, making an odious and unjust distinction between the different states of this Union. [Applause] I hold it to be a fundamental principle in our republican form of government that all the states of this Union, old and new, free and slave, stand on an exact equality. Equality among the different states is a cardinal principle on which all our institutions rest. Wherever, therefore, you make a discrimination, saying to a slave state that it shall be admitted with 35,000 inhabitants, and to a free state, that it shall not be admitted until it has 93,000 or 100,000 inhabitants, you are throwing the whole weight of the federal government into the scale in

---

3. Under the provisions of the English bill, the Lecompton Constitution was submitted to a vote in Kansas on Aug. 2, when it was rejected by 11,812 to 1,926.

favor of one class of states against the other. Nor would I, on the other hand, any sooner sanction the doctrine that a free state could be admitted into the Union with 35,000 people, while a slave state was kept out until it had 93,000.

I have always declared in the Senate my willingness, and I am willing now to adopt the rule, that no territory shall ever become a state until it has the requisite population for a member of Congress, according to the then existing ratio. But while I have always been, and am now willing to adopt that general rule, I was not willing and would not consent to make an exception of Kansas as a punishment for her obstinacy in demanding the right to do as she pleased in the formation of her constitution.

It is proper that I should remark here, that my opposition to the Lecompton Constitution did not rest upon the peculiar position taken by Kansas on the subject of slavery. I held then, and hold now, that if the people of Kansas want a slave state, it is their right to make one and be received into the Union under it. If, on the contrary, they want a free state, it is their right to have it, and no man should ever oppose their admission because they ask it under the one or the other. I hold to that great principle of self-government which asserts the right of every people to decide for themselves the nature and character of the domestic institutions and fundamental law under which they are to live.

The effort has been and is now being made in this state by certain postmasters and other federal office holders to make a test of faith on the support of the English bill. These men are now making speeches all over the state against me and in favor of Lincoln, either directly or indirectly, because I would not sanction a discrimination between slave and free states by voting for the English bill. But while that bill is made a test in Illinois for the purpose of breaking up the Democratic organization in this state, how is it in the other states? Go to Indiana, and there you find English himself, the author of the English bill, who is a candidate for re-election to Congress, has been forced by public opinion to abandon his own darling project and to give a promise that he will vote for the admission of Kansas at once, whenever she forms a constitution in pursuance of law and ratifies it by a majority vote of her people. Not only is this the case with English himself, but I am informed that every Democratic candidate for Congress in Indiana takes the same ground. Pass to Ohio, and there you find that Groesbeck and Pendleton and Cox and all the other anti-Lecompton men who stood shoulder to shoulder with me against the Lecompton Constitution, but voted for the English bill, now repudiate it and take the same ground that I do on that question. So it is with the Joneses and others of Pennsylvania, and so it is with every other Lecompton Democrat in the free states. They now abandon even the English bill and come back to the true platform which I proclaimed at the time in the Senate, and upon which the Democracy of Illinois now stand.

And yet, notwithstanding the fact that every Lecompton and anti-Lecompton Democrat in the free states has abandoned the English bill, you are told that it is to be made a test upon me, while the power and patronage of the government are all exerted to elect men to Congress in the other states who occupy the same position with reference to it that I do. It seems that my political offence consists in the fact that I first did not vote for the English bill, and thus pledge myself to keep Kansas out of the Union until she has a population of 93,420, and then return home, violate that pledge, repudiate the bill, and take the opposite ground. If I had done this, perhaps the administration would now be advocating my re-election, as it is that of the others who have pursued this course.∘ I did not choose to give that pledge, for the reason that I did not intend to carry out that principle. I never will consent, for the sake of conciliating the frowns of power, to pledge myself to do that which I do not intend to perform. I now submit the question to you as my constituency, whether I was not right, first, in resisting the adoption of the Lecompton Constitution; and secondly, in resisting the English bill. *[Cries of "yes"]* I repeat, that I opposed the Lecompton Constitution because it was not the act and deed of the people of Kansas and did not embody their will. I denied the right of any power on earth, under our system of government, to force a constitution on an unwilling people. *[Cheers, applause]*

There was a time when some men could pretend to believe that the Lecompton Constitution embodied the will of the people of Kansas, but that time has passed. The question was referred to the people of Kansas under the English bill last August, and then, at a fair election, they rejected the Lecompton Constitution by a vote of from eight to ten against it to one in its favor. Since it has been voted down by so overwhelming a majority, no man can pretend that it was the act and deed of that people. *[Cheers]* I submit the question to you whether or not, if it had not been for me, that constitution would have been crammed down the throats of the people of Kansas against their consent. *[Cheers]* While at least ninety-nine out of every hundred people here present agree that I was right in defeating that project, yet my enemies use the fact that I did defeat it, by doing right, to break me down and put another man in the U.S. Senate in my place. *[Cheers, applause]*

The very men who acknowledge that I was right in defeating Lecompton, now form an alliance with federal office holders, professed Lecompton men, to defeat me, because I did right. My political opponent, Mr. Lincoln, has no hope on earth, and has never dreamed that he had a chance of success, were it not for the aid he is receiving from federal office holders, who are using their influence and the patronage of the government against me in revenge for my having defeated the Lecompton Constitution.[4] *[Cheers, applause]* What do you Republicans

---

4. See "National Democrats" in the glossary, p. 328.

think of a political organization that will try to make an unholy and unnatural combination with its professed foes to beat a man merely because he has done right? You know such is the fact with regard to your own party. You know that the axe of decapitation is suspended over every man in office in Illinois, and the terror of proscription is threatened every Democrat by the present administration unless he supports the Republican ticket in preference to my Democratic associates and myself. *[Cheers]* I could find an instance in the postmaster of the city of Galesburg, and in every other postmaster in this vicinity, all of whom have been stricken down simply because they discharged the duties of their offices honestly and supported the regular Democratic ticket in this state in the right.[5] The Republican party is availing itself of every unworthy means in the present contest to carry the election, because its leaders know that if they let this chance slip, they will never have another and their hopes of making this a Republican state will be blasted forever.

Now, let me ask you whether the country has any interest in sustaining this organization known as the Republican party? That party is unlike all other political organizations in this country. All other parties have been national in their character, have avowed their principles alike in the slave and the free states, in Kentucky as well as in Illinois, in Louisiana as well as in Massachusetts. Such was the case with the old Whig party, and such was and is the case with the Democratic party. Whigs and Democrats could proclaim their principles boldly and fearlessly in the North and in the South, in the East and in the West, wherever the Constitution ruled and the American flag waved over American soil.

But now you have a sectional organization, a party which appeals to the Northern section of the Union against the Southern, a party which appeals to Northern passion, Northern pride, Northern ambition, and Northern prejudices, against Southern people, the Southern states and Southern institutions. The leaders of that party hope that they will be able to unite the Northern states in one great sectional party, and inasmuch as the North is the strongest section, that they will thus be enabled to out-vote, conquer, govern, and control the South. Hence you find that they now make speeches advocating principles and measures which cannot be defended in any slaveholding state of this Union. Is there a Republican residing in Galesburg who can travel into Kentucky and carry his principles with him across the Ohio? What Republican from Massachusetts can visit the Old Dominion without leaving his principles behind him when he crosses Mason and Dixon's line? Permit me to say to you in perfect good humor, but in all sincerity, that no political creed is sound which cannot be proclaimed fearlessly in every state of this

---

5. In Sept. 1858, George C. Lanphere, a Douglas Democrat, was replaced as postmaster in Galesburg by Josiah Gale, a Buchanan supporter.

Union where the federal Constitution is the supreme law of the land.° *[Cheers]*
Not only is this Republican party unable to proclaim its principles alike in the
North and in the South, in the free states and in the slave states, but it cannot
even proclaim them in the same forms and give them the same strength and
meaning in all parts of the same state. My friend Lincoln finds it extremely difficult to manage a debate in the center part of the state, where there is a mixture
of men from the North and the South. In the extreme Northern part of Illinois,
he can proclaim as bold and radical abolitionism as ever Giddings, Lovejoy, or
Garrison enunciated, but when he gets down a little farther South, he claims
that he is an old line Whig, *[Laughter]* a disciple of Henry Clay, and declares
that he still adheres to the old line Whig creed, and has nothing whatever to do
with abolitionism, or negro equality, or negro citizenship. *[Cheers]* I once before
hinted this of Mr. Lincoln in a public speech, and at Charleston he defied me to
show that there was any difference between his speeches in the North and in the
South, and that they were not in strict harmony.

I will now call your attention to two of them, and you can then say whether
you would be apt to believe that the same man ever uttered both. *[Laughter, cheers]*
In a speech in reply to me at Chicago in July last, Mr. Lincoln, in speaking of the
equality of the negro with the white man, used the following language:[6]

> I should like to know if taking this old Declaration of Independence, which de-
> clares that all men are equal upon principle, and making exceptions to it where
> will it stop. If one man says it does not mean a negro, why may not another say
> it does not mean some other man? If that declaration is not the truth, let us get
> the statute book in which we find it and tear it out! Who is so bold as to do it!
> If it is not true let us tear it out!°

You find that Mr. Lincoln there proposed that if the doctrine of the Declaration of Independence, declaring all men to be born equal, did not include the
negro and put him on an equality with the white man, that we should take the
statute book and tear it out. *[Laughter, cheers]* He there took the ground that the
negro race is included in the Declaration of Independence as the equal of the
white race, and that there could be no such thing as a distinction in the races,
making one superior and the other inferior. I read now from the same speech.[7]
"My friends," he says,

> I have detained you about as long as I desired to do; and I have only to say, let us
> discard all this quibbling about this man and the other man, this race and that

---

6. From AL's Chicago speech of July 10, 1858, in Roy P. Basler et al., eds., *The Collected
Works of Abraham Lincoln* (New Brunswick: Rutgers University Press, 1953), 2:500–501.
    7. Ibid.

race, and the other race being inferior, and, therefore, they must be placed in an inferior position, discarding our standard that we have left us. Let us discard all these things, and unite as one people throughout this land, until we shall once more stand up declaring that all men are created equal. °

Voice: That's right.

Douglas: Yes, I have no doubt that you think it is right, but the Lincoln men down in Coles, Tazewell, and Sangamon Counties *do not* think it is right. *[Applause, laughter]* In the conclusion of the same speech, talking to the Chicago abolitionists, he said: "I leave you, hoping that the lamp of liberty will burn in your bosoms until there shall no longer be a doubt that all men are created free and equal." °

Voices: Good, good.

Douglas: Well, you say "good" to that, and you are going to vote for Lincoln because he holds that doctrine. I will not blame you for supporting him on that ground, but I will show you, in immediate contrast with that doctrine, what Mr. Lincoln said down in Egypt in order to get votes in that locality, where they do not hold to such a doctrine. *[Applause]* In a joint discussion between Mr. Lincoln and myself, at Charleston, I think, on the 18th of last month, Mr. Lincoln, referring to this subject, used the following language:[8]

> I will say then, that I am not nor ever have been in favor of bringing about in any way, the social and political equality of the white and black races; that I am not, nor ever have been in favor of making voters of the free negroes, or jurors, or qualifying them to hold office, or having them to marry with white people. I will say in addition, that there is a physical difference between the white and black races, which, I suppose, will forever forbid the two races living together upon terms of social and political equality, and inasmuch, as they cannot so live, that while they do remain together, there must be the position of superior and inferior, that I as much as any other man am in favor of the superior position being assigned to the white man. °

Voices: "Good for Lincoln," "Hurrah for Lincoln."

Douglas: Fellow citizens, here you find men hurrahing for Lincoln and saying that he did right, when in one part of the state he stood up for negro equality, and in another part, for political effect, discarded the doctrine and declared that there always must be a superior and inferior race. Abolitionists up North are expected and required to vote for Lincoln because he goes for the equality of the races, holding that, by the Declaration of Independence, the white man and the negro were created equal and endowed by the divine law with that equality. And down South he tells the old Whigs, the Kentuckians, Virginians, and Ten-

---

8. From AL's opening speech at the Charleston debate. See p. 131.

nesseeans that there is a physical difference in the races, making one superior and the other inferior, and that he is in favor of maintaining the superiority of the white race over the negro.

Now, how can you reconcile those two positions of Mr. Lincoln? He is to be voted for in the South as a pro-slavery man, and he is to be voted for in the North as an abolitionist. *[Cheers]* Up here he thinks it is all nonsense to talk about a difference between the races, and says that we must "discard all quibbling about this race and that race and the other race being inferior and therefore they must be placed in an inferior position." Down South he makes this "quibble" about this race and that race and the other race being inferior as the creed of his party, and declares that the negro can never be elevated to the position of the white man. You find that his political meetings are called by different names in different counties in the state. Here they are called Republican meetings, but in old Tazewell, where Lincoln made a speech last Saturday I think it was, but perhaps it was Monday, they don't have any such thing as Republican meetings.

Lincoln: Nor Democratic here. °

Douglas: He did not address a *Republican* meeting, but "a grand rally of the *Lincoln men*." *[Laughter]* There are very few Republicans there, because Tazewell County is filled with old Virginians and Kentuckians, all of whom are Whigs or Democrats, and if Mr. Lincoln had called an abolition or Republican meeting there, he would not get many votes. *[Laughter]* Go down into Egypt and you find that he and his party are operating under an alias there, which his friend Trumbull has given them, in order that they may cheat the people. When I was down in Monroe County a few weeks ago addressing the people, I saw handbills posted announcing that Mr. Trumbull was going to speak in behalf of Lincoln, and what do you think the name of his party was there? Why the "*Free Democracy*." *[Laughter]* Mr. Trumbull and Mr. Jehu Baker were announced to address the "Free Democracy of Monroe County," and the bill was signed "Many Free Democrats." The reason that Lincoln and his party adopted the name of "Free Democracy" down there was because Monroe County has always been an old-fashioned Democratic county, and hence it was necessary to make the people believe that they were Democrats, sympathized with them, and were fighting for Lincoln as Democrats. Come up to Springfield, where Lincoln now lives, and always has lived, and you find that the convention of his party which assembled to nominate candidates for the °legislature, who are expected to vote for him if elected, dare not adopt the name of Republican, but assembled under the title of "all opposed to the Democracy." *[Laughter, cheers]* Thus you find that Mr. Lincoln's creed cannot travel through even one half of the counties of this state, but that it changes its hues and becomes lighter and lighter, as it travels from the extreme North, until it is nearly white, when it reaches the extreme South end of the state.

I ask you, my friends, why cannot Republicans avow their principles alike everywhere? I would despise myself if I thought that I was procuring your votes by concealing my opinions, and by avowing one set of principles in one part of the state and a different set in another part. If I do not truly and honorably represent your feelings and principles, then I ought not to be your senator, and I will never conceal my opinions, or modify or change them a hair's breadth in order to get votes.

I tell you that this Chicago doctrine of Lincoln's—declaring that the negro and the white man are made equal by the Declaration of Independence and by Divine Providence—is a monstrous heresy. *[Applause]* The signers of the Declaration of Independence never dreamed of the negro when they were writing that document. They referred to white men, to men of European birth and European descent, when they declared the equality of all men. I see a gentleman there in the crowd shaking his head. Let me remind him that when Thomas Jefferson wrote that document, he was the owner, and so continued until his death, of a large number of slaves. Did he intend to say in that Declaration that his negro slaves, which he held and treated as property, were created his equals by divine law, and that he was violating the law of God every day of his life by holding them as slaves? It must be borne in mind that when that Declaration was put forth, every one of the thirteen colonies were slaveholding colonies, and every man who signed that instrument represented a slaveholding constituency. Recollect, also, that no one of them emancipated his slaves, much less put them on an equality with himself, after he signed the Declaration. On the contrary, they all continued to hold their negroes as slaves during the Revolutionary War. Now, do you believe— are you willing to have it said—that every man who signed the Declaration of Independence declared the negro his equal, and then was hypocrite enough to continue to hold him as a slave, in violation of what he believed to be the divine law? *[Cries of "no"]* And yet when you say that the Declaration of Independence includes the negro, you charge the signers of it with hypocrisy.

I say to you, frankly, that in my opinion this government was made by our fathers on the white basis. It was made by the white men for the benefit of white men and their posterity forever and was intended to be administered by white men in all time to come. *[Cheers]* But while I hold that under our Constitution and political system the negro is not a citizen, cannot be a citizen, and ought not to be a citizen, it does not follow by any means that he should be a slave. On the contrary it does follow that the negro, as an inferior race, ought to possess every right, every privilege, every immunity which he can safely exercise consistent with the safety of the society in which he lives. *[Cheers]* Humanity requires, and Christianity commands, that you shall extend to every inferior being, and every dependent being, all the privileges, immunities and advantages which can be granted to them, consistent with the safety of society.

If you ask me the nature and extent of these privileges, I answer that that is a question which the people of each state must decide for themselves. Illinois has decided that question for herself. We have said that in this state the negro shall not be a slave, nor shall he be a citizen. Kentucky holds a different doctrine. New York holds one different from either, and Maine one different from all. Virginia, in her policy on this question, differs in many respects from the others, and so on, until there are° hardly two states whose policy is exactly alike in regard to the relation of the white man and the negro. Nor can you reconcile them and make them alike.[9] Each state must do as it pleases. Illinois had as much right to adopt the policy which we have on that subject as Kentucky had to adopt a different policy. The great principle of this government is that each state has the right to do as it pleases on all these questions, and no other state, or power on earth, has the right to interfere with us or complain of us merely because our system differs from theirs.

In the compromise measures of 1850, Mr. Clay declared that this great principle ought to exist in the territories as well as in the states, and I reasserted his doctrine in the Kansas and Nebraska bill in 1854. But Mr. Lincoln cannot be made to understand, and those who are determined to vote for him, no matter whether he is a pro-slavery man in the South and a negro equality advocate in the North, cannot be made to understand how it is that in a territory the people can do as they please on the slavery question under the Dred Scott decision. Let us see whether I cannot explain it to the satisfaction of all impartial men. Chief Justice Taney has said in his opinion in the Dred Scott case, that a negro slave, being property, stands on an equal footing with other property, and that the owner may carry them into United States territory the same as he does other property. Suppose any two of you, neighbors, should conclude to go to Kansas, one carrying $100,000 worth of negro slaves and the other $100,000 worth of mixed merchandise, including quantities of liquors. You both agree that under that decision you may carry your property to Kansas, but when you get it there, the merchant who is possessed of the liquors is met by the Maine Liquor Law, which prohibits the sale or use of his property, and the owner of the slaves is met by equally unfriendly legislation, which makes his property worthless after he gets there. What is the right to carry your property into the territory worth to either, when unfriendly legislation in the territory renders it worthless after you get it there?

---

9. Maine allowed suffrage rights to its male black citizens; New York allowed them to black holders of $250 worth of property. Kentucky and Virginia, as slave states, allowed few privileges to free blacks.

How can the owner of the slave be more fortunate?° The slaveholder, when he gets his slaves there, finds that there is no local law to protect him in holding them, no slave code, no police regulation maintaining and supporting him in his right, and he discovers at once that the absence of such friendly legislation excludes his property from the territory, just as irresistibly as if there was a positive constitutional prohibition excluding it. Thus you find it is with any kind of property in a territory; it depends for its protection on the local and municipal law. If the people of a territory want slavery, they make friendly legislation to introduce it, but if they do not want it, they withhold all protection from it, and then it cannot exist there.

Such was the view taken on the subject by different Southern men when the Nebraska bill passed. See the speech of Mr. Orr, of South Carolina, the present Speaker of the House of Representatives of Congress, made at that time, and there you will find this whole doctrine argued out at full length. Read the speeches of other Southern congressmen, senators and representatives, made in 1854, and you will find that they took the same view of the subject as Mr. Orr—that slavery could never be forced on a people who did not want it.[10] I hold that in this country there is no power, there should be no power° on the face of the globe, that can force any institution on an unwilling people. The great fundamental principle of our government is that the people of each state and each territory shall be left perfectly free to decide for themselves what shall be the nature and character of their institutions.

When this government was made, it was based on that principle. At the time of its formation, there were twelve slaveholding states and one free state in this Union.[11] Suppose this doctrine of Mr. Lincoln and the Republicans, of uniformity of the laws of all the states on the subject of slavery, had prevailed. Suppose Mr. Lincoln himself had been a member of the convention which framed the Constitution, and that he had risen in that august body, and addressing the Father of his Country, had said as he did at Springfield:[12] "a house divided against itself cannot stand, this government divided into free and slave states cannot permanently endure, that they must be all free or all slave, all the one thing or all the other." (I don't pretend to quote his exact language but I give his idea.)° What do you think would have been the result? [Cheers] Suppose he had made that convention

---

10. See speeches by Samuel Smith of Tennessee and James L. Orr in *Congressional Globe*, 34th Cong., 3rd Sess., Dec. 9, 1856, Dec. 11, 1856, 3:67, 103–4.

11. By the time of the Constitutional Convention in 1787, slavery had been abolished outright in Vermont, Massachusetts, and New Hampshire, and provisions had been made for its gradual extinction in Pennsylvania, Rhode Island, and Connecticut.

12. From AL's "House Divided" speech to the Illinois Republican state convention on June 16, 1858.

believe that doctrine and they had acted upon it. What do you think would have been the result? Do you believe that the one free state would have out-voted the twelve slaveholding states, and thus abolished slavery? *[Cheers]* On the contrary, would not the twelve slaveholding states have out-voted the one free state and, under his doctrine, have fastened slavery by an irrevocable constitutional provision upon every inch of the American Republic. Thus you see that the doctrine he now advocates, if proclaimed at the beginning of the government, would have established slavery everywhere throughout the American continent.

And are you willing, now that we have the majority section, to exercise a power which we never would have submitted to when we were in the minority? *[Applause]* If the Southern states had attempted to control our institutions, and make the states all slave when they had the power, I ask, would you have submitted to it? If you would not, are you willing, now that we have become the strongest, under the great principle of self-government that allows each state to do as it pleases, to attempt to control the Southern institutions? Then, my friends, I say to you that there is but one path of peace in this republic, and that is to administer this government as our fathers made it, divided into free and slave states, allowing each state to decide for itself whether it wants slavery or not. If Illinois will settle the slavery question for herself, mind her own business and let her neighbors alone, we will be at peace with Kentucky, and every other Southern state. If every other state in the Union will do the same, there will be peace between the North and the South, and in the whole Union.

I am told that my time has expired. *[Applause]*

LINCOLN'S REPLY

My fellow citizens: A very large portion of the speech which Judge Douglas has addressed to you has previously been delivered and put in print. *[Laughter]* I do not mean that for a hit upon the Judge at all. *[Laughter]* If I had not been interrupted, I was going to say that such an answer as I was able to make to a very large portion of it had already been more than once made and published. There has been an opportunity already° afforded to the public to see our respective views upon the topics discussed in a large portion of the speech which he has just delivered. I make these remarks for the purpose of excusing myself for not passing over the entire ground that the Judge has traversed. I however desire to take up some of the points that he has attended to, and ask your attention to them, and I shall follow him backwards upon some notes which I have taken, reversing the order by beginning where he concluded.

The Judge has alluded to the Declaration of Independence and insisted that negroes are not included in that Declaration, and that it is a slander upon the framers of that instrument to suppose that negroes were meant therein. And he asks you: Is it possible to believe that Mr. Jefferson, who penned the immortal paper, could have supposed himself applying the language of that instrument to the negro race, and yet have° held a portion of that race in slavery? Would he not at once have freed them? I only have to remark upon this part of the Judge's speech—and that, too, very briefly, for I shall not detain myself, or you, upon that point for any great length of time—that I believe the entire records of the world, from the date of the Declaration of Independence up to within three years ago, may be searched in vain for one single affirmation, from one single man, that the negro was not included in the Declaration of Independence. I think I may defy Judge Douglas to show that he ever said so, that Washington ever said so, that any president ever said so, that any member of Congress ever said so, or that any living man upon the whole earth ever said so, until the necessities of the present policy of the Democratic party, in regard to slavery, had to invent that affirmation. *[Applause]* And I will remind Judge Douglas and this audience, that while Mr. Jefferson was the owner of slaves, as undoubtedly he was, in speaking upon this very subject, he used the strong language that he trembled for his country when he remembered that God was just.[13] And I will offer the highest premium in my power to Judge Douglas if he will show that he, in all his life, ever uttered a sentiment at all akin to that of Jefferson. *[Applause, cheers]*

The next thing to which I will ask your attention is the Judge's comments upon the fact, as he assumes it to be, that we cannot call our public meetings as Republican meetings, and he instances Tazewell County as one of the places where the friends of Lincoln have called a public meeting and have not dared to name it a Republican meeting. He instances Monroe County as another where Judge Trumbull and Jehu Baker addressed the persons whom the Judge assumes to be the friends of Lincoln, calling them the "Free Democracy." I have the honor to inform Judge Douglas that he spoke in that very county of Tazewell last Saturday, and I was there on Tuesday last, and when he spoke there, he spoke under a call not venturing to use the word "Democrat." *[Cheers, laughter] [Addressing Douglas]* What do you think of this? *[Applause, laughter]*

So again, there is another thing to which I would ask the Judge's attention upon this subject. In the contest of 1856, his party delighted to call themselves together as the "National Democracy," but now, if there should be a notice put up anywhere for a meeting of the "National Democracy," Judge Douglas and his friends would not come. *[Laughter]* They would not suppose themselves invited.

---

13. See Thomas Jefferson, *Notes on the State of Virginia,* in *Writings* (New York: Library of America, 1984), 289.

[Laughter, cheers] They would understand that it was a call for those hateful post-masters whom he talks about.[14] *[Laughter, applause]*

Now a few words in regard to these extracts from speeches of mine, which Judge Douglas has read to you and which he supposes are in very great contrast to each other. Those speeches have been before the public for a considerable time, and if they have any inconsistency in them, if there is any conflict in them, the public have been able to detect it. When the Judge says, in speaking on this subject, that I make speeches of one sort for the people of the Northern end of the state, and of a different sort for the Southern people, he assumes that I do not understand that my speeches will be put in print and read North and South. I knew all the while that the speech that I made at Chicago, and the one I made at Jonesboro, and the one at Charleston, would all be put in print, and all the reading and intelligent men in the community would see them and know all about my opinions. And I have not supposed, and do not now suppose, that there is any conflict whatever between them. *[Cheers]*

But the Judge will have it that if we do not confess that there is a sort of inequality between the white and black races which justifies us in making them slaves, we must, then, insist that there is a degree of equality that requires us to make them our wives. *[Applause, cheers]* Now, I have all the while taken a broad distinction in regard to that matter, and that is all there is in these different speeches which he arrays here, and the entire reading of either of the speeches will show that that distinction was made. Perhaps by taking two parts of the same speech, he could have got up as much of a conflict as the one he has found. I have all the while maintained that insofar as it should be insisted that there was an equality between the white and black races that should produce a perfect social and political equality, it was an impossibility. This you have seen in my printed speeches, and with it I have said, that in their right to "life, liberty and the pursuit of happiness," as proclaimed in that old Declaration, the inferior races are our equals. *[Cheers]*

And these declarations I have constantly made in reference to the abstract moral question, to contemplate and consider when we are legislating about any new country which is not already cursed with the actual presence of the evil—slavery. I have never manifested any impatience with the necessities that spring from the actual presence of black people amongst us, and the actual existence of slavery amongst us where it does already exist. But I have insisted that, in legislating for new countries, where it does not exist, there is no just rule other than that of moral and abstract right! With reference to those new countries, those

---

14. See "National Democrats" in the glossary, p. 328.

maxims as to the right of a people to "life, liberty and the pursuit of happiness," were the just rules to be constantly referred to.

There is no misunderstanding this, except by men interested to misunderstand it. *[Applause]* I take it that I have to address an intelligent and reading community, who will peruse what I say, weigh it, and then judge whether I advance improper or unsound views, or whether I advance hypocritical, and deceptive, and contrary views in different portions of the country. I believe myself to be guilty of no such thing as the latter, though, of course, I cannot claim that I am entirely free from all error in the opinions I advance.

The Judge has also detained us a while in regard to the distinction between his party and our party. His he assumes to be a national party, ours, a sectional one. He does this in asking the question whether this country has any interest in the maintenance of the Republican party. He assumes that our party is altogether sectional—that the party to which he adheres is national. And the argument is that no party can be a rightful party, can be based upon rightful principles, unless it can announce its principles everywhere. Now, it is the first time, I believe, that I have ever heard it announced as being true, that a man could always announce rightful principles everywhere!° I presume that Judge Douglas could not go into Russia and announce the doctrine of our national democracy. He could not denounce the doctrine of kings, and emperors, and monarchies, in Russia. And it may be true of this country that in some places we may not be able to proclaim a doctrine as clearly true as the truth of democracy, because there is a section so directly opposed to it that they will not tolerate us in doing so. Is it the true test of the soundness of a doctrine that in some places people won't let you proclaim it? Is that the way to test the truth of any doctrine? Why, I understood that at one time the people of Chicago would not let Judge Douglas preach a certain favorite doctrine of his. *[Laughter, cheers]* I commend to his consideration the question, whether he takes that as a test of the unsoundness of what he wanted to preach.[15] *[Cheers]*

There is another thing to which I wish to ask attention for a little while on this occasion. What has always been the evidence brought forward to prove that the Republican party is a sectional party? The main one was that in the Southern portion of the Union, the people did not let the Republicans proclaim their doctrine amongst them. That has been the main evidence brought forward, that they had no supporters, or substantially none, in the slave states. The South have not taken hold of our principles as we announce them, nor does Judge Douglas now grapple with those principles. We have a Republican state platform, laid down

---

15. When defending the Kansas-Nebraska Act in a speech in Chicago on Sept. 1, 1854, SAD was shouted down by an angry crowd.

in Springfield in June last, stating our position all the way through the questions before the country. We are now far advanced in this canvass. Judge Douglas and I have made perhaps forty speeches apiece, and we have now for the fifth time met face to face in debate, and up to this day I have not found either Judge Douglas or any friend of his taking hold of the Republican platform or laying his finger upon anything in it that is wrong. *[Cheers]* I ask you all to recollect that. Judge Douglas turns away from the platform of principles to the fact that he can find people somewhere who will not allow us to announce those principles. *[Applause]* If he had great confidence that our principles were wrong, he would take hold of them and demonstrate them to be wrong. But he does not do so. The only evidence he has of their being wrong is in the fact that there are people who won't allow us to preach them. I ask again, is that the way to test the soundness of a doctrine?

I ask his attention also to the fact that by the rule of nationality, he is himself fast becoming sectional. *[Cheers, laughter]* I ask his attention to the fact that his speeches would not go as current now south of the Ohio River as they have formerly gone there. *[Cheers]* I ask his attention to the fact that he felicitates himself today that all the Democrats of the free states are agreeing with him, *[Applause]* while he omits to tell us that the Democrats of any slave state agree with him. If he has not thought of this, I commend to his consideration the evidence in his own declarations, on this day, of his becoming sectional too. *[Cheers]* I see it rapidly approaching. Whatever may be the result of this ephemeral contest between Judge Douglas and myself, I see the day rapidly approaching when his pill of sectionalism, which he has been thrusting down the throats of Republicans for years past, will be crowded down his own throat. *[Applause]*

Now in regard to what Judge Douglas said in the beginning of his speech about the Compromise of 1850 containing the principle of the Nebraska bill. Although I have often presented my views upon that subject, yet as I have not done so in this canvass, I will, if you please, detain you a little with them. I have always maintained, so far as I was able, that there was nothing of the principle of the Nebraska bill in the Compromise of 1850 at all, nothing whatever. Where can you find the principle of the Nebraska bill in that Compromise? If anywhere, in the two pieces of the compromise organizing the territories of New Mexico and Utah. It was expressly provided in these two acts that, when they came to be admitted into the Union, they should be admitted with or without slavery, as they should choose, by their own constitutions. Nothing was said in either of those acts as to what was to be done in relation to slavery during the territorial existence of those territories, while Henry Clay constantly made the declaration— Judge Douglas recognizing him as a leader—that, in his opinion, the old Mexican laws would control that question during the territorial existence, and that these old Mexican laws excluded slavery. How can that be used as a principle for declaring that during the territorial existence, as well as at the time of framing the constitution, the people, if you please, might have slaves if they wanted them? I am not discussing the question whether it is right or wrong, but how are the New Mexican and Utah laws patterns for the Nebraska bill? I maintain that the organization of Utah and New Mexico *did not* establish a general principle at all. It had no feature of establishing a general principle.

The acts to which I have referred were a part of a general system of compromises. They did not lay down what was proposed as a regular policy for the territories, only an agreement in this particular case to do in that way, because other things were done that were to be a compensation for it. They were allowed to come in in that shape, because in another way it was paid for, considering that as a part of that system of measures called the Compromise of 1850, which finally included half a dozen acts. It included the admission of California as a free state, which was kept out of the Union for half a year because it had formed a free constitution. It included the settlement of the boundary of Texas, which had been undefined before, which was in itself a slavery question, for, if you pushed the line farther west, you made Texas larger, and made more slave territory, while, if you drew the line towards the east, you narrowed the boundary and diminished the domain of slavery, and by so much increased free territory. It included the abolition of the slave trade in the District of Columbia. It included the passage of a new Fugitive Slave Law.

All these things were put together, and though passed in separate acts, were nevertheless in legislation, as the speeches at the time will show, made to depend upon each other. Each got votes, with the understanding that the other measures were to pass, and by this system of compromise, in that series of measures, those two bills—the New Mexico and Utah bills—were passed. And I say for that reason they could not be taken as models, framed upon their own intrinsic principle, for all future territories. And I have the evidence of this in the fact that Judge Douglas, a year afterwards, or more than a year afterwards, perhaps, when he first introduced bills for the purpose of framing new territories, did not attempt to follow these bills of New Mexico and Utah. And even when he introduced this Nebraska bill, I think you will discover that he did not exactly follow them. But I do not wish to dwell at great length upon this branch of the discussion. My own opinion is that a thorough investigation will show most plainly that the New Mexico and Utah bills were part of a system of compromise, and not designed as patterns for future territorial legislation, and that this Nebraska bill did not follow them as a pattern at all.[16]

---

16. It appears that not until the introduction of the Kansas-Nebraska bill, in January 1854, was the Compromise of 1850 discussed as affording a precedent for subsequent territorial

The Judge tells, in proceeding, that he is opposed to making any odious distinctions between free and slave states. I am altogether unaware that the Republicans are in favor of making any odious distinctions between the free and slave states. But there still is a difference, I think, between Judge Douglas and the Republicans in this.° I suppose that the real difference between Judge Douglas and his friends, and the Republicans on the contrary, is that the Judge is not in favor of making any difference between slavery and liberty, that he is in favor of eradicating, of pressing out of view, the question of preference in this country for free over slave institutions. And consequently every sentiment he utters discards the idea that there is any wrong in slavery. Everything that emanates from him or his coadjutors in their course of policy carefully excludes the thought that there is anything wrong in slavery. All their arguments, if you will consider them, will be seen to exclude the thought that there is anything whatever wrong in slavery. If you will take the Judge's speeches, and select the short and pointed sentences expressed by him—as his declaration that he "don't care whether slavery is voted up or down"—you will see at once that this is perfectly logical, if you do not admit that slavery is wrong. If you do admit that it is wrong, Judge Douglas cannot logically say that he don't care whether a wrong is voted up or down. Judge Douglas declares that if any community wants slavery, they have a right to have it. He can say that logically, if he says that there is no wrong in slavery. But if you admit that there is a wrong in it, he cannot logically say that anybody has a right to do wrong. He insists that, upon the score of equality, the owners of slaves and owners of property—of horses and every other sort of property—should be alike and hold them alike in a new territory. That is perfectly logical if the two species of property are alike and are equally founded in right.

But if you admit that one of them is wrong, you cannot institute any equality between right and wrong. And from this difference of sentiment—the belief on the part of one that the institution is wrong, and a policy springing from that belief which looks to the arrest of the enlargement of that wrong; and this other sentiment, that it is no wrong, and a policy springing° from that sentiment which will tolerate no idea of preventing that wrong from growing larger, and looks to there never being an end of it through all the existence of things—arises the real difference between Judge Douglas and his friends, on the one hand, and the Republicans on the other.

Now, I confess myself as belonging to that class in the country who contemplate slavery as a moral, social, and political evil, having due regard for its actual existence amongst us and the difficulties of getting rid of it in any satisfactory way,

---

organization. Robert W. Johannsen, *Stephen A. Douglas* (Urbana: University of Illinois Press, 1997), 400, 403–5.

and to all the constitutional obligations which have been thrown about it, but, nevertheless, desire a policy that looks to the prevention of it as a wrong, and looks hopefully to the time when, as a wrong, it may come to an end. *[Applause]*

Judge Douglas has again, for, I believe, the fifth time, if not the seventh, in my presence, reiterated his charge of a conspiracy or combination between the National Democrats[17] and Republicans. What evidence Judge Douglas has upon this subject I know not, inasmuch as he never favors us with any. *[Laughter, cheers]* I have said upon a former occasion, and I do not choose to suppress it now, that I have no objection to the division in the Judge's party. *[Cheers]* He got it up himself. It was all his and their work. He had, I think, a great deal more to do with the steps that led to the Lecompton Constitution than Mr. Buchanan had, *[Applause]* though at last, when they reached it, they quarreled over it, and their friends divided upon it. *[Applause]* I am very free to confess to Judge Douglas that I have no objection to the division. *[Applause, laughter]* But I defy the Judge to show any evidence that I have in any way promoted that division, unless he insists on being a witness himself in merely saying so. *[Laughter]* I can give all fair friends of Judge Douglas here to understand exactly the view that Republicans take in regard to that division. Don't you remember how two years ago the opponents of the Democratic party were divided between Fremont and Fillmore?[18] I guess you do. *[Cheers]* Any Democrat who remembers that division will remember also that he was at the time very glad of it. *[Laughter]* And then he will be able to see all there is between the National Democrats and the Republicans. What we now think of the two divisions of Democrats, you then thought of the Fremont and Fillmore divisions. *[Cheers]* That is all there is of it.

We are glad of the division,° but if the Judge continues to put forward the declaration that there is an unholy and unnatural alliance between the Republicans and the National Democrats, I now want to enter my protest against receiving him as an entirely competent witness upon that subject. *[Cheers]* I want to call to the Judge's attention an attack he made upon me in the first one of these debates, at Ottawa, on the 21st of August. In order to fix extreme abolitionism upon me, Judge Douglas read a set of resolutions which he declared had been passed by a Republican state convention in October, 1854 at Springfield, Illinois, and he declared I had taken part in that convention. It turned out that, although a few men calling themselves an anti-Nebraska state convention had sat at Springfield about

---

17. The National Democrats were the small Democratic faction that opposed SAD's position on the Lecompton Constitution and the English bill. See glossary, p. 328.

18. The three major presidential contestants in 1856 were James Buchanan (Democrat), John C. Fremont (Republican), and former President Millard Fillmore (of the nativist American Party). The "division" AL speaks of was between the Republicans and the Americans.

that time, yet neither did I take any part in it, nor did it pass the resolutions or any such resolutions as Judge Douglas read. *[Applause]* So apparent had it become that the resolutions which he read had not been passed at Springfield at all, nor by a state convention in which I had taken part, that six° days afterwards, at Freeport, Judge Douglas gave it up, but° declared that he had been misled by Charles H. Lanphier, editor of the *State Register,* and Thomas L. Harris, member of Congress in that district, and he promised in that speech that when he went to Springfield, he would investigate the matter. Since then Judge Douglas has been to Springfield, and I presume has made the investigation. But a month has passed since he has been there, and so far as I know, he has made no report of the result of his investigation. *[Applause]* I have waited, as I think, sufficient time for the report of that investigation, and I have some curiosity to see and hear it. *[Applause]*

A fraud, an absolute forgery was committed, and the perpetration of it was traced to the three: Lanphier, Harris, and Douglas. *[Applause, laughter]* Whether it can be narrowed in any way so as to exonerate any one of them is what Judge Douglas's report would probably show. *[Applause, laughter]* It is true that the set of resolutions read by Judge Douglas were published in the *Illinois State Register* on the 16th October, 1854, as being the resolutions of an anti-Nebraska convention, which had sat in that same month of October at Springfield. But it is also true that the publication in the *Register* was a forgery then *[Cheers],* and the question is still behind[19]—which of the three, if not all of them, committed that forgery? *[Applause]*

The idea that it was done by mistake is absurd. The article in the *Illinois State Register* contains part of the real proceedings of that Springfield convention, showing that the writer of the article had the real proceedings before him, and purposely threw out the genuine resolutions passed by the convention and fraudulently substituted the others. Lanphier then, as now, was the editor of the *Register,* so that there seems to be but little room for his escape. But then it is to be borne in mind that Lanphier had less interest in the object of that forgery than either of the other two. *[Cheers]* The main object of that forgery at that time was to beat Yates and elect Harris to Congress, and that object was known to be exceedingly dear to Judge Douglas at that time. *[Laughter]* Harris and Douglas were both in Springfield when the convention was in session, and although they both left before the fraud appeared in the *Register,* subsequent events show that they have both had their eyes fixed upon that convention.

The fraud having been apparently successful upon the occasion, both Harris and Douglas have more than once since then been attempting to put it to new

---

19. "behind": e.g., "in arrears" or "unanswered."

uses. As the fisherman's wife, whose drowned husband was brought home with his body full of eels,° said when she was asked what was to be done with him? *"Take the eels out and set him again."* [Laughter] So Harris and Douglas have shown a disposition to take the eels out of that stale fraud by which they gained Harris's election, and set the fraud again more than once. [Cheers, laughter] On the 9th of July, 1856, Douglas attempted a repetition of it upon Trumbull on the floor of the Senate of the United States, as will appear from the appendix of the *Congressional Globe* of that date.[20] On the 9th of August, Harris attempted it again upon Norton in the House of Representatives, as will appear by the same documents, the appendix of the *Congressional Globe* of that date.[21] On the 21st of August last,° all three—Lanphier, Douglas and Harris—re-attempted it upon me at Ottawa. [Applause] It has been clung to and played out again and again as an exceedingly high trump by this blessed trio. [Laughter, applause]

And now that it has been discovered publicly to be a fraud, we find that Judge Douglas manifests no surprise at it at all. [Laughter, cheers] He makes no complaint of Lanphier, who must have known it to be a fraud from the beginning. He,° Lanphier and Harris are just as cozy° now, and just as active in the concoction of new schemes, as they were before the general discovery of this fraud. Now all this is very natural if they are all alike guilty in that fraud, [Laughter, cheers] and it is very unnatural if any one of them is innocent. [Laughter, cheers] Lanphier perhaps insists that the rule of honor among thieves does not quite require him to take all upon himself, [Laughter] and consequently my friend Judge Douglas finds it difficult to make a satisfactory report upon his investigation. [Laughter, applause] But meanwhile the three are agreed that each is *"a most honorable man."* [Cheers, laughter]

Judge Douglas requires an indorsement of his truth and honor by a re-election to the United States Senate, and he makes and repeats° against me and against Judge Trumbull, day after day, charges which we know to be utterly untrue, without for a moment seeming to think that this one unexplained fraud, which he promised to investigate, will be the least drawback to his claim to belief. Harris ditto. He asks a re-election to the lower house of Congress without seeming to remember at all that he is involved in this dishonorable fraud! The *Illinois State Register,* edited by Lanphier, then, as now, the central organ of both Harris and Douglas, continues to din the public ear with this assertion without seeming to suspect that these assertions are at all lacking in title to belief.

---

20. AL refers to a debate between SAD and Trumbull, which is reported in *Congressional Globe, Appendix,* 34th Cong., 1st Sess., July 9, 1856, 860–61.

21. Such an exchange between Harris and Jesse O. Norton took place on Aug. 9, 1856. See ibid., Aug. 9, 1856, 1274.

After all, the question still recurs upon us: how did that fraud originally get into the *State Register?* Lanphier then, as now, was the editor of that paper. Lanphier knows. Lanphier cannot be ignorant of how and by whom it was originally concocted. Can he be induced to tell, or if he has told, can Judge Douglas be induced to tell how it originally was concocted? It may be true that Lanphier insists that the two men for whose benefit it was originally devised shall at least bear their share of it! How that is, I do not know, and while it remains unexplained after the express promise of Judge Douglas to investigate it,° I hope to be pardoned if I insist that the mere fact of Judge Douglas making charges against Trumbull and myself is not quite sufficient evidence to establish them! *[Cheers]*

While we were at Freeport, in one of these joint discussions, I answered certain interrogatories which Judge Douglas had propounded to me, and there in turn propounded some to him, which he, in a sort of way, answered. The third one of these interrogatories I have with me and wish now to make some comments upon it. It was in these words: "If the Supreme Court of the United States shall decide that states can not exclude slavery from their limits, are you in favor of acquiescing in, adopting, and following such decision as a rule of political action?"° To this interrogatory Judge Douglas made no answer in any just sense of the word. He contented himself with sneering at the thought that it was possible for the Supreme Court ever to make such a decision. He sneered at me for propounding the interrogatory. I had not propounded it without some reflection, and I wish now to address to this audience some remarks upon it.

In the second clause of the sixth article, I believe it is, of the Constitution of the United States, we find the following language: "This Constitution, and the laws of the United States which shall be made in pursuance thereof; and all treaties made, or° which shall be made, under the authority of the United States, shall be the supreme law of the land; and the judges in every State shall be bound thereby, anything in the Constitution or laws of any state to the contrary notwithstanding."° The essence of the Dred Scott case is compressed° into the sentence which I will now read: "Now, as we have already said in an earlier part of this opinion, upon a different point, the right of property in a slave is distinctly and expressly affirmed in the Constitution."[22] I repeat it, *"The right of property in a slave is distinctly and expressly affirmed in the Constitution."* What is *affirmed*° in the Constitution? Made firm in the Constitution, so made that it cannot be separated from the Constitution without breaking the Constitution, durable as the Constitution, and part of the Constitution. Now, remembering the provision of the Constitution which I have read affirming that that instrument is the supreme law of the land, that the judges of every state shall be bound by it, any

---

22. *Scott v. Sandford,* 60 U.S., 451–52.

law or constitution of any state to the contrary notwithstanding, that the right of property in a slave is affirmed in that Constitution, is made firm in it,° and cannot be separated from it without breaking it, durable as the instrument, part of the instrument, what follows as a short and even syllogistic argument from it? I think it follows, and I submit to the consideration of men capable of arguing, whether, as I state it in syllogistic form, the argument has any fault in it:

Nothing in the constitution or laws of any state can destroy a right distinctly and expressly affirmed in the Constitution of the United States.

The right of property in a slave is distinctly and expressly affirmed in the Constitution of The United States.

Therefore, nothing in the constitution or laws of any state can destroy the right of property in a slave.

I believe that no fault can be pointed out in that argument. Assuming the truth of the premises, the conclusion, so far as I have capacity at all to understand it, follows inevitably.

There is a fault in it, as I think, but the fault is not in the reasoning, but the fault is the falsehood in fact of one of the premises.° I believe that the right of property in a slave *is not* distinctly and expressly affirmed in the Constitution, and Judge Douglas thinks it *is*. I believe that the Supreme Court and the advocates of that decision may search in vain for the place in the Constitution where the right of property in a slave is distinctly and expressly affirmed.° I say, therefore, that I think one of the premises is not true in fact. But it is true with Judge Douglas. It is true with the Supreme Court who pronounced it. They are estopped from denying it, and being estopped from denying it, the conclusion follows that the Constitution of the United States, being the supreme law, no constitution or law of a state° can interfere with it.[23] It being affirmed in the decision that the right of property in a slave is distinctly and expressly affirmed in the Constitution, the conclusion inevitably follows that no state law or constitution can destroy that right. I then say to Judge Douglas and to all others that I think it will take a better answer than a sneer to show that those who have said that the right of property in a slave is distinctly and expressly affirmed in the Constitution are not prepared to show that no constitution or law can destroy that right. I say I believe it will take a far better argument than a mere sneer to show to the minds of intelligent men that whoever has so said is not prepared, whenever public sentiment is so far advanced as to justify it, to say the other.

This is but an opinion, and the opinion of one very humble man. But it is my opinion that the Dred Scott decision, as it is, never would have been made in its

---

23. In law, to be estopped is to be prevented from asserting a fact or claim that is inconsistent with a position previously taken.

present form if the party that made it had not been sustained previously by the elections. My own opinion is that the new Dred Scott decision, deciding against the right of the people of the states to exclude slavery, will never be made, if that party is not sustained by the elections. [Cheers] I believe, further, that it is just as sure to be made as tomorrow is to come, if that party shall be sustained.[24] [Cheers]

I have said, upon a former occasion, and I repeat it now, that the course of argument that Judge Douglas makes use of upon this subject—I charge not his motives in this—but the course of argument that he makes day by day° is preparing the public mind for the new Dred Scott decision. I have asked him again to point out to me the reasons for his firm adherence to the Dred Scott decision as it is. I have turned his attention to the fact that General Jackson differed with him in regard to the political obligation of a Supreme Court decision. I have asked his attention to the fact that Jefferson differed with him in regard to the political obligation of a Supreme Court decision. Jefferson said, that "judges are as honest as other men, and not more so."[25] And he said, substantially, that whenever a free people should give up in absolute submission to any department of government, retaining for themselves no appeal from it, their liberties were gone. I have asked his attention to the fact that the Cincinnati platform, upon which he says he stands, disregards a time-honored decision of the Supreme Court, in denying the power of Congress to establish a national bank. I have asked his attention to the fact that he himself was one of the most active instruments at one time in breaking° down the Supreme Court of the State of Illinois, because it had made a decision distasteful to him, a struggle ending in the remarkable circumstance of his sitting down as one of the new judges who were to overslaugh that decision, [Applause] getting his title of Judge in that very way. [Applause, laughter] So

24. AL's discussion here suggests the extent to which the finality of Supreme Court decisions was still not settled doctrine by 1858. In *McCulloch v. Maryland* (1819) the Supreme Court had upheld the power of Congress under the Constitution to charter the Bank of the United States, but in the message accompanying his veto of the bill to recharter that institution in 1832, President Jackson wrote that he believed that the bank was unconstitutional, and he denied that "the opinion of the judges" had authority over Congress or the president. That position, that the national bank was unconstitutional, remained the Democratic position in that party's Cincinnati platform in 1856. It is true that the action involved in the *McCulloch* case (the chartering of a bank) was voluntary, as opposed to that in the *Dred Scott* decision, which required that slaveholders have access to the territories, as SAD would suggest below in his claim that the two cases were not parallel (p. 269). Yet AL's point, that Supreme Court decisions were not untouchable, retained its rhetorical force. See David Zarefsky, *Lincoln, Douglas and Slavery: In the Crucible of Public Debate* (Chicago: University of Chicago Press, 1990), 114.

25. Thomas Jefferson to William Charles Jarvis, Sept. 28, 1820, in Paul L. Ford, ed., *The Works of Thomas Jefferson*, 12 vols. (New York: Putnam's, 1905), 12:162–63.

far in this controversy I can get no answer at all from Judge Douglas upon these subjects. Not one can I get from him, except that he swells himself up and says, "All of us who stand by the decision of the Supreme Court are the friends of the Constitution; all you fellows that dare question it in any way, are the enemies of the Constitution." *[Laughter, cheers]*

Now, in this very devoted adherence to this decision, in opposition to all the great political leaders whom he has recognized as leaders, in opposition to his former self and history, there is something very marked. And the manner in which he adheres to it—not as being right upon the merits, as he conceives, because he did not discuss that at all, but as being absolutely obligatory upon every one simply because of the source from whence it comes, as that which no man can gainsay, whatever it may be—this is another marked feature of his adherence to that decision. It marks it in this respect, that it commits him to the next decision, whenever it comes, as being as obligatory as this one. Since he does not investigate it, and won't inquire whether this opinion is right or wrong, so he takes the next one without inquiring whether it is right or wrong. *[Applause]* He teaches men this doctrine, and in so doing prepares the public mind to take the next decision when it comes, without any inquiry. In this I think I argue fairly, without questioning motives at all, that Judge Douglas is most ingeniously and powerfully preparing the public mind to take that decision when it comes.

And not only so, but he is doing it in various other ways. In these general maxims about liberty, in his assertions that he don't care whether slavery is voted up or voted down, that whoever wants slavery has a right to have it, that upon principles of equality it should be allowed to go everywhere, that there is no inconsistency between free and slave institutions. In this he is also preparing, whether purposely or not, the way for making the institution of slavery national! *[Cheers]* I repeat again, for I wish no misunderstanding, that I do not charge that he means it so. But I call upon your minds to inquire: if you were going to get the best instrument you could, and then set it to work in the most ingenious way, to prepare the public mind for this movement, operating in the free states where there is now an abhorrence of the institution of slavery, could you find an instrument so capable of doing it as Judge Douglas? Or one employed in so apt a way to do it? *[Cheers]*

I have said once before, and I will repeat it now, that Mr. Clay, when he was once answering an objection to the Colonization Society, that it had a tendency to the ultimate emancipation of the slaves, said that those who would repress all tendencies to liberty and ultimate emancipation must do more than put down the benevolent efforts of the Colonization Society. They must go back to the era of our liberty and independence, and muzzle the cannon that thunders its annual joyous return; they must blow° out the moral lights around us; they must penetrate the human soul, and eradicate the light of reason and the love of liberty!° And I do think, I repeat, though I said it on a former occasion,[26] that Judge Douglas, and whoever like him teaches that the negro has no share, humble though it may be, in the Declaration of Independence, is going back to the era of our liberty and independence, and, so far as in him lies, muzzling the cannon that thunders its annual joyous return; that he is blowing° out the moral lights around us, when he contends that whoever wants slaves has a right to hold them; that he is penetrating, so far as lies in his power, the human soul, and eradicating the light of reason and the love of liberty, when he is in every possible way preparing the public mind, by his vast influence, for making the institution of slavery perpetual and national. *[Applause, cheers]*

There is, my friends, only one other point to which I will call your attention for the remaining time that I have left me, and perhaps I shall not occupy the entire time that I have, as that one point may not take me clear through it. Among the interrogatories that Judge Douglas propounded to me at Freeport, there was one in about this language: "Are you opposed to the acquisition of any further territory to the United States, unless slavery shall first be prohibited therein?"° I answered as I thought, in this way, that I am not generally opposed to the acquisition of additional territory, and that I would support a proposition for the acquisition of additional territory, according as my supporting it was or was not calculated to aggravate this slavery question amongst us. I then proposed to Judge Douglas another interrogatory, which was correlative to that: "Are you in favor of acquiring additional territory in disregard of how it may affect us upon the slavery question?"° Judge Douglas answered, that is, in his own way he answered it. *[Laughter]* I believe that, although he took a good many words to answer it, it was a little more fully answered than any other. The substance of his answer was that this country would continue to expand, that it would need additional territory, that it was as absurd to suppose that we could continue upon our present territory, enlarging in population as we are, as it would be to hoop a boy twelve years of age, and expect him to grow to man's size without bursting the hoops. *[Laughter]* I believe it was something like that. Consequently he was in favor of the acquisition of further territory, as fast as we might need it, in disregard of how it might affect the slavery question. I do not say this as giving his exact language, but he said so substantially, and he would leave the question of slavery, where the territory was acquired, to be settled by the people of the acquired territory.

Voice: That's the doctrine.

Lincoln: Maybe it is. Let us consider that for a while. This will probably, in the run of things, become one of the concrete manifestations of this slavery ques-

---

26. See the Ottawa debate, note 38, p. 34.

tion. If Judge Douglas's policy upon this question succeeds and gets fairly settled down until all opposition is crushed out, the next thing will be a grab for the territory of poor Mexico, an invasion of the rich lands of South America, then the adjoining islands will follow, each one of which promises additional slave fields. And this question is to be left to the people of those countries for settlement. When we shall get Mexico, I don't know whether the Judge will be in favor of the Mexican people that we get with it settling that question for themselves and all others, because we know the Judge has a great horror for mongrels *[Laughter]*, and I understand that the people of Mexico are most decidedly a race of mongrels. *[Laughter]* I understand that there is not more than one person there out of eight who is pure white, and I suppose from the Judge's previous declaration, that when we get Mexico or any considerable portion of it, that he will be in favor of these mongrels settling the question, which would bring him somewhat into collision with his horror of an inferior race.

It is to be remembered, though, that this power of acquiring additional territory is a power confided to the President and Senate of the United States. It is a power not under the control of the representatives of the people any further than they, the President and the Senate, can be considered the representatives of the people. Let me illustrate that by a case we have in our history. When we acquired the territory from Mexico in the Mexican War, the House of Representatives, composed of the immediate representatives of the people, all the time insisted that the territory thus to be acquired should be brought in upon condition that slavery should be forever prohibited therein, upon the terms and the language that slavery had been prohibited from coming into this country. That was insisted upon constantly and never failed to call forth an assurance that any territory thus acquired should have that prohibition in it, so far as the House of Representatives was concerned.[27] But at last the President and Senate acquired the territory without asking the House of Representatives anything about it, and took it without that prohibition. They have the power of acquiring territory without the immediate representatives of the people being called upon to say anything about it, and thus furnishing a very apt and powerful means of bringing new territory into the Union, and when it is once brought into the country, involving us anew in this slavery agitation.

It is, therefore, as I think, a very important question for the consideration of the American people, whether the policy of bringing in additional territory without considering at all how it will operate upon the safety of the Union, in reference to this one great disturbing element in our national polities, shall be adopted as the policy of the country. You will bear in mind that it is to be acquired, according

---

27. AL alludes to the Wilmot Proviso (see glossary, pp. 333–34).

to the Judge's view, as fast as it is needed, and the indefinite part of this proposition is that we have only Judge Douglas and his class of men to decide how fast it is needed. We have no clear and certain way of determining or demonstrating how fast territory is needed by the necessities of the country. Whoever wants to go out filibustering,[28] then, thinks that more territory is needed. Whoever wants wider slave fields feels sure that some additional territory is needed as slave territory. Then it is as easy to show the necessity of additional slave territory as it is to assert anything that is incapable of absolute demonstration. Whatever motive a man or a set of men may have for making annexation of property or territory, it is very easy to assert, but much less easy to disprove, that it is necessary for the wants of the country.

And now it only remains for me to say that I think it is a very grave question for the people of this Union to consider whether, in view of the fact that this slavery question has been the only one that has ever endangered our republican institutions, the only one that has ever threatened or menaced a dissolution of the Union, that has ever disturbed us in such a way as to make us fear for the perpetuity of our liberty, in view of these facts, I think it is an exceedingly interesting and important question for this people to consider, whether we shall engage in the policy of acquiring additional territory, disregarding altogether from our consideration, while obtaining new territory, the question how it may affect us in regard to this, the only endangering element to our liberties and national greatness. The Judge's view has been expressed. I, in my answer to his question, have expressed mine. I think it will become an important and practical question. Our views are before the public. I am willing and anxious that they should consider them fully, that they should turn it about and consider the importance of the question, and arrive at a just conclusion as to whether it is or is not wise in the people of this Union, in the acquisition of new territory, to consider whether it will add to the disturbance that is existing amongst us, whether it will add to the one only danger that has ever threatened the perpetuity of the Union or our own liberties. I think it is extremely important that they shall decide, and rightly decide, that question before entering upon that policy.

And now, my friends, having said the little I wish to say upon this head, whether I have occupied the whole of the remnant of my time or not, I believe I could not enter upon any new topic so as to treat it fully without transcending my time, which I would not for a moment think of doing. I give way to Judge Douglas.

---

28. "filibustering": carrying on unauthorized military ventures in a foreign country. In the 1850s, such activity by Americans in Mexico, Central America, and Cuba was especially conspicuous.

DOUGLAS'S REJOINDER

Gentlemen, the highest compliment you can pay me during the brief half hour that I have to conclude is by observing a strict silence. I desire to be heard rather than to be applauded.

The first criticism that Mr. Lincoln makes on my speech was that it was in substance what I have said everywhere else in the state where I have addressed the people. I wish I could say the same of his speeches. ° [Cheers, laughter] Why, the reason I complain of him is because he makes one speech North and another South, because he has one set of sentiments for the abolition counties and another set for the counties opposed to abolitionism. My point of complaint against him is that I cannot induce him to hold up the same standard, to carry the same flag in all parts of the state. He does not pretend, and no other man will, that I have one set of principles for Galesburg and another for Charleston. He does not pretend that I hold to one doctrine in Chicago and to an opposite one in Jonesboro. I have proved that he has a different set of principles for each of these localities. [Cries of opposition] Silence, if you please. ° All I asked of him was that he should deliver the speech that he has made here today in Coles County instead of in old Knox. It would have settled the question between us in that doubtful county, if the speech delivered here had been made there. ° Here I understand him to reaffirm the doctrine of negro equality, and to assert that, by the Declaration of Independence, the negro is declared equal to the white man. He tells you today that the negro was included in the Declaration of Independence when it asserted that all men were created equal.

Voice: We believe it.

Douglas: You believe it. ° Very well. [Other voices] Gentlemen, I ask you to remember that Mr. Lincoln was listened to respectfully, and I have the right to insist that I shall not be interrupted during my reply.

Lincoln: I hope that silence will be preserved.

Douglas: Mr. Lincoln asserts today, as he did at Chicago, that the negro was included in that clause of the Declaration of Independence which says all men were created equal and endowed by the Creator with certain inalienable rights, among which are life, liberty and the pursuit of happiness. If the negro was made his equal and mine, if that equality was established by divine law, and was the negro's inalienable right, how came he to say at Charleston to the Kentuckians residing in that section of our state that the negro was physically inferior to the white man, belonged to an inferior race, and he was for keeping him always in that inferior condition? I wish you to bear these things in mind. At Charleston he said that the negro belonged to an inferior race, and that he was for keeping him in that inferior condition. There he gave the people to understand that there was no moral question involved, because the inferiority being established, it was only a question of degree and not a question of right. Here today, instead of making it a question of degree, he makes it a moral question, says that it is a great crime to hold the negro in that inferior condition.

Voice: He's right.

Douglas: Is he right now or was he right in Charleston?

Voice: Both.

Douglas: He is right then, sir, in your estimation, not because he is consistent, but because he can trim his principles any way in any section, so as to secure votes. All I desire of him is that he will declare the same principles in the South that he does in the North, and wherever the Constitution rules. °

But did you notice how he answered my position that a man should hold the same doctrines throughout the length and breadth of this republic? He said, "Would Judge Douglas go to Russia and proclaim the same principles he does here?" I would remind him that Russia is not under the American Constitution. *[Cheers, laughter]* If Russia was a part of the American republic, under our federal Constitution, and I was sworn to support that Constitution, I would maintain the same doctrine in Russia that I do in Illinois. *[Cheers, applause]* The slaveholding states are governed by the same federal Constitution as ourselves, and hence, a man's principles, in order to be in harmony with the Constitution, must be the same in the South as they are in the North, the same in the free states as they are in the slave states. Whenever a man advocates one set of principles in one section, and another set in another section, his opinions are in violation of the spirit of the Constitution which he has sworn to support. *[Cheers]* When Mr. Lincoln went to Congress in 1847, and laying his hand upon the holy evangelists, made a solemn vow in the presence of high heaven that he would be faithful to the Constitution, what did he mean? The Constitution as he expounds it in Galesburg, or the Constitution as he expounds it in Charleston. *[Cheers, laughter]*

Mr. Lincoln has devoted considerable time to the circumstance that, at Ottawa, I read a series of resolutions as having been adopted at Springfield, in this state, on the 4th or 5th of October, 1854, which happened not to have been adopted there. He has used hard names, has dared to talk about fraud, *[Laughter]* about forgery, and has insinuated that there was a conspiracy between Mr. Lanphier, Mr. Harris, and myself to perpetrate a forgery. *[Laughter]* Now, bear in mind that he does not deny that these resolutions were adopted in a majority of all the Republican counties of this state in that year. He does not deny that they were declared to be the platform of this Republican party in the First Congressional District, in the Second, in the Third, and in many counties of the Fourth, and that they thus became the platform of his party in a majority of the counties upon which he now relies for support. He does not deny the truthfulness of the resolutions, but takes exception to the *spot* on which they were adopted. He takes to himself great merit because he thinks they were not adopted on the right spot for me to use them against him, just as he was very severe in Congress upon the government of his country when he thought that he had discovered that the Mexican War was not begun in the right *spot,* and was therefore unjust.[29] *[Laughter]* He tries very hard to make out that there is something very extraordinary in the place where the thing was done, and not in the thing itself.

I never believed before that Abraham Lincoln would be guilty of what he has done this day in regard to those resolutions. *[Applause]* In the first place, the moment it was intimated to me that they had been adopted at Aurora and Rockford instead of Springfield, I did not wait for him to call my attention to the fact, but led off and explained in my first meeting after the Ottawa debate, what the mistake was, and how it had been made.[30] I supposed that for an honest man, conscious of his own rectitude, that explanation would be sufficient. I did not wait for him, after the mistake was made, to call my attention to it, but frankly explained it at once as an honest man would. *[Cheers, applause]*[31] I also gave the authority on which I had stated that these resolutions were adopted by the Springfield Republican convention; that I had seen them quoted by Major Harris in a debate in Congress, as having been adopted by the first Republican state convention in Illinois, and that I had written to him and asked him for the authority as to the time and place of their adoption; that Major Harris being extremely ill, Charles H. Lanphier had written to me for him, that they were adopted at Springfield, on the 5th of October, 1854, and had sent me a copy of the Springfield paper containing them. I read them from the newspaper, just as Mr. Lincoln reads the proceedings of meetings held years ago from the newspapers. After giving that explanation, I did not think there was an honest man in the state of Illinois who doubted that I had been led into the error, if it was such, innocently, in the way I detailed. And I will now say that I do not now believe that there is an honest man on the face of the globe who will not regard with abhorrence and disgust Mr. Lincoln's insinuations of my complicity in that forgery, if it was a forgery. *[Cheers]*

Does Mr. Lincoln wish to push these things to the point of personal difficulties here? I commenced this contest by treating him courteously and kindly. I

---

29. See "spot resolutions" in the glossary, p. 331.

30. At Galena on Aug. 25, SAD admitted to having erroneously attributed a set of Republican resolutions from northern Illinois to a Springfield Anti-Nebraska meeting on Oct. 5, 1854. He complained that as a result he had been charged "not with an error, but with forgery." *Chicago Times,* Aug. 28, 1858.

31. At this point the *Chicago Press and Tribune* inserts within brackets: "Here Judge Douglas turned round to Mr. Lincoln and spoke to him."

always spoke of him in words of respect, and in return he has sought, and is now seeking, to divert public attention from the enormity of his revolutionary principles by impeaching men's sincerity and integrity, and inviting personal quarrels. *[Cheers]* I desired to conduct this contest with him like a gentleman, but I spurn the insinuation of complicity and fraud made upon the simple circumstance of an editor of a newspaper having made a mistake as to the place where a thing was done, but not as to the thing itself. These resolutions were the platform of this Republican party of Mr. Lincoln's of that year. They were adopted in a majority of the Republican counties in the state; and when I asked him at Ottawa whether they formed the platform upon which he stood, he did not answer, and I could not get an answer out of him. He then thought, as I thought, that those resolutions were adopted at the Springfield convention, but excused himself by saying that he was not there when they were adopted, but had gone to Tazewell court in order to avoid being present at the convention. He saw them published as having been adopted at Springfield, and so did I, and he knew that if there was a mistake in regard to them, that I had nothing under heaven to do with it. Besides, you find that in all these Northern counties where the Republican candidates are running pledged to him, that the conventions which nominated them adopted that identical platform. One cardinal point in that platform which he shrinks from is this—that there shall be no more slave states admitted into the Union, even if the people want them. Lovejoy stands pledged against the admission of any more slave states.

Voice: Right, so do we.

Douglas: So do you, you say. Farnsworth stands pledged against the admission of any more slave states. Washburne stands pledged the same way. The candidate for the legislature who is running on Lincoln's ticket in Henderson and Warren stands committed by his vote in the legislature to the same thing, and I am informed, but do not know of the fact, that your candidate here is also so pledged.[32]

Voice: Hurrah for him.

Douglas: Now, you Republicans all hurrah for him, and for the doctrine of no more slave states, and yet Lincoln tells you that his conscience will not permit him to sanction that doctrine, *[Applause]* and complains because the resolutions I read at Ottawa made him, as a member of the party, responsible for sanctioning the doctrine of no more slave states. You are one way, you confess, and he is, or pretends to be, the other, and yet you are both governed by *principle* in supporting one another. If it be true, as I have shown it is, that the whole Republican

---

32. William C. Rice was the Republican candidate to represent Warren and Henderson counties in the Illinois General Assembly. Rufus Miles was running as the Republican legislative candidate in Knox County, where Galesburg is located.

party in the Northern part of the state stands committed to the doctrine of no more slave states, and that this same doctrine is repudiated by the Republicans in the other part of the state, I wonder whether Mr. Lincoln and his party do not present the case which he cited from the scriptures, of a house divided against itself which cannot stand! *[Applause]*

I desire to know what are Mr. Lincoln's principles and the principles of his party? I hold, and the party with which I am identified hold, that the people of each state, old and new, have the right to decide the slavery question for themselves, *[Cheers, applause]* and when I used the remark that I did not care whether slavery was voted up or down, I used it in the connection that I was for allowing Kansas to do just as she pleased on the slavery question. I said that I did not care whether they voted slavery up or down, because they had the right to do as they pleased on the question, and therefore my action would not be controlled by any such consideration. Why cannot Abraham Lincoln, and the party with which he acts, speak out their principles so that they may be understood? Why do they claim to be one thing in one part of the state and another in the other part? Whenever I allude to the abolition doctrines, which he considers a slander to be charged with being in favor of, you all endorse them, and hurrah for them, not knowing that your candidate is ashamed to acknowledge them. *[Cheers]*

I have a few words to say upon the Dred Scott decision, which has troubled the brain of Mr. Lincoln so much. *[Laughter]* He insists that that decision would carry slavery into the free states, notwithstanding that the decision says directly the opposite, and goes into a long argument to make you believe that I am in favor of, and would sanction the doctrine that would allow slaves to be brought here and held as slaves contrary to our constitution and laws. Mr. Lincoln knew better when he asserted this. He knew that one newspaper, and so far as is within my knowledge, but one ever asserted that doctrine, and that I was the first man in either house of Congress that read that article in debate, and denounced it on the floor of the Senate as revolutionary. When the *Washington Union,* on the 17th of last November published an article to that effect, I branded it at once, and denounced it, and hence the *Union* has been pursuing me ever since. Mr. Toombs, of Georgia, replied to me, and said that there was not a man in any of the slave states South of the Potomac River that held any such doctrine.[33] Mr. Lincoln knows that there is not a member of the Supreme Court who holds that doctrine. He knows that every one of them, as shown by their opinions, holds the reverse.[34] Why this attempt, then, to bring the Supreme Court into disre-

---

33. For SAD's denunciation of the *Washington Union* article and Toombs's response, see *Congressional Globe, Appendix,* 35th Cong., 1st Sess., Mar. 22, 1858, 194–202.

34. At least one authority has concluded the opposite to SAD's contention. Don E. Fehrenbacher believed that if given the opportunity, a majority of the justices on the Supreme Court

pute among the people? It looks as if there was an effort being made to destroy public confidence in the highest judicial tribunal on earth. Suppose he succeeds in destroying public confidence in the Court, so that the people will not respect its decisions, but will feel at liberty to disregard them, and resist the laws of the land. What will he have gained? He will have changed the government from one of laws into that of a mob, in which the strong arm of violence will be substituted for the decisions of the courts of justice. *[Cheers]*

He complains because I did not go into an argument reviewing Chief Justice Taney's opinion, and the other opinions of the different judges, to determine whether their reasoning is right or wrong on the questions of law. What use would that be? He wants to take an appeal from the Supreme Court to this meeting to determine whether the questions of law were decided properly. He is going to appeal from the Supreme Court of the United States to every town meeting in the hope that he can excite a prejudice against that Court, and on the wave of that prejudice ride into the Senate of the United States, when he could not get there on his own principles, or his own merits. *[Laughter, cheers]* Suppose he should succeed in getting into the Senate of the United States. What, then, will he have to do with the decision of the Supreme Court in the Dred Scott case? Can he reverse that decision when he gets there? Can he act upon it? Has the Senate any right to reverse it or revise it? He will not pretend that it has. Then why drag the matter into this contest, unless for the purpose of making a false issue, by which he can direct public attention from the real issue?

He has cited General Jackson in justification of the war he is making on the decision of the Court. Mr. Lincoln misunderstands the history of the country if he believes there is any parallel in the two cases. It is true that the Supreme Court once decided that if a bank of the United States was a necessary fiscal agent of the government, it was constitutional, and if not, that it was unconstitutional. And also, that whether or not it was necessary for that purpose, was a political question for Congress, and not a judicial one for the courts to determine. Hence the Court would not determine the bank unconstitutional. Jackson respected the decision, obeyed the law, executed it and carried it into effect during its existence. But after the charter of the bank expired and a proposition was made to create a new bank, General Jackson said, it is unnecessary, and improper, and therefore, I am against it on constitutional grounds, as well as those of expediency.[35]

Is Congress bound to pass every act that is constitutional? Why, there are a thousand things that are constitutional, but yet are inexpedient and unnecessary,

would have rendered a proslavery decision if confronted by a case giving federal protection to slaveholders in a free state. *The Dred Scott Decision: Its Significance in Law and Politics* (New York: Oxford University Press, 1978), 444–45.

35. See note 24, p. 199.

and you surely would not vote for them merely because you had the right to? And because General Jackson would not do a thing which he had a right to do, but did not deem expedient or proper, Mr. Lincoln is going to justify himself in doing that which he has no right to do. *[Laughter]* I ask him, whether he is not bound to respect and obey the decisions of the Supreme Court as well as me?

The Constitution has created that Court to decide all constitutional questions in the last resort, and when such decisions have been made, they become the law of the land, and you, and he, and myself, and every other good citizen are bound by them. Yet, he argues that I am bound by their decisions and he is not. He says that their decisions are binding on Democrats, but not on Republicans. *[Laughter, applause]* Are not Republicans bound by the laws of the land, as well as Democrats? And when the court has fixed the construction of the Constitution on the validity of a given law, is not their decision binding upon Republicans as well as upon Democrats? Is it possible that you Republicans have the right to raise your mobs and oppose the laws of the land and the constituted authorities, and yet hold us Democrats bound to obey them? My time is within half a minute of expiring, and all I have to say is, that I stand by the laws of the land. *[Cheers]* I stand by the Constitution as our fathers made it, by the laws as they are enacted, and by the decisions of the Court upon all points within their jurisdiction as they are pronounced by the highest tribunal on earth, and any man who resists these must resort to mob law and violence to overturn the government of laws. *[Applause]*

QUINCY

INTRODUCTION

With a population of thirteen thousand, Quincy, Illinois, site of the sixth Lincoln-Douglas debate on October 13, 1858, was the metropolis of western Illinois and the largest town of any of the debate locations. Senator Douglas had once claimed the town as his residence, and he represented the surrounding Fifth Congressional District during his three terms in the House of Representatives in the 1840s. As both railroad terminus and Mississippi River port, Quincy had business and travel connections with the East through Chicago, and with St. Louis and New Orleans to the south. The Great River, a highway to the outside world at Quincy, was also a border, and the nearness of slaveholding Missouri directly across that border was deeply felt in Quincy; indeed the town was known to be a stop on the Underground Railroad. Quincy and Adams County had long been safely if not overwhelmingly Democratic in political sentiment, and significant inroads had been made on the county's old Whig vote by the nativist American Party in 1856. For Republicans to gain a local majority in 1858 was therefore at best a modest hope, but Lincoln and Douglas had their eyes on the much larger moderate majority of voters in Illinois's surrounding central area.

Both Lincoln and Douglas had been campaigning in western Illinois since their meeting at Galesburg on October 7, resting only on the intervening Sunday. Douglas arrived in Quincy the night before the debate, to be met by a torchlight procession, and Lincoln's arrival the next morning was greeted by a parade that was reputedly half an hour in passing its point of departure. Carl Schurz, who came to Quincy on the same train as Lincoln, gave due attention in his memoirs to the festive local preparations, and though partisan, he thought "the Democratic displays were much more elaborate and gorgeous than those of the Republicans."

Schurz also remembered Lincoln's shrill voice and awkward gestures, which could easily and negatively be contrasted to Douglas's sonorous baritone and his vigorous mode of expression, but Schurz considered the force and sincerity of Lincoln's message to have compensated for his liabilities as an orator.[1] The debate audience at Quincy was more heterogeneous than most, as Illinois spectators were joined by boatloads from Hannibal, Missouri, and Keokuk, Iowa. Estimates of the crowd's size varied widely, from eight thousand to almost twice that, and though there was general agreement that the Galesburg audience had been larger, it was said that "the excitement and enthusiasm on both sides were more marked and vociferous" at Quincy.[2] The proceedings were delayed somewhat by the collapse of a part of the overloaded platform which had been erected on the public square to accommodate speakers and feminine spectators.

Campaign rigors were beginning to tell on Lincoln and Douglas at Quincy; an unfriendly correspondent thought Douglas "looked very much the worse for wear," and both contestants betrayed more irritation with each other than at any previous time during the debates.[3] Each spent time refuting some of the other's frequently stated charges: that Lincoln stood for the complete equality of blacks and whites or that Lincoln and the Republicans had "one set of principles in the abolition counties, and a different and contradictory set in the other counties"; that Douglas had confronted Lincoln at Ottawa with a set of forged and spurious resolutions to which he insisted that Lincoln respond, or that Douglas, along with Presidents Pierce and Buchanan and Chief Justice Taney, was party to a conspiracy to nationalize slavery in the United States. Each respectively defended and attacked the Supreme Court and the Dred Scott decision. Lincoln again undertook to distinguish between his denial that Negroes ought to have full American citizenship, and his affirmation that they were due the natural rights defined in the Declaration of Independence. As he managed to do in almost every debate, Douglas reasserted what amounted to his Freeport Doctrine, and he went further, declaring that if Republicans were successful in their drive to place limits on the expansion of slavery, slaves would die of starvation as a result of overpopulation. In this way slavery would be placed "in the course of ultimate extinction."

Lincoln revived the moral appeal he first enunciated at Galesburg, proclaiming slavery a wrong, which Republicans, though recognizing constitutional obligations, would deal with as an evil that should not be allowed to spread. Douglas and his fellow Democrats, said Lincoln, simply did not propose to deal with slavery as a wrong. Douglas responded that since the federal Constitution

---

1. Carl Schurz, *The Reminiscences of Carl Schurz* (New York: McClure, 1907) I:192–94.

2. *Chicago Press and Tribune*, Oct. 15, 1858.

3. *St. Louis Missouri Democrat*, Oct. 15, 1858.

guaranteed to each state the right to do as it pleased with regard to slavery, he forbore discussing the morality of the institution, for slavery was a question on which Congress had no right to act. Indeed, at the end of his speech, Douglas, in a moment of unguarded enthusiasm, looked forward to a time when each state would mind its own business on the slavery issue, when the Union might exist forever divided into free and slave states. Lincoln in his rejoinder seized on this, thanking Douglas for finally acknowledging that he anticipated that slavery would last forever.

As had happened after each previous debate, the partisan newspapers reporting the meeting declared victory for their own candidate and ignominious defeat for his adversary at Quincy. "Taken together," said the Democratic Springfield *Illinois State Register,* "the arguments of Judge Douglas were of so overwhelmning [*sic*] a character, as to carry conviction to the heart of many a man that day," while that paper's local Republican rival considered the Quincy debate "as the most damaging to Douglas of the series."[4] Lincoln's own notion of the way things were going may have been provided by him in a conversation with David Ross Locke, later the creator of the humorous character Petroleum V. Nasby, when Locke visited him at his hotel after the debate. As Locke remembered almost thirty years later, Lincoln thought that the Republicans would carry the state in the election to come, but the existing legislative apportionment would nonetheless insure that Douglas would return to the Senate. "You can't overturn a pyramid," he was remembered to have said, "but you can undermine it; that's what I have been trying to do."[5]

---

4. *Illinois State Register,* Oct. 18, 1858; *Daily Illinois State Journal* (Springfield), Oct. 18, 1858.

5. Locke in Allen Thorndike Rice, ed., *Reminiscences of Abraham Lincoln by Distinguished Men of His Time, Collected and Edited by Allen Thorndike Rice* (New York: North American, 1886), 441–43.

LINCOLN'S OPENING SPEECH

L adies and gentlemen: I have had no immediate conference with Judge Douglas, but I will venture to say he and I will perfectly agree that your entire silence, both when I speak and when he speaks, will be most agreeable to us.

In the month of May, 1856, the elements in the State of Illinois, which have since been consolidated into the Republican party, assembled together in a state convention at Bloomington. They adopted at that time what, in political language, is called a platform. In June of the same year, the elements of the Republican party in the nation assembled together in a national convention at Philadelphia. They adopted what is called the national platform. In June, 1858—the present year—the Republicans of Illinois reassembled at Springfield, in state convention, and adopted again their platform, as I suppose not differing in any essential particular from either of the former ones, but perhaps adding something in relation to the new developments of political progress in the country.

The convention that assembled in June last did me the honor, if it be one, and I esteem it such, to nominate me as their candidate for the United States Senate. I have supposed that in entering upon this canvass I stood generally upon these platforms. We are now met together on the 13th of October of the same year, only four months from the adoption of the last platform, and I am unaware that in this canvass, from the beginning until today, any one of our adversaries has taken hold of our platforms or laid his finger upon anything that he calls wrong in them.

In the very first one of these joint discussions between Senator Douglas and myself, Senator Douglas, without alluding at all to these platforms, or any one of them, of which I have spoken, attempted to hold me responsible for a set of resolutions passed long before the meeting of either one of these conventions of which I have spoken. And as a ground for holding me responsible for these resolutions, he assumed that they had been passed at a state convention of the Republican party, and that I took part in that convention. It was discovered afterwards that this was erroneous, that the resolutions which he endeavored to hold me responsible for had not been passed by any state convention anywhere, had not been passed at Springfield, where he supposed they had, or assumed that they had, and that they had been passed in no convention in which I had taken part.[1] The Judge, nevertheless, was not willing to give up the point that he was endeavoring to make upon me, and he therefore thought to still hold me to the point that he was endeavoring to make, by showing that the resolutions that he read had been passed at a local

---

1. See "Springfield resolutions controversy" in the glossary, pp. 331–32.

convention in the Northern part of the state, although it was not a local convention that embraced my residence at all, nor one that reached, as I suppose, nearer than 150 or 200 miles of where I was when it met, nor one in which I took any part at all. He also introduced other resolutions passed at other meetings, and by combining the whole, although they were all antecedent to the two state conventions, and the one national convention I have mentioned, still he insisted and now insists, as I understand, that I am in some way responsible for them.

At Jonesboro, on our third meeting, I insisted to the Judge that I was in no way rightfully held responsible for the proceedings of this local meeting or convention in which I had taken no part, and in which I was in no way embraced, but I insisted to him that if he thought I was responsible for every man or every set of men everywhere who happen to be my friends, the rule ought to work both ways, and he ought to be responsible for the acts and resolutions of all men or sets of men who were or are now his supporters and friends, *[Cheers]* and gave him a pretty long string of resolutions, passed by men who are now his friends, and announcing doctrine for which he does not desire to be held responsible.[2]

This still does not satisfy Judge Douglas. He still adheres to his proposition that I am responsible for what some of my friends in different parts of the state have done, but that he is not responsible for what his have done. At least so I understand him. But in addition to that, the Judge, at our meeting in Galesburg last week, undertakes to establish that I am guilty of a species of double-dealing with the public—that I make speeches of a certain sort in the North, among the abolitionists, which I would not make in the South, and that I make speeches of a certain sort in the South which I would not make in the North. I apprehend in the course I have marked out for myself that I shall not have an opportunity° to dwell at very great length upon this subject.

As this was done in the Judge's opening speech at Galesburg, I had an opportunity, as I had the middle speech then, of saying something in answer to it. He brought forward a quotation or two from a speech of mine delivered at Chicago, and then, to contrast with it, he brought forward an extract from a speech of mine at Charleston, in which he insisted that I was greatly inconsistent, and insisted that his conclusion followed that I was playing a double part, and speaking in one region one way, and in another region, another way.[3] I have not time now to dwell on this as long as I would like, and I wish only now to re-quote that portion of my speech at Charleston which the Judge quoted, and then make some comments upon it. This he quotes from me as being delivered at Charleston and I believe correctly:[4]

---

2. See the Jonesboro debate, pp. 105–10.

3. See Galesburg debate, pp. 181–83.

4. The following is from AL's speech at Charleston, p. 131, and SAD's speech at Galesburg, p. 182.

I will say, then, that I am not, nor ever have been, in favor of bringing about in any way the social and political equality of the white and black races—that I am not nor ever have been in favor of making voters or jurors of negroes, nor of qualifying them to hold office, nor to intermarry° with white people; and I will say in addition to this that there is a physical difference between the white and black races which will ever forbid the two races living together on terms of social and political equality. And inasmuch as they cannot so live, while they do remain together, there must be the position of superior and inferior,° I am as much as any other man in favor of having the superior position assigned to the white race.° [Cheers]

This, I believe, is the entire quotation from the Charleston speech as the Judge made it. His comments are as follows:[5]

Yes here you find men who hurrah for Lincoln, and say he is right when he discards all distinction between races, or when he declares that he discards the doctrine that there is such a thing as a superior and inferior race; and abolitionists are required and expected to vote for Mr. Lincoln because he goes for the equality of the races, holding that in the Declaration of Independence the white man and the negro were declared equal, and endowed by Divine law with equality. And down South with old line Whigs, with the Kentuckians, the Virginians, and the Tennesseeans, he tells you that there is a physical difference between the races, making the one superior, the other inferior, and he is in favor of maintaining the superiority of the white race over the negro.°

Those are the Judge's comments. Now I wish to show you that a month, or only lacking three days of a month, before I made the speech at Charleston, which the Judge quotes from, he had himself heard me say substantially the same thing. It was in our first meeting, at Ottawa, and I will say a word about where it was and the atmosphere it was in, after a while. But at our first meeting at Ottawa, I read an extract from an old speech of mine, made nearly four years ago, not merely to show my sentiments, but to show that my sentiments were long entertained and openly expressed. In which extract I expressly declared that my own feelings would not admit of° a social and political equality between the white and black races, and that even if my own feelings would admit of it, I still knew that the public sentiment of the country would not, and that such a thing was an utter impossibility, or substantially that.[6] That extract from my old speech the reporters, by some sort of accident, passed over, and it was not reported. I lay no blame upon anybody. I suppose they thought that I would hand it over to them, and dropped reporting while I was reading it, but afterwards went away without

5. From SAD's speech at Galesburg, pp. 182–83.
6. AL read at Ottawa from his 1854 Peoria speech, pp. 18–20.

getting it from me. At the end of that quotation from my old speech, which I read at Ottawa, I made the comments which were reported at that time, and which I will now read, and ask you to notice how very nearly they are the same as Judge Douglas says were delivered by me down in Egypt.

After reading I added these words:[7]

> Now gentlemen, I don't want to read at any greater length, but this is the true complexion of all I have ever said in regard to the institution of slavery and the black race. This is the whole of it, and anything that argues me into his idea of perfect social and political equality with the negro, is but a specious and fantastic arrangement of words, by which a man can prove a horse chestnut to be a chestnut horse. I will say here, while upon this subject, that I have no purpose directly or indirectly to interfere with the institution of slavery in the states where it exists. I believe I have no lawful right to do so, and I have no inclination to do so. I have no purpose to introduce political and social equality between the white and the black races. There is a physical difference between the two, which in my judgment will probably forever forbid their living together upon the footing of perfect equality, and inasmuch as it becomes a necessity that there must be a difference, I, as well as Judge Douglas, am in favor of the race to which I belong, having the superior position. *[Cheers]* I have never said anything to the contrary, but I hold that notwithstanding all this, there is no reason in the world why the negro is not entitled to all the natural rights enumerated in the Declaration of Independence, the right to life, liberty and the pursuit of happiness. I hold that he is as much entitled to these as the white man. I agree with Judge Douglas he is not my equal in many respects—certainly not in color, perhaps not in moral or intellectual endowment. But in the right to eat the bread, without leave of anybody else, which his own hand earns, *he is my equal and the equal of Judge Douglas, and the equal of every living man.*° *[Cheers]*

I have chiefly introduced this for the purpose of meeting the Judge's charge that the quotation he took from my Charleston speech was what I would say down South among the Kentuckians, the Virginians, and so on,° but would not say in the regions in which was supposed to be more of the abolition element. I now make this comment: That speech from which I have now read the quotation, and which is there given correctly, perhaps too much so for good taste, was made away up North in the abolition district of this state *par excellence*—in the Lovejoy district—in the personal presence of Lovejoy, for he was on the stand with us when I made° it. It had been made and put in print in that region only three days less than a month before the speech made at Charleston, the like of which Judge Douglas thinks I would not make where there was any abolition element.

I only refer to this matter to say that I am altogether unconscious of having

---

7. From AL's speech at Ottawa, pp. 20–21.

attempted any double dealing anywhere, that upon one occasion I may say one thing and leave other things unsaid, and *vice versa.* But that I have said anything on one occasion that is inconsistent with what I have said elsewhere, I deny. At least I deny it so far as the intention is concerned.

I find that I have devoted to this topic a larger portion of my time than I had intended. I wished to show, but I will pass it upon this occasion, that in the sentiment I have occasionally advanced upon the Declaration of Independence, I am entirely borne out by the sentiments advanced by our old Whig leader, Henry Clay, and I have the book here to show it from. But because I have already occupied more time than I intended to do on that topic, I pass over it.

At Galesburg, I tried to show that by the Dred Scott decision, pushed to its legitimate consequences, slavery would be established in all the states, as well as in the territories. I did this because, upon a former occasion, I had asked Judge Douglas whether, if the Supreme Court should make a decision declaring that the states had not the power to exclude slavery from their limits, he would adopt and follow that decision as a rule of political action. And because he had not directly answered that question, but had merely contented himself with sneering at it, I again introduced it and tried to show that the conclusion that I stated followed inevitably and logically from the proposition already decided by the Court. Judge Douglas had the privilege of replying to me at Galesburg, and again he gave me no direct answer as to whether he would or would not sustain such a decision if made. I give° him this third chance to say "yes" or "no." He is not obliged to do either. Probably he will not do either, [Laughter] but I give him the third chance. I tried to show then that this result, this conclusion, inevitably followed from the point already decided by the Court. The Judge, in his reply, again sneers at the thought of the Court making any such decision, and in the course of his remarks upon this subject, uses the language which I will now read. Speaking of me, the Judge says:[8]

> He goes on and insists that the Dred Scott decision would carry slavery into the free States, notwithstanding the decision itself says the contrary.

And he adds:

> Mr. Lincoln knows that there is no member of the Supreme Court that holds that doctrine. He knows that every one of them in their opinions held the reverse.°

I especially introduce this subject again for the purpose of saying that I have the Dred Scott decision here, and I will thank Judge Douglas to lay his finger upon the place in the entire opinions of the Court where any one of them "says

---

8. From AL's speech at Galesburg, p. 208.

the contrary." It is very hard to affirm a negative with entire confidence. I say, however, that I have examined that decision with a good deal of care, as a lawyer examines a decision, and so far as I have been able to do so, the Court has nowhere in its opinions said that the states have the power to exclude slavery, nor have they used other language substantially that. I also say, so far as I can find, not one of the concurring judges has said that the states can exclude slavery, nor said anything that was substantially that. The nearest approach that any one of them has made to it, so far as I can find, was by Judge Nelson, and the approach he made to it was exactly, in substance, the Nebraska bill—that the states had the exclusive power over the question of slavery, so far as they are not limited by the Constitution of the United States. I asked the question, therefore, if the non-concurring judges, McLean or Curtis, had asked to get an express declaration that the states could absolutely exclude slavery from their limits, what reason have we to believe that it would not have been voted down by the majority of the judges, just as Chase's amendment was voted down by Judge Douglas and his compeers when it was offered to the Nebraska bill. [Cheers]

Also at Galesburg, I said something in regard to those Springfield resolutions that Judge Douglas had attempted to use upon me at Ottawa, and commented at some length upon the fact that they were, as presented, not genuine. Judge Douglas in his reply to me seemed to be somewhat exasperated. He said he would never have believed that Abraham Lincoln, as he kindly called me, would have attempted such a thing as I had attempted upon that occasion, and among other expressions which he used toward me, was that I dared to say "forgery"— that I had *dared* to say "forgery." [Turning to Douglas] Yes, Judge, I did dare to say "forgery." [Applause, laughter] But in this political canvass, the Judge ought to remember that I was not the first who *dared* to say "forgery." At Jacksonville Judge Douglas made a speech in answer to something said by Judge Trumbull, and at the close of what he said upon that subject, he *dared* to say that Trumbull had forged his evidence from beginning to end.° He said, too, that he should not concern himself with Trumbull any more, but thereafter he should hold Lincoln responsible for the slanders upon him.[9] [Laughter, applause] When I met him at Charleston after that—although I think that I should not have noticed the subject if he had not said he would hold me responsible for it—I spread out before him the statements of the evidence that Judge Trumbull had used, and I asked Judge Douglas, piece by piece, to put his finger upon one piece of all that evidence that he would say was a forgery! When I went through with each and every piece,

---

9. AL refers to SAD's Sept. 6 speech at Jacksonville, which is excerpted in the *Chicago Times*, Sept. 10, 1858, in AL's Debates Scrapbook (146), and in *Chicago Press and Tribune*, Sept. 9, 1858. See also Charleston debate, pp. 132–33.

Judge Douglas did not *dare* then to say that any piece of it was a forgery. *[Laughter, cheers]* So it seems that there are some things that Judge Douglas dares to do, and some that he dares not to do. *[Applause, laughter]*

Voice: It's the same thing with you.

Lincoln: Yes, sir, it's the same thing with me. I do dare to say "forgery" when it's true, and I don't dare to say "forgery" when it's false. *[Applause, cheers]*

Now, I will say here to this audience and to Judge Douglas, I have not dared to say he committed a forgery, and I never shall until I know it. But I did dare to say—just to suggest to the Judge—that a forgery had been committed, which by his own showing had been traced to him and two of his friends. *[Laughter, cheers]* I dared to suggest to him that he had expressly promised in one of his public speeches to investigate that matter, and I dared to suggest to him that there was an implied promise that when he investigated it, he would make known the result. I dared to suggest to the Judge that he could not expect to be quite clear of suspicion of that fraud, for since the time that promise was made, he had been with those friends and had not kept his promise in regard to the investigation and the report upon it.[10] *[Laughter, cheers]* I am not a very daring man, *[Laughter]* but I dared that much, Judge, and I am not much scared about it yet. *[Laughter, applause]*

When the Judge says he wouldn't have believed of Abraham Lincoln that he would have made such an attempt as that, he reminds me of the fact that he entered upon this canvass with the purpose to treat me courteously. That touched me somewhat. *[Laughter]* It sets me to thinking. I was aware, when it was first agreed that Judge Douglas and I were to have these seven joint discussions, that they were the successive acts of a drama, perhaps I should say, to be enacted not merely in the face of audiences like this, but in the face of the nation, and to some extent, by my relation to him, and not from anything in myself, in the face of the world. And I am anxious that they should be conducted with dignity and in the good temper which would be befitting the vast audience before which it was conducted. But when Judge Douglas got home from Washington and made his first speech in Chicago, the evening afterwards, I made some sort of reply to it. His second speech was made at Bloomington, in which, he commented upon my speech at Chicago, and said, that I had used language ingeniously contrived to conceal my intentions, or words to that effect.[11]

Now, I understand that this is an imputation upon my veracity and my candor. I do not know what the Judge understood by it, but in our first discussion

---

10. See the Galesburg debate, note 30, p. 206. The "friends" that AL alludes to were Congressman Thomas H. Harris of the Springfield district, and Charles H. Lanphier, editor of the *Register* in Springfield.

11. For SAD's July 17 speech at Bloomington, see *Chicago Times*, July 22, 1858, and AL's Debates Scrapbook, 49–67.

at Ottawa, he led off by charging a bargain, somewhat corrupt in its character, upon Trumbull and myself—that we had entered into a bargain, one of the terms of which was that Trumbull was to abolitionize the old Democratic party, and I, Lincoln, was to abolitionize the old Whig party, I pretending to be as good an old line Whig as ever. Judge Douglas may not understand that he implicated my truthfulness and my honor, when he said I was doing one thing and pretending another, and I misunderstood him if he thought he was treating me in a dignified way, as a man of honor and truth, as he now claims he was disposed to treat me.

Even after that time, at Galesburg, when he brings forward an extract from a speech made at Chicago, and an extract from a speech made at Charleston, to prove that I was trying to play a double part—that I was trying to cheat the public, and get votes upon one set of principles at one place and upon another set of principles at another place—I do not understand but what he impeaches my honor, my veracity, and my candor. And because *he* does this, I do not understand that I am bound, if I see a truthful ground for it, to keep my hands off of him.[12]

As soon as I learned that Judge Douglas was disposed to treat me in this way, I signified in one of my speeches that I should be driven to draw upon whatever of humble resources I might have—to adopt a new course with him. I was not entirely sure that I should be able to hold my own with him, but I at least had the purpose made to do as well as I could upon him. And now I say that I will not be first to cry "hold." I think it originated with the Judge, and when he quits, I probably will. *[Laughter]* But I shall not ask any favors at all. He asks me, or he asks the audience, if I wish to push this matter to the point of personal difficulty. I tell him "no." He did not make a mistake, in one of his early speeches, when he called me an "amiable" man, though perhaps he did when he called me an "intelligent" man. *[Laughter]* It really hurts me very much to suppose that I have wronged anybody on earth. I again tell him "no"! I very much prefer, when this canvass shall be over, however it may result, that we at least part without any bitter recollections of personal difficulties.

Voice: We don't want to hear your long yarns.

Lincoln: Now, is my friend entirely sure that these people agree with him? *[Laughter]* Don't waste my time. °

The Judge, in his concluding speech at Galesburg, says that I was pushing this matter to a personal difficulty, to avoid the responsibility for the enormity of my principles. I say to the Judge, and to this audience now, that I will again state our principles as well as I hastily can in all their enormity, and if the Judge hereafter chooses to confine himself to a war upon these principles, he will probably not find me departing from it. °

---

12. See Galesburg debate, pp. 181–84.

We have in this nation this element of domestic slavery. It is a matter of absolute certainty that it is a disturbing element. It is the opinion of all the great men who have expressed an opinion upon it that it is a dangerous element. Why° keep up a controversy in regard to it? That controversy necessarily springs from difference of opinion, and if we can learn exactly, can reduce to the lowest elements, what that difference of opinion is, we perhaps shall be better prepared for discussing the different systems of policy that we would propose in regard to the disturbing element. I suggest that the difference of opinion, reduced to its lowest terms, is no other than the difference between the men who think slavery a wrong and those who do not think it wrong. I suppose that is the whole thing. It is the difference between those who think it wrong and those who do not think it wrong.°

The Republican party think it wrong. We think it is a moral, a social, and a political wrong. We think it is a wrong not confining itself merely to the persons or the states where it exists, but that it is a wrong in its tendency, to say the least, that extends itself to the existence of the whole nation. Because we think it wrong, we propose a course of policy that shall deal with it as a wrong. We deal with it as with any other wrong, insofar as we can prevent its growing any larger, and so deal with it that in the run of time, there may be some promise of an end to it. We have a due regard to the actual presence of it amongst us and the difficulties of getting rid of it in any satisfactory way, and all the constitutional obligations thrown about it. I suppose that in reference both to its actual existence in the nation, and to our constitutional obligations, we have no right at all to disturb it in the states where it exists, and we profess that we have no more inclination to disturb it than we have the right to do it.

We go further than that. We don't propose to disturb it where, in one instance, we think the Constitution would permit us. We think the Constitution would permit us to disturb it in the District of Columbia. Still we do not propose to do that, unless it should be in terms which I don't suppose the nation is very likely soon to agree to—the terms of making the emancipation gradual and compensating the unwilling owners. Where we suppose we have the constitutional right, we restrain ourselves in reference to the actual existence of the institution and the difficulties thrown about it. We also oppose it as an evil so far as it seeks to spread itself. We insist on the policy that shall restrict it to its present limits. We don't suppose that in doing this we violate anything due to the actual presence of the institution, or anything due to the constitutional guarantees thrown around it.

We oppose the Dred Scott decision in a certain way, upon which I ought perhaps to address you a few words. We do not propose that when Dred Scott has been decided to be a slave by the court, we, as a mob, will decide him to be free. We do not propose that, when any other one, or one thousand, shall be decided by that court to be slaves, we will in any violent way disturb the rights of property thus settled. But we nevertheless do oppose that decision as a political rule which shall be binding on the voter to vote for nobody who thinks it wrong, which shall be binding on the members of Congress or the president to favor no measure that does not actually concur with the principles of that decision. We do not propose to be bound by it as a political rule in that way, because we think it lays the foundation, not merely of enlarging and spreading out what we consider an evil, but it lays the foundation for spreading that evil into the states themselves. We propose so resisting it as to have it reversed, if we can, and a new judicial rule established upon this subject.[13]

I will add this that if there be any man who does not believe that slavery is wrong in the three aspects which I have mentioned, or in any one of them, that man is misplaced and ought to leave us. While, on the other hand, if there be any man in the Republican party who is impatient over the necessity springing from its actual presence, and is impatient of the constitutional guarantees thrown around it, and would act in disregard of these, he, too, is misplaced standing with us. He will find his place somewhere else, for we have a due regard, so far as we are capable of understanding them, for all these things. This, gentlemen, as well as I can give it, is a plain statement of our principles in all their enormity.

I will say now that there is a sentiment in the country contrary to ours,° a sentiment which holds that slavery is not wrong. And therefore it goes for policy that does not propose dealing with it as a wrong. That policy is the Democratic policy, and the sentiment is the Democratic sentiment. If there be a doubt in the mind of any one of this vast audience that this is really the central idea of the Democratic party, in relation to this subject, I ask him to bear with me while I state a few things tending, as I think, to prove that proposition. In the first place, the leading man—I think I may do my friend Judge Douglas the honor of call-ing him such—advocating the present Democratic policy never himself says it is wrong. He has the high distinction, so far as I know, of never having said slavery is either right or wrong. [*Laughter*] Almost everybody else says one or the other, but the Judge never does. If there be a man in the Democratic party who thinks it is wrong, and yet clings to that party, I suggest to him in the first place that his leader don't talk as he does, for he never says that it is wrong. In the second place, I suggest to him that if he will examine the policy proposed to be carried forward, he will find that it° carefully excludes the idea that there is anything wrong in it. If you will examine the arguments that are made in it, you will find that every one carefully excludes the idea that there is anything wrong in slavery.

Perhaps that Democrat who says he is as much opposed to slavery as I am

---

13. See glossary, "another Dred Scott decision," p. 319.

will tell me that I am wrong about this. I wish him to examine his own course in regard to this matter a moment, and then see if his opinion will not be changed a little. You say it is wrong, but don't you constantly object to anybody else saying so? Do you not constantly argue that this is not the right place to oppose it? You say it must not be opposed in the free states, because slavery is not here. It must not be opposed in the slave states, because it is there. It must not be opposed in politics, because that will make a fuss. It must not be opposed in the pulpit, because it is not religion. [Cheers] Then where is the place to oppose it? There is no suitable place to oppose it. There is no plan in the country to oppose this evil overspreading the continent, which you say yourself is coming. You sometimes say that if the states or any state would free itself it would be all well enough, but consider awhile.° Frank Blair and Gratz Brown tried to get up a system of gradual emancipation in Missouri, had an election in August and got beat, and you, Mr. Democrat, threw up your hat, and halloed "hurrah for Democracy."[14] [Cheers] So I say again that in regard to the arguments that are made, when Judge Douglas says he "don't care whether slavery is voted up or voted down," whether he means that as an individual expression of sentiment, or only as a sort of statement of his view on national policy, it is alike true to say that he can thus argue logically if he don't see anything wrong in it. But he cannot say so logically if he admits that slavery is wrong. He cannot say that he would as soon see a wrong voted up as voted down.

When Judge Douglas says that whoever, or whatever community, wants slaves, they have a right to have them, he is perfectly logical, if there is nothing wrong in the institution. But if you admit that it is wrong, he cannot logically say that anybody has a right to do wrong. When he says that slave property and horse and hog property are alike to be allowed to go into the territories upon the principles of equality, he is reasoning truly, if there is no difference between them as property. But if the one is property held rightfully and the other is wrong, then there is no equality between the right and wrong.

Voice: Douglas is right!

Lincoln: That is just the question that we are going to try.° So that, turn it in any way you can, in all the arguments sustaining the Democratic policy, and in that policy itself, there is a careful, studied exclusion of the idea that there is

---

14. In February of 1857, B. Gratz Brown called for the gradual compensated emancipation of Missouri's slaves in a speech in the Missouri House of Representatives, arguing that Missouri should rid itself of slave labor and replace it with free white labor. Brown was allied with Missouri Congressman Frank Blair, who seconded him and at the same time actively promoted the colonization of emancipated blacks in Central America. The reelection campaigns of the two men in 1858 can be taken as a referendum on their emancipation and colonization proposals. As AL indicates, both candidates lost.

anything wrong in slavery. Let us understand this. I am not, just here, trying°
to prove that we are right and they are wrong. I have been stating where we and
they stand, and trying to show what is the real difference between us. And I now
say that whenever we can get the question distinctly stated—can get all these
men who believe that slavery is, in some of these respects, wrong to stand and
act with us in treating it as a wrong—then, and not till then, I think we will in
some way come to an end of this slavery agitation. *[Cheers]*

DOUGLAS'S REPLY

L adies and gentlemen: Permit me to say that unless silence is observed it will
be impossible for me to be heard by this immense crowd, and my friends
can confer no higher favor upon me than by omitting all expressions of
applause or approbation. I desire to be heard rather than to be applauded. I wish
to address myself to your reason, your judgment, your sense of justice, and not
to your passions.

I regret that Mr. Lincoln should have deemed it proper for him to again
indulge in gross personalities and base insinuations in regard to the Springfield
resolutions. It has imposed upon me the necessity of using some portion of my
time for the purpose of calling your attention to the facts of the case, and it will
then be for you to say what you think of a man who can predicate such a charge
under those circumstances.°

I had seen the platform adopted by a Republican congressional convention
held in Aurora, the Second Congressional district, in September, 1854, published
as purporting to be the platform of the Republican party. That platform declared
that the Republican party was pledged never to admit another slave state into
the Union, and also that it pledged to prohibit slavery in all the territories of the
United States, not only all that we then had, but all that we should thereafter
acquire, and to repeal unconditionally the Fugitive Slave Law, abolish slavery
in the District of Columbia, and prohibit the slave trade between the different
states. These and other articles against slavery were contained in this platform
and unanimously adopted by the Republican congressional convention in that
district. I had also seen that the Republican congressional conventions at Rockford, in the First District, and at Bloomington, in the Third, had adopted the same
platform that year, nearly word for word, and had declared it to be the platform
of the Republican party. I had noticed that Major Thomas L. Harris, a member of
Congress from the Springfield district, had referred to that platform in a speech in
Congress as having been adopted by the first Republican state convention which
assembled in Illinois. When I had occasion to use the fact in this canvass, I wrote
to Major Harris to know on what day that convention was held, and to ask him

to send me its proceedings. He being sick, Charles H. Lanphier answered my letter by sending the published proceedings of the convention held at Springfield
on the 5th of October, 1854, as they appeared in the report of the *State Register*. I
read those resolutions from that newspaper the same as any of you would refer
back and quote any fact from the files of a newspaper which had published it.

Mr. Lincoln pretends that, after I had so quoted those resolutions, he discovered that they had never been adopted at Springfield. He does not deny their
adoption by the Republican party at Aurora, at Bloomington, and at Rockford,
and by nearly all the Republican county conventions in Northern Illinois, where
his party is in a majority. But merely because they were not adopted on the *"spot"*
on which I said they were, he chooses to quibble about the place, rather than meet
and discuss the merits of the resolutions themselves.[15] I stated when I quoted
them that I did so from the *State Register*. I gave my authority. Lincoln believed at
the time, as he has since admitted, that they had been adopted at Springfield, as
published. Does he believe now, that I did not tell the truth when I quoted those
resolutions? He knows, in his heart, that I quoted them in good faith, believing,
at the time, that they had been adopted at Springfield. I would consider myself
an infamous wretch, if under such circumstances, I could charge any man with
being a party to a trick or a fraud. *[Applause]* And I will tell him, too, that it will
not do to charge a forgery on Charles H. Lanphier or Thomas L. Harris. No man
on earth who knows them, and knows Lincoln, would take his oath against their
word. *[Cheers, applause]* There are not two men in the State of Illinois who have
higher characters for truth, for integrity, for moral character, and for elevation of
tone as gentlemen, than Mr. Lanphier and Mr. Harris. Any man who attempts to
make such charges as Mr. Lincoln has indulged in against them, only proclaims
himself a slanderer. *[Applause]*

I will now show you that I stated with entire fairness, as soon as it was made
known to me, that there was a mistake about the spot where the resolutions had
been adopted, although their truthfulness, as a declaration of the principles of the
Republican party had not, and could not be questioned. I did not wait for Lincoln
to point out the mistake, but the moment I discovered it, I made a speech and
published it to the world, correcting the error.[16] I corrected it myself, as a gentleman, and an honest man, and as I always feel proud to do when I have made a
mistake. I wish Mr. Lincoln could show that he has acted with equal fairness and
truthfulness when I have convinced him that he has been mistaken. *[Cheers]*

I will give you an illustration to show you how he acts in a similar case. In a
speech at Springfield, he charged Chief Justice Taney and his associates, President

---

15. "spot": an allusion to AL's unpopular opposition to the Mexican War. See "spot resolutions," in the glossary, p.331.

16. See the Galesburg debate, note 30, p. 206.

Pierce, President Buchanan, and myself with having entered into a conspiracy at the time the Nebraska bill was introduced, by which the Dred Scott decision was to be made by the Supreme Court, in order to carry slavery everywhere under the constitution.[17] I called his attention to the fact that, at the time alluded to—to wit, the introduction of the Nebraska bill—it was not possible that such a conspiracy could have been entered into, for the reason that the Dred Scott case had never been taken before the Supreme Court, and was not taken before it for a year after. And I asked him to take back that charge. Did he do it? I showed him that it was impossible that the charge could be true. I proved it by the record, and I then called upon him to retract his false charge. What was his answer? Instead of coming out like an honest man and doing so, he reiterated the charge, and said that if the case had not gone up to the Supreme Court from the courts of Missouri at the time he charged, that the judges of the Supreme Court entered into the conspiracy, yet, that there was an understanding with the Democratic owners of Dred Scott, that they would take it up. I have since asked him who the Democratic owners of Dred Scott were, but he could not tell. And why? Because there were no such Democratic owners in existence. Dred Scott at the time was owned by the Rev. Dr. Chaffee, an abolition member of Congress of Springfield, Massachusetts, in right of his wife. He was owned by one of Lincoln's friends, and not by Democrats at all. [Cheers] His case was conducted in court by abolition lawyers, so that both the prosecution and the defense were in the hands of the abolition political friends of Mr. Lincoln.[18] [Cheers]

Notwithstanding I thus proved by the record that his charge against the Supreme Court was false, instead of taking it back, he resorted to another false charge to sustain the infamy of it. [Cheers, applause] He also charged President Buchanan with having been a party to the conspiracy. I directed his attention to the fact that the charge could not possibly be true, for the reason that at the time specified, Mr. Buchanan was not in America, but was three thousand miles off, representing the United States at the Court of St. James, and had been there for a year previous, and did not return until three years afterwards. Yet, I never could get Mr. Lincoln to take back his false charge, although I have called upon him over and over again. He refuses to do it, and either remains silent or resorts to other tricks to try and palm his slander off on the country. [Cheers] Therein you will find the difference between Mr. Lincoln and myself. When I make° a mistake, as an honest man, I correct it without being asked to do so, but when he makes a false charge, he sticks to it, and never corrects it. [Cheers]

One more word in regard to these resolutions. I quoted them at Ottawa

17. An allusion to AL's "House Divided" speech.
18. See the Charleston debate, note 28, p. 152.

merely to ask Mr. Lincoln whether he stood on that platform. That was the purpose for which I quoted them. I did not think that I had a right to put idle questions to him, and I first laid a foundation for my questions by showing that the principles which I wished him either to affirm or deny had been adopted by some portion of his friends, at least as their creed. Hence I read the resolutions, and put the questions to him, and he then refused to answer them. *[Laughter]* Subsequently, one week afterwards, he did answer a part of them, but the other he has not answered up to this day. *[Cheers]* My friends, if you are my friends, you will be silent, instead of interrupting me by your applause.

Now, let me call your attention for a moment to the answers which Mr. Lincoln made at Freeport to the questions which I propounded him at Ottawa, based upon the platform adopted by a majority of the abolition counties of the state, which now as then supported him. In answer to my question whether he endorsed the Black Republican principle of no more slave states, he answered that he was not pledged against the admission of any more slave states, but that he would be very sorry if he should ever be placed in a position where he would have to vote on the question, that he would rejoice to know that no more slave states would be admitted into the Union. "But," he added, "if slavery shall be kept out of the territories during territorial existence of any one given territory, and then the people shall, having a fair chance and a clear field when they come to adopt the constitution, do such an extraordinary thing as to adopt a slave constitution, uninfluenced by the actual presence of the institution among them, I see no alternative, if we own the country, but to admit them into the Union."° The point I wish him to answer is this: Suppose Congress should not prohibit slavery in the territory, and it applied for admission with a constitution recognizing slavery, then how would he vote? His answer at Freeport does not apply to any territory in America. I ask you, *[turning to Lincoln]* will you vote to admit Kansas into the Union, with just such a constitution as her people want, with slavery or without as they shall determine? He will not answer. *[Cheers]* I have put that question to him time and time again, and have not been able to get an answer out of him.

I ask you again, Lincoln, will you vote to admit New Mexico when she has the requisite population with such a constitution as her people adopt, either recognizing slavery or not as they shall determine? He will not answer. I put the same question to him in reference to Oregon and the new states to be carved out of Texas and the United States, and he will not answer. He will not answer these questions in reference to any territory now in existence, but says that if Congress should prohibit slavery in a territory, and when its people asked for admission as a state, they should adopt slavery as one of their institutions, that he supposes he would have to let it come in. *[Laughter]*

I submit to you whether that answer of his to my question does not justify me in saying that he has a fertile genius in devising language to conceal his thoughts. I ask you whether there is an intelligent man in America who does not believe that that answer was made for the purpose of concealing what he intended to do. *[Cheers]* He wished to make the old line Whigs believe that he would stand by the compromise measures of 1850, which declared that the states might come into the Union with slavery, or without as they pleased, while Lovejoy and his abolition allies up North explained to the abolitionists that in taking this ground, he preached good abolition doctrine, because his proviso would not apply to any territory in America, and therefore there was no chance of his being governed by it. It would have been quite easy for him to have said that he would let the people of a state do just as they pleased, if he desired to convey such an idea. Why did he not do it? He would not answer my question directly, because up North, the abolition creed declares that there shall be no more slave states, while down South in Adams County, in Coles, and in Sangamon, he and his friends are afraid to advance that doctrine. Therefore, he gives an evasive and equivocal answer, to be construed one way in the South and another way in the North, which, when analyzed, it is apparent is not an answer at all with reference to any territory now in existence. *[Cheers]*

Mr. Lincoln complains that, in my speech the other day at Galesburg, I read an extract from a speech delivered by him at Chicago, and then another from his speech at Charleston, and compared them, thus showing the people that he had one set of principles in one part of the state and another in the other part. And how does he answer that charge? Why, he quotes from his Charleston speech as I quoted from it, and then quotes another extract from a speech which he made at another place, which he says is the same as the extract from his speech at Charleston. But he does not quote the extract from his Chicago speech, upon which I convicted him of double dealing.[19] *[Cheers]* I quoted from his Chicago speech to prove that he held one set of principles up North among the abolitionists, and from his Charleston speech to prove that he held another set down at Charleston and in Southern Illinois. In his answer to this charge, he ignores entirely his Chicago speech, and merely argues that he said the same thing which he said at Charleston at another place. If he did, it follows that he has twice, instead of once, held one creed in one part of the state and a different creed in another part. *[Cheers]* Up at Chicago, in the opening of the campaign, he reviewed my reception speech, and undertook to answer my argument attacking his favorite doctrine of negro equality. I had shown that it was a falsification of

---

19. The speech that AL made "at another place" refers to the Ottawa debate, pp. 20–24.

the Declaration of Independence to pretend that that instrument applied to and included negroes in the clause declaring that all men were created equal. What was Lincoln's reply? I will read from his Chicago speech, and the one which he did not quote, and dare not quote in this part of the state. He said:[20]

> I should like to know if taking this old Declaration of Independence, which declares that all men are equal upon principle, and making exceptions to it where will it stop. If one man says it does not mean a negro, why may not another say it does not mean some other man? If that declaration is not the truth, let us get the statute book in which we find it and tear it out! Who is so bold as to do it! If it is not true let us tear it out!°

There you find that Mr. Lincoln told the abolitionists of Chicago that if the Declaration of Independence did not declare that the negro was created by the Almighty the equal of the white man, that you ought to take that instrument and tear out the clause which says that all men were created equal. But let me call your attention to another part of the same speech. You know that in his Charleston speech, an extract from which he has read, he declared that the negro belongs to an inferior race, is physically inferior to the white man, and should always be kept in an inferior position. I will now read to you what he said at Chicago on that point. In concluding his speech at that place, he remarked:[21]

> My friends, I have detained you about as long as I desired to do, and I have only to say, let us discard all this quibbling about this man and the other man, this race and that race, and the other race being inferior, and, therefore, they must be placed in an inferior position, discarding our standard that we have left us. Let us discard all these things, and unite as one people throughout this land, until we shall once more stand up declaring that all men are created equal.°

Thus you see that when addressing the Chicago abolitionists, he declared that all distinction of race must be discarded and blotted out, because the negro stood on an equal footing with the white man, that if one man said the Declaration of Independence did not mean a negro when it declared all men created equal, that another man would say that it did not mean another man. And hence we ought to discard all difference between the negro race and all other races and declare them all created equal. Did old Giddings, when he came down among you four years ago, preach more radical abolitionism than that? Did Lovejoy or Lloyd Garrison or Wendell Phillips or Fred Douglass ever take higher abolition ground° than that?

Lincoln told you that I had charged him with getting up these personal attacks to conceal the enormity of his principles, and then commenced talking about

---

20. From AL's Chicago speech, July 10, 1858. See textual note at p. 312.
21. Ibid.

something else, omitting to quote this part of his Chicago speech which contained the enormity of his principles to which I alluded. He knew that I alluded to his negro equality doctrines when I spoke of the enormity of his principles, yet he did not find it convenient to answer on that point. Having shown you what he said in his Chicago speech in reference to negroes being created equal to white men, and about discarding all distinctions between the two races, I will again read to you what he said at Charleston in order that the two may go out side by side. Here is what he said at Charleston:°

> I will say then, that I am not nor ever have been in favor of bringing about in any way, the social and political equality of the white and black races; that I am not nor ever have been in favor of making voters of the free negroes, or jurors, or qualifying them to hold office, or having them to marry with white people. I will say in addition, that there is a physical difference between the white and black races, which I suppose, will forever forbid the two races living together upon terms of social and political equality, and inasmuch, as they cannot so live, that while they do remain together, there must be the position of superior and inferior, that I as much as any other man am in favor of the superior position being assigned to the white man.°

Voice: That's good° doctrine.

Douglas: Yes, sir, that is good doctrine, but Mr. Lincoln is afraid to advocate it in the latitude of Chicago, where he hopes to get his votes. *[Cheers, laughter]* It is good doctrine in the anti-abolition counties for him, and his Chicago speech is good doctrine in the abolition counties. I assert, on the authority of these two speeches of Mr. Lincoln, that he holds one set of principles in the abolition counties, and a different and contradictory set in the other counties. *[Cheers]* I do not question that he said at Ottawa what he quoted, but that only convicts him further, by proving that he has twice contradicted himself instead of once. *[Applause]*

Let me ask him why he cannot avow his principles the same in the North as in the South, the same in every county, if he has a conviction that they are just? But I forgot. He would not be a Republican if his principles would apply alike to every part of the country. The party to which he belongs is bounded and limited by geographical lines. With their principles they cannot even cross the Mississippi River on your ferry boats. *[Laughter, applause]* They cannot cross over the Ohio into Kentucky. Lincoln himself cannot visit the land of his fathers, the scenes of his childhood, the graves of his ancestors, and carry his abolition principles, as he declared them at Chicago, with him. *[Cheers]*

This Republican organization appeals to the North against the South. It appeals to Northern passion, Northern prejudice, and Northern ambition, against Southern people, Southern states, and Southern institutions, and its only hope of success is by that appeal. Mr. Lincoln goes on to justify himself in making a war upon slavery upon the ground that Frank Blair and Gratz Brown did not succeed in their warfare upon the institution in Missouri. *[Laughter, applause]* Let us see what right Frank Blair had to believe he would succeed in Missouri.° Frank Blair was elected to Congress in 1856 from the State of Missouri as a Buchanan Democrat, and he turned Fremonter after the people elected him, thus belonging to one party before his election, and another afterwards. What right, then, had he to expect, after having thus cheated his constituency, that they would support him at another election.

Mr. Lincoln thinks that it is his duty to preach a crusade in the free states against slavery because it is a crime, as he believes, and ought to be extinguished, and because the people of the slave states will never abolish it. How is he going to abolish it? Down in the Southern part of the state he takes the ground openly that he will not interfere with slavery where it exists, and says that he is not now and never was in favor of interfering with slavery where it exists in the states. Well, if he is not in favor of that, how does he expect to bring slavery in a course of ultimate extinction? How can he extinguish it in Kentucky, in Virginia, in all the slave states by his policy, if he will not pursue a policy which will interfere with it in the states where it exists? In his speech at Springfield before the abolition or Republican convention, he declared his hostility to any more slave states in this language:[22]

> Under the operation of that policy, that agitation has not only, not ceased, but has constantly augmented. In my opinion, it will not cease, until a crisis shall have been reached and passed. "A house divided against itself cannot stand." I believe this government cannot endure permanently half slave and half free. I do not expect the Union to be dissolved—I do not expect the house to fall—but I do expect it will cease to be divided. It will become all one thing, or all the other. Either the opponents of slavery, will arrest the further spread of it, and place it where the public mind shall rest in the belief that it is in the course of ultimate extinction; or its advocates will push it forward, till it shall become alike lawful in all the States, old as well as new—North as well as South.°

Mr. Lincoln there told his abolition friends that this government could not endure permanently divided into free and slave states, as our fathers made it, and that it must become all free or all slave, otherwise, that the government could not exist. How then does Lincoln propose to save the Union, unless by compelling all the states to become free, so that the house shall not be divided against itself? He intends making them all free. He will preserve the Union in that way, and yet he is not going to interfere with slavery anywhere it now exists. How is he going to bring that about? Why, he will agitate, he will induce the North to agitate, until the South shall be worried out and forced to abolish slavery.

---

22. From AL's "House Divided" speech.

Let us examine the policy by which that is to be done. He first tells you that he would prohibit slavery everywhere in the territories. He would thus confine slavery within its present limits. When he thus gets it confined, and surrounded, so that it cannot spread, the natural laws of increase will go on until the negroes will be so plenty that they cannot live on the soil. He will hem them in until starvation seizes them, and by starving them to death, he will put slavery in the course of ultimate extinction. If he is not going to interfere with slavery in the states, but intends to interfere and prohibit it in the territories, and thus smother slavery out, it naturally follows that he can extinguish it only by extinguishing the negro race, for his policy would drive them to starvation. This is the humane and Christian remedy that he proposes for the great crime of slavery.

He tells you that I will not argue the question whether slavery is right or wrong. I tell you why I will not do it. I hold that, under the Constitution of the United States, each state of this Union has a right to do as it pleases on the subject of slavery. In Illinois we have exercised that sovereign right by prohibiting slavery within our own limits. I approve of that line of policy. We have performed our whole duty in Illinois. We have gone as far as we have a right to go under the Constitution of our common country. It is none of our business whether slavery exists in Missouri or not. Missouri is a sovereign state of this Union and has the same right to decide the slavery question for herself that Illinois has to decide it for herself. Hence I do not choose to occupy the time allotted to me in discussing a question that we have no right to act upon. I thought that you desired to hear us upon those questions coming within our constitutional power of action. Lincoln will not discuss these. What one question has he discussed that comes within the power or calls for the action or interference of an United States Senator? He is going to discuss the rightfulness of slavery when Congress cannot act upon it either way.

He wishes to discuss the merits of the Dred Scott decision when, under the Constitution, a senator has no right to interfere with the decision of judicial tribunals. He wants your exclusive attention to two questions that he has no power to act upon, to two questions that he could not vote upon if he was in Congress, to two questions that are not practical, in order to conceal your attention from other questions which he might be required to vote upon should he ever become a member of Congress. He tells you that he does not like the Dred Scott decision. Suppose he does not, how is he going to help himself? He says that he will reverse it. How will he reverse it? I know of but one mode of reversing judicial decisions, and that is by appealing from the inferior to the superior court. But I have never yet learned how or where an appeal could be taken from the Supreme Court of the United States! The Dred Scott decision was pronounced by the highest tribunal on earth. From that decision there is no appeal this side of Heaven. Yet, Mr.

Lincoln says he is going to reverse that decision. By what tribunal will he reverse it? Will he appeal to a mob? Does he intend to appeal to violence, to Lynch law? Will he stir up strife and rebellion in the land and overthrow the Court by violence? He does not deign to tell you how he will reverse the Dred Scott decision, but keeps appealing each day from the Supreme Court of the United States to political meetings in the country. *[Laughter]*

He wants me to argue with you the merits of each point of that decision before this political meeting. I say to you, with all due respect, that I choose to abide by the decisions of the Supreme Court as they are pronounced. It is not for me to inquire after a decision is made whether I like it in all the points or not. When I used to practice law with Lincoln, I never knew him to be beat in a case that he did not get mad at the judge and talk about appealing. *[Laughter]* And when I got beat I generally thought the court was wrong, but I never dreamed of going out of the court house and making a stump speech to the people against the judge, merely because I had found out that I did not know the law as well as he did. *[Laughter]* If the decision did not suit me, I appealed until I got to the Supreme Court, and then if that Court, the highest tribunal in the world, decided against me, I was satisfied, because it is the duty of every law-abiding man to obey the Constitution, the laws, and the constituted authorities. He who attempts to stir up odium and rebellion in the country against the constituted authorities is stimulating the passions of men to° resort to violence and to mobs instead of to the law. Hence, I tell you that I take the decisions of the Supreme Court as the law of the land, and I intend to obey them as such.

But Mr. Lincoln says that I will not answer his question as to what I would do in the event of the Court making so ridiculous a decision as he imagines they would by deciding that the free state of Illinois could not prohibit slavery within her own limits. I told him at Freeport why I would not answer such a question. I told him that there was not a man possessing any brains in America, lawyer or not, who ever dreamed that such a thing could be done. I told him then, as I say now, that by all the principles set forth in the Dred Scott decision, it is impossible. I told him then, as I do now, that it is an insult to men's understanding, and a gross calumny on the Court, to presume in advance that it was going to degrade itself so low as to make a decision known to be in direct violation of the Constitution.

Voice: That same thing was said about the Dred Scott decision before it passed.

Douglas: Perhaps you think that the Court did the same thing in reference to the Dred Scott decision. I have heard a man talk that way before. The principles contained in the Dred Scott decision had been affirmed previously in various other decisions. What court or judge ever held that a negro was a citizen? *[Laughter]* The state courts had decided that question over and over again, and the Dred Scott decision on that point only affirmed what every court in the land knew to be the law.

But I will not be drawn off into an argument upon the merits of the Dred Scott decision. It is enough for me to know that the Constitution of the United States created the Supreme Court for the purpose of deciding all disputed questions touching the true construction of that instrument, and when such decisions are pronounced, they are the law of the land, binding on every good citizen. Mr. Lincoln has a very convenient mode of arguing upon the subject. He holds that because he is a Republican, that he is not bound by the decisions of the Court, but that I being a Democrat am so bound. *[Laughter, cheers]* It may be that Republicans do not hold themselves bound by the laws of the land and the Constitution of the country as expounded by the courts. It may be an article in the Republican creed that men who do not like a decision have a right to rebel against it. But when Mr. Lincoln preaches that doctrine, I think he will find some honest Republicans, some law-abiding men° in that party, who will repudiate such a monstrous doctrine. The decision in the Dred Scott case is binding on every American citizen alike, and yet Mr. Lincoln argues that the Republicans are not bound by it, because they are opposed to it, *[Laughter]* whilst Democrats are bound by it, because we will not resist it. A Democrat cannot resist the constitutional authorities of this country. A Democrat is a law-abiding man. A Democrat stands by the Constitution and the laws, and relies upon liberty as protected by law, and not upon mob or political violence.

I have never yet been able to make Mr. Lincoln understand, nor° can I make any man who is determined to support him, right or wrong, understand how it is that under the Dred Scott decision the people of a territory, as well as a state, can have slavery or not, just as they please. I believe that I can explain that proposition to all Constitution-loving, law-abiding men in a way that they cannot fail to understand it. Chief Justice Taney, in his opinion in the Dred Scott case, said that slaves being property, the owner of them has a right to take them into a territory, the same as he would any other property. In other words, that slave property, so far as the right to enter a territory is concerned, stands on the same footing with other property. Suppose we grant that proposition. Then any man has a right to go to Kansas and take his property with him. But when he gets there, he must rely upon the local law to protect his property, whatever it may be. In order to illustrate this, imagine that three of you conclude to go to Kansas. One takes $10,000 worth of slaves, another $10,000 worth of liquors, and the third $10,000 worth of dry goods. When the man who owns the dry goods arrives out there and commences selling them, he finds that he is stopped and prohibited from selling until he gets a license, which will destroy all the profits he can make on his goods to pay for. When the man with the liquors gets there and tries to sell, he finds a Maine liquor law in force which prevents him. Now, of what use is his right to go there with his property unless he is protected in the enjoyment of that right after he gets there? The man who goes there with his slaves finds that there is no law to protect him when he arrives there. He has no remedy if his slaves run away to another country. There is no slave code or police regulations, and the absence of them excludes his slaves from the territory just as effectually and as positively as a constitutional prohibition could.

Such was the understanding when the Kansas and Nebraska bill was pending in Congress. Read the speech of Speaker Orr, of South Carolina, in the House of Representatives, in 1856, on the Kansas question, and you will find that he takes the ground that, while the owner of a slave has a right to go into a territory and carry his slaves with him, that he cannot hold them one day or hour unless there is a slave code to protect him. He tells you that slavery would not exist a day in South Carolina, or any other state, unless there was a friendly people and friendly legislation. Read the speeches of that giant in intellect, Alexander H. Stephens, of Georgia, and you will find them to the same effect. Read the speeches of Sam Smith, of Tennessee, and of all Southern men, and you will find that they all understood this doctrine then as we understand it now.[23]

Mr. Lincoln cannot be made to understand it however. Down at Jonesboro, he went on to argue that if it be the law that a man has a right to take his slaves into the° territory of the United States under the Constitution, that then a member of Congress was perjured if he did not vote for a slave code. I ask him whether the decision of the Supreme Court is not binding upon him as well as on me? If so, and he holds that he would be perjured if he did not vote for a slave code under it, I ask him whether, if elected to Congress, he will so vote? I have a right to his answer, and I will tell you why. He put that question to me down in Egypt, and did it with an air of triumph. This was about the form of it: "In the event of a slaveholding citizen of one of the territories should need and demand a slave code to protect his slaves, will you vote for it?"[24] I answered him that a fundamental article in the Democratic creed, as put forth in the Nebraska bill and the Cincinnati platform, was non-intervention by Congress with slavery in the states and territories, [Cheers] and hence, that I would not vote in Congress for any code of laws either for or against slavery in any territory. I will leave the people perfectly free to decide that question for themselves. [Cheers]

Mr. Lincoln and the *Washington Union* both think this a monstrous bad doctrine. Neither Mr. Lincoln nor° the *Washington Union* like my Freeport speech on that subject. The *Union*, in a late number, has been reading me out of the

---

23. See the Galesburg debate, note 10, p. 186.
24. See the Jonesboro debate, p. 115.

Democratic party because I hold that the people of a territory, like those of a state, have the right to have slavery or not, as they please. It has devoted three and a half columns to prove certain propositions, one of which I will read.[25] It says:

> We propose to show that Judge Douglas's action in 1850 and 1854 was taken with especial reference to the announcement of doctrine and programme which was made at Freeport. The declaration at Freeport was, that "in his opinion the people can, *by lawful means,* exclude slavery from a Territory *before* it comes in as a State*,*" and he declared that his competitor had "heard him *argue the Nebraska bill on that principle* all over Illinois in 1854, 1855, and 1856, and had no *excuse to pretend to have any doubt upon that subject.* °

The *Washington Union* there charges me with the monstrous crime of now proclaiming on the stump the same doctrine that I carried out in 1850, by supporting Clay's compromise measures. The *Union* also charges that I am now proclaiming the same doctrine that I did in 1854 in support of the Kansas and Nebraska bill. It is shocked that I should now stand where I stood in 1850, when I was supported by Clay, Webster, Cass and the great men of that day, and where I stood in 1854, and in 1856, when Mr. Buchanan was elected President. It goes on to prove, and succeeds in proving from my speeches in Congress on Clay's compromise measures, that I held the same doctrine at that time that I do now, and then proves that by the Kansas and Nebraska bill, I advanced the same doctrine that I now advance. It remarks:

> So much for the course taken by Judge Douglas on the compromises of 1850. The record shows, beyond the possibility of cavil or dispute, that he expressly intended in those bills to give the territorial legislatures power to exclude slavery. How stands his record in the memorable session of 1854 with reference to the Kansas-Nebraska bill itself?
>
> We shall not overhaul the votes that were given on that notable measure. Our space will not afford it. We have his own words, however, delivered in his speech closing the great debate on that bill on the night of March 3, 1854, to show that *he meant* to do in 1854 precisely what *he had meant* to do in 1858. The Kansas-Nebraska bill being upon its passage, he said:

It then quotes my remarks upon the passage of the bill as follows:

> The principle which we propose to carry into effect by this bill is this: That Congress shall neither legislate slavery into any Territory or State nor out of the same; but the people shall be left free to regulate their domestic concerns in their own way, subject only to the constitution of the United States. In order to carry this principle into practical operation, it becomes necessary *to remove whatever*

---

25. This and the succeeding quotations are from the *Washington Union,* Oct. 5, 1858.

legal obstacles might be found in the way of its *free exercise.* It is only for the purpose of carrying out this great fundamental principle of self-government that the bill renders the eighth section of the Missouri act inoperative and void.

Now, let me ask, will those senators who have arraigned me, or any one of them, have the assurance to rise in his place and declare that this great principle was never thought of or advocated as applicable to territorial bills, in 1850; that, from that session until the present, nobody ever thought of incorporating this principle in all new territorial organizations, &c., &c? I will begin with the compromises of 1850. Any senator who will take the trouble to examine our journals will find that on the 25th of March of that year I reported from the Committee on Territories two bills, including the following measures: the admission of California, a territorial government for Utah, a territorial government for New Mexico, and adjustment of the Texas boundary. These bills proposed to leave the people of Utah and New Mexico free to decide the slavery question for themselves, *in the precise language of the Nebraska bill* now under discussion. A few weeks afterwards the committee of thirteen took those bills and put a wafer between them and reported them back to the Senate as one bill, with some slight amendments. *One of those amendments was, that the territorial legislature should not legislate upon the subject of African slavery. I objected to this provision,* upon the ground that it subverted the great principle of self-government, *upon which the bill had been originally framed by the Territorial Committee.* On the first trial the Senate refused to strike it out, but subsequently did so, upon full debate, in order to establish that principle as the rule of action in territorial organizations.

The *Union* comments thus upon my speech on that occasion:

> Thus it is seen that, in framing the Nebraska-Kansas bill, Judge Douglas framed it in the terms and upon the model of those of Utah and New Mexico, and that in the debate he took pains expressly to revive the recollection of the voting which had taken place upon amendments affecting the powers of the territorial legislatures over the subject of slavery in the bills of 1850, in order to give the same meaning, force, and effect to the Nebraska-Kansas bill on this subject as had been given to those of Utah and New Mexico.°

The *Union* proves the following propositions: First, that I sustained Clay's compromise measures on the ground that they established the principle of self-government in the territories, giving the legislature the right to have slavery or not, as it pleased.° Secondly, that I brought in the Kansas and Nebraska bill founded upon the same principles as Clay's compromise measures of 1850. And thirdly, that my Freeport speech is in exact accordance with those principles. And what do you think is the imputation that the *Union* casts upon me for all this? It says that my Freeport speech is not Democratic, and that I was not a Democrat in 1854 or in 1850! Now, is not that funny? *[Laughter, cheers]* To° think that the author of the Kansas and Nebraska bill was not a Democrat when he introduced it. The *Union* says I was not a sound Democrat in 1850, nor in 1854, nor in 1856, nor am I in 1858, because I have always taken and now occupy the ground that the people of a territory, like those of a state, have the right to decide for themselves whether slavery shall or shall not exist in a territory.

I wish to cite, for the benefit of the *Washington Union* and the followers of that sheet, one authority on that point, and I hope the authority will be deemed satisfactory to that class of politicians. I will read from Mr. Buchanan's letter accepting the nomination of the Democratic convention for the presidency. You know that Mr. Buchanan, after he was nominated, declared to the Keystone Club, in a public speech, that he was no longer James Buchanan, but the embodiment of the Democratic platform.[26] In his letter to the committee which informed him of his nomination, accepting it he defined the meaning of the Kansas and Nebraska bill and the Cincinnati platform in these words:[27]

> The recent legislation of Congress respecting domestic slavery, derived, as it has been, from the original and pure fountain of legitimate political power, the will of the majority, promises ere long to allay the dangerous excitement. This legislation is founded upon principles as ancient as free government itself, and, in accordance with them, has simply declared that the people of a territory, like those of a State, shall decide for themselves whether slavery shall or shall not exist within their limits. °

Thus you see that James Buchanan accepted the nomination at Cincinnati on the condition that the people of a territory, like those of a state, should be left to decide for themselves whether slavery should or should not exist within their limits. I sustained James Buchanan for the presidency on that platform, as adopted at Cincinnati and expounded by himself. He was elected president on that platform, and now we are told by the *Washington Union* that no man is a true Democrat who stands on the platform on which Mr. Buchanan was nominated, and which he has explained and expounded himself. *[Laughter]*

We are told that a man is not a Democrat who stands by Clay, Webster, and Cass, and the compromise measures of 1850, and the Kansas and Nebraska bill of 1854. Whether a man be Democrat or not on that platform, I intend to stand there as long as I have life. *[Cheers]* I intend to cling firmly to that great principle which declares the right of each state and each territory to settle the question

---

26. In Buchanan's speech to the Keystone Club speech of June 9, 1856, he said: "Being the representative of the great Democratic party, and not simply James Buchanan, I must square my conduct according to the platform of the party, and insert no new plank, nor take one from it." John Bassett Moore, ed., *The Works of James Buchanan* (Philadelphia: Lippincott, 1910), 10:81.

27. "To the Committee of Notification," June 16, 1856, ibid., 10:83.

of slavery, and every other domestic question, for themselves. I hold that if they want a slave state, they have a right under the Constitution of the United States to make it so, and if they want a free state, it is their right to have it. But the *Union,* in advocating the claims of Lincoln over me to the Senate, lays down two un-pardonable heresies which it says I advocate. The first is the right of the people of a territory, the same as a state, to decide for themselves the question whether slavery shall exist "within their limits," in the language of Mr. Buchanan. And the second is that a constitution shall be submitted to the people of a territory for its adoption or rejection before their admission as a state under it. It so happens that Mr. Buchanan is pledged to both these heresies, for supporting which the *Washington Union* has read me out of the Democratic church. In his annual message he said that he trusted that the example of the Minnesota case would be followed in all future cases, requiring a submission of the constitution. And in his letter of acceptance, he said that the people of a territory, the same as a state, had the right to decide for themselves whether slavery should exist within their limits. Thus you find that this little corrupt gang who control the *Union,* and wish to elect Lincoln in preference to me because, as they say, of these two heresies which I support, denounce President Buchanan when they denounce me, if he stands now by the principles upon which he was elected.

Will they pretend that he does not now stand by the principles on which he was elected? Do they hold that he has abandoned the Kansas-Nebraska bill, the Cincinnati platform, and his own letter accepting his nomination, all of which declare the right of the people of a territory, the same as a state, to decide the slavery question for themselves? I will not believe that he has betrayed or intends to betray the platform which elected him. But if he does, I will not follow him. I will stand by that great principle, no matter who may desert it. I intend to stand by it for the purpose of preserving peace between the North and the South, the free and the slave states.

If each state will only agree to mind its own business, and let its neighbors alone, there will be peace forever between us. We in Illinois tried slavery when a territory, and found it was not good for us in this climate and with our sur-roundings, and hence, we abolished it. We then adopted a free state constitution, as we had a right to do. In this state we have declared that a negro shall not be a citizen, and we have also declared that he shall not be a slave. We had a right to adopt that policy. Missouri has just as good a right to adopt the other policy.[28] I am now speaking of rights under the Constitution, and not of moral or religious

---

28. See in glossary "slavery in Illinois Territory," p. 331, and "Illinois and the rights of blacks," pp. 325–26.

rights. I do not discuss the morals of the people of Missouri, but let them settle that matter for themselves.

I hold that the people of the slaveholding states are civilized men as well as ourselves; that they have° consciences as well as we, and that they are accountable to God and their posterity and not to us. It is for them to decide therefore the moral and religious right of the slavery question for themselves within their own limits. But as to the constitutional question, I do decide.° I assert that they had as much right under the Constitution to adopt the system of policy which they have as we had to adopt ours. So it is with every other state in this Union. Let each state stand firmly by that great constitutional right. Let each state mind its own business and let its neighbors alone, and there will be no trouble on this question.

If we will stand by that principle, then Mr. Lincoln will find that this republic can exist forever divided into free and slave states, as our fathers made it and the people of each state have decided. Stand by that great principle and we can go on as we have done, increasing in wealth, in population, in power, and in all the elements of greatness, until we shall be the admiration and terror of the world. We can go on and enlarge as our population increases and we require more room, until we make this continent one ocean-bound republic. Under that principle, the United States can perform that great mission, that destiny which Providence has marked out for us. Under that principle, we can receive with entire safety that stream of intelligence which is constantly flowing from the Old World to the New, filling up our prairies, clearing our wildernesses, and building cities, towns, railroads and other internal improvements, and thus make this the asylum of the oppressed of the whole earth.

We have this great mission to perform, and it can only be performed by adhering faithfully to that principle of self-government on which our institutions were all established. I repeat that the principle is the right of each state, each territory, to decide this slavery question for itself, to have slavery or not, as it chooses, and it does not become Mr. Lincoln, or anybody else, to tell the people of Kentucky that they have no conscience, that they are living in a state of iniquity, and that they are cherishing an institution to their bosoms in violation of the law of God. Better for him to adopt the doctrine of "judge not lest ye be judged." [Applause] Let him perform his own duty at home, and he will have a better fate in the future. I think there are objects of charity enough in the free states to excite the sympathies and open the pockets of all the benevolence we have amongst us, without going abroad in search of negroes, of whose condition we know nothing. We have enough objects of charity at home, and it is our duty to take care of our own poor, and our own suffering, and make them comfortable and happy,° before we go abroad to intermeddle with other people's business.

My friends, I am told that my time is within two minutes of expiring. I have omitted many topics that I would like to have discussed before you at length. There were many points touched by Mr. Lincoln that I have not been able to take up for the want of time. I have hurried over each subject that I have discussed as rapidly as possible so as to omit but few, but one hour and a half is not time sufficient for a man to discuss at length one half of the great questions which are now dividing the public mind.

In conclusion, I desire to return to you my grateful acknowledgements for the kindness and the courtesy with which you have listened to me. It is something remarkable that in an audience as vast as this, composed of men of opposite politics and views, with their passions highly excited, there should be so much courtesy, kindness, and respect exhibited not only towards one another, but towards the speakers, and I feel that it is due to you that I should thus express my gratitude for the kindness with which you have treated me. *[Cheers, applause]*

LINCOLN'S REJOINDER

My friends: Since Judge Douglas has said to you in his conclusion that he had not time in an hour and a half to answer all I had said in an hour, it follows of course that I will not be able to answer in half an hour all that he said in an hour and a half. *[Cheers, laughter]*

I wish to return to Judge Douglas my profound thanks for his public annunciation here today, to be put on record, that his system of policy in regard to the institution of slavery *contemplates that it shall last forever.* *[Cheers]* We are getting a little nearer the true issue of this controversy, and I am profoundly grateful for this one sentence. Judge Douglas asks you why cannot the institution of slavery, or rather, why cannot the nation, part slave and part free, continue as our fathers made it *forever?* In the first place, I insist that our fathers *did not* make this nation half slave and half free, or part slave and part free. *[Applause]* I insist that they found the institution of slavery existing here. They did not make it so, but they left it so because they knew of no way to get rid of it at that time. When Judge Douglas undertakes to say that, as a matter of choice, the fathers of the government made this nation part slave and part free, *he assumes what is, historically, a falsehood.* *[Applause]* More than that, when the fathers of the government cut off the source of slavery by the abolition of the slave trade, and adopted a system of restricting it from the new territories where it had not existed, I maintain that they placed it where they understood, and all sensible men understood, it was in the course of ultimate extinction.[29] And when Judge Douglas asks me why it

29. AL refers to the federal Constitution's provision (Art. I, Sect. 9), which could permit

cannot continue as our fathers made it, I ask him why he and his friends could not let it remain as our fathers made it? *[Cheers]*

It is precisely all I ask of him in relation to the institution of slavery, that it shall be placed upon the basis that our fathers placed it upon. Mr. Brooks, of South Carolina, once said, and truly said, that when this government was established, no one expected the institution of slavery to last until this day, and that the men who formed the government were wiser and better men than the men of these days. But the men of these days had experience which the fathers had not, and that experience had taught them the invention of the cotton gin, and this had made the perpetuation of the institution of slavery a necessity in this country. Judge Douglas could not let it stand upon the basis upon which our fathers placed it, but removed it and *put it upon the cotton-gin basis. [Laughter, applause]* It is a question, therefore, for him and his friends to answer—why they could not let it remain where the fathers of the government originally placed it.[30] *[Cheers]*

I hope nobody has understood me as trying to sustain the doctrine that we have a right to quarrel with Kentucky, or Virginia, or any of the slave states, about the institution of slavery, thus giving the Judge an opportunity to make himself eloquent and valiant against us in fighting for their rights. I expressly declared in my opening speech that I had neither the inclination to exercise, nor the belief in the existence of, the right to interfere with the states of Kentucky or Virginia in doing as they pleased with slavery or any other existing institution. *[Applause]* Then what becomes of all his eloquence in behalf of the rights of states, which are assailed by no living man? *[Applause]*

But I have to hurry on, for I have but a half hour. The Judge has informed me, or informed this audience, that the *Washington Union* is laboring for my election to the United States Senate. *[Cheers, laughter]* That is news to me—not very ungrateful news either. *[Turning to Mr. W. H. Carlin, seated on the platform]* I hope that Carlin will be elected to the State Senate and will vote for me.

W. H. Carlin: Carlin don't fall in.°

Lincoln: Carlin don't fall in, I perceive, and I suppose he will not do much for me. *[Laughter]* But I am glad of all the support I can get anywhere, if I can get it without practicing any deception to obtain it. In respect to this large portion of Judge Douglas's speech, in which he tries to show that in the controversy between himself and the administration party he is in the right, I do not feel myself at all competent or inclined to answer him. I say to him, "Give it to them. *[Laughter]*

---

the outlawing of the overseas slave trade after 1808, and to the exclusion of slaves from the Northwest Territory by the Northwest Ordinance. .

30. Congressman Preston Brooks's speech is recorded in *Congressional Globe, Appendix,* 33rd Cong., 1st Sess., Mar. 15, 1854, 372.

Give it to them just all you can." *[Laughter, cheers]* And, on the other hand, I say to Carlin, and Jake Davis, and to this man Wagley up here in Hancock, "Give it to Douglas.[31] *[Laughter]* Just pour it into him. You know him and he knows you." It is a fair fight, just clear the way and let them have it.° *[Cheers, laughter]*

Now in regard to this matter of the Dred Scott decision, I wish to say a word or two. After all, the Judge will not say whether, if a decision is made holding that the people of the *states* cannot exclude slavery, he will support it or not. He obstinately refuses to say what he will do in that case. The judges of the Supreme Court as obstinately refused to say what they would do on this subject. Before this, I reminded him that at Galesburg he had said the judges had expressly declared the contrary, and you remember that in my opening speech I told him I had the book containing that decision here, and I would thank him to lay his finger on the place where any such thing was said. He has occupied his hour and a half, and he has not ventured to try to sustain his assertion. *[Cheers]* He never will. *[Cheers]*

But he is desirous of knowing how we are going to reverse the Dred Scott decision. Judge Douglas ought to know how. Did not he and his political friends find a way to reverse the decision of that same Court in favor of the constitutionality of the National Bank?[32] *[Cheers, laughter]* Didn't they find a way to do it so effectually that they have reversed it as completely as any decision ever was reversed, so far as its practical operation is concerned? *[Cheers]* And let me ask you, didn't Judge Douglas find a way to reverse the decision of our Supreme Court, when it decided that Carlin's father—old Governor Carlin—had not the constitutional power to remove a secretary of state? *[Cheers, laughter]* Did he not appeal to the "mobs," as he calls them? Did he not make speeches in the lobby to show how villainous that decision was, and how it ought to be overthrown? Did he not succeed, too, in getting an act passed by the legislature to have it overthrown? And didn't he himself sit down on that bench as one of the five added judges, who were to overslaugh the four old ones, getting his name of "Judge" in that way and no other?[33] *[Cheers, laughter]* If there is a villainy in using disrespect or making opposition to Supreme Court decisions, I commend it to Judge Douglas's earnest consideration. *[Cheers, laughter]* I know of no man in the State of Illinois who ought to know so well about *how much* villainy it takes to oppose a decision of the Supreme Court as our honorable friend, Stephen A. Douglas. *[Applause]*

Judge Douglas also makes the declaration that I say the Democrats are bound

---

31. AL refers here to several Democratic candidates for the Illinois General Assembly from western Illinois who were antagonistic to SAD, and humorously offers encouragement to their antagonism.

32. See the Ottawa debate, note 36, pp. 32–33.

33. See the Ottawa debate, note 37, p. 33.

by the Dred Scott decision while the Republicans are not. In the sense in which he argues, I never said it, but I will tell you what I have said and what I do not hesitate to repeat today. I have said that as the Democrats believe that decision to be correct and that the extension of slavery is affirmed in the national Constitution, they are bound to support it as such; but as we do not believe it is a correct decision, we are not bound to support it as such. ° And I will tell you here that General Jackson once said each man was bound to support the Constitution "as he understood it." Now, Judge Douglas understands the Constitution according to the Dred Scott decision, and he is bound to support it as he understands it. *[Cheers]* I understand it another way, and therefore I am bound to support it in the way in which I understand it. *[Applause]* And as Judge Douglas believes that decision to be correct, I will remake the argument if I have time to do so.

Let me talk to some gentleman down there among you who looks me in the face. We will say you are a member of the territorial legislature, and like Judge Douglas, you believe that the right to take and hold slaves there is a constitutional right. The first thing you do is to *swear you will support the Constitution* and all rights guaranteed therein, that you will, whenever your neighbor needs your legislation to support his constitutional right, not withhold that legislation. If you withhold that necessary legislation for the support of the Constitution and constitutional rights, do you not commit perjury? I ask every sensible man, if that is not so? *[Mixed response]* That is undoubtedly just so, say what you please. Now that is precisely what Judge Douglas says, that this is a constitutional right. Does the Judge mean to say that the territorial legislature in legislating may, by withholding necessary laws, or by passing unfriendly laws, *nullify that constitutional right?* Does he mean to say that? Does he mean to ignore the proposition so long known and well established in the law, that what you cannot do directly, you cannot do indirectly? Does he mean that?

The truth about the matter is this: Judge Douglas has sung paeans to his "popular sovereignty" doctrine until his Supreme Court, cooperating with him, has *squatted* his "squatter sovereignty" out. *[Laughter, applause]* But he will keep up this species of humbuggery about "squatter sovereignty." He has at last invented this sort of "*do-nothing sovereignty,*" *[Laughter]* that the people may exclude slavery by a sort of "sovereignty" that is exercised by doing nothing at all. *[Laughter]* Is not that running his "popular sovereignty" down awfully? *[Laughter]* Has it not got down as thin as the homeopathic soup that was made by boiling the shadow of a pigeon that had starved to death? *[Laughter, cheers]* But at last, when it is brought to the test of close reasoning, there is not even that thin decoction of it left. It is a presumption impossible in the domain of thought. It is precisely no other than the putting of that most unphilosophical proposition, that two bodies may occupy the same space at the same time. The Dred Scott decision covers the whole ground, and while it occupies it, there is no room even for the shadow of a starved pigeon to occupy the same ground. *[Cheers, laughter]*

Voice from the platform: Your time is almost out.

Lincoln: Well, I'll talk to you a little longer. Judge Douglas, in reply to what I have said about having, upon a previous occasion, made the same° speech at Ottawa as the one he took an extract from, at Charleston, says it only shows that I practiced the deception twice. Now, my friends, are any of you obtuse enough to swallow that? Judge Douglas had said I had made a speech at Charleston that I would not make up North, and I turned around and answered him by showing I *had* made that same speech up North, had made it at Ottawa, made it in his hearing, made it in *the* abolition district, Lovejoy's district, in the personal presence of Lovejoy himself, in the same atmosphere exactly in which I had made my Chicago speech of which he complains so much.

Now, in relation to my not having said anything about the quotation from the Chicago speech. He thinks that is a terrible subject for me to handle. Why, gentlemen, I can show you that the substance of the Chicago speech, I delivered two years ago in "Egypt," as he calls it. It was down at Springfield.[34] That speech is here in this book, and I could turn to it and read it to you but for the lack of time. I have not now the time to read it.

Voices: Read it.

Lincoln: No, gentlemen, I am obliged to use discretion in disposing most advantageously of my brief time. The Judge has taken great exception to my adopting the heretical statement in the Declaration of Independence that all men are created equal, and he has a great deal to say about negro equality. I want to say that, in sometimes alluding to the Declaration of Independence, I have only uttered the sentiments that Henry Clay used to hold. Allow me to occupy your time a moment with what he said. Mr. Clay was at one time called upon in Indiana, and in a way that I suppose was very insulting, to liberate his slaves, and he made a written reply to that application, and one portion of it is in these words:[35]

> What is the *foundation* of this appeal to me in Indiana, to liberate the slaves under my care in Kentucky? It is a general declaration in the act announcing to the world the independence of the thirteen American colonies, that all° *men are created equal.* Now, as an abstract principal, *there is no doubt of the truth of that*

---

34. AL probably refers to his speech in response to the *Dred Scott* decision. See "Speech at Springfield, Illinois," June 26, 1857, in Roy P. Basler et al., eds., *The Collected Works of Abraham Lincoln* (New Brunswick: Rutgers University Press, 1953), 2:405–10.

35. AL quotes from Clay's "Speech in Richmond, Indiana," Oct. 1, 1842. See Robert Porter Seager II and Melba Porter Hay, eds., *The Papers of Henry Clay* (Lexington: University Press of Kentucky, 1988), 9:778–79. Italics not in original.

declaration; and it is desirable, in the *original construction* of society, and in organized societies, to keep it in view as a great fundamental principle.° *[Cheers]*

When I sometimes, in relation to the organization of new societies in new countries where the soil is clean and clear, insisted that we should keep that principle in view, Judge Douglas will have it that I want a nigger° wife.[36] *[Laughter]* He never can be brought to understand that there is any middle ground on this subject. I have lived until my fiftieth year and have never had a negro woman either for a slave or a wife, *[Cheers]* and I think I can live fifty centuries, for that matter, without having had one for either. *[Cheers, laughter]* I maintain that you may take Judge Douglas's quotations from my Chicago speech, and from my Charleston speech, and the Galesburg speech in his speech of today, and compare them over, and I am willing to trust them with you upon his proposition that they show rascality or double dealing. I deny that they do. *[Applause]*

I suppose I have occupied ten minutes.°

The Judge does not seem at all disposed to have peace, but I find he is disposed to have a personal warfare with me. He says that my oath would not be taken against the bare word of Charles H. Lanphier or Thomas L. Harris. Well, that is altogether a matter of opinion. *[Laughter]* It is certainly not for me to vaunt my word against oaths of these gentlemen, but I will tell Judge Douglas again the facts upon which I *dared* to say they proved a forgery. I pointed out at Galesburg that the publication of these resolutions in the *Illinois State Register* could not have been the result of accident, as the proceedings of that meeting bore unmistakable evidence of being done by a man who *knew* it was a forgery, that it was a publication partly taken from the real proceedings of the convention, and partly from the proceedings of a convention at another place, which showed that he had the real proceedings before him. And taking one part of the resolutions, he threw out another part and substituted false and fraudulent ones in their stead.[37] I pointed that out to him, and also that his friend Lanphier, who was editor of the *Register* at that time and now is, must have known how it was done. Now whether *he* did it or got some friend to do it for him, I could not tell, but he certainly knew all about it. I pointed out to Judge Douglas that, in his Freeport speech, he had promised to *investigate* that matter. Does he now say he did not make that promise?[38] I have a right to ask *why he did not keep it?* *[Applause]* I call upon him to tell here today why he did not keep that promise? That fraud has been traced up so that it lies between him, Harris, and Lanphier. There is little room for escape for Lanphier.

---

36. For SAD's practice of construing AL's position on the Declaration of Independence as advocating racial amalgamation, see the Ottawa debate, note 23, p. 24.

37. The resolutions in question were published in the *Illinois State Register,* Oct. 16, 1854.

38. See the Freeport debate, p. 64.

[Laughter] Lanphier is doing the Judge good service, and Douglas desires his word to be taken for the truth. He desires Lanphier to be taken as authority in what he states in his newspaper. He desires Harris to be taken as a man of vast credibility, and when this thing lies among them, they will not press it to show where the guilt really belongs. Now, as he has said that he would investigate it, and implied that he would tell us the result of his investigation, I demand of him to tell why he did not investigate it, if he did not. And if he did, *why he won't tell the result.* *[Cheers]* I call upon him for that.

This is the third time that Judge Douglas has assumed that he learned about these resolutions by Harris's attempting to use them against Norton on the floor of Congress. I tell Judge Douglas the public records of the country show that *he himself* attempted it upon Trumbull a month before Harris tried them on Norton, *[Applause]* that Harris had the opportunity of *learning it from him,* rather than he from Harris. I now ask his attention to that part of the record on the case. My friends, I am not disposed to detain you longer in regard to that matter.[39]

I am told that I still have five minutes left. There is another matter I wish to call attention to. He says, when he discovered there was a mistake in that case, he came forward magnanimously, without my calling his attention to it, and explained it. I will tell you how he became so magnanimous. When the newspapers of our side had discovered and published it, and put it beyond his power to deny it, then he came forward and made a virtue of necessity by acknowledging it. *[Applause]* Now he argues that all the point there was in those resolutions, although never passed at Springfield, is retained by their being passed at other localities. Is that true? He said I had a hand in passing them in his opening speech, that I was in the convention and helped to pass them. Do the resolutions touch me at all? It strikes me there is some difference between holding a man responsible for an act which he *has not* done, and holding him responsible for an act that he *has* done. You will judge whether there is any difference in the *spots.* *[Laughter, cheers]* And he has taken credit for great magnanimity in coming forward and acknowledging what is proved on him beyond even the capacity of Judge Douglas to deny, and he has more capacity in that way than any other living man. *[Laughter, cheers]*

Then he wants to know why I won't withdraw the charge in regard to a conspiracy to make slavery national, as he has withdrawn the one he made. May it please his worship, I will withdraw it *when it is proven on me as that was proved on him.* ° *[Applause, laughter]* I will add a little more than that. I will withdraw it whenever a reasonable man shall be brought to believe that the charge is not

---

39. The debate between SAD and Trumbull is reported in *Congressional Globe, Appendix,* 34th Cong., 1st Sess., July 9, 1856, 860–61. The exchange between Harris and Norton is reported in ibid., Aug. 9, 1856, 1274.

true. *[Applause]* I have asked Judge Douglas's attention to certain matters of fact tending to prove the charge of a conspiracy to nationalize slavery, and he says he convinces me that this is all untrue because Buchanan was not in the country at that time, and because the Dred Scott case had not then got into the Supreme Court. And he says that I say the *Democratic* owners of Dred Scott got up the case. I never did say that. *[Applause]* I defy Judge Douglas to show that I ever said so, *for I never uttered it.*

[Press & Tribune: One of Mr. Douglas's reporters gesticulated affirmatively at Mr. Lincoln.]

Lincoln: I don't care if your hireling does say I did, I tell you myself that *I never said the "Democratic" owners of Dred Scott got up the case. [Press & Tribune: "Tremendous enthusiasm" Times: "Great confusion"]* I have never pretended to know whether Dred Scott's owners were Democrats or abolitionists or Free Soilers or border ruffians. I have said that there is evidence about the case tending to show that it was a made up case, for the purpose of getting that decision. I have said that that evidence was very strong in the fact that when Dred Scott was declared to be a slave, the owner of him made him free, showing that he had had the case tried and the question settled for such° use as could be made of that decision. He cared nothing about the property thus declared to be his by that decision. *[Applause]* But my time is out and I can say no more.

ALTON

INTRODUCTION

After their sixth debate, Lincoln and Douglas both booked passage on the steamboat *City of Louisiana* and traveled downriver from Quincy to the final debate site at Alton, Illinois, making the 115-mile trip on the Mississippi on the night of October 14–15, 1858. They reached a town of six thousand population which, like Quincy, was both a railroad terminal and a Mississippi River port. The proximity of slaveholding Missouri to Alton was noted by both Lincoln and Douglas in their speeches on October 15—St. Louis was only twenty miles downriver and furnished two steamboat loads of listeners to the debate crowd—and Lincoln observed that he and Douglas were "before an audience, having strong sympathies southward by relationship, place of birth, and so on." This was probably true enough, but the local political situation was nonetheless quite complex. Surrounding Madison County delivered 77 percent of its vote to Lyman Trumbull, who, though nominally a Democrat, ran as an Anti-Nebraska candidate for the House of Representatives in 1854. Two years later both Democrats and Republicans were eclipsed and the large local German immigrant population was intimidated by a heavily antiforeign Know-Nothing turnout in favor of Millard Fillmore. And inadvertently giving credence to a claim often made by Douglas about Republicans in central and southern Illinois, the Madison County Republican Party did not identify itself by name as late as 1858; it sought support by calling itself the "People's Party" instead.

By the mutual agreement of the local debate organizers, neither Lincoln nor Douglas were met by a welcoming reception upon their arrival at 5:00 AM on the debate day. They repaired to their respective hotels instead and during the morning received visitors, while bands played outside, a Springfield military company performed, and the crowd began to assemble. Otherwise, fewer organized partisan demonstrations or displays were visible at Alton than at any other debate site save Jonesboro. A speakers' stand had been placed on the east side of Alton's new city hall, and by the scheduled debate time perhaps five thousand listeners had congregated there, the second-smallest audience of the debates series. Voter interest in the debates seems already to have peaked. Perhaps that happened at Galesburg, eight days before.

Leading off, Douglas enumerated what he considered to be the main points that separated him from Lincoln, relating to the nature of the Union, the meaning of the Dred Scott decision, and the comparative status of whites and Negroes in America. He repeated an assertion that Lincoln had earlier attacked at Quincy, that the U.S. government could last forever divided into free and slave states. In an argument not made before, he angled for antislavery sympathies by claiming that the practical workings of self-rule on the slavery issue in new states and territories had allowed the current balance of free and slave states to develop in favor of the free states. More forcibly than ever before in the debates, he acknowledged his contention with the Buchanan administration over the Lecompton Constitution and the English bill. And he affirmed once again his conviction that the promise of the rights to life, liberty, and the pursuit of happiness in the Declaration of Independence applied only to white people, and that the rights and privileges of blacks should be determined only by their immediate communities.

Lincoln rebutted by contending that only recently had the Declaration of Independence been said to apply only to whites, that indeed to say so was to tend to dehumanize black people and to prepare the public mind to consider them mere property. Declaring once again that the Founding Fathers had desired to place slavery on a course to ultimate extinction, Lincoln in ringing terms defined the main question separating him and Douglas as involving the wrongfulness of slavery. The real issue between the two was "the eternal struggle between these two principles—right and wrong—throughout the world." He considered slavery to be an institution that, because it was wrong, was dangerous and should thus not be allowed to expand into new territories, whereas Douglas and the Democrats refused ever to identify slavery as a wrong. Lincoln concluded by condemning Douglas's Freeport Doctrine as "lawless" and "monstrous" for what it seemed to allow territorial legislators to do in defiance of a right guaranteed by the Dred Scott decision.

Douglas's rejoinder contained much that was in his opening speech, and much that was in his Quincy speech. Going further, he reminded the audience of Lincoln's opposition to the Mexican War and the lack of patriotism that that opposition suggested. In tangential reference to Lincoln's identification of the main issue separating the two contestants, Douglas declared that he cared more for the principle of self-rule than for "all the niggers in Christendom." And he concluded with what amounted to another reaffirmation of the Freeport Doctrine, ignoring Lincoln's assessment of it.

A Madison County editor, having had enough of bipolar partisan descriptions of the Alton debate, wrote that the result of the meeting was "that we now have no candidates left for the United States Senate. According to the papers, Lincoln was "skinned alive and his hide hung on a fence, whilst the 'Little Giant' was rubbed completely out, not a grease spot left."[1] Most certainly, after three months of full-time campaigning and speechmaking, at the debate sites to be sure but also at dozens of other places, it should not be surprising that both campaigners might seem jaded and worn by mid-October, if not totally wiped out. Douglas's voice in particular seemed to some to be "completely shattered."[2] Nonetheless, a New York reporter who had attended most of the debates thought that despite the relatively small attendance, the meeting at Alton was "in many respects . . . the greatest discussion yet held."[3] If greatness resides in eloquence and appeals to morality, unquestionably Lincoln's moral position was one that he had unfolded and expanded between the Galesburg and Alton gatherings, and proclaimed in a kind of peroration at Alton. But unlike Lincoln, though he made a couple of new points, Douglas had become almost predictable at Alton. As one observer has said, "His attacks and constructive positions were about the same in Alton as in Ottawa."[4]

---

1. *Weekly Madison Press* (Edwardsville, Illinois), Oct. 20, 1858.
2. *Alton Weekly Courier,* Oct. 16, 1858.
3. *New York Evening Post,* Oct. 20, 1858
4. David Zarefsky, *Lincoln, Douglas and Slavery: In the Crucible of Public Debate* (Chicago: University of Chicago Press, 1990), 66.

DOUGLAS'S OPENING SPEECH

Thomas M. Hope: Judge, before you commence speaking, allow me to ask you a question.

Douglas: If you will not occupy too much of my time.

Hope: Only an instant.

Douglas: What is your question?

Hope: Do you believe that the territorial legislatures ought to pass laws to protect slavery in the territories?

Douglas: You will get an answer in the course of my remarks. *[Applause]*

Ladies and gentlemen: It is now nearly four months since the canvass between Mr. Lincoln and myself commenced. On the 16th of June the Republican convention assembled at Springfield and nominated Mr. Lincoln as their candidate for the Presidency and° the U. S. Senate, and he, on that occasion, delivered a speech in which he laid down what he understood to be the Republican creed and the platform on which he proposed to stand during the contest. The principal points in that speech of Mr. Lincoln's were: First, that this government could not endure permanently divided into free and slave states, as our fathers made it; that they must all become free or all become slave; all become one thing or all become the other, otherwise this Union could not continue to exist. I give you his opinions almost in the identical language he used. His second proposition was a crusade against the Supreme Court of the United States because of the Dred Scott decision, urging as an especial reason for his opposition to that decision, that it deprived the negroes of the rights and benefits of that clause in the Constitution of the United States which guarantees to the citizens of each state all the rights, privileges, and immunities of the citizens of the several states.[1]

On the 10th of July° I returned home, and delivered a speech to the people of Chicago, in which I announced it to be my purpose to appeal to the people of Illinois to sustain the course I had pursued in Congress.[2] In that speech, I joined issue with Mr. Lincoln on the points° which he had presented. Thus there was an issue clear and distinct made up between us on these two propositions laid down in the speech of Mr. Lincoln at Springfield, and controverted by me in my reply to him at Chicago. On the next day the 11th of July° Mr. Lincoln replied to

---

1. SAD alludes to Lincoln's "House Divided" speech to the Illinois Republican state convention on June 16, 1858, Roy P. Basler et al., eds., *The Collected Works of Abraham Lincoln* (New Brunswick: Rutgers University Press, 1953), 2:461–69.

2. SAD's July 9 (not July 10) Chicago speech is in the *Chicago Times*, July 10, 1858.

me at Chicago, explaining at some length, and re-affirming, the positions which he had taken in his Springfield speech.[3] In that Chicago speech, he even went further than he had before and uttered sentiments in regard to the negro being on an equality with the white man. He adopted in support of this position the argument which Lovejoy and Codding and other abolition lecturers had made familiar in the Northern and central portions of the state, to wit: that the Declaration of Independence having declared all men free and equal, by divine law also, that negro equality was an inalienable right, of which they could not be deprived. He insisted, in that speech, that the Declaration of Independence included the negro in the clause asserting that all men were created equal and went so far as to say that if one man was allowed to take the position that it did not include the negro, others might take the position that it did not include other men. He said that all these distinctions between this man and that man, this race and the other race, must be discarded, and we must all stand by the Declaration of Independence, declaring that all men were created equal.

The issue thus being made up between Mr. Lincoln and myself on three points, we went before the people of the state. During the following seven weeks, between the Chicago speeches and our first meeting at Ottawa, he and I addressed large assemblages of the people in many of the central counties. In my speeches I confined myself closely to those three positions which he had taken, controverting his proposition that this Union could not exist as our fathers made it, divided into free and slave states; controverting his proposition of a crusade against the Supreme Court because of the Dred Scott decision; and controverting his proposition that the Declaration of Independence included and meant the negroes as well as the white men, when it declared all men to be created equal. *[Cheers]*

I supposed at that time that these propositions constituted a distinct issue between us and that the opposite positions we had taken upon them we would be willing to be held to in every part of the state. I never intended to waver one hair's breadth from that issue, either in the North or the South, or wherever I should address the people of Illinois. I hold that when the time arrives that I cannot proclaim my political creed in the same terms, not only in the Northern but the Southern part of Illinois, not only in the Northern but the Southern states, and wherever the American flag waves over American soil, that then there must be something wrong in that creed. *[Cheers, applause]* So long as we live under a common Constitution, so long as we live in a confederacy of sovereign and equal states, joined together as one for certain purposes, I shall consider° that any political creed is radically wrong which cannot be proclaimed in every state, and every section of that Union alike.

---

3. AL, "Speech at Chicago, Illinois," July 10, 1858, Basler et al., *Collected Works*, 2:499–501.

I took up Mr. Lincoln's three propositions in my several speeches, analyzed them, and pointed out what I believed to be the radical errors contained in them. First, in regard to his doctrine that this government was in violation of the law of God which says that a house divided against itself cannot stand, I repudiated it as a slander upon the immortal framers of our Constitution. *[Applause]* I then said, have often repeated, and now again assert, that in my opinion this government can endure forever, divided into free and slave states as our fathers made it, each state having the right to prohibit, abolish, or sustain slavery, just as it pleases. *[Cheers]* This government was made upon the great basis of the sovereignty of the states— the right of each state to regulate its own domestic institutions to suit itself—and that right was conferred with the° understanding and expectation that, inasmuch as each locality had separate interests, each locality must have different and distinct local and domestic institutions, corresponding to its wants and interests. Our fathers knew when they made the government that the laws and institutions which were well adapted to the green mountains of Vermont were unsuited to the rice plantations of South Carolina. They knew then, as well as we know now, that the laws and institutions which would be well adapted to the beautiful prairies of Illinois would not be suited to the mining regions of California. They knew that in a republic as broad as this—having such a variety of soil, climate, and interests— there must necessarily be a corresponding variety of local laws, the policy and institutions of each state adapted to its condition and wants. For this reason, this Union was established on the right of each state to do as it pleased on the question of slavery, and every other question, and the various states were not allowed to complain of, much less interfere with, the policy of their neighbors. *[Cheers]*

Suppose the doctrine advocated by Mr. Lincoln and the abolitionists of this day had prevailed when the Constitution was made. What would have been the result? Imagine for a moment that Mr. Lincoln had been a member of the convention that framed the Constitution of the United States, and that when its members were about to sign that wonderful document, he had risen in that convention, as he did at Springfield this summer, and addressing himself to the President, had said "a house divided against itself cannot stand. *[Laughter]* This government divided into free and slave states cannot endure. They must all be free or all be slave; they must all be one thing or all be the other. Otherwise, it is a violation of the law of God and cannot continue to exist." Suppose Mr. Lincoln had convinced that body of sages that that doctrine was sound. What would have been the result? Remember that the Union was then composed of thirteen states, twelve of which were slaveholding and one free.[4] Do you think that the

---

4. By the time of the federal constitutional convention in 1787, slavery had been abolished outright in Massachusetts and New Hampshire, and provisions had been made for its gradual extinction in Pennsylvania, Rhode Island, and Connecticut.

one free state would have outvoted the twelve slaveholding states, and thus have secured the abolition of slavery? *[Cries of "No, no"]* On the other hand, would not the twelve slaveholding states have outvoted the one free state and thus have fastened slavery, by a constitutional provision, on every foot of the American republic forever?

You see that if this abolition doctrine of Mr. Lincoln had prevailed when the government was made, it would have established slavery as a permanent institution, in all the states whether they wanted it or not. And the question for us to determine in Illinois now, as one of the free states is, whether or not we are willing, having become the majority section, to enforce a doctrine on the minority which we would have resisted with our heart's blood had it been attempted on us when we were in a minority. *[Cheers]* How has the South lost her power as the majority section in this Union, and how have the free states gained it, except under the operation of that principle which declares the right of the people of each state and each territory to form and regulate their domestic institutions in their own way? It was under that principle that slavery was abolished in New Hampshire, Rhode Island, Connecticut, New York, New Jersey, and Pennsylvania. It was under that principle that one half of the slaveholding states became free. It was under that principle that the number of free states increased until from being one out of twelve states, we have grown to be the majority of states of the whole Union, with the power to control the House of Representatives and Senate, and the power, consequently, to elect a president by Northern votes, without the aid of a Southern state. Having obtained this power under the operation of that great principle, are you now prepared to abandon the principle and declare that merely because we have the power, you will wage a war against the Southern states and their institutions until you force them to abolish slavery everywhere? *[Applause]*

After having pressed these arguments home on Mr. Lincoln for seven weeks, publishing a number of my speeches, we met at Ottawa in joint discussion, and he then began to crawfish a little, and let himself down. *[Applause]* I there propounded certain questions to him. Amongst others, I asked him whether he would vote for the admission of any more slave states in the event the people wanted them. He would not answer. *[Applause, laughter]* I then told him that if he did not answer the question there, I would renew it at Freeport, and would then trot him down into Egypt and again put it to him. *[Cheers, applause]* Well, at Freeport, knowing that the next joint discussion took place in Egypt, and being in dread of it, he did answer my question in regard to no more slave states in a mode which he hoped would be satisfactory to me, and accomplish the object he had in view. I will show you what his answer was. After saying that he was not pledged to the Republican doctrine of "no more slave states," he declared: "I state to you freely, frankly, that I should be exceedingly sorry to ever be put in the position of having to pass upon that question." Here, permit me to remark, that I do not think the people will ever force him into a position against his will. *[Laughter, applause]* He went on to say:°

> I should be exceedingly glad to know that there never would be another slave State admitted into this Union. But I must add in regard to this, that if slavery shall be kept out of the territory during the territorial existence of any one given territory and then the people should, having a fair chance and clear field when they come to adopt a constitution, if they should do the extraordinary thing of adopting a slave constitution, uninfluenced by the actual presence of the institution among them, I see no alternative, if we own the country, but we must admit it into the Union.° *[Applause, cheers]*

Gentlemen, your silence is more acceptable than your applause, for I desire to address exclusively your judgment.°

That answer Mr. Lincoln supposed would satisfy the old line Whigs, composed of Kentuckians and Virginians, down in the Southern part of the state. Now, what does it amount to? I desired to know whether he would vote to allow Kansas to come into the Union with slavery or not, as her people desired. He would not answer, but in a roundabout way said that if slavery should be kept out of a territory during the whole of its territorial existence, and then the people, when they adopted a state constitution, asked admission as a slave state, he supposed he would have to let the state come in. The case I put to him was an entirely different one. I desired to know whether he would vote to admit a state if Congress had not prohibited slavery in it during its territorial existence, as Congress never pretended to do under Clay's compromise measures of 1850.[5] He would not answer, and I have not yet been able to get an answer from him. *[Laughter, applause]* I have asked him whether he would vote to admit Nebraska if her people asked to come in as a state with a constitution recognizing slavery, and he refused to answer. *[Cheers]* I have put the question to him with reference to New Mexico, and he has not uttered a word in answer. I have enumerated the territories, one after another, putting the same question to him with reference to each, and he has not said, and will not say, whether, if elected to Congress, he will vote to admit any territory now in existence with such a constitution as her people may adopt. He invents a case which does not exist, and cannot exist, under this government, and answers it, but he will not answer the question I put to him in connection with any of the territories now in existence. *[Cheers]*

The contract we entered into with Texas when she entered the Union obliges us to allow four states to be formed out of the old state and admitted with or without slavery, as the respective inhabitants of each may determine. I have asked

---

5. See Freeport debate, pp. 60–61.

Mr. Lincoln three times in our joint discussions whether he would vote to redeem that pledge, and he has never yet answered. He is as silent as the grave on the subject. *[Laughter]* He would rather answer as to a state of the case which will never arise than commit himself by telling what he would do in a case which would come up for his action soon after his election to Congress. *[Laughter]*

Why can he not say whether he is willing to allow the people of each state to have slavery or not as they please, and to come into the Union when they have the requisite population as a slave or a free state, as they decide? I have no trouble in answering the question. I have said everywhere, and now repeat it to you, that if the people of Kansas want a slave state they have a right, under the Constitution of the United States, to form such a state, and I will let them come into the Union with slavery or without, as they determine. *[Cheers]* If the people of any other territory desire slavery, let them have it. If they do not want it, let them prohibit it. It is their business not mine. *[Cheers]* It is none of our business in Illinois whether Kansas is a free state or a slave state. It is none of your business in Missouri whether Kansas shall adopt slavery or reject it. It is the business of her people and none of yours. The people of Kansas have as much right to decide that question for themselves as you have in Missouri to decide it for yourselves, or we in Illinois to decide it for ourselves. *[Cheers]*

And here I may repeat what I have said in every speech I have made in Illinois, that I fought the Lecompton Constitution to its death, not because of the slavery clause in it, but because it was not the act and deed of the people of Kansas. *[Applause]* I said, then, in Congress, and I say now, that if the people of Kansas want a slave state, they have a right to have it. If they wanted the Lecompton Constitution, they had a right to have it. I was opposed to that constitution because I did not believe that it was the act and deed of the people, but on the contrary, the act of a small, pitiful minority acting in the name of the majority. When at last it was determined to send that constitution back to the people, and accordingly, in August last, the question of admission under it was submitted to a popular vote, the citizens rejected it by nearly ten to one, thus showing conclusively that I was right when I said that the Lecompton Constitution was not the act and deed of the people of Kansas and did not embody their will.[6] *[Cheers]*

I hold that there is no power on earth, under our system of government, which has the right to force a constitution upon an unwilling people. Suppose there had been a majority of ten to one in favor of slavery in Kansas, and suppose there had been an abolition president, and an abolition administration, and by some means the abolitionists succeeded in forcing an abolition constitution on

---

6. Under the provisions of the English bill, the Lecompton Constitution was submitted to a vote in Kansas on Aug. 2, when it was rejected by 11,812 to 1,926.

those slaveholding people. Would the people of the South have submitted to that act for one instant? *[Cries of "No, no"]* Well, if you of the South would not have submitted to it a day, how can you, as fair, honorable, and honest men, insist on putting a slave constitution on a people who desire a free state? *[Cheers]* Your safety and ours depend upon both of us acting in good faith and living up to that great principle which asserts the right of every people to form and regulate their domestic institutions to suit themselves, subject only to the Constitution of the United States. *[Applause]*

Most of the men who denounced my course on the Lecompton question objected to it, not because I was not right, but because they thought it expedient at that time, for the sake of keeping the party together, to do wrong. *[Cheers, applause]* I never knew the Democratic party to violate any one of its principles, out of policy or expediency, that it did not pay the debt with sorrow. There is no safety or success for our party unless we always do right and trust the consequences to God and the people. I chose not to depart from principle for the sake of expediency in the Lecompton question, and I never intend to do it on that or any other question.

But I am told that I would have been all right if I had only voted for the English bill after Lecompton was killed. *[Laughter, cheers]* You know a general pardon was granted to all political offenders on the Lecompton question, provided they would only vote for the English bill. I did not accept the benefits of that pardon, for the reason that I had been right in the course I had pursued, and hence did not require any forgiveness.[7] Let us see how the result has been worked out. English brought in his bill referring the Lecompton Constitution back to the people, with the provision that if it was rejected, Kansas should be kept out of the Union until she had the full ratio of population required for a member of Congress, thus in effect declaring that if the people of Kansas would only consent to come into the Union under the Lecompton Constitution, and have a slave state when they did not want it, they should be admitted with a population of 35,000, but that if they were so obstinate as to insist upon having just such a constitution as they thought best, and to desire admission as a free state, then they should be kept out until they had 93,420 inhabitants. I then said, and I now repeat to you, that whenever Kansas has people enough for a slave state, she has people enough for a free state. *[Cheers, applause]* I was and am willing to adopt the rule that no state shall ever come into the Union until she has the full ratio of population for a member of Congress, provided that rule is made uniform. I made that proposition in the Senate last winter, but a majority of the senators

---

7. Given strong Buchanan administration support of the English bill, SAD's opposition to it precluded any possible reconciliation between him and the president.

would not agree to it, and I then said to them: "If you will not adopt the general rule, I will not consent to make an exception of Kansas."[8]

I hold that it is a violation of the fundamental principles of this government to throw the weight of federal power into the scale, either in favor of the free or the slave states. Equality among all the states of this Union is a fundamental principle in our political system. We have no more right to throw the weight of the federal government into the scale in favor of the slaveholding than the free states, and least° of all should our friends in the South consent for a moment that Congress should wield° its powers either way, when they know that there is a majority against them in both houses of Congress.

Fellow citizens, how have the supporters of the English bill stood up to their pledges not to admit Kansas until she obtained a population of 93,420 in the event she rejected the Lecompton Constitution? How? The newspapers inform us that English himself, whilst conducting his canvass for re-election, and in order to secure it, pledged himself to his constituents that if returned, he would disregard his own bill and vote to admit Kansas into the Union with such population as she might have when she made application. *[Laughter, applause]* We are informed that every Democratic candidate for Congress, in all the states where elections have recently been held, was pledged against the English bill, with perhaps one or two exceptions. Now, if I had only done as these anti-Lecompton men who voted for the English bill in Congress, pledging themselves to refuse to admit Kansas if she refused to become a slave state until she had a population of 93,420, and then returned to their people, forfeited their pledge, and made a new pledge to admit Kansas at any time she applied, without regard to population, I would have had no trouble. You saw the whole power and patronage of the federal government wielded in Indiana, Ohio, and Pennsylvania to re-elect anti-Lecompton men to Congress who voted against Lecompton, then voted for the English bill, and then denounced the English bill and pledged themselves to their people to disregard it. My sin consists in not having given a pledge, and then in not having afterwards forfeited it.

For that reason, in this state, every postmaster, every route agent, every collector of the ports, and every federal office-holder, forfeits his head the moment he expresses a preference for the Democratic candidates against Lincoln and his abolition associates. *[Cheers, applause]* A Democratic administration, which we helped to bring into power, deems it consistent with its fidelity to principle

---

8. SAD's insistence that he will not "make an exception of Kansas" here means that he will not go along with the scheme, incorporated into the English bill, to offer special incentives to Kansas to come into the Union as a slave state, a proposition offered to no other states, and therefore making Kansas an exception. This can be a source of confusion, for in the matter of population requirements for statehood, he clearly is willing to "make an exception of Kansas."

and its regard to duty to wield its power in this state in behalf of the Republican abolition candidates in every county and every congressional district, against the Democratic party. All I have to say in reference to the matter is, that if that administration have not regard enough for principle, if they are not sufficiently attached to the creed of the Democratic party to bury forever their personal hostilities in order to succeed in carrying out our glorious principles, I have.[9] *[Cheers]* I have no personal difficulties with Mr. Buchanan or his cabinet. He chose to make certain recommendations to Congress, as he had a right to do on the Lecompton question. I could not vote in favor of them. I had as much right to judge for myself how I should vote as he had as to° how he should recommend. He undertook to say to me, "If you do not vote as I tell you, I will take off the heads of your friends." *[Laughter]* I replied to him, "You did not elect me. I represent Illinois, and I am accountable to Illinois as my constituency, and to God, but not to the President or to any other power on earth." *[Cheers, applause]*

And now this warfare is made on me because I would not surrender my connections of duty, because I would not abandon my constituency, and receive the orders of the executive authorities how I should vote in the Senate of the United States. *[Cheers]* I hold that an attempt to control the Senate on the part of the Executive is subversive of the principles of our Constitution. The Executive department is independent of the Senate, and the Senate is independent of the President. In matters of legislation, the President has a veto on the action of the Senate, and in appointments and treaties the Senate has a veto on the President. He has no more right to tell me how I shall vote on his appointments than I have to tell him whether he shall veto or approve a bill that the Senate has passed. Whenever you recognize the right of the Executive to say to a senator, "Do this, or I will take off the heads of your friends," you convert this government from a republic into a despotism. *[Cheers]* Whenever you recognize the right of a President to say to a member of Congress, "Vote as I tell you, or I will bring a power to bear against you at home which will crush you," you destroy the independence of the representative, and convert him into a tool of executive power. *[Applause]* I resisted this invasion of the constitutional rights of a senator, and I intend to resist it as long as I have a voice to speak or a vote to give. Yet, Mr. Buchanan cannot provoke me to abandon one iota of Democratic principles out of revenge or hostility to his course. *[Cheers]* I stand by the platform of the Democratic party, and by its organization, and support its nominees. If there are any who choose to bolt, the fact only shows that they are not as good Democrats as I am. *[Applause]*

My friends, there never was a time when it was as important for the Democratic party, for all national men, to rally and stand together as it is today. We find

9. See "National Democrats" in the glossary, p. 328.

all sectional men giving up past differences and combining on ° the one question of slavery, and when we find sectional men thus uniting, we should unite to resist them and their treasonable designs. Such was the case in 1850, when Clay left the quiet and peace of his home and again entered upon public life to quell agitation and restore peace to a distracted Union. Then we Democrats, with Cass at our head, welcomed Henry Clay, whom the whole nation regarded as having been preserved by God for the times. He became our leader in that great fight, and we rallied around him the same as the Whigs rallied around Old Hickory in 1832 to put down nullification. *[Cheers]* Thus you see that whilst Whigs and Democrats fought fearlessly in old times about banks, the tariff, distribution, the specie circular, and the sub-treasury, all united as a band of brothers when the peace, harmony, or integrity of the Union was imperiled. *[Applause]* It was so in 1850, when abolitionism had even so far divided this country, North and South, as to endanger the peace of the Union. Whigs and Democrats united in establishing the compromise measures of that year, and restoring tranquility and good feeling. These measures passed on the joint action of the two parties. They rested on the great principle that the people of each state and each territory should be left perfectly free to form and regulate their domestic institutions to suit themselves. You Whigs and we Democrats justified them in that principle.

In 1854, when it became necessary to organize the territories of Kansas and Nebraska, I brought forward the bill on the same principle. In the Kansas-Nebraska bill you find it declared to be °"the true intent and meaning of the act not to legislate slavery into any state or territory, nor to exclude it therefrom, but to leave the people thereof perfectly free to form and regulate their domestic institutions in their own way."[10] *[Cheers]* I stand on that same platform in 1858 that I did in 1850, 1854, and 1856. The *Washington Union,* pretending to be the organ of the administration, in the number of the 5th of this month, devotes three columns and a half to establish these propositions: first, that Douglas, in his Freeport speech, held the same doctrine that he did in his Nebraska bill in 1854; second, that in 1854, Douglas justified the Nebraska bill upon the ground that it was based upon the same principle as Clay's compromise measures of 1850. The *Union* thus proved that Douglas was the same in 1858 that he was in 1856, 1854, and 1850, and consequently argued that he was never a Democrat. *[Laughter, applause]* Is it not funny that I was never a Democrat? *[Laughter]* There is no pretence that I have changed a hair's breadth. The *Union* proves by my speeches that I explained the compromise measures of 1850 just as I do now and that I explained the Kansas and Nebraska bill in 1854 just as I did in my Freeport speech, and yet says that I am not a Democrat, and cannot be trusted, because I have not changed during

---

10. *U.S. Statutes at Large* 10, 283.

the whole of that time. It has occurred to me that in 1854, the author of the Kansas and Nebraska bill was considered a pretty good Democrat. *[Cheers]* It has occurred to me that in 1856, when I was exerting every nerve and every energy for James Buchanan, standing on the same platform then that I do now, that I was a pretty good Democrat. *[Applause]* They now tell me that I am not a Democrat, because I assert that the people of a territory, as well as those of a state, have the right to decide for themselves whether slavery can or can not exist in such territory. Let me read what James Buchanan said on that point when he accepted the Democratic nomination for the Presidency in 1856. In his letter of acceptance,[11] he used the following language:

> The recent legislation of Congress respecting domestic slavery, derived, as it has been from the original and pure fountain of legitimate political power, the will of the majority, promises ere long to allay the dangerous excitement. This legislation is founded upon principles as ancient as free government itself, and, in accordance with them, has simply declared that the people of a territory, like those of a State, shall decide for themselves WHETHER SLAVERY SHALL OR SHALL NOT EXIST WITHIN THEIR LIMITS.°

Dr. Hope will there find my answer to the question he propounded to me before I commenced speaking. *[Applause]* Of course no man will consider it an answer who is outside of the Democratic organization, bolts Democratic nominations, and indirectly aids to put abolitionists into power over Democrats.[12] But whether Dr. Hope considers it an answer or not, every fair-minded man will see that James Buchanan has answered the question, and has asserted that the people of a territory, like those of a state, shall decide for themselves whether slavery shall or shall not exist within their limits. I answer specifically, if you want a further answer, and say that while under the decision of the Supreme Court, as recorded in the opinion of Chief Justice Taney,[13] slaves are property like all other property and can be carried into a° territory of the United States, the same as any other description of property, yet when you get them there, they are subject to the local law of the territory, just like all other property. You will find in a recent speech delivered by that able and eloquent statesman, Hon. Jefferson Davis, at Bangor, Maine, that he took the same view of this subject that I did in my Freeport speech. He there said:[14]

---

11. "To the Committee of Notification," June 16, 1856. See John Bassett Moore, ed., *The Works of James Buchanan* (Philadelphia: Lippincott, 1910), 10:83. Capitalization of the concluding words not in original.

12. SAD here implies that Hope belongs to the faction of Democrats opposing his candidacy.

13. SAD refers to the *Dred Scott* decision.

14. From a speech by U.S. Senator Jefferson Davis of Mississippi to a Democratic meeting

If the inhabitants of any territory should refuse to enact such laws and police regulations as would give security to their property or to his, it would be rendered more or less valueless in proportion to the difficulty of holding it without such protection. In the case of property in the labor of man or what is usually called slave property, the insecurity would be so great that the owner could not ordinarily retain it. Therefore, though the right would remain, the remedy being withheld, it would follow that the owner would be practically debarred, by the circumstances of the case, from taking slave property into a territory where the sense of the inhabitants was opposed to its introduction. So much for the oft repeated fallacy of forcing slavery upon any community.°

You will also find that the distinguished Speaker of the present House of Representatives, Hon. James L. Orr, construed the Kansas and Nebraska bill in this same way in 1856, and also that great intellect of the South, Alexander H. Stephens, put the same construction upon it in Congress that I did in my Freeport speech.[15] The whole South are rallying to the support of the doctrine that if the people of a territory want slavery, they have a right to have it, and if they do not want it, that no power on earth can force it upon them. I hold that there is no principle on earth more sacred to all the friends of freedom than that which says that no institution, no law, no constitution, should be forced on an unwilling people contrary to their wishes, and I assert that the Kansas and Nebraska bill contains that principle. It is the great principle contained in that bill. It is the principle on which James Buchanan was made President. Without that principle, he never would have been made President of the United States.

I will never violate or abandon that doctrine, if I have to stand alone. I have resisted the blandishments and threats of power on the one side, and seduction on the other, and have stood immovably for that principle, fighting for it when assailed by Northern mobs, or threatened by Southern hostility. [*Cheers*] I have defended it against the North and South, and I will defend it against whoever assails it, and I will follow it wherever its logical conclusions lead me. [*Cheers*] I say to you that

at Portland, Maine, in early Sept. 1858. See "Speech at Portland" [Sept. 11, 1858], Lynda Lasswell Crist and Mary Seaton Dix, eds., *The Papers of Jefferson Davis* (Baton Rouge: Louisiana State University Press, 1989) 6:218. Though Davis was voicing sentiments expressed by other Southern spokesmen as late as 1856, and akin to SAD's Freeport Doctrine (see note 15, p. 265), SAD's tacit cooperation with Republicans in 1858 against the Lecompton Constitution and the English bill had greatly reduced his standing with Southern Democrats. Davis probably had not heard of SAD's Freeport speech when he spoke at Portland, and he was roundly criticized upon returning to Mississippi. See Don E. Fehrenbacher, *Prelude to Greatness: Lincoln in the 1850's* (Stanford: Stanford University Press, 1962), 137–39.

15. See speeches by James L. Orr and Alexander H. Stephens in *Congressional Globe*, 34th Cong., 3rd Sess., House, Dec. 11, 1856, 3: 103–4, and ibid., *Appendix*, 34th Cong., Jan. 6, 1857, 133–35.

there is but one hope, one safety for this country, and that is to stand immovably by that principle which declares the right of each state and each territory to decide these questions for themselves. This government was founded on that principle and must be administered in the same sense in which it was founded.

But the abolition party really think that under the Declaration of Independence the negro is equal to the white man, and that negro equality is an inalienable right conferred by the Almighty, and hence, that all human laws in violation of it are null and void. With such men, it is no use for me to argue. I hold that the signers of the Declaration of Independence had no reference to negroes at all when they declared all men to be created equal. They did not mean negro, nor the savage Indians, nor the Fejee islanders, nor any other barbarous race. They were speaking of white men. *[Cheers]* They alluded to men of European birth and European descent, to white men and to none others, when they declared that doctrine. I hold that this government was established on the white basis. It was established by white men for the benefit of white men and their posterity forever, and should be administered by white men, and none others. But it does not follow, by any means, that merely because the negro is not a citizen, and merely because he is not our equal, that therefore he should be a slave. On the contrary, it does follow that we ought to extend to the negro race, and to all other dependent races, all the rights, all the privileges, and all the immunities which they can exercise consistently with the safety of society. Humanity requires that we should give them all these privileges. Christianity commands that we should extend those privileges to them.

The question then arises, what are those privileges, and what is the nature and extent of them? My answer is that that is a question which each state must answer for itself. We in Illinois have decided it for ourselves. We tried slavery, kept it up for twelve years, and finding that it was not profitable, we abolished it for that reason and became a free state. We adopted in its stead the policy that a negro in this state shall not be a slave and shall not be a citizen.[16] We have a right to adopt that policy. For my part I think it is a wise and sound policy for us. You in Missouri must judge for yourselves whether it is a wise policy for you. If you choose to follow our example, very good; if you reject it, still well. It is your business, not ours. So with Kentucky. Let Kentucky adopt a policy to suit herself. If we do not like it we will keep away from it, and if she does not like ours, let her stay at home, mind her own business and let us alone. If the people of all the states will act on that great principle, and each state mind its own business, attend to its own affairs, take care of its own negroes, and not meddle with its

---

16. See glossary: "slavery in Illinois Territory," p. 331, and "Illinois and the rights of blacks," pp. 325–26.

neighbors, then there will be peace between the North and the South, the East and the West, throughout the whole Union. *[Cheers]*

Why can we not thus have peace? Why should we thus allow a sectional party to agitate this country and convulse it,° to array the North against the South, and convert us into enemies instead of friends, merely that a few ambitious men may ride into power on a sectional hobby? How long is it since these ambitious Northern men wished for a sectional organization? Did any one of them dream of a sectional party as long as the North was the weaker section and the South the stronger? Then all were opposed to sectional parties. But the moment the North obtained the majority in the House and Senate by the admission of California, and could elect a President without the aid of Southern votes, that moment ambitious Northern men formed a scheme to excite the North against the South, and make the people be governed in their votes by geographical lines, thinking that the North, being the stronger section, would out-vote the South, and consequently they, the leaders, would ride into office on a sectional hobby. I am told that my hour is out. It was very short. *[Applause]*

LINCOLN'S REPLY

L adies and gentlemen.

Voice: There are no ladies here.

Lincoln: You are mistaken about that. There is a fine chance of them back here.[17] *[Laughter]*°

I have been somewhat, in my own mind, complimented by a large portion of Judge Douglas's speech. I mean that portion which he devotes to the controversy between himself and the present administration. *[Cheers, laughter]* This is the seventh time Judge Douglas and myself have met in these joint discussions, and he has been gradually improving in regard to his war with the administration. *[Laughter]* At Quincy, day before yesterday, he was a little more severe upon the administration than I had heard him upon any former occasion, and I took pains to compliment him for it. I told him that I altogether commended him to a most vigorous prosecution of that war.° I then told him to give it to them with all the power he had, and as some of them were present, I told them I would be very much obliged if they would *give it to him* in about the same way. *[Laughter, cheers]* I take it he has now vastly improved upon the attack he made then upon the administration. I flatter myself he has really taken my advice on this subject. All I can say now is to re-commend to him and to them what I then commended—

---

17. AL's wife, Mary Todd Lincoln, was in the crowd, which might have been at least part of his motivation for responding thus.

to prosecute the war against one another in the most vigorous manner. I say to them again, "Go it, husband! Go it, bear!" *[Laughter]*

There is one other thing I will mention before I leave this branch of the discussion, although I do not consider it much of my business anyway. I refer to that part of the Judge's remarks where he undertakes to involve Mr. Buchanan in an inconsistency. He reads something from Mr. Buchanan, from which he undertakes to involve him in an inconsistency, and he gets something of a cheer for having done so. I would only remind the Judge that while he is very valiantly fighting for the Nebraska bill and the repeal of the Missouri Compromise, it has been but a little while since he was the *valiant advocate of* the Missouri Compromise.[18] *[Cheers]* I want to know if Buchanan has not as much right to be inconsistent as Douglas has? *[Applause, laughter]* Has Douglas the *exclusive right,* in this country, of being *on all sides of all questions?* Is nobody allowed that high privilege but himself? Is he to have an entire *monopoly* on that subject? *[Laughter]*

So far as Judge Douglas addressed his speech to me, or so far as it was about me, it is my business to pay some attention to it. I have heard the Judge state two or three times what he has stated today—that in a speech which I made at Springfield, Illinois, I had in a very especial manner complained that the Supreme Court in the Dred Scott case had decided that a negro could never be a citizen of the United States.[19] I have omitted by some accident heretofore to analyze this statement, and it is required of me to notice it now. In point of fact it is *untrue.* I never have complained *especially* of the Dred Scott decision because it held that a negro could not be a citizen, and the Judge is always wrong when he says I ever did so complain of it. I have the speech here, and I will thank him or any of his friends to show where I said that a negro should be a citizen, and complained especially of the Dred Scott decision because it declared he could not be one. I have done no such thing, and Judge Douglas's so persistently insisting that I have done so has strongly impressed me with the belief of a pre-determination on his part to misrepresent me. He could not get his foundation for insisting that I was in favor of this negro equality anywhere else as well as he could by assuming that untrue proposition.

Let me tell this audience what is true in regard to that matter and the means by which they may correct me, if I do not tell them truly, is by a recurrence to the speech itself. I spoke of the Dred Scott decision in my Springfield speech, and I was then endeavoring to prove that the Dred Scott decision was a portion

18. In a speech at Springfield on Oct. 23, 1849, SAD eulogized the Missouri Compromise as a measure that "had an origin akin to that of the Constitution of the United States," and which "had become canonized in the hearts of the American people, as a sacred thing, which no ruthless hand would ever be reckless enough to disturb." See *Illinois State Register,* Nov. 2, 1849.

19. AL's "House Divided" speech, June 16, 1858, Basler et al., *Collected Works,* 2:461–69.

of a system or scheme to make slavery national in this country. I pointed out what things had been decided by the court. I mentioned as a fact that they had decided that a negro could not be a citizen, that they had done so, as I supposed, to deprive the negro, under all circumstances, of the remotest possibility of ever becoming a citizen and claiming the rights of a citizen of the United States under a certain clause of the Constitution, which guarantees to the citizens of each state all the privileges and immunities of citizens in the several states.° I stated that without making any complaint of it at all. I then went on and stated the other points decided in the case, namely, that the bringing of a negro into the State of Illinois and holding him in slavery for two years here was a matter in regard to which they would not decide whether it made him free or not; that they decided the further point that taking him into a United States territory, where slavery was prohibited by act of Congress, did not make him free because that act of Congress, as they held, was unconstitutional. I mentioned these three things as making up the points decided in that case. I mentioned them in a lump, taken in connection with the introduction of the Nebraska bill and the amendment of Chase, offered at the time, declaratory of the right of the people of the territories to *exclude slavery,* which was voted down by the friends of the bill. I mentioned all these things together as evidence tending to prove a combination and conspiracy to make the institution of slavery national. In that connection, and in that way, I mentioned the decision on the point that a negro could not be a citizen, and in no other connection. Out of this, Judge Douglas builds up his beautiful fabrication of my purpose to introduce a perfect social and political equality between the white and black races. His assertion that I made an "especial objection" (that is his exact language) to the decision on this account is untrue in point of fact.

Now, while I am upon this subject, and as Henry Clay has been alluded to, I desire to place myself, in connection with Mr. Clay, as nearly right before this people as may be. I am quite aware what the Judge's object is here by all these allusions. He knows that we are before an audience having strong sympathies southward by relationship, place of birth, and so on. He desires to place me in an extremely abolition attitude. He read upon a former occasion, and alludes without reading today, to a portion of a speech which I delivered in Chicago. In his quotations from that speech, as he has made them upon former occasions, the extracts were taken in such a way as, I suppose, brings them within the definition of what is called *garbling*—taking portions of a speech which, when taken by themselves, do not present the entire sense of the speaker as expressed at the time. I propose, therefore, out of that same speech, to show how one portion of it which he skipped over—taking an extract before and an extract after—will give a different idea, and the true idea I intended to convey. It will take me some little time to read it, but I believe I will occupy the time in that way.

You have heard him frequently allude to my controversy with him in regard to the Declaration of Independence. I confess that I have had a struggle with Judge Douglas on that matter, and I will try briefly to place myself right in regard to it on this occasion. I said—and it is between the extracts Judge Douglas has taken from this speech and put in his published speeches—I said: °

> It may be argued that there are certain conditions that make necessities and impose them upon us, and to the extent that a necessity is imposed upon a man he must submit to it. I think that was the condition in which we found ourselves when we established this government. We had slavery among us, we could not get our Constitution unless we permitted them to remain in slavery, we could not secure the good we did secure if we grasped for more, and having by necessity submitted to that much, it does not destroy the principle that is the charter of our liberties. Let that charter stand as our standard. ° [20]

Now I have upon all occasions declared as strongly as Judge Douglas against the disposition to interfere with the existing institution of slavery. You hear me read it from the same speech from which he takes garbled extracts for the purpose of proving upon me a disposition to interfere with the institution of slavery and establish a perfect social and political equality between negroes and white people.

Allow me while upon this subject briefly to present one other extract from a speech of mine,[21] more than a year ago, at Springfield, in discussing this very same question, soon after Judge Douglas took his ground that negroes were not included in the Declaration of Independence:

> I think the authors of that notable instrument intended to include *all* men, but they did not intend to declare all men equal *in all respects.* They did not mean to say all men were equal in color, size, intellect, moral developments, or social capacity. They defined with tolerable distinctness, in what respects they did consider all men created equal—equal in "certain inalienable rights, among which are life, liberty and the pursuit of happiness." This they said, and this they° meant. They did not mean to assert the obvious untruth, that all were then actually enjoying that equality, nor yet, that they were about to confer it immediately upon them. In fact they had no power to confer such a boon. They meant simply to declare the *right,* so that the *enforcement* of it might follow as fast as circumstances should permit. They meant to set up a standard maxim for free society, which should be familiar to all, and revered by all; constantly looked to, constantly labored for, and even though never perfectly attained, constantly approximated, and thereby constantly spreading and deepening its influence, and augmenting the happiness and value of life to all people, of all colors everywhere. °

---

20. "Speech at Chicago, Illinois," July 10, 1858, Basler et al., *Collected Works,* 2:501.

21. From AL's speech in response to the *Dred Scott* decision, "Speech at Springfield, Illinois," June 26, 1857, Basler et al., *Collected Works,* 2:405–6.

There again are the sentiments I have expressed in regard to the Declaration of Independence upon a former occasion, sentiments which have been put in print and read wherever anybody cared to know what so humble an individual as myself chose to say in regard to it.

At Galesburg the other day, I said in answer to Judge Douglas, that three years ago there never had been a man, so far as I knew or believed, in the whole world, who had said that the Declaration of Independence did not include negroes in the term "all men." I reassert it today. I assert that Judge Douglas and all his friends may search the whole records of the country, and it will be a matter of great astonishment to me if they shall be able to find that one human being three years ago had ever uttered the astounding sentiment that the term "all men" in the Declaration did not include the negro.

Do not let me be misunderstood. I know that more than three years ago there were men who, finding this assertion constantly in the way of their schemes to bring about the ascendancy and perpetuation of slavery, *denied the truth of it*. I know that Mr. Calhoun and all the politicians of his school denied the truth of the Declaration. I know that it ran along in the mouths of some Southern men for a period of years, ending at last in that shameful though rather forcible declaration of Pettit of Indiana, upon the floor of the United States Senate, that the Declaration of Independence was in that respect "a self-evident lie," rather than a self-evident truth.[22] But I say, with a perfect knowledge of all this hawking at the Declaration without directly attacking it, that three years ago there never had lived a man who had ventured to assail it in the sneaking way of pretending to believe it and then asserting it did not include the negro. *[Cheers]* I believe the first man who ever said it was Chief Justice Taney in the Dred Scott case, and the next to him was our friend Stephen A. Douglas. *[Cheers, laughter]* And now it has become the catch-word of the entire party. I would like to call upon his friends everywhere to consider how they have come in so short a time to view this matter in a way so entirely different from their former belief? To ask whether they are not being borne along by an irresistible current, whither they know not? *[Applause]*

In answer to my proposition at Galesburg last week, I see that some man in Chicago has got up a letter addressed to the *Chicago Times,* to show, as he professes, that somebody *had* said so before. And he signs himself "An Old Line Whig," if I remember correctly.[23] In the first place I would say he *was not* an old line Whig. I am somewhat acquainted with old line Whigs. I was with the old line Whigs from the origin to the end of that party. I became pretty well acquainted

---

22. For this famous affirmation by Senator John Pettit, see *Congressional Globe, Appendix,* 33rd Cong., 1st Sess., Feb. 20, 1854, 214.

23. This letter is in the *Chicago Times,* Oct. 10, 1858.

with them, and I know they always had some sense, whatever else you could ascribe to them. *[Laughter]* I know there never was one who had not more sense than to try to show by the evidence he produces° that some man had, prior to the time I named, said that negroes were not included in the term "all men" in the Declaration of Independence.

What is the evidence he produces? I will bring forward *his* evidence and let you see what *he* offers by way of showing that somebody more than three years ago had said negroes were not included in the Declaration. He brings forward part of a speech from Henry Clay, *the* part of *the* speech of Henry Clay which I used to bring forward to prove precisely the contrary. *[Laughter]* I guess we are surrounded to some extent today by the old friends of Mr. Clay, and they will be glad to hear anything from that authority. While he was in Indiana, a man presented him a petition to liberate his negroes, and he, Mr. Clay, made a speech in answer to it, which I suppose he carefully wrote out himself and caused to be published. I have before me an extract from that speech which constitutes the evidence this pretended "Old Line Whig" at Chicago brought forward to show that Mr. Clay didn't suppose the negro was included in the Declaration of Independence. Hear what Mr. Clay said:[24]

> What is the *foundation* of this appeal to me in Indiana, to liberate the slaves under my care in Kentucky? It is a general declaration in the act announcing to the world the independence of the thirteen American colonies, that *all "men are created equal."* Now, as an abstract principle, *there is no doubt of the truth of that declaration,* and it is desirable *in the original construction of society, and in organized societies,* to keep it in view as a great fundamental principle. But then I apprehend that in no society that ever did exist, or ever shall be formed, was or can the equality asserted among the members of the human race be practically enforced and carried out. There are portions of it, large portions, women, minors, insane, culprits, transient sojourners, that will always probably remain subject to the government of another portion of the community.
>
> That declaration, whatever may be the extent of its import, was made by the delegations of the Thirteen States. In most of them slavery existed, and had long existed, and was established by law. It was introduced and forced upon the colonies by the paramount law of England. Do you believe that in making that declaration the States that concurred in it intended that it should be tortured into a virtual emancipation of all the slaves within their respective limits? Would Virginia and the other Southern States have ever united in a declaration which was to be interpreted into an abolition of slavery among them? Did any one of the

---

24. From Clay's "Speech in Richmond, Indiana," Oct. 1, 1842, as printed in the *Chicago Times*, Oct. 10, 1858. For an authoritative modern text, see Robert Porter Seager II and Melba Porter Hay, eds., *The Papers of Henry Clay* (Lexington: University Press of Kentucky, 1988), 9:778–79.

Thirteen States entertain such a design or expectation? To impute such a secret and unavowed purpose, would be to charge a political fraud upon the noblest band of patriots that ever assembled in council; a fraud upon the confederacy of the revolution; a fraud upon the union of these States whose constitution not only recognized the lawfulness of slavery, but permitted the importation of slaves from Africa until the year 1808.°

This is the entire quotation[25] brought forward to prove that somebody previous to three years ago had said the negro was not included in the term "all men" in the Declaration. How does it do so? In what way has it a tendency to prove that? Mr. Clay says *it is true as an abstract principle* that all men are created equal, but that we cannot practically apply it in all cases. He illustrates this by bringing forward the cases of females, minors and insane persons with whom it cannot be enforced. But he says it is true as an abstract principle in the organization of society as well as in organized society and it should be kept in view as a fundamental principle. Let me read a few words more before I add some comments of my own. Mr. Clay says a little further on:[26]

I desire no concealment of my opinions in regard to the institution of slavery. I look upon it as a great evil; and deeply lament that we have derived it from the parental government; and from our ancestors. I wish every slave in the United States was in the country of his ancestors.° But here they are, and the question is, how they can be best dealt with? If a state of nature existed, and we were about to lay the foundations of society, *no man would be more strongly opposed than I should be, to incorporate the institution of slavery among its elements.*°

These were the sentiments of Henry Clay. He says, "if a state of nature existed, and we were about to lay the foundation of society, no man would be more strongly opposed than I should be to incorporate the institution of slavery among its elements."° Now here we have°—in this same book, in this same speech, in this same extract brought forward to prove that Mr. Clay held that the negro was not included in the Declaration of Independence—no such statement on his part, but the declaration *that it is a great fundamental truth* which should be constantly kept in view in the organization of society and in societies already organized. But

---

25. AL failed to quote the final sentence of the portion of Clay's speech that was in the letter to the *Chicago Times,* and which is quite pertinent to the letter writer's point: "And I am bold to say that if the doctrines of ultra political Abolitionists, (meaning, of course, such doctrines as he was then discussing,) had been seriously promulgated at the epoch of our Revolution, our glorious Independence would never have been achieved—never, NEVER!" The words in parentheses belong not to Clay but to the letter writer.

26. AL may have found this passage in a standard edition of the day, *The Speeches of Henry Clay,* ed. Calvin Colton, 2 vols. (New York: Barne, 1857), 2:387. For a modern edition, see Seager and Hay, *Papers of Henry Clay,* 9:779.

if I say a word about it—if I attempt, as Mr. Clay said all good men ought to do, to keep it in view; if, in this "organized society," I ask to have the public eye turned upon it; if I ask, in relation to the organization of new territories, that the public eye should be turned upon it—forthwith I am vilified, as you hear me today.

What have I done in regard to the Declaration of Independence° that I have not the license of Henry Clay's illustrious example here in doing? Have I done aught that I have not his authority for, while maintaining that in organizing new territories and societies, this fundamental principle should be regarded and, in organized society, holding it up to the public view and recognizing what *he* recognized as the great principle of free government? *[Applause, cheers]* And when this new principle, this new proposition that no human being ever thought of three years ago, is brought forward, *I combat it* as having an evil tendency, if not an evil design. I combat it as having a tendency to dehumanize the negro, to take away from him the right of ever striving to be a man. I combat it as being one of the thousand things constantly done in these days to prepare the public mind to make property—and nothing but property—of the *negro in all the states of this Union. [Applause, cheers]*

But there is a point that I wish, before leaving this part of the discussion, to ask attention to. I have read, and I repeat the words of Henry Clay:[27]

> I desire no concealment of my opinions in regard to the institution of slavery. I look upon it as a great evil, and deeply lament that we have derived it from the parental government, and from our ancestors. I wish every slave in the United States was in the country of his ancestors. But here they are, and the question is, how they can be best dealt with? If a state of nature existed, and we were about to lay the foundation of society, no man would be more strongly opposed than I should be, to incorporate the institution of slavery among its elements.°

The principle upon which I have insisted from the Declaration of Independence, as applicable to this discussion and° this canvass, is in relation to laying the foundations of new societies. I have never sought to apply these principles to the old states where slavery exists° for the purpose of abolishing slavery in those states. It is nothing but a miserable perversion of what I *have* said, to assume that I have brought forth the Declaration of Independence to ask that° Missouri, or any other slave state, shall emancipate her slaves. I have proposed no such thing. But when Mr. Clay says that, in laying the foundations of societies in our territories where it does not exist, he would be opposed to the introduction of slavery as an element, I insist that we have *his warrant,* his license for insisting upon the exclusion of that element, which he declared in such strong and emphatic language *was most hateful to him. [Applause]*

---

27. See previous note.

Judge Douglas, in this connection,° has again referred to a Springfield speech in which I said "a house divided against itself cannot stand." Now, if you please, I will address myself for a little while to something that springs from that Springfield speech.° The Judge has so often made the entire quotation from that speech that I can make it from memory. I used this language:[28]

> We are now far into the fifth year, since a policy was initiated with the avowed object, and confident promise, of putting an end to the slavery agitation. Under the operation of that policy, that agitation has not only, not ceased, but has constantly augmented. In my opinion, it will not cease, until a crisis shall have been reached and passed. "A house divided against itself cannot stand." I believe this government cannot endure permanently half slave and half free. I do not expect the Union to be dissolved—° I do not expect the house to fall—but I do expect it will cease to be divided. It will become all one thing, or all the other. Either the opponents of slavery, will arrest the further spread of it, and place it where the public mind shall rest in the belief that it is in the course of ultimate extinction; or its advocates will push it forward, till it shall become alike lawful in all the states, old as well as new—North as well as South.°

That extract and the sentiments expressed in it have been extremely offensive to Judge Douglas. He has warred upon them as Satan does upon the Bible. *[Laughter]* He has never given it up, and° his perversions upon it are endless. Here now are my views upon it in brief. I said we were now far into the fifth year since a policy was initiated with the avowed object and confident promise of putting an end to the slavery agitation. Is it not so? When that Nebraska bill was brought forward four years ago last January, was it not for the "avowed object" of putting an end to the slavery agitation? We were to have no more agitation in Congress, no more in the states, and° it was all to be banished to the territories. By the way, I will remark here that, as Judge Douglas is very fond of complimenting Mr. Crittenden in these days, Mr. Crittenden has said there was a falsehood in that whole business, for there was *no slavery agitation at that time to allay.*[29] We were for a little while *quiet* on the troublesome thing and that very allaying plaster of Judge Douglas stirred it up again. *[Applause, laughter]* But was it not understood or intimated with the "confident promise" of putting an end to the slavery agitation? Surely it was. In every speech you heard Judge Douglas make, until he got into this "imbroglio," as they call it, with the administration about the Lecomp-

---

28. From AL's "House Divided" speech.
29. Reports had been circulating that the venerable Senator John J. Crittenden favored SAD over AL in the Illinois senatorial campaign. See AL's July 7, 1858, letter to Crittenden in Basler et al., *Collected Works,* 2:483–84; Crittenden to AL, July 29, 1858, Abraham Lincoln Papers, Library of Congress. AL here alludes to a speech in Congress by Crittenden (*Congressional Globe,* 35th Cong., 1st Sess., Senate, March 17, 1858, 2: 1158).

ton Constitution, every speech on that Nebraska bill was full of his felicitations that we were *just at the end* of the slavery agitation. The last tip of the last joint of the old serpent's tail was just drawing out of view. *[Cheers, laughter]* But has it proved so? I have asserted that under that policy that agitation "has not only not° ceased, but has constantly augmented." When was there ever a greater agitation in Congress than last winter? When was it as great in the country as today?

There was a collateral object in the introduction of that Nebraska policy, which was to clothe the people of the territories with a superior degree of self-government, beyond what they had ever had before. The first object, and the main one, of putting an end to slavery agitation has not succeeded. The second and collateral one° of conferring upon the people a higher degree of "self-government" is a question of fact to be determined by you in answer to a single question. Have you ever heard or known of a people anywhere on earth who had as little to do, as, in the first instance of its use, the people of Kansas had with this same right of "self-government?" *[Applause]* In its main policy, and in its collateral object, *it has been nothing but a living, creeping lie from the time of its introduction till today.* *[Cheers]*

I have intimated that I thought the agitation would not cease until a crisis should have been reached and passed. I have stated in what way I thought it would be reached and passed. I have said that it might go one way or the other. We might, by arresting the further spread of it and placing it where the fathers originally placed it, put it where the public mind should rest in the belief that it was in the course of ultimate extinction. Thus the agitation may cease. It may be pushed forward until it shall become alike lawful in all the states, old as well as new, North as well as South. I have said and I repeat, my wish is that the further spread of it may be arrested and that it may be placed where the public mind shall rest in the belief that it is in the course of ultimate extinction. *[Applause]* I have expressed that as my wish, and I have no disposition to shrink from it, but I have a disposition to be not misrepresented about it. I have a disposition to not have it believed by any honest man that I desire to go to war with Missouri. Not at all!°

I entertain the opinion, upon evidence sufficient to my mind, that the fathers of this government placed that institution where the public mind *did* rest in the belief that it was in the course of ultimate extinction. Let me ask why they made provision that the source of slavery—the African slave trade—should be cut off at the end of twenty years? Why did they make provision that, in all the new territory we owned at that time, slavery should be forever inhibited?[30] Why

---

30. AL refers to the federal Constitution's provision (Art. I, Sect. 9), which could permit the outlawing of the overseas slave trade after 1808, and the Ordinance of 1787, which forbade slavery in the Northwest Territory.

stop its spread in one direction and cut off its source in another, if they did not look to its being placed in the course of ultimate extinction?

Again, the institution of slavery is only mentioned in the Constitution of the United States two or three times, and in neither of these cases does the word "slavery" or "negro race" occur, but covert language is used each time, and for a purpose full of significance. What is the language in regard to the prohibition of the African slave trade? It runs in about this way:[31] "The migration or importation of such persons as any of the states now existing shall think proper to admit, shall not be prohibited by the Congress prior to the year one thousand eight hundred and eight, but a tax or duty may be imposed on such importation, not exceeding ten dollars for each person."°

The next allusion in the Constitution to the question of slavery and the black race is on the subject of the basis of representation, and there the language used is, "Representatives and direct taxes shall be apportioned among the several states which may be included within this Union, according to their respective numbers, which shall be determined by adding to the whole number of free persons, including those bound to service for a term of years, and excluding Indians not taxed, three-fifths of all other persons."[32] It says "persons," not slaves, not negroes, but this "three-fifths" can be applied to no other class among us than the negroes.

Lastly, in the provision for the reclamation of fugitive slaves it is said: "No Person held to service or labor in one state, under the laws thereof, escaping into another, shall, in consequence of any law or regulation therein, be discharged from such service or labor, but shall be° delivered up on claim of the party to whom such service or labor may be due."[33] There again, there is no mention of the word "negro" or of slavery. In all three of these places, being the only allusions to slavery in the instrument, covert language is used. Language is used not suggesting that slavery existed or that the black race were among us. And I understand the contemporaneous history of those times to be that covert language was used with a purpose, and that purpose was that in our Constitution, which it was hoped and is still hoped will endure forever—when it should be read by intelligent and patriotic men, after the institution of slavery had passed from among us—there should be nothing on the face of the great charter of liberty suggesting that such a thing as negro slavery had ever existed among us. *[Applause]*

This is part of the evidence that the fathers of the government expected and intended the institution of slavery to come to an end. They expected and intended that it should be in the course of ultimate extinction. And when I say that I desire

---

31. AL quotes from the Constitution of the United States, Art. I, Sect. 9.
32. Ibid., Sect. 2.
33. Ibid., Art. IV, Sect. 2.

to see the further spread of it arrested, I only say I desire to see that done which the fathers have first done. When I say I desire to see it placed where the public mind will rest in the belief that it is in the course of ultimate extinction, I only say I desire to see it placed where they placed it.

It is not true that our fathers, as Judge Douglas assumes, made this government part slave and part free. Understand the sense in which he puts it. He assumes that slavery, as° a rightful thing within itself, was introduced by the framers of the Constitution. In that sense, then, it is not true that the framers of our Constitution made this government part slave and part free.° The exact truth is, that they found the institution existing among us, and they left it as they found it. But in making the government, they left this institution with many clear marks of disapprobation upon it. They found slavery among them, and they left it among them because of the difficulty, the absolute impossibility, of its immediate removal. And when Judge Douglas asks me why we cannot let it remain part slave and part free as the fathers of the government made it,° he asks a question based upon an assumption which is itself a falsehood. And I turn upon him and ask him the question, when the policy that the fathers of the government had adopted in relation to this element among us was the best policy in the world, the only wise policy, the only policy that we can ever safely continue upon, that will ever give us peace unless this dangerous element masters us all and becomes a national institution—*I turn upon him and ask him why he could not let it alone? [Cheers]*

I turn and ask him why he was driven to the necessity of introducing a *new policy* in regard to it? He has himself said he introduced a new policy. He said so in his speech on the 22d of March of the present year, 1858.[34] I ask him why he could not let it remain where our fathers placed it? I ask, too, of Judge Douglas and his friends why we shall not again place this institution upon the basis on which the fathers left it? I ask no more than that, and now° I ask you, when he infers that I am in favor of setting the free and slave states at war, does he not do me injustice?° When the institution was placed in that attitude by those who made the Constitution, *did they make any war? [Crises of "no, no" and cheers]* If we had no war out of it when thus placed, wherein is the ground of belief that we shall have war out of it if we return to that policy? Have we had any peace upon this matter springing from any other basis? I maintain that we have not. I have proposed nothing more than a return to the policy of the fathers.

Now, I confess very frankly that° when I propose a certain measure of policy, it is not enough for me that I do not intend° anything evil in the result, but it is incumbent on me to show that it has not a *tendency* to that result. I have met Judge Douglas in that point of view. I have not only made the declaration that I

---

34. AL read from this speech in the Ottawa debate, p. 29.

do not *mean* to produce a conflict between the states, but I have tried to show by fair reasoning—and I think I have shown to the minds of fair men—that I propose nothing but what has a most peaceful tendency. The quotation that I happened to make in that Springfield speech, that "a house divided against itself cannot stand," and which has proved so offensive to the Judge, was part and parcel of the same thing. He tries to show that variety in the domestic institutions of the different states is necessary and indispensable. I do not dispute it. I have no controversy with Judge Douglas about that. I shall very readily agree with him that it would be foolish for us to insist upon having a cranberry law here in Illinois, where we have no cranberries, because they have a cranberry law in Indiana, where they have cranberries. *[Laughter]* I should insist that it would be exceedingly wrong in us to deny to Virginia the right to enact oyster laws where they have oysters, because we want no such laws here. *[Laughter]* I understand, I hope, quite as well as Judge Douglas or anybody else, that the variety in the soil and climate and face of the country, and consequent variety in the industrial pursuits and productions of a country, require systems of law conforming to this variety in the natural features of the country. I understand quite as well as Judge Douglas that if we here raise a barrel of flour more than we want, and the Louisianians raise a barrel of sugar more than they want, it is of mutual advantage to exchange. That produces commerce, brings us together, and makes us better friends. We like one another the more for it. And I understand as well as Judge Douglas or anybody else that these mutual accommodations are the cements which bind together the different parts of this Union—that instead of being a thing to "divide the house," figuratively expressing the Union, they tend to sustain it. They are the props of the house tending always to hold it up.

But when I have admitted all this, I ask if there is any parallel between these things and this institution of slavery? I do not see that there is any parallel at all between them. Consider it. When have we had any difficulty or quarrel amongst ourselves about the cranberry laws of Indiana, or the oyster laws of Virginia, or the pine lumber laws of Maine, or the fact that Louisiana produces sugar, and Illinois flour? When have we had any quarrels over these things?

When have we had perfect peace in regard to this thing which I say is an element of discord in this Union? We have sometimes had peace, but when was it? It was when the institution of slavery remained quiet where it was. We have had difficulty and turmoil whenever it has made a struggle to spread itself where it was not. I ask then, if experience does not speak in thunder tones, telling us that the policy which has given peace to the country heretofore, being returned to, gives the greatest promise of peace again. You may say, and Judge Douglas has intimated the same thing, that all this difficulty in regard to the institution of slavery is the mere agitation of office seekers and ambitious Northern politicians. He thinks we want to get "his place," I suppose. *[Cheers, laughter]* I agree that there are office seekers amongst us. The Bible says somewhere that we are desperately selfish. I think we would have discovered that fact without the Bible. I do not claim that I am any less so than the average of men, but I do claim that I am not more selfish than Judge Douglas. *[Laughter, applause]*

But is it true that all the difficulty and agitation we have in regard to this institution of slavery springs from office-seeking, from the mere ambition of politicians? Is that the truth? How many times have we had danger from this question? Go back to the day of the Missouri Compromise. Go back to the nullification question, at the bottom of which lay this same slavery question. Go back to the time of the annexation of Texas. Go back to the troubles that led to the Compromise of 1850. You will find that every time, with the single exception of the nullification question, they sprung from an endeavor to spread this institution. There never was a party in the history of this country, and there probably never will be, of sufficient strength to disturb the general peace of the country. Parties themselves may be divided and quarrel on minor questions, yet it extends not beyond the parties themselves. But does *not* this question make a disturbance outside of political circles? Does it not enter into the churches and rend them asunder? What divided the great Methodist Church into two parts, North and South? What has raised this constant disturbance in every Presbyterian General Assembly that meets? What disturbed the Unitarian Church in this very city two years ago? What has jarred and shaken the great American Tract Society recently, not yet splitting it, but sure to divide it in the end.[35] Is it not this same mighty, deep-seated power that somehow operates on the minds of men, exciting and stirring them up in every avenue of society—in politics, in religion, in literature, in morals, in all the manifold relations of life? *[Applause]* Is this the work of politicians? Is that irresistible power which for fifty years has shaken the government and agitated the people to be stilled and subdued by pretending that it is an exceedingly simple thing, and we ought not to talk about it? *[Cheers, laughter]* If you will get everybody else to stop talking about it, I assure you° I will quit before they have half done so. *[Laughter]*

But where is the philosophy or statesmanship which assumes that you can quiet that disturbing element in our society, which has disturbed us for more than

---

35. The Methodist Episcopal Church had divided into northern and southern branches by 1848, and the two major divisions of the Presbyterian Church were riven by the slavery controversy in the 1840s and 1850s. The Unitarian congregation in Alton was divided over an antislavery sermon by its pastor, Rev. William D. Haley, in July 1856. The American Tract Society, which had an intersectional presence, was under constant attack in the 1850s for not opposing slavery.

half a century, which has been the only serious danger that has threatened our institutions. I say, where is the philosophy or the statesmanship based on the assumption that we are to quit talking about it *[Applause]* and that the public mind is all at once to cease being agitated by it? Yet this is the policy here in the North that Douglas is advocating—that we are to care nothing about it! I ask you if it is not a false philosophy? Is it not a false statesmanship that undertakes to build up a system of policy upon the basis of caring nothing about *the very thing that everybody does care the most about?* *[Cries of "yes, yes," applause]* A thing which all experience has shown we care a very great deal about? *[Laughter, applause]*

The Judge alludes very often in the course of his remarks to the exclusive right which the states have to decide the whole thing for themselves. I agree with him very readily that the different states have that right. He is but fighting a man of straw when he assumes that I am contending against the° right of the states to do as they please about it. Our controversy with him is in regard to the new territories. We agree that when the states come in as states, they have the right and the power to do as they please. We have no power as citizens of the free states, or in our federal capacity as members of the federal Union through the general government, to disturb slavery in the states where it exists. We profess constantly that we have no more inclination than belief in the power of the government to disturb it, yet we are driven constantly to defend ourselves from the assumption that we are warring upon the rights of the *states.*

What I insist upon is that the new territories shall be kept free from it while in the territorial condition. Judge Douglas assumes that we have no interest in them, that we have no right whatever to interfere. I think we have some interest. I think that as white men we have. Do we not wish for an outlet for our surplus population, if I may so express myself? Do we not feel an interest in getting to that outlet with such institutions as we would like to have prevail there? If *you* go to the territory opposed to slavery, and another man comes upon the same ground with his slave, upon the assumption that the things are equal, it turns out that he has the equal right all his way, and you have no part of it your way. If he goes in and makes it a slave territory, and by consequence a slave state, is it not time that those who desire to have it a free state were on equal ground?

Let me suggest it in a different way. How many Democrats are there about here who have left slave states and come into the free State of Illinois to get rid of the institution of slavery?

Voice: A thousand and one.

Lincoln: I reckon there are a thousand and one. *[Laughter]* I will ask you, if the policy you are now advocating had prevailed when this country was in territorial condition, where would you have gone to get rid of it? *[Applause]* Where would you have found your free state or territory to go to? And when, hereafter, for any cause, the people in this place shall desire to find new homes, if they wish to be rid of the institution, where will they find the place to go to? *[Cheers]*

Now irrespective of the moral aspect of this question as to whether there is a right or wrong in enslaving a negro, I am still in favor of our new territories being in such a condition that white men may find a home, may find some spot where they can better their condition, where they can settle upon new soil and better their condition in life. *[Cheers]* I am in favor of this not merely—I must say it here as I have elsewhere—for our own people who are born amongst us, but as an outlet for *free white people everywhere,* the world over, in which Hans and Baptiste and Patrick and all other men from all the world may find new homes and better their conditions in life. *[Applause]*

I have stated upon former occasions, and I may as well state again, what I understand to be the real issue in this controversy between Judge Douglas and myself. On the point of my wanting to make war between the free and the slave states, there has been no issue between us. So, too, when he assumes that I am in favor of introducing a perfect social and political equality between the white and black races. These are false issues upon which Judge Douglas has tried to force the controversy. There is no foundation in truth for the charge that I maintain either of these propositions. The real issue in this controversy—the one pressing upon every mind—is the sentiment on the part of one class that looks upon the institution of slavery *as a wrong,* and of another class that *does not* look upon it as a wrong. The sentiment that contemplates the institution of slavery in this country as wrong is the sentiment of the Republican party. It is the sentiment around which all their actions, all their arguments, circle, from which all their propositions radiate. They look upon it as being a moral, social, and political wrong, and while they contemplate it as such, they nevertheless have due regard for its actual existence among us, and the difficulties of getting rid of it in any satisfactory way, and to all the constitutional obligations thrown about it. Yet having a due regard for these, they desire a policy in regard to it that looks to its not creating any more danger. They insist that it should, as far as may be, *be treated* as a wrong, and one of the methods of treating it as a wrong is to *make provision that it shall grow no larger. [Applause]* They also desire a policy that looks to a peaceful end of slavery, at some time, as being wrong.

These are the views they entertain in regard to it, as I understand them, and all their sentiments, all their arguments and propositions, are brought within this range. I have said, and I repeat it here, that if there be a man amongst us who does not think that the institution of slavery is wrong in any one of the aspects of which I have spoken, he is misplaced, and ought not to be with us. And if there be a man amongst us who is so impatient of it as a wrong as to disregard its actual presence among us and the difficulty of getting rid of it suddenly in a satisfactory way, and to disregard the constitutional obligations thrown about it, that man is misplaced if he is on our platform. We disclaim sympathy with him in practical action. He is not placed properly with us.

On this subject of treating it as a wrong, and limiting its spread, let me say a word. Has any thing ever threatened the existence of this Union save and except this very institution of slavery? What is it that we hold most dear amongst us? Our own liberty and prosperity. What has ever threatened our liberty and prosperity save and except this institution of slavery? If this is true, how do you propose to improve the condition of things? By enlarging slavery, by spreading it out and making it bigger? You may have a wen or a cancer upon your person and not be able to cut it out lest you bleed to death. But surely it is no way to cure it, to engraft it and spread it over your whole body. That is no proper way of treating what you regard a wrong. You see this peaceful way of dealing with it as a wrong, restricting the spread of it, and not allowing it to go into new countries where it has not already existed. That is the peaceful way, the old-fashioned way, the way in which the fathers themselves set us the example.

On the other hand, I have said there is a sentiment which treats it as *not* being wrong. That is the Democratic sentiment of this day. I do not mean to say that every man who stands within that range positively asserts that it is right. That class will include all who positively assert that it is right, and all who, like Judge Douglas, treat it as indifferent and do not say it is either right or wrong. These two classes of men fall within the general class of those who do not look upon it as a wrong. And if there be among you anybody who supposes that he as a Democrat, can consider himself "as much opposed to slavery as anybody," I would like to reason with him. You never treat it as a wrong. What other thing that you consider as a wrong do you deal with as you deal with that? Perhaps you say it is wrong, *but your leader never does, and you quarrel with anybody who says it is wrong.* Although you pretend to say so yourself, you can find no fit place to deal with it as a wrong. You must not say anything about it in the free states, *because it is not here.* You must not say anything about it in the slave states, *because it is there.* You must not say anything about it in the pulpit, because that is religion and has nothing to do with it. You must not say anything about it in politics, *because that will disturb the security of "my place." [Laughter, cheers]* There is no place to talk about it° as being a wrong, although you say yourself it is a wrong. But finally you will screw yourself up to the belief that if the people of the slave states should adopt a system of gradual emancipation on the slavery question, you would be in favor of it. You would be in favor of it. You say that is getting it in the right place, and you would be glad to see it succeed.

But you are deceiving yourself. You all know that Frank Blair and Gratz

Brown, down there in St. Louis, undertook to introduce that system in Missouri. They fought as valiantly as they could for the system of gradual emancipation, which you pretend you would be glad to see succeed. Now I will bring you to the test. After a hard fight they were beaten, and when the news came over here, you threw up your hats and *hurrahed for Democracy*.[36] *[Applause, laughter]* More than that, take all the argument made in favor of the system you have proposed, and it carefully excludes the idea that there is anything wrong in the institution of slavery. The arguments to sustain that policy carefully excluded it. Even here today you heard Judge Douglas quarrel with me because I uttered a wish that it might sometime come to an end. Although Henry Clay could say he wished every slave in the United States was in the country of his ancestors, I am denounced by those pretending to respect Henry Clay for uttering a wish that it might sometime, in some peaceful way, come to an end.[37]

The Democratic policy in regard to that institution will not tolerate the merest breath, the slightest hint, expressive° of the least degree of wrong about it. Try it by some of Judge Douglas's arguments. He says he don't care whether it is voted up or voted down in the territories. I do not care myself, in dealing with that expression, whether it is intended to be expressive of his individual sentiments on the subject or only of the national policy he desires to have established. It is alike valuable for my purpose. Any man can say that who does not see anything wrong in slavery, but no man can logically say it who does see a wrong in it, because no man can logically say he don't care whether a wrong is voted up or voted down. He may say he don't care whether an indifferent thing is voted up or down, but he must logically have a choice between a right thing and a wrong thing. He contends that whatever community wants slaves has a right to have them. So they have, if it is not a wrong. But if it is a wrong, he cannot say people have a right to do wrong. He says that upon the score of equality, slaves should be allowed to go in a new territory like other property. This is strictly logical if there is no difference between it and other property. If it and other property are equal, his argument is entirely logical. But if you insist that one is wrong and the other right, there is no use to institute a comparison between right and wrong. You may turn over everything in the Democratic policy from beginning to end, whether in the shape it takes on the statute book, in the shape it takes in the Dred Scott decision, in the shape it takes in conversation, or the shape it takes in short maxim-like arguments. It everywhere carefully excludes the idea that there is anything wrong in it.

That is the real issue. That is the issue that will continue in this country when

---

36. See the Quincy debate, note 14, p. 224.
37. See pp. 256–59.

these poor tongues of Judge Douglas and myself shall be silent. It is the eternal struggle between these two principles, right and wrong, throughout the world. They are the two principles that have stood face to face from the beginning of time, and will ever continue to struggle. The one is the common right of humanity, and the other the divine right of kings. It is the same principle in whatever shape it develops itself. It is the same old serpent° that says, "You work and toil and earn bread, and I'll eat it." *[Applause]* No matter in what shape it comes, whether from the mouth of a king who seeks to bestride the people of his own nation and live by the fruit of their labor, or from one race of men as an apology for enslaving another race, it is the same tyrannical principle.

I was glad to express my gratitude at Quincy, and I re-express it here to Judge Douglas, *that he looks to no end of the institution of slavery.* That will help the people to see where the struggle really is. It will, hereafter, place with us all men who really do wish the wrong may have an end. And whenever we can get rid of the fog which obscures the real question—when we can get Judge Douglas and his friends to avow a policy looking to its perpetuation—we can get out from among them that class of men and bring them to the side of those who treat it as a wrong. Then there will soon be an end of it, and that end will be its "ultimate extinction." Whenever the issue can be distinctly made, and all extraneous matter thrown out so that men can fairly see the real difference between the parties, this controversy will soon be settled, and it will be done peaceably too. There will be no war, no violence. It will be placed again where the wisest and best men of the world placed it.

Brooks of South Carolina once declared that when this Constitution was framed, its framers did not look to the institution existing until this day. When he said this, I think he stated a fact that is fully borne out by the history of the times. But he also said they were better and wiser men than the men of these days. Yet the men of these days had experience which they had not, and by the invention of the cotton gin, it became a necessity in this country that slavery should be perpetual.[38] I now say that willingly or unwillingly, purposely or without purpose, Judge Douglas has been the most prominent instrument in changing the position of the institution of slavery, which the fathers of the government expected to come to an end ere this, *and putting it upon Brooks's cotton-gin basis, [Applause]* placing it where he openly confesses he has no desire there shall ever be an end of it. *[Applause]*

I understand I have ten minutes yet. I will employ it in saying something about this argument Judge Douglas uses, while he sustains the Dred Scott deci-

---

38. AL refers to Congressman Preston Brooks's speech as reported in *Congressional Globe, Appendix,* 33rd Cong., 1st Sess., Mar. 15, 1854, 372.

sion, that the people of the territories can still somehow exclude slavery. The first thing I ask attention to is the fact that Judge Douglas constantly said, before the decision, that whether they could or not *was a question for the Supreme Court.* *[Cheers]* But after the Court has made the decision, he virtually says it is *not* a question for the Supreme Court, but for the people. *[Applause]* And how is it he tells us they can exclude it? He says it needs "police regulations," and that admits of "unfriendly legislation." Although it is a right established by the Constitution of the United States to take a slave into a territory of the United States and hold him as property, yet unless the territorial legislature will give friendly legislation, and, more especially, if they adopt unfriendly legislation, they can practically exclude him.

Now, without meeting this proposition as a matter of fact, I pass to consider the real constitutional obligation. Let me take the gentlemen who looks me in the face before me, and let us suppose that he is a member of the territorial legislature. The first thing he will do will be to swear that he will support the Constitution of the United States. His neighbor by his side in the territory has slaves and needs territorial legislation to enable him to enjoy that constitutional right. Can he withhold the legislation which his neighbor needs for the enjoyment of a right which is fixed in his favor in the Constitution of the United States, which he has sworn to support? Can he withhold it without violating his oath? And more especially, can he pass unfriendly legislation to violate his oath? Why this is a *monstrous* sort of talk about the Constitution of the United States! *[Applause]* *There has never been as outlandish or lawless a doctrine from the mouth of any respectable man on earth.* *[Cheers]* I do not believe it is a constitutional right to hold slaves in a territory of the United States. I believe the decision was improperly made, and I go for reversing it. Judge Douglas is furious against those who go for reversing a decision. But he is for legislating it out of all force while the law itself stands. I repeat that there has never been so monstrous a doctrine uttered from the mouth of a respectable man. *[Cheers]*

I suppose most of us—I know it of myself—believe that the people of the Southern states are entitled to a congressional fugitive slave law, that it is a right fixed in the Constitution. But it cannot be made available to them without congressional legislation. In the Judge's language, it is a "barren right" which needs legislation before it can become efficient and valuable to the persons to whom it is guaranteed. And as the right is constitutional, I agree that the legislation shall be granted to it—and that, not that we like the institution of slavery. We profess to have no taste for running and catching niggers—at least I profess no taste for that job at all. Why then do I yield support to a fugitive slave law? Because I do not understand that the Constitution, which guarantees that right, can be supported without it. And if I believed that the right to hold a slave in a territory was equally fixed in the Constitution with the right to reclaim fugitives, I should be bound to give it the legislation necessary to support it.

I say that no man can deny his obligation to give the necessary legislation to support slavery in a territory, who believes it is a constitutional right to have it there. No man can, who does not give the abolitionist an argument to deny the obligation enjoined by the Constitution to enact a fugitive slave law. Try it now. It is the strongest abolition argument ever made. I say if that Dred Scott decision is correct, then the right to hold slaves in a territory is equally a constitutional right with the right of a slaveholder to have his runaway returned. No one can show the distinction between them. The one is express, so that we cannot deny it. The other is construed to be in the Constitution, so that he who believes the decision to be correct believes in the right. And the man who argues that by unfriendly legislation, in spite of that constitutional right, slavery may be driven from the territories, cannot avoid furnishing an argument by which abolitionists may deny the obligation to return fugitives, and claim the power to pass laws unfriendly to the right of the slaveholder to reclaim his fugitive. I do not know how such an argument may strike a popular assembly like this, but I defy anybody to go before a body of men whose minds are educated to estimating evidence and reasoning, and show that there is an iota of difference between the constitutional right to reclaim a fugitive, and the constitutional right to hold a slave, in a territory, provided this Dred Scott decision is correct. *[Cheers]*

I defy any man to make an argument that will justify unfriendly legislation to deprive a slaveholder of his right to hold his slave in a territory, that will not equally, in all its length, breadth and thickness, furnish an argument for nullifying the Fugitive Slave Law. Why there is not such an abolitionist in the nation as Douglas, after all. *[Applause]*

DOUGLAS'S REJOINDER

Mr. Lincoln has concluded his remarks by saying that there is not such an abolitionist as I am in all America. *[Laughter]* If he could make the abolitionists of Illinois believe that, he would not have much show for the Senate. *[Laughter, applause]* Let him make the abolitionists believe the truth of that statement and his political back is broken. *[Laughter]* The back of his party is broken when abolitionism is withdrawn. °

His first criticism upon me is the expression of his hope that the war of the administration will be prosecuted against me and the Democratic party of this state with vigor. He wants that war prosecuted with vigor, I have no doubt of it. His hopes of success, and the hopes of his party, depend solely upon it. They have no chance of destroying the Democracy of this state except by the aid of federal patronage. *[Cheers]* He has all the federal office-holders here, as his allies, running separate tickets against the Democracy to divide the party, although the leaders all intend to vote directly the abolition ticket, and only leave the green-horns to vote this separate ticket, who refuse to go into the abolition camp.[39] *[Laughter, cheers]*

There is something really refreshing in the thought that Mr. Lincoln is in favor of prosecuting one war vigorously. *[Laughter]* It is the first war I ever knew him to be in favor of prosecuting. *[Laughter, applause]* It is the first war that I ever knew him to believe to be just or constitutional. *[Laughter, cheers]* When the Mexican War was° being waged, and the American army was surrounded by the enemy in Mexico, he thought that war was unconstitutional, unnecessary, and unjust. He thought it was not commenced on the right *spot.*[40] *[Laughter]* When I made an incidental allusion of that kind in the joint discussion over at Charleston some weeks ago, Lincoln, in replying, said that I, Douglas, had charged him with voting against supplies for the Mexican war.[41] And then he reared up full length, and swore that he never voted against the supplies, that it was a slander, and caught hold of Ficklin, who sat on the stand, and said, "Here, Ficklin, tell the people that it is a lie." *[Laughter, applause]* Well, Ficklin, who had served in Congress with him, stood up and told them all that he recollected about it. It was that when George Ashmun, of Massachusetts, brought forward a resolution declaring the war unconstitutional, unnecessary, and unjust, that Lincoln had voted for it. "Yes," said Lincoln, "I did." Thus he confessed that he voted that the war was wrong, that our country was in the wrong, and consequently that the Mexicans were in the right, but charged that I had slandered him by saying that he voted against the supplies. I never charged him with voting against the supplies in my life, because I knew that he was not in Congress when they were voted. *[Laughter]* The war was commenced on the 13th day of May, 1846, and on that day we appropriated in Congress ten millions of dollars and fifty thousand men to prosecute it. During the same session we voted more men and more money, and at the next session we voted more men and more money, so that by the time Mr. Lincoln entered Congress, we had enough men and enough money to carry on the war, and had no occasion to vote any more. *[Laughter, cheers]*

When he got into the House, being opposed to the war and not being able to stop the supplies, because they had all gone forward, all he could do was to follow the lead of Corwin, and prove that the war was not begun on the right spot, and that it was unconstitutional, unnecessary, and wrong. Remember, too, that this he did after the war had been begun. It is one thing to be opposed to the

---

39. See "National Democrats" in the glossary, p. 328.
40. See "spot resolutions" in the glossary, p. 331.
41. See the Charleston debate, pp. 167–68.

declaration of a war, another and very different thing to take sides with the enemy against your own country after the war has been commenced. *[Cheers]* Our army was in Mexico at the time, many battles had been fought. Our citizens, who were defending the honor of their country's flag, were surrounded by the daggers, the guns, and the poison of the enemy. Then it was that Corwin made his speech in which he declared that the American soldiers ought to be welcomed by the Mexicans with bloody hands and hospitable graves.[42] Then it was that Ashmun and Lincoln voted in the House of Representatives that the war was unconstitutional and unjust. And Ashmun's resolution, Corwin's speech, and Lincoln's vote were sent to Mexico and read at the head of the Mexican Army, to prove to them that there was a Mexican party in the Congress of the United States who were doing all in their power to aid them. *[Applause]* That a man who takes sides with the common enemy against his own country in time of war should rejoice in a war being made on me now, is very natural. *[Applause]* And in my opinion, no other kind of a man would rejoice in it. *[Cheers]*

Mr. Lincoln has told you a great deal today about his being an old line Clay Whig. Bear in mind that there are a great many old Clay Whigs down in this region. It is more agreeable, therefore, for him to talk about the old Clay Whig party than it is for him to talk abolitionism. We did not hear much about the old Clay Whig party up in the abolition districts. How much of an old line Henry Clay Whig was he? Have you read Gen. Singleton's speech at Jacksonville?[43] *[Cheers]* You know that Gen. Singleton was, for twenty-five years, the confidential friend of Henry Clay in Illinois. And he testified that in 1847, when the constitutional convention of this state was in session, the Whig members were invited to a Whig caucus at the house of Mr. Lincoln's brother-in-law, where Mr. Lincoln proposed to throw Henry Clay overboard and take up Gen. Taylor in his place, giving, as his reason, that if the Whigs did not take up Gen. Taylor, the Democrats would. *[Cheers, laughter]* Singleton testifies that Lincoln, in that speech, urged, as another reason for throwing Henry Clay overboard, that the Whigs had fought long enough for principle and ought to begin to fight for success. Singleton also testifies that Lincoln's speech did have the effect of cutting Clay's throat, and that he, Singleton, and others withdrew from the caucus in indignation. He further states that when they got to Philadelphia to attend the national convention of

---

42. Senator Thomas Corwin of Ohio famously attacked the Mexican War as a simple act of stealing a neighbor's property. In a speech delivered on Feb. 11, 1847, he said, "If I were a Mexican I would tell you: Have you not room in your own country to bury your dead men? If you come into mine we will greet you with bloody hands and welcome you to hospitable graves." *Congressional Globe, Appendix,* 29th Cong., 2nd Sess., Feb. 11, 1847, 216–17.

43. James W. Singleton's Jacksonville speech is excerpted in the *Illinois State Register* (Springfield), Sept. 24, 1858, copied from the *St. Louis Republican.*

the Whig party, that Lincoln was there, the bitter and deadly enemy of Clay, and that he tried to keep him, Singleton, out of the convention because he insisted on voting for Clay, and Lincoln was determined to have Taylor. *[Laughter, applause]* Singleton says that Lincoln rejoiced with very great joy when he found the mangled remains of the murdered Whig statesman lying cold before him. Now, Mr. Lincoln tells you that he is an old line Clay Whig! *[Laughter, cheers]* Gen. Singleton testifies to the facts I have narrated in a public speech which has been printed and circulated broadcast over the state for weeks, yet not a lisp have we heard from Mr. Lincoln on the subject, except that he is an old Clay Whig.

What part of Henry Clay's policy did Lincoln ever advocate? He was in Congress in 1848–49 when the Wilmot Proviso warfare disturbed the peace and harmony of the country until it shook the foundation of the republic from the center to its circumference. It was that agitation that brought Clay forth from his retirement at Ashland again to occupy his seat in the Senate of the United States to see if he could not, by his great wisdom and experience, and the renown of his name, do something to restore peace and quiet to a disturbed country. Who got up that sectional strife that Clay had to be called upon to quell? I have heard Lincoln boast that he voted forty-two times for the Wilmot Proviso, and that he would have voted as many times more if he could.[44] *[Laughter]* Lincoln is the man, in connection with Seward, Chase, Giddings, and other abolitionists, who got up that strife that I helped Clay to put down. *[Applause]* Henry Clay came back to the Senate in 1849, and saw that he must do something to restore peace to the country. The Union Whigs and the Union Democrats welcomed him the moment he arrived, as the man for the occasion. We believed that he, of all men on earth, had been preserved by Divine Providence to guide us out of our difficulties, and we Democrats rallied under Clay then, as you Whigs in nullification time rallied under the banner of old Jackson, forgetting party when the country was in danger, in order that we might have a country first and parties afterwards. *[Cheers, applause]*

And this reminds me that Mr. Lincoln told you that the slavery question was the only thing that ever disturbed the peace and harmony of the Union. Did not nullification once raise its head and disturb the peace of this Union in 1832?[45]

---

44. Of the Wilmot Proviso, AL said, "I may venture to say that I voted for it at least forty times," though it is not clear that he would have had that many opportunities so to vote during his congressional term. See "Speech at Peoria, Illinois," Oct. 16, 1854, Basler et al., *Collected Works*, 2:252.

45. A South Carolina convention in 1832 adopted ordinances nullifying the controversial federal tariffs of 1828 and 1832. President Jackson proclaimed that the assumption of such a power by a state was "incompatible with the existence of the Union." A compromise tariff promoted by Henry Clay and passed by Congress defused the resulting constitutional crisis the next year.

Was that the slavery question, Mr. Lincoln? Did not disunion raise its monster head during the last war with Great Britain?[46] Was that the slavery question, Mr. Lincoln? The peace of this country has been disturbed three times, once during the war with Great Britain, once on the tariff question, and once on the slavery question. His argument, therefore, that slavery is the only question that has ever created dissention in the Union falls to the ground. It is true that agitators are enabled now to use this slavery question for the purpose of sectional strife. He admits that in regard to all things else, the principle that I advocate, making each state and territory free to decide for itself, ought to prevail. He instances the cranberry laws, and the oyster laws, and he might have gone though the whole list with the same effect. I say that all these laws are local and domestic, and that local and domestic concerns should be left to each state and each territory to manage for itself. If agitators would acquiesce in that principle, there never would be any danger to the peace and harmony of this Union. *[Cheers]*

Mr. Lincoln tries to avoid the main issue by attacking the truth of my proposition that our fathers made this government divided into free and slave states, recognizing the right of each to decide all its local questions for itself. Did they not thus make it? It is true that they did not establish slavery in any of the states, or abolish it in any of them. But finding thirteen states, twelve of which were slave and one free, they agreed to form a government uniting them together, as they stood divided into free and slave states, and to guarantee forever to each state the right to do as it pleased on the slavery question.[47] *[Cheers]* Having thus made the government, and conferred this right upon each state forever, I assert that this government can exist as they made it, divided into free and slave states, if any one state chooses to retain slavery. *[Cheers]*

He says that he looks forward to a time when slavery shall be abolished everywhere. I look forward to a time when each state shall be allowed to do as it pleases. If it chooses to keep slavery forever, it is not my business, but its own. If it chooses to abolish slavery, it is its own business, not mine. I care more for the great principle of self-government, the right of the people to rule, than I do for all the niggers° in Christendom. *[Cheers]* I would not endanger the perpetuity of this Union. I would not blot out the great inalienable rights of the white men for all the niggers° that ever existed. *[Applause]* Hence, I say, let us maintain this

46. Very near the end of the War of 1812, in Dec. 1814, a convention of New England delegates disaffected with that war met at Hartford, Connecticut, to consider their region's best response to it and to their sense that New England had been neglected during the administrations of Jefferson and Madison. An extremist group within the convention was prepared for secession from the Union. The end of the war insured that the Hartford Convention's deliberations came to naught.

47. See note 4, p. 256.

government on the principles that our fathers made it, recognizing the right of each state to keep slavery as long as its people determined, or to abolish it when they please. *[Cheers]*

But Mr. Lincoln says that when our fathers made this government, they did not look forward to the state of things now existing, and therefore he thinks the doctrine was wrong. And he quotes Brooks, of South Carolina, to prove that our fathers then thought that probably slavery would be abolished by each state acting for itself before this time.[48] Suppose they did. Suppose they did not foresee what has occurred. Does that change the principles of our government? They did not probably foresee the telegraph that transmits intelligence by lightning, nor did they foresee the railroads that now form the bonds of union between the different states, or the thousand mechanical inventions that have elevated mankind. But do these things change the principles of the government? Our fathers, I say, made this government on the principle of the right of each state to do as it pleases in its own domestic affairs, subject to the Constitution, and allowed the people of each to apply to every new change of circumstances such remedy as they may see fit to improve their condition. This right they have for all time to come. *[Cheers]*

Mr. Lincoln went on to tell you that he does not at all desire to interfere with slavery in the states where it exists, nor does his party. I expected him to say that down here. *[Laughter]* Let me ask him then how he is going to put slavery in the course of ultimate extinction everywhere, if he does not intend to interfere with it in the states where it exists? *[Laughter, applause]* He says that he will prohibit it in all territories, and the inference is then that unless they make free states out of them, he will keep them out of the Union. For, mark you, he did not say whether or not he would vote to admit Kansas with slavery or not, as her people might apply. He did not say whether or not he was in favor of bringing the territories now in existence into the Union on the principle of Clay's compromise measures on the slavery question. I told you that he would not. *[Applause]* His idea is that he will prohibit slavery in all the territories, and thus force them all to become free states, surrounding the slave states with a cordon of free states, and hemming them in, keeping the slaves confined to their present limits, whilst they go on multiplying until the soil on which they live will no longer feed them, and he will thus be able to put slavery in a course of ultimate extinction by starvation. *[Cheers, applause]*

He will extinguish slavery in the Southern states as the French general exterminated the Algerines, when he smoked them out.[49] He is going to extinguish slavery by surrounding the slave states, hemming in the slaves, and starving them

---

48. See note 30, p. 276.

49. During a revolt in the 1840s, French forces in Algeria burned or asphyxiated noncombatants who had sheltered themselves in caves.

out of existence as you smoke a fox out of his hole. And he intends to do that in the name of humanity and Christianity, in order that we may get rid of the terrible crime and sin entailed upon our fathers of holding slaves. *[Laughter, cheers]* Mr. Lincoln marks° out that line of policy, and appeals to the moral sense and° justice and to the Christian feeling of the community to sustain him. He says that any man who holds to the contrary doctrine is in the position of the king who claimed to govern by divine right. Let us examine for a moment and see what principle it was that overthrew the divine right of George the Third to govern us. Did not these colonies rebel because the British Parliament had no right to pass laws concerning our property and domestic and private institutions without our consent? We demanded that the British government should not pass such laws unless they gave us representation in the body passing them, and this the British government insisting on doing. We went to war on the principle that the home government should not control and govern distant colonies without giving them a representation. Now, Mr. Lincoln proposes to govern the territories without giving the people a representation, and calls on Congress to pass laws controlling their property and domestic concerns without their consent and against their will. Thus, he asserts for his party the identical principle asserted by George III and the tories of the Revolution. *[Cheers]*

I ask you to look into these things and then to tell me whether the Democracy or the abolitionists are right. I hold that the people of a territory like those of a state—I use the language of Mr. Buchanan in his letter of acceptance—have the right "to decide for themselves whether slavery shall or shall not exist within their limits."[50] *[Cheers]* The point upon which Chief Justice Taney expresses his opinion is simply this, that slaves, being property, stand on an equal footing with other property, and consequently that the owner has the same right to carry that property into a territory that he has any other, subject to the same conditions. Suppose that one of your merchants was to take fifty or one hundred thousand dollars worth of liquors to Kansas. He has a right to go there under that decision, but when he gets there he finds the Maine Liquor Law in force, and what can he do with his property after he gets it there? He cannot sell it; he cannot use it. It is subject to the local law, and that law is against him. And the best thing he can do with it is to bring it back into Missouri or Illinois and sell it.

If you take negroes to Kansas, as Col. Jeff. Davis said in his Bangor speech from which I have quoted today, you must take them there subject to the local law. If the people want the institution of slavery, they will protect and encourage it, but if they do not want it, they will withhold that protection. And the absence of local legislation protecting slavery excludes it as completely as a positive prohibition.

---

50. See note 26, p. 239.

[Cheers] You slaveholders of Missouri might as well understand what you know practically, that you cannot carry slavery where the people do not want it. All you have a right to ask is that the people shall do as they please. If they want slavery let them have it. If they do not want it, allow them to refuse to encourage it.[51]

My friends, if, as I have said before, we will only live up to this great fundamental principle, there will be peace between the North and South. Mr. Lincoln admits that under the Constitution on all domestic questions, except slavery, we ought not to interfere with the people of each state. What right have we to interfere with slavery any more than we have to interfere with any other question? He says that this slavery question is now the bone of contention. Why? Simply because agitators have combined in all the free states to make war upon it. Suppose the agitators in the states should combine in one-half of the Union to make war upon the railroad system of the other half? They would thus be driven to the same sectional strife. Suppose one section makes war upon any other peculiar institution of the opposite section, and the same strife is produced. The only remedy and safety is that we shall stand by the Constitution as our fathers made it, obey the laws as they are passed, while they stand the proper test, and sustain the decisions of the Supreme Court and the constitutional authorities. I am told my time is up. °

---

51. SAD closes the debates with a reiteration of the Freeport doctrine.

ACKNOWLEDGMENTS

The Lincoln Studies Center Publication Series, of which this volume is the second to appear, owes its origin to a suggestion by the late Professor William Gienapp, an early member of the center's board of advisors, that a series dedicated to the publication of Lincoln source materials be established under the center's sponsorship. The co-directors of the center continue to be indebted to their advisors for their counsel and encouragement as the Series has developed. The members of the board as this volume went through the press were Michael Burlingame, Jennifer Fleischner, William C. Harris, James M. McPherson, Edna Greene Medford, William Lee Miller, Lucas Morel, Phillip S. Paludan, Matthew Pinsker, Gerald J. Prokopowicz, John R. Sellers, Ronald C. White Jr., and Kenneth J. Winkle. We are pleased to acknowledge timely support from the Lehrman Institute. We are happy too to acknowledge the early support of personnel at the Chicago Historical Society (now the Chicago History Museum), who helped us gain access to original or microfilm newspaper texts of the debates that were otherwise hard to find. Russell Lewis, executive vice president and chief historian at the museum, and staffers Jennifer Hartz and Lesley Martin all assisted in this manner. John Hoffmann, director of the Illinois Historical Survey at the University of Illinois Library at Urbana-Champaign, performed a similar service for us with newspapers available at his facility, and Guy C. Fraker of Bloomington, Illinois, also provided us with photocopies of newspaper debate coverage. Kathryn Harris and Thomas F. Schwartz at the Abraham Lincoln Presidential Library and Museum in Springfield were accommodating as usual, as we sought access to journalistic accounts of the debates that are held there. J. Jefferson Looney, editor of Thomas Jefferson's Retirement Papers, offered expert counsel and advice on editorial matters. For answers to research questions we are grateful to Becky Green, Church Administrator, First Unitarian-Universalist Church of Alton, Illinois, and Chris Gordy, Executive Director of the Stephenson County Historical Society at Freeport, Illinois. Michael Burlingame shared early drafts of appropriate chapters of his forthcoming biography of Abraham Lincoln with us, for which we are extremely grateful. Jane Davis researched some law cases for us, for which we are obliged. At Knox College, the staff of Seymour Library has been helpful and supportive, as always. We are grateful to Sharon Clayton, Jeffrey Douglas, Anne Giffey, Matthew Norman, Irene Ponce, Carley Robison, Laurie Sauer and Kay Vander Meulen for providing assistance in research and in finding source materials. Roger Taylor, Lawrence Breitborde, and Ralph Walter are due particular thanks for sustaining and encouraging the projects of the Lincoln Studies Center at Knox College. Other Knox friends, Owen Muelder and Ross Vander Meulen, shared sources and translation expertise with us. We are indebted to Anne Taylor for timely advice. Special thanks to our student assistant Jessa Kennedy Dahl. We are pleased to extend special thanks to Dr. Willis Regier, Director of the University of Illinois Press, for his support of the Lincoln Studies Center Publication Series and to others on his staff whose exertions made it possible for this volume to appear in time for the 150th anniversary of the debates. And our wives, Norma G. Davis and Sharon E. Wilson, provided indispensable late-stage proofreading, and they also provided constant moral support, without which this project would have been much the poorer. We thank them again.

TEXTUAL ANNOTATION

The following notes pertain to textual considerations in the editorial rendering of the newspaper accounts of the Lincoln-Douglas debates. In most cases, they relate to variations in the wording of the primary text—*Chicago Press and Tribune (P&T)* for Lincoln's speeches, *Chicago Times (Times)* for Douglas's. Reference is frequently made to the collection of debates texts assembled in a scrapbook and edited by Abraham Lincoln, which has been reproduced in facsimile in David C. Mearns, ed., *The Illinois Political Campaign in 1858: A Facsimile of the Printer's Copy of His Debates with Senator Stephen Arnold Douglas as Edited and Prepared for the Press by Abraham Lincoln* (Washington, D.C.: Library of Congress, 1958); cited here as Debates Scrapbook.

The presence of editorial alterations or commentary is indicated in the text itself by the raised reference mark ° and given in the notes below by page and line number (p. 000 /L. 00).

TEXTUAL NOTES FOR THE OTTAWA DEBATE

P. 7 / L. 21 — "It being the true intent . . . to the federal Constitution." The text of the Kansas-Nebraska Act, given here, concluded this passage with "subject only to the constitution of the United States." As both *Times* and *P&T* report SAD as saying "subject only to the federal Constitution," the editorial assumption is that, in speaking, he here diverged from the text of the act.

P. 8 / L. 16 — "Fred" from *P&T*; *Times* has "Ford."

P. 8 / L. 17 — "and Farnsworth" from *P&T*.

P. 8 / L. 21 — "constructed out of the old Whig party . . . and transferring them to abolitionism" from *P&T*; *Times* has "which was to be thus constructed."

P. 9 / L. 14 — "2. *Resolved*, That the times . . . shall have been prohibited." SAD read from the text printed in *Illinois State Register,* Oct. 16, 1854, the text given here. All of the issues that SAD referred to in his subsequent remarks are from the second of the three numbered sections that were printed in *Times.* As SAD said he would only read "part of them, and cause the others to be printed," and as *P&T* published only the second item, together with the fact that SAD later read the third section in his rejoinder as something new (see p. 38), the editors conclude that the second section is likely the only item he read to the crowd. The first section, which appeared at this point along with the second and third in *Times,* is given below from the source text:

> 1. *Resolved,* That we believe this truth to be self-evident, that when parties become subversive of the ends for which they are established, or incapable of restoring the government to the true principles of the constitution, it is the right and duty of the people to dissolve the political bands by which they may have been connected therewith, and to organize new parties upon such principles and with such views as the circumstances and exigencies of the nation may demand.

P. 10 / L. 7 — "Giddings and Fred Douglass." *P&T* has "Giddings and Chase."

P. 10 / L. 24 — "win" from *P&T; Times* has "ruin." The context is competitive activity, where to "win" liquor (presumably the prize in these sports) makes much more sense than "ruin."

P. 10 / L. 25 — "put" from *P&T.*

P. 12 / L. 18 — "Judd was not to be considered" from *P&T.*

P. 12 / L. 26 — "the slavery agitation" from *P&T; Times* has "it."

P. 12 / L. 34 — "In my opinion . . . North as well as South." SAD is undoubtedly reading from the text printed in the *P&T,* June 19, 1858, which is the one given here. The italicization shown here is that of the *Times,* does not correspond to Lincoln's printed text, and likely reflects Douglas's way of reading it.

P. 13 / L. 6 — "eighty" from *P&T; Times* has "seventy." See AL's reference on p. 22.

P. 13 / L. 9 — "as the President of the convention" from *P&T.*

P. 14 / L. 32 — "could receive baptism" from *P&T; Times* has "is worthy of a medal," which accords less well with "Father" Giddings.

P. 14 / L. 39 — "six thousand years" from *P&T; Times* has "thousands of years."

P. 14 / L. 40 — "that whole six thousand years" from *P&T; Times* has "all that time."

P. 18 / L. 29 — "materials": emendation by AL in his Debates Scrapbook (97); clipping has "materially."

P. 19 / L. 37 — "What": a misprint corrected by AL in his Debates Scrapbook; clipping had "Whas."

P. 19 / L. 41 — "Let the Judge . . . our equals?" The evidence of the *P&T* report indicates that AL made the interjection given here and then repeated the sentence he had just read.

P. 20 / L. 16 — "This is the repeal . . . of the latter." AL here read a passage of 817 words from his 1854 speech at Peoria, a passage both newspapers declined to print in its entirety. *P&T* printed 315 words; *Times* account is much garbled and even more abbreviated. In the Quincy debate, AL complained of the negligible coverage of this passage (see p. 216).

In his scrapbook of the debates, AL inserted, in place of the *P&T* account, a newspaper clipping of the entire passage, accompanied by a handwritten note: "This extract from Mr. Lincoln's Peoria Speech of 1854, was read by him in the Ottawa debate, but was not reported fully or accurately in either *Times* or *Press &Tribune.* It is inserted now as necessary to a complete report of the debates" (97). The text given here follows the scrapbook clipping, as corrected there by AL.

P. 23 / L. 13 — "Well, you are a fool . . . two of us that are that way." from *Times.*

P. 24 / L. 23 — The text Lincoln read here can be identified by the italicization and the word "lick" as that printed in Lincoln's home newspaper, the *Illinois State Journal*, June 18, 1858. See Basler et al., *Collected Works*, 2:465–66.

P. 24 / L. 29 — "insinuates" is a conjectural reading; *P&T's* word "eliminates" does not fit the context.

P. 25 / L. 3 — "and one that the world . . . that in mockery" from *Times*.

P. 25 / L. 10 — "I had incidentally said" from *Times*; *P&T* has "the next time I met him, which was at Springfield." See pp. xxxv–vi for further information on this passage.

P. 25 / L. 14 — "and there ought to be . . . I would not go" from *Times*; *P&T* has "under the Constitution, nor had I any inclination, to enter into the Slave States and interfere with the institutions of slavery. He says upon that: Lincoln will not enter."

P. 25 / L. 18 — "unless he shall . . . shall be dissolved." from SAD's Springfield speech, *Illinois State Register*, July 19, 1858; *P&T* has "Unless he shall be successful in firing his batteries until he has extinguished slavery in all the States, the Union shall be dissolved."

P. 26 / L. 9 — "and that" from *Times*.

P. 27 / L. 11 — "As to his statement . . . call somebody a liar about it." from *Times*.

P. 27 / L. 29 — Quoted from the Kansas-Nebraska bill, the text given here.

P. 28 / L. 32 — "And then the Judge, after I have dropped a part of the quotation, added that he "had" from *Times*; *P&T* has "I have."

P. 28 / L. 33 — "I did not answer . . . in making the charge." AL read from *Times*, July 30, 1858, the text given here.

P. 29 / L. 25 — "In this connection there is another topic . . . the article to which I allude." AL here, and in the passages that follow, read from a pamphlet version of SAD's Senate speech (see p. 29, note 33), the text given here. The words "authoritatively," "authoritative," and "fatal blow" are not italicized in the original.

P. 29 / L. 27 — "This is a speech . . . read it for yourselves" from *Times*; *P&T* has "This is a part of the speech."

P. 30 / L. 26 — "and every man is branded . . . not subscribe to them." appears only in *Times*, where the text differs only in capitalization from the source text, given here.

P. 30 / L. 36 — "a death blow to State rights . . . they will ever stand." appears only in *Times*, where the text shows a slight variation ("wish it" instead of "trust they") from the source text, given here.

P. 32 / L. 20 — "This being borne . . . Dred Scott decision?" from *Times*.

P. 32 / L. 24 — "he, as a good citizen, and you, as good citizens," from *Times*; *P&T* has "he is, and you."

P. 32 / L. 33 — "the great binding force of Supreme Court" from *Times*; *P&T* has "the binding force of."

P. 34 / L. 5 — "*Voice: Give us something besides Dred Scott.*" This interruption from the crowd is reported only in *P&T*, where the speaker is described as "A Hibernian." *Times* gives Lincoln's reply without specifying that it was in response to something from the crowd.

P. 34 / L. 18 — "no share" from *Times*; *P&T* has "nothing."

P. 34 / L. 22 — "don't care" from *Times*; *P&T* has "cares not." *Times* version is what Lincoln usually said in this context; "cares not" is more likely the work of an editor who forgot that "Douglas don't care" was one of AL's most persistent lines of attack.

P. 35 / L. 7 — "I have told him . . . of these interrogatories" from *P&T*; *Times* has "and ask for a specific answer."

P. 35 / L. 33 — "I know he did not." from *Times*; *P&T* has "I do know it." See note at p. 40. The *Times*, at this point, reports: "Two of the Republican committee here seized Mr. Lincoln, and by a sudden jerk caused him to disappear from the front of the stand, one of them saying quite audibly, 'What are you making such a fuss for. Douglas didn't interrupt you, and can't you see that the people don't like it?'"

P. 36 / L. 2 — "his milk" from *P&T*.

P. 36 / L. 7 — "the Declaration of Independence that niggers were equal to white men" from *P&T*; *Times* has "negro equality under the Declaration of Independence." For the use and reporting of the words "negro" and "nigger," see pp. 4–5.

P. 37 / L. 5 — "States" from *P&T*

P. 37 / L. 9 — "He has not answered that, has he?" from *P&T*.

P. 37 / L. 18 — "Why, he says that a man . . . each state having slavery" from *P&T*; *Times* has "He goes on to say that the man who would talk about giving each State the right to have slavery."

P. 37 / L. 37 — "acquirement": *P&T* has "acquisition." SAD previously uses "acquisition" in this context, but the passage he is citing, and from which he read in his opening speech, has "acquirement." See p. 9.

P. 38 / L. 19 — *Resolved,* That in furtherance . . . old party allegiance and ties." SAD read from the *Illinois State Register,* Oct. 16, 1854, the text given here.

P. 39 / L. 36 — "could prohibit, but could not introduce" from *P&T*; *Times* has "could prohibit by not introducing."

P. 40 / L. 28 — "He is an ignorant man." This provocative sentence is absent from the *P&T* account.

P. 40 / L. 32 — "right": *P&T* has "truth."

TEXTUAL NOTES FOR THE FREEPORT DEBATE

P. 46 / L. 12 — "on condition only that he should agree to answer as many for me.": emendation from AL's Debates Scrapbook (109); *Times* has "upon the terms that he would answer as many for me."

P. 46 / L. 16 — "absolutely and unconditionally" from *Times*.

P. 46 / L. 21 — "I shall make no objection . . . chooses to remain silent" from *Times*; *P&T* has "I give him an opportunity to respond. The Judge remains silent."

P. 46 / L. 25 — "I desire to say . . . any man or set of men." from *Times*.

P. 47 / L. 38 — "aggravate" from *Times*; *P&T* has "agitate." This (as "agravate") appears as AL's marginal emendation in his Debates Scrapbook (109).

P. 49 / L. 2 — "foul blot": both newspaper reports put quotations marks around the words "sweep from our Capital that foul blot upon our nation," but "foul blot" is likely the only language of Clay's that Lincoln is citing. See note 2, p. 49.

P. 49 / L. 10 — "and" from *Times*; *P&T* has "to."

P. 49 / L. 13 — "the slave trade" from *Times*; *P&T* has "tlavery." AL adopted the *Times's* wording in his Debates Scrapbook (109).

P. 49 / L. 29 — "offensive": emendation in AL's Debates Scrapbook (109); *P&T* has "affirmed."

P. 50 / L. 7 — "decide" from *Times; P&T* has "decree." AL adopted the *Times* reading in his Debates Scrapbook (109).

P. 52 / L. 1 — "I have arrayed, from time to time, the evidence which I think—I have thought—tends to establish and prove the truth of this charge." This sentence represents an editorial fusion of a sentence that appears in *P&T* and its counterpart in *Times. P&T* version: "I have arranged from time to time the evidence which establishes and proves the truth of this charge." *Times* version (which is closer to AL's position): "I have arrayed, from time to time, the evidence which I think—I have thought—tends to prove the truth of this charge."

P. 52 / L. 17 — "in" is an editorial emendation; *P&T* has "of."

P. 52 / L. 24 — "—and I am afraid I shall be offensive to the Judge by quoting it again—" from *Times.*

P. 52 / L. 26 — AL here quotes from the Kansas-Nebraska bill, presumably from memory, as both newspapers report him as saying "state or territory," whereas the act reads "territory or state."

P. 53 / L. 6 — "that cannot be understood" from *Times.*

P. 53 / L. 33 — "it" from *Times.*

P. 53 / L. 35 — "I believe I fairly state Judge Douglas's answer." from *Times.*

P. 53 / L. 36 — "This is substantially all of his reply." appears within parentheses one sentence earlier in *P&T* (two sentences earlier in the present text), but seems to be out of place and has been repositioned.

P. 53 / L. 37 — "of the record" from *Times.*

P. 54 / L. 11 — "some way" from *Times; P&T* has "somewhere."

P. 55 / L. 7 — "to" from *Times.*

P. 55 / L. 11 — "or upon my word" from *Times.*

P. 55 / L. 21 — "was": editorial emendation; *P&T* has "as."

P. 56 / L. 11 — "of all" from *P&T.*

P. 56 / L. 24 — "upon every question" from *P&T.*

P. 58 / L. 18 — "furnishing remedies and means of enforcing the right to hold slaves" from *P&T.*

P. 60 / L. 5 — "December": from both *P&T* and *Times.*

P. 60 / L. 9 — "was" from *P&T; Times* has "were."

P. 61 / L. 10 — "bank": *Times* has "branch," which may indicate SAD intended to refer to the Red River.

P. 61 / L. 39 — "Good, good": *Times* has "Good, good, &c. Renewed laughter, in which Mr. Lincoln feebly joined, saying that he hoped with their aid to get seven questions, the number asked him by Judge Douglas, and so make *conclusions* even."

P. 62 / L. 10 — "What of it!" from *P&T.*

P. 62 / L. 18 — "nigger" from *P&T; Times* has "negro." For the reporting of this word in the debates, see pp. 4–5. For testimony that SAD here used this word and not "negro," see Walter B. Stevens, *A Reporter's Lincoln,* ed. Michael Burlingame (Lincoln: University of Nebraska, 1994), 75.

P. 64 / L. 11 — "During the late discussions . . . our readers to it." SAD read from the *Illinois State Register,* Oct. 16, 1854, the text given here.

P. 65 / L. 6 — "All right. . . . Now for the next." from *P&T.*

P. 65 / L. 22 — "That's all right . . . until I read it. The next is" from *P&T.*

P. 65 / L. 26 — "Good. Good. . . . Now for the next." from *P&T.*

P. 66 / L. 4 — "Now I will read another resolution:" from *P&T.*

P. 66 / L. 13 — "*Resolved,* That we cordially invite . . . in carrying them into effect." only in *Times.* At this point, *Times* has Douglas saying substantially the same thing that the *P&T* reported him as saying intermittently during his reading of the resolutions. See the passage above beginning "Well, you think that is a very good platform. . . ." For this passage on the reading of the resolutions, *P&T* order is followed as more likely, though the *Times* text is adhered to, except as noted.

P. 66 / L. 19 — "Yes, you say exactly" from *P&T.*

P. 66 / L. 30 — "White Republicans!" from *P&T.*

P. 66 / L. 32 — "as laid down in the compromise measures of 1850, and carried out in the Kansas-Nebraska bill" from *P&T.*

P. 68 / L. 3 — "I drew these resolutions" from *P&T.*

P. 68 / L. 10 — "Turner says they are his—that is the Black Republican creed—exactly" from *P&T.*

P. 68 / L. 15 — "position where he will have to vote on the admission of a slave state" from *P&T.*

P. 70 / L. 3 — "I will read the resolutions and hand the preamble to the reporters, that they may publish the whole" from *P&T.* The preamble was apparently not read from the platform; it was printed only in the *Times.* See p. 70n for the source and the text of the preamble. The text from which SAD read, given here, is from *Journal of the House of Representatives of the Nineteenth General Assembly of the State of Illinois* (Springfield: Lanphier & Walker, 1855), Feb. 6, 1855, 284.

P. 71 / L. 19 — "and here are the votes, which I will hand to the reporter to copy" from *P&T.*

P. 71 / L. 32 — "25" from *P&T,* which is correct; *Times* has "35."

P. 72 / L. 5 — "cast your vote for him?" At this point, *Times* has a parenthetical aside: "Mr. Lincoln here started forward, and grasping Mr. Turner, shook him nervously, and said, 'Don't answer, Turner, you have no right to answer.'"

P. 72 / L. 7 — "Not only is the name of Turner here, but there are names from the adjoining counties" from *P&T.*

P. 72 / L. 9 — "with two exceptions" from *P&T.*

P. 73 / L. 2 — "Will he vote for or against the admission of a slave state?" from *P&T.*

P. 73 / L. 14 — The likeliest source for the passage that follows is the "House Divided" speech as printed in the *P&T,* June 19, 1858, the text given here.

P. 73 / L. 15 — "(the slavery agitation)" was presumably added by SAD.

P. 73 / L. 18 — "I do not expect the house to fall": the first part of this sentence in the original ("I do not expect the Union to be dissolved—") is absent in both *Times* and *P&T* and presumably was omitted by SAD.

P. 78 / L. 24 — "But there is one particular branch . . . occurs to me, and it is this:" from *Times.*

P. 78 / L. 29 — "When he shall see my speech in print," from *Times.*

P. 78 / L. 35 — "I said that in very plain language." from *Times.*

P. 79 / L. 17 — "And now, then, there is one subject to which I wish to call your attention." from *Times*.

P. 79 / L. 31 — "has" from *Times*; *P&T* has "was."

P. 79 / L. 37 — "(I don't know that I give the Judge's exact language,)" from *Times*. Note that the surrounding sentence is almost identical in both accounts.

P. 79 / L. 39 — "merely because Mr. Toombs got up and made a speech" from *Times*, which has AL repeating this phrase, but substituting "simply" for "merely" the second time.

P. 80 / L. 5 — "when" from *Times*.

P. 80 / L. 11 — "Turn this way . . . shan't be this way!" from *Times*.

P. 80 / L. 12 — "he said when they had done their day's work, why," from *Times*.

P. 80 / L. 18 — "and stuck no pins. . . . drayman came by and he asked him" from *Times*. *P&T*, in giving the "go-it-ometer" result as ten miles, seems to confuse what AL said about this result being off by as much as nine or ten times. The *P&T* account shows evidence of being a stripped down version of what AL said. See John Phoenix [George Horatio Derby], *Phoenixiana; or, Sketches and Burlesques*, (New York: D. Appleton, 1856), 20.

P. 80 / L. 26 — "There is another thing . . . I think that the man that" from *Times*; *P&T* has "Yet it is a fact that the man who."

p. 80 /L. 30—"Well, now my friends, . . . on the 22d of March" from *Times*; *P&T* has "Now, gentlemen, you may take Judge Douglas' speech of March 22d, 1858."

p. 80 /L. 31—"beginning about the middle of page 21, and reading to the bottom of page 24": AL here cites pagination from the same pamphlet version of SAD's Mar. 22, 1858, speech he used at Ottawa. See note 33, p. 29.

p. 80 /L. 34—"I cannot stop to read it, but I will give it to the reporters.": *P&T* here printed the pertinent part of SAD's speech, but *Times* did not. AL apparently did not think he could afford the time to read the entire excerpt, as he had done at Ottawa, but rather proceeded to analyze some of its statements. Therefore the entire excerpt is not included here but can be seen in the Ottawa debate on pp. 29–30. The text is the same somewhat truncated version of this passage of SAD's speech as was printed in *P&T*'s account of the Ottawa debate.

P. 80 / L. 35 — "After he had quoted the article from the editor of the *Union*, he then said:" from *Times*; *P&T* has "Judge Douglas said."

P. 81 / L. 1 — "Mr. President, you here find several distinct propositions advanced boldly, and apparently *authoritatively*.": abbreviated from "Mr. President, you here find several distinct propositions advanced boldly by the Washington Union editorially and apparently authoritatively, . . ." (p. 23). Italics added in *P&T* to reflect AL's emphasis.

P. 81 / L. 6 — "in the Washington Union . . . who does not subscribe to them." from *Times*, *Speech of Senator Douglas, of Illinois*, p. 23. Italics added in *P&T* to reflect AL's emphasis.

P. 81 / L. 16 — "I ask you to read it yourselves." from *Times*.

P. 81 / L. 23 — "a death blow to State rights . . . they will ever stand." from *Times*, where the text shows a slight variation ("wish it" instead of "trust they") from the source text, given here.

P. 82 / L. 2 — "I repeat here . . . that such was the fact." from *Times*.

P. 82 / L. 7 — "head of": editorial emendation; *P&T* has "head our."

TEXTUAL NOTES FOR THE JONESBORO DEBATE

P. 86 / L. 18 — "when" from *P&T*.

P. 87 / L. 38 — "nigger" from *P&T*; *Times* has "negro." For discussion of the use and reporting of these words, see pp. 4–5.

P. 88 / L. 10 — "It is true according to the evidence and the history of the transaction, that" from *P&T*.

P. 88 / L. 16 — "then": editorial emendation—both *Times* and *P&T* give this word as "when."

P. 88 / L. 29 — "in connection" from *P&T*; *Times* has "in the connection."

P. 89 / L. 20 — "shot" from *P&T*; *Times* has "short."

P. 90 / L. 10 — "Signed: "The Monroe Free Democrat[s]" from *P&T*; *Times* has "The Monroe Free Democracy."

P. 91 / L. 15 — "was first" from *P&T*; *Times* has "was at first."

P. 92 / L. 9 — "that two years ago this fall" from *P&T*, and is part of the newspaper article SAD is reading from. SAD's source text (see note 5, p. 92) is followed here.

P. 93 / L. 15 — "to be discarded" from *P&T*; *Times* has "degraded."

P. 93 / L. 35 — "We are now far into the fifth year . . . North as well as South." The text presented here as the likeliest source SAD read from is that of *P&T*, June 19, 1858, the text that appears AL's Debates Scrapbook.

P. 95 / L. 4 — "Where" from *P&T*; *Times* has "When."

P. 95 / L. 5 — "made by our fathers" from *P&T*.

P. 95 / L. 12 — "naval and military" from *P&T*.

P. 98 / L. 6 — "natural" from *P&T*; *Times* has "national."

P. 99 / L. 5 — "I say that our institutions rest on that great principle." from *P&T*.

P. 99 / L. 20 — "I am told my time is out." from *P&T*.

P. 100 / L. 5 — "the policy" from *Times*; *P&T* has "them."

P. 101 / L. 19 — "We all knew it was a lie." from *Times*, attributed to "Pedlar in the crowd"; *P&T* has "That's right." "Hit him again."

P. 104 / L. 15 — "expressed in the extract which" from *Times*.

P. 104 / L. 17 — "Upon that subject . . . as I best can." from *Times*. Both reporters seem to have had difficulty with this portion of AL's speech, and it may indeed have been one of the occasions, sometimes referred to, where the wind or other conditions made it hard for them to follow.

P. 104 / L. 21 — "and those who act with me" from *Times*.

P. 104 / L. 24 — "why" from *Times*; *P&T* has "whether."

P. 106 / L. 6 — "That is one and . . . in the affirmative." from *Times*.

P. 106 / L. 17 — "I read the answers, leaving out the first ones that I have read:" from Times.

P. 106 / L. 30 — "he was elected to Congress over a very good man named" from *Times*; *P&T* has "against."

P. 106 / L. 36 — "Whether defeated or not nominated, I do not know." At this point, *P&T*

inserted in brackets: "Mr. Campbell was nominated for re-election by the Democratic party, by acclamation."

P. 106 / L. 37 — "of election upon this platform" from *Times*.

P. 107 / L. 6 — "sneaking about—I take back that ugly word, [to the reporters] you must not put that in—" from *Times*. See note 16, p. 107.

P. 107 / L. 18 — "*Resolved,* That we are . . . expounder of our faith." AL's source text is unknown. The text of *P&T* and *Times* are virtually identical and do not differ verbally from the text published in the *Chicago Democrat,* Oct. 11, 1850.

P. 107 / L. 22 — "I received the within interrogatories . . . Yours, &c., R. S. Molony." AL's source text is not known. The texts of *P&T* and *Times* are virtually identical, but they omit two sentences (see note below) of the text that appeared in the *Chicago Democrat* of Oct. 11, 1858, where Molony's statement is dated Oct. 8, 1850.

P. 107 / L. 35 — ". . . would *never* receive my vote." Two sentences that follow here in the text carried by the *Chicago Democrat,* Oct. 11, 1858, are absent in this text: "My mind is not made up on this point, not having examined the resolution with reference to it. Still I must view the whole matter now, and for a long time to come, as an abstraction, for no such States will ask to be admitted for a long while."

P. 108 / L. 19 — "Ike" from *Times*.

P. 109 / L. 1 — "which, according to the custom . . . without reading" from *Times*.

P. 109 / L. 15 — "There is some portion . . . wish to comment upon." from *Times*.

P. 109 / L. 20 — "I was not present . . . some error in it." from *Times*.

P. 109 / L. 27 — *P&T* here inserts in brackets: "DeKalb County *Sentinel*."

P. 110 / L. 6 — "In this I agree with him." AL's interjection appears in *P&T* within brackets in the running text of the clipping he is reading from.

P. 110 / L. 10 — "Our education has been such . . . more of than some white men." A newspaper clipping bearing this text is present in one of the notebooks that AL's law partner, William H. Herndon, says was used in the debates (Herndon-Weik Collection, Library of Congress, Container 1). In the margin, a pencil notation says: "DeKalb Sentinel/Quoted at Jonesboro Debate p. 355." (The page number relates to the Nicolay and Hay edition of AL's *Complete Works,* 2 vols. [New York: Century, 1894], 1:355.) The clipping is presumed to be AL's source text and is the one given here. The italicization is from *P&T* and probably reflects emphasis applied by AL on the platform.

P. 110 / L. 15 — "which I will give to the reporter," from *Times*.

P. 110 / L. 18 — "Your time is half over!" from *Times*.

P. 110 / L. 19 — "I now understand that my time is half out." from *Times*. Not included here is an accompanying prejudicial remark given in *Times*—"*I did not know that I was wasting time in that way.*"—which, while dubious as an accurate report, may suggest that the announcement about time induced AL to shift tactics and move on.

P. 111 / L. 17 — "Question 1. If the people . . . vote to admit them?" AL here read from the *P&T*'s published account of Aug. 30, 1858, the text given here.

P. 111 / L. 27 — "in disregard of": emendation from AL's Debates Scrapbook (135); *P&T* has "according to."

P. 111 / L. 34 — "Question 2. Can the people . . . formation of a State Constitution?" AL here read from the *P&T*'s published account of Aug. 30, 1858, the text given here.

P. 112 / L. 25 — "I am not sure that I have the page, but that is the date." from *Times*.

P. 112 / L. 34 — "He shakes his head!" from *Times.*

P. 113 / L. 3 — "Trumbull" from *Times; P&T* has "us."

P. 113 / L. 5 — "then" from *Times.*

P. 113 / L. 8 — "This is not all with regard to that answer of his." from *Times.*

P. 114 / L. 14 — "How could you?" from *Times.*

P. 115 / L. 2 — "withhold" from *Times; P&T* has "withheld."

P. 116 / L. 27 — "He would not answer these questions." After this sentence, the source text (*Missouri Republican,* Sept. 9, 1858) contains the following passage, omitted in AL's presentation:

> (a voice, "he did not understand the language.") He ought to have understood it. It was good Abolition language, it was written in the true dialect of the party. I hope the party is not running a man who does not understand the dialect of the party. He would not answer the questions I put to him over and over again.

P. 116 / L. 34 — "You know at Ottawa I read . . . came up to Freeport last Friday." This text from *Missouri Republican,* Sept. 9, 1858, with the deletion noted above.

P. 117 / L. 4 — "There!" The exclamation point is from *Times,* which has "Yes, sir!!"; *P&T* has "There;."

P. 117 / L. 11 — "I did." from *Times.*

P. 119 / L. 28 — "In regard to the other question . . . admit them into the Union." Douglas is here reading from the *P&T* account at Freeport, which is the text followed here.

P. 121 / L. 3 — "and wire worker? / Mr. Lincoln—Yes, sir." from *P&T.*

P. 121 / L. 11 — "If you will name the witnesses I will bring them to you." from *P&T.*

P. 122 / L. 34 — "because he was raised in Indiana." from *P&T.*

P. 124 / L. 1 — "If the slaveholding . . . against such legislation?" See AL's speech above, p. 115.

P. 124 / L. 17 — "not" from *P&T*

P. 124 / L. 30 — "true" from *P&T; Times* has "time."

P. 125 / L. 27 — "your" from *P&T; Times* has "our."

P. 125 / L. 27 — "a": editorial emendation.

P. 125 / L. 37 — "who lost his case and liked the decision" from *P&T.*

P. 126 / L. 1 — "who did not think the decision unjust." from *P&T; Times* has "lose his case that he approved the decision of the court."

P. 126 / L. 4 — "sustain the constitutional authorities as they exist," from *P&T.*

TEXTUAL NOTES FOR THE CHARLESTON DEBATE

P. 132 / L. 33 — "that" from *Times.*

P. 133 / L. 4 — "Judge Douglas proceeded . . . responsible for the slanders." AL's source text for SAD's speech at Jacksonville, Sept. 6, 1858, given here, is from the unidentified newspaper (not *Times*), whose account of it is included in AL's Debates Scrapbook, 146.

P. 133 / L. 9 — "I say to the just extent I take the responsibility." (second utterance) from *Times.*

P. 133 / L. 19 — "*Now, the charge is . . . Mr. Douglas was in the plot.*" The source text for AL's quotations for Trumbull's Speech at Alton, given here and in the excerpts from that speech that follow, are from the extracts in AL's Debates Scrapbook, 142–44, 146; for the quotation cited here, 142.

P. 134 / L. 6 — "He then brings forward . . . the vote of the people." from *Times*.

P. 134 / L. 17 — "Suppose it were true . . . against their will?" from SAD's Jacksonville speech, AL's Debates Scrapbook, 146.

P. 134 / L. 19 — "And he argues from that . . . vote upon their constitution." from *Times*.

P. 134 / L. 30 — "why" from *Times*; *P&T* has "when."

P. 135 / L. 36 — "Judge Douglas did not . . . in which I have stated. Trumbull" from *Times*.

P. 136 / L. 5 — "That the following propositions . . . said State of Kansas.": from Trumbull's Alton speech, AL's Debates Scrapbook, 143. Except for the capitalization added by the newspaper to focus attention on the disputed passage, this is an accurate quotation from the original. See Senate bill S. 172 offered by Douglas on Mar. 17, 1856, "Bills and Resolutions," Library of Congress Web site, "A Century of Lawmaking for a New Nation: U.S. Congressional Documents and Debates, 1774–1875."

P. 136 / L. 10 — "Would it have been possible . . . was to be held.": from extracts of Trumbull's Alton speech, Debates Scrapbook, 143.

P. 136 / L. 12 — "provision" from *Times*; *P&T* has "proposition."

P. 137 / L. 18 — "It would not touch the question at all." from *Times*.

P. 137 / L. 32 — "Let me not be misunderstood . . . between him (Judge Douglas) and Mr. Toombs." from *Times*.

P. 138 / L. 1 — "until the complete . . . in said Territory": from SAD's Jacksonville speech, Debates Scrapbook, 146. The quotation derives from the wording of the bill (S. 356) Douglas reported to the Senate on June 30, 1856. The *Times* preceded this quotation with the sentence in Trumbull's speech leading up to it, but the account of SAD's Jacksonville speech that AL is here analyzing does not contain this sentence, and it has not been included here.

P. 138 / L. 27 — "He says I am speaking of the bill . . . as he brought it back.": AL's characterizations in these two sentences were treated in both papers as a direct quotation from Trumbull's Alton speech, but they are, in fact, only approximations.

P. 139 / L. 5 — "it may have become apparent enough to any one that these were his cubs," from *Times*.

P. 139 / L. 9 — "close" from *Times*; *P&T* has "clause."

P. 139 / L. 11 — "He forged his evidence . . . bolster up his false charge." from SAD's speech at Jacksonville, Debates Scrapbook, 146.

P. 139 / L. 32 — "if I have time to do so. One piece of evidence I have already read." from *Times*.

P. 140 / L. 2 — "That the following propositions . . . the said State of Kansas.": from Trumbull's Alton speech, Debates Scrapbook, 143.

P. 140 / L. 7 — "and then adds, 'I read from part 1, *Congressional Globe* of last session, page 21:'" from *Times*.

P. 140 / L. 15 — "I was present when . . . submitting it to the popular vote." This text from Trumbull's Alton speech (Debates Scrapbook, 143), which passage is virtually identical to its source in the *Congressional Globe*.

P. 141 / L. 8 — "bill" from *Times*.

P. 141 / L. 12 — "Nothing was farther from my mind . . . had been stricken out." This text from Trumbull's Alton speech, Debates Scrapbook, 143.

P. 141 / L. 24 — "That during the last session . . . passed by the Senate." This text from Trumbull's Alton speech, Debates Scrapbook, 143–44.

P. 141 / L. 28 — "That is what I want him to do." from *Times.*

P. 142 / L. 5 — "I will ask the Senator . . . fairness to have been done." This text from Trumbull's Alton speech, Debates Scrapbook, 144. This passage is from SAD's reply to Bigler on Dec. 9, 1857 and is virtually identical to its source in the *Congressional Globe.*

P. 142 / L. 19 — "Judge Douglas, however, on the same . . . would be submitted to the people." This text from Trumbull's Alton Speech, *P&T,* Aug. 31. This passage is from SAD's reply to Bigler on Dec. 9, 1857 and is virtually identical to its source in the *Congressional Globe.*

P. 142 / L. 20 — "Trumbull adds upon that" from *Times.*

P. 142 / L. 24 — "Whether this statement . . . so far as I am concerned." This text from Trumbull's Alton speech, Debates Scrapbook, 144. The last part of this quotation—"for if the public records do not convict and condemn him, he may go uncondemned, so far as I am concerned"—does not appear in P&T's account of the Charleston debate but is present in *Times.*

P. 145 / L. 25 — "Why don't you reply to the charge?" from *P&T.*

P. 145 / L. 29 — "Now, I propose to first state the charge in Trumbull's own language." from *P&T.*

P. 146 / L. 4 — "Now, fellow citizens . . . a constitution upon that people." This text from Trumbull's Chicago speech, as printed in the *P&T,* Aug. 9, 1858. *Times* account of the Charleston debate omitted "not submitted to the people to have a constitution," but these words were part of the Trumbull's speech being quoted and were probably read by SAD, as they are present in the *P&T* account.

P. 146 / L. 13 — "And you want to satisfy . . . claim credit for it." This text from Trumbull's Chicago speech, *P&T,* Aug. 9. The final sentence is not in *P&T's* report of the Charleston debate.

P. 148 / L. 13 — SAD read from *Senate Reports,* 34th Congress, 1st Session, No. 198, 7, the text given here.

P. 149 / L. 23 — "on" from *P&T; Times* has "in."

P. 150 / L. 5 — "There is nothing said . . . provisions of the bill." This text is from Trumbull's speech in the Senate on the Toombs bill for the admission of Kansas, *CG Appendix,* 34th Congress, 1st Session, 779. *P&T* omits the last sentence.

P. 150 / L. 23 — "MR. DOUGLAS—I have an amendment . . . which I hold in my hand." This text from Douglas's remarks on the floor of the Senate, July 2, 1856, as printed in the *CG Appendix,* 34th Congress, 1st Session, 795.

P. 151 / L. 3 — "MR. DOUGLAS—I have another amendment . . . failure to come into the Union." This text from ibid., 796. The concluding passage—"so that they can appoint the day in the event that there should be a failure to come into the Union"—is not in *P&T.*

P. 151 / L. 20 — "prosecute" from *P&T; Times* has "persecute."

P. 151 / L. 31 — "expression of a" from *P&T; Times* has "determination of."

P. 151 / L. 35 — "to have the Dred Scott case decided in such a manner as" from *P&T.*

P. 151 / L. 36 — "He charged a conspiracy between us." from *P&T.*

P. 153 / L. 23 — "for I was not aware that he was a candidate, *[Laughter]*" from *P&T.*

P. 158 / L. 13 — "wearied" from *P&T; Times* has "worried out."

P. 159 / L. 9 — "the whigs, abolitionists, know-nothings . . . conspires or contracts with rogues.'" As with the same quotation read by SAD at Jonesboro, the text followed here is that of SAD's presumed original, as published in *Times*, June 24, 1858, crediting the *Menard Index*, which "brings forth from its files the following extract from a report of a speech delivered by Mr. M just before the [1856] Presidential election."

P. 160 / L. 27 — "just as fast" from *P&T.*

P. 160 / L. 38 — "13th" from *P&T; Times* has "12th." Monday was the 13th.

P. 160 / L. 38 — "Jehu" from *P&T; Times* has "John."

P. 162 / L. 28 — "I should like to know . . . and bear it out!" The text of AL's July 10, 1858, Chicago speech SAD read from was probably the one printed by *Times*, July 13, 1858, which is followed here.

P. 163 / L. 34 — "people on the face of the globe" from *P&T; Times* has "other."

P. 167 / L. 2 — "I made that answer off-hand . . . Ford's history upon the subject." from *Times.*

P. 168 / L. 31 — "he should not hereafter . . . responsible for the slanders." From SAD's speech at Jacksonville, AL's Debates Scrapbook, 146.

P. 169 / L. 20 — "That is what I want to know." from *Times.*

P. 171 / L. 5 — "If you have ever studied geometry . . . and therefore I close." These sentences containing the example of Euclid and the closing sentence that follows it do not appear in *Times.*

TEXTUAL NOTES FOR THE GALESBURG DEBATE

P. 176 / L. 18 — "the true intent and meaning . . . the Constitution of the United States." SAD here probably quotes from memory the text of the Kansas-Nebraska Act.

P. 179 / L. 10 — "If I had done this . . . have pursued this course." This sentence does not appear in the *P&T*, though its text closely follows the *Times* up to this point.

P. 181 / L. 1 — "the federal Constitution is the supreme law of the land." *Times* has "the Federal Constitution is not the supreme law of the land"—which is presumably a mistake. *P&T* does not have this word.

P. 181 / L. 25 — "I should like to know . . . tear it out!" As at Charleston, SAD is probably reading from the text of AL's July 10, 1858, Chicago speech as printed in *Times*, July 13, 1858, the text followed here, with one exception. SAD has apparently taken notice, since his Charleston speech, of the superior applicability of the word "tear" over the word "bear" and has substituted accordingly. See p. 162, note 37.

P. 182 / L. 4 — "I have detained you . . . are created equal." From AL's July 10, 1858, speech at Chicago as published in *Times*, July 3.

P. 182 / L. 11 — "I leave you . . . created free and equal." From AL's July 10, 1858, speech at Chicago as published in *Times*, July 3.

P. 182 / L. 28 — "I will say then . . . assigned to the white man." SAD reads from the *Times* report of what AL said at Charleston, which is very close to *P&T.*

P. 183 / L. 16 — "Saturday I think . . . Nor Democratic here." from *P&T.* There it includes the word "and" between "Monday," and "they."

P. 183 / L. 34 — "the" from *P&T.*

P. 185 / L. 9 — "are" from *P&T; Times* has "is."

P. 186 / L. 1 — "How can the owner of the slave be more fortunate?" from *P&T.*

P. 186 / L. 18 — "there should be no power" from *P&T.*

P. 186 / L. 32 — "'a house divided . . . I give his idea.)" from *P&T.* There it also includes, prior to the parenthetical material the words "what do you think would have been the result?" That sentence has been omitted here because it appears slightly later in the primary (*Times*) text.

P. 187 / L. 30 — "already" from *Times,* where the phrase "already afforded" is actually repeated.

P. 188 / L. 4 — "have" from *Times.*

P. 190 / L. 18 — "Now, it is the first time . . . rightful principles everywhere!" from *Times.*

P. 193 / L. 5 — At this point *Times* has "For instance—(here some men running off to see some kind of a hubbub in the vicinity of the crowd.) Well, that is very beautiful—."

P. 193 / L. 30 — "springing" from *Times; P&T* has "sprung."

P. 194 / L. 25 — "We are glad of the division" from *Times.*

P. 195 / L. 4 — "six" from *Times; P&T* has "seven."

P. 195 / L. 5 — "gave it up, but" from *Times.*

P. 196 / L. 2 — "drowned husband was brought home with his body full of eels": incorporates AL's emendation in his Debates Scrapbook, 171; *P&T* has "drowned husband's body was brought home with the pockets full of eels"; *Times* has "husband's body was brought home full of eels."

P. 196 / L. 11 — "last": emendation from AL's Debates Scrapbook, 171.

P. 196 / L. 16 — "He,": emendation from AL's Debates Scrapbook, 171; *P&T* has "Both"; *Times* has "He and."

P. 196 / L. 17 — "cozy" from *Times; P&T* has "crazy." AL adopted the *Times* reading in his Debates Scrapbook, 171.

P. 196 / L. 27 — "repeats" from *Times; P&T* has "reports."

P. 197 / L. 8 — "after the express promise of Judge Douglas to investigate it" from *Times.*

P. 197 / L. 18 — "If the Supreme Court . . . rule of political action?" The text of this question is here given in the form in which it was offered at Freeport, which is almost identical to that reported for the Galesburg debate in *Times.* The Galesburg version reported in *P&T,* which was presumably reported stenographically, includes variations: "If the Supreme Court of the United States shall decide that the states cannot exclude slavery from their limits, are you in favor of acquiescing in, adhering to and following such decision, as a rule of political action?"

P. 197 / L. 26 — "all treaties made, or" from *Times; P&T* has "all the treaties for." AL adopted the *Times'* reading in his Debates Scrapbook, 171.

P. 197 / L. 29 — "This Constitution . . . contrary notwithstanding.": from text of Article VI, U.S. Constitution.

P. 197 / L. 29 — "compressed" from *Times; P&T* has "comprised." AL adopted the *Times* reading in his Debates Scrapbook, 171.

P. 197 / L. 33 — "What is *affirmed*" is reported in both *P&T* and *Times.* This suggests that AL's marginal emendation in his Debates Scrapbook (171)—"What is it to be '*affirmed*'"—is most likely an after-the-fact clarification and is therefore not adopted here.

P. 198 / L. 2 — "firm in it," from *Times; P&T* has "made, formed into."

P. 198 / L. 17 — "the fault is the falsehood in fact of one of the premises." from *Times; P&T* has "the falsehood in fact is a fault of the premises."

P. 198 / L. 21 — "affirmed": emendation by AL in his Debates Scrapbook, 173; *P&T* has "affirmen."

P. 198 / L. 26 — "of a state" from *Times.*

P. 199 / L. 8 — "but the course of argument that he makes day by day" from *Times.*

P. 199 / L. 22 — "breaking": emendation by AL in his Debates Scrapbook, 173; *P&T* has "backing."

P. 200 / L. 40 — "blow" from *Times; P&T* has "blot." Clay's original text has "blow," and a marginal mark in Debates Scrapbook (173) may have been intended as a substitution of "blow" for "blot."

P. 201 / L. 1 — "would repress all tendencies to liberty . . . light of reason and the love of liberty!" This is a condensed version of a passage in Clay's speech, largely in his own language. See note 38, p. 34.

P. 201 / L. 6 — "blowing" from *Times; P&T* has "blotting." AL adopted the *Times* reading in his Debates Scrapbook (173).

P. 201 / L. 17 — "Are you opposed to the acquisition . . . first be prohibited therein?" See p. 47.

P. 201 / L. 24 — "Are you in favor of acquiring . . . upon the slavery question?" See p. 50.

P. 204 / L. 7 — "speeches" from *P&T; Times* has "speech."

P. 204 / L. 16 — "Silence, if you please." from *P&T.*

P. 204 / L. 19 — "if the speech delivered here had been made there." from *P&T.*

P. 204 / L. 25 — "You believe it." from *P&T.*

P. 205 / L. 12 — "and wherever the Constitution rules." from *P&T.*

TEXTUAL NOTES FOR THE QUINCY DEBATE

P. 215 / L. 25 — "an opportunity" from *Times.*

P. 216 / L. 4 — "intermarry": emendation from AL's Debates Scrapbook, 179; *P&T* has "intermingling."

P. 216 / L. 8 — "and inferior": emendation ("& inferior") from AL's Debates Scrapbook, 179.

P. 216 / L. 10 — "I will say, then . . . the white race." What text Lincoln reads from (*Times* or *P&T,* Charleston or Galesburg) is unclear, especially since he says in the next line he has given "the entire quotation from the Charleston speech as the Judge made it." The differences are quite minor, and since he corrected this quotation in his Debates Scrapbook (179), that text has been followed here.

P. 216 / L. 22 — "Yes here you find men . . . white race over the negro." Except for a slight condensation of the first sentence, AL seems here to be quoting directly from the *P&T* account of SAD's Charleston remarks, the text followed here. Compare the original at pp. 182–83.

P. 216 / L. 31 — "of" from *Times;* not present in *P&T* but its presence is implied in what Lincoln says immediately below.

P. 217 / L. 27 — "Now gentlemen, I don't . . . *equal of every living man.*" The *P&T* account of this passage is imperfect and bears the marks of having been taken down by the reporter, rather than having been simply transcribed from a printed copy of the Ottawa text. For example, "a specious and fantastic arrangement of words" becomes "a species of fantastical arrangement of words" or "the equal of every living man" is rendered as "the equal of any other man." AL, in his Debates Scrapbook (179), corrected some but not all of the errors. The *Times* account, however, is taken directly from the *P&T's* report of the Ottawa debate (see pp. 20–21), as is the text given here. The cheers occurring during and after the speech are those at Quincy, not Ottawa.

P. 217 / L. 30 — "and so on" from *Times; P&T* has "&c."

P. 217 / L. 36 — "made" from *Times; P&T* has "read." AL adopted the *Times* reading in his Debates Scrapbook, 179.

P. 218 / L. 22 — "give" from *Times; P&T* has "gave." AL adopted the *Times* reading in his Debates Scrapbook, 181.

P. 218 / L. 33 — "He goes on and insists . . . their opinions held the reverse." These two passages from SAD's Galesburg rejoinder were read from the *P&T* account of the Galesburg debate, the text given here.

P. 219 / L. 29 — "from beginning to end" from *Times.*

P. 221 / L. 32 — "We don't want to hear . . . Don't waste my time." The voice from the crowd and AL's response is from *Times.*

P. 221 / L. 38 — "departing from it." In his Debates Scrapbook (181), AL struck the last word in this sentence, "it," and substituted "the same course." But inasmuch as *Times* has the entire sentence in exactly the same words as *P&T,* including "it," AL's emendation would appear to be an after-the-fact alteration and is therefore not adopted here.

P. 222 / L. 3 — "Why" from *Times; P&T* has "We."

P. 222 / L. 12 — "I suppose that is . . . who do not think it wrong." from *Times.*

P. 223 / L. 20 — "ours" from *Times; P&T* has "me."

P. 223 / L. 35 — "it" from *Times: P&T* has "he."

P. 224 / L. 12 — "You sometimes say that . . . but consider awhile." from *Times.*

P. 224 / L. 31 — "Douglas is right! . . . question that we are going to try." The voice from the crowd and AL's response from *Times.*

P. 225 / L. 1 — "not, just here, trying": emendation from AL's Debates Scrapbook (183), presumably adapted from *Times* "have not been trying"; *P&T* has "I am here."

P. 225 / L. 20 — "under those circumstances." from P&T; Times has "upon the circumstances he has this."

P. 227 / L. 34 — "make" from P&T; Times has "made."

P. 228 / L. 23 — "But," he added, "if slavery . . . admit them into the Union.": from the *P&T* account of the Freeport debate, the text given here.

P. 230 / L. 10 — "I should like to know . . . let us tear it out!" The text of AL's Chicago speech SAD read from here, as at Charleston and Galesburg, was most likely that printed in *Times* on July 13, 1858, the text (with one exception) given here. As at Galesburg, SAD opted to substitute the word "tear" for the less probable word printed by *Times,* "bear." *P&T* seems to have deliberately altered the text from "some other man" to "a German?" The last two sentences appear only in *P&T.* When SAD quoted this passage at Galesburg, he had included these two sentences, lending credence to *P&T's* account.

P. 230 / L. 25 — "My friends, I have . . . all men are created equal." from the same source as the previous quotation.

P. 230 / L. 34 — "ground" from *P&T*; *Times* has "grounds."

P. 231 / L. 8 — "in order that the two may go out side by side. Here is what he said at Charleston" from *P&T*.

P. 231 / L. 18 — "I will say then . . . assigned to the white man.": from the text of AL's Charleston speech as printed in the *Times*, Sept. 21, 1858.

P. 231 / L. 19 — "good" from *P&T*; *Times* has "the."

P. 232 / L. 3 — "Let us see what right . . . succeed in Missouri." from *P&T*.

P. 232 / L. 29 — "Under the operation . . . North as well as South." SAD here read from the text of AL's "House Divided" speech of June 16, 1858, presumably that printed in *P&T*, June, 19, 1858, the text given here.

P. 234 / L. 21 — "to" from *P&T*.

P. 235 / L. 15 — "Republicans" and "men" from *P&T*; *Times* has "Republican" and "man."

P. 235 / L. 23 — "nor" from *P&T*; *Times* has "or."

P. 236 / L. 21 — "the" from *P&T*.

P. 236 / L. 36 — "nor" from P&T; *Times* has "or."

P. 237 / L. 10 — "We propose to show . . . *doubt upon that subject.*" The text given here and in succeeding quotations is from the *Washington Union*, Oct. 5, 1858. Except for some quotation marks and italicization added to indicate SAD's emphasis, the *Times* text is virtually identical.

P. 238 / L. 30 — "So much for the course taken . . . of Utah and New Mexico.": the *Washington Union*, Oct. 5, 1858. The text printed in the *Times* account, here and in the excerpts that follow, contains only a few deviations. The final paragraph is the only part of the Union article Douglas read from that appears in the *P&T* account.

P. 238 / L. 34 — "giving the Legislature the right to have slavery or not, as it pleased." from *P&T*.

P. 238 / L. 39 — "To": word added by the editors.

P. 239 / L. 20 — "The recent legislation . . . within their limits." The text given here is from John Bassett Moore, ed., *The Works of James Buchanan* (Philadelphia: Lippincott, 1910), 10:81. Except for a few minor variations, the *Times* account is identical.

P. 241 / L. 4 — "have" from *P&T*; *Times* has "bare."

P. 241 / L. 7 — "But as to the constitutional question, I do decide." from *P&T*.

P. 241 / L. 39 — "and make them comfortable and happy," from *P&T*.

P. 243 / L. 29 — "Carlin don't fall in." from *Times*.

P. 244 / L. 4 — "You know him . . . let them have it." from *Times*.

P. 245 / L. 6 — "but as we do not believe . . . support it as such." from *Times*.

P. 246 / L. 6 — "same" from Times.

P. 246 / L. 33 — "all" from *Times*.

P. 247 / L. 2 — "What is the *foundation* . . . . a great fundamental principle." The exact source of the text AL read from is unknown, but *P&T* is likely responsible for the italics shown here.

P. 247 / L. 5 — "nigger" from *Times*; *P&T* has "negro." See discussion of the occurrences of this word at pp. 4–5. It is impossible to be certain that AL said this here, but this is the word he used in this context previously at Ottawa, and the *Times* reports this word very sparingly.

P. 247 / L. 4 — "I suppose I have occupied ten minutes." from *Times*.

P. 247 / L. 35 — "*when it is proven on me as that was proved on him.*" In his Debates Scrapbook (193), AL has inserted the word "false" twice into this passage so as to make it read: "*when it is proven false on me as that was proved false on him.*" As the *Times* has "when it is proved like that was proved on him," it seems more likely that the two insertions of the word "false" constitute an after-the-fact revision than a restoration. For this reason, AL's change is not adopted.

P. 249 / L. 18 — "such" from Times; *P&T* has "as much." AL adopted the *Times* reading in his Debates Scrapbook, 193.

TEXTUAL NOTES FOR THE ALTON DEBATE

P. 254 / L. 12 — "the Presidency and" from *P&T*.

P. 254 / L. 26 — "10th of July": SAD spoke on the 9th of July; *P&T* has "11th."

P. 254 / L. 29 — "points" from *P&T*; *Times* has "point."

P. 254 / L. 32 — "11th of July": mistake for July 10th. See above.

P. 255 / L. 36 — "I shall consider" from *P&T*.

P. 256 / L. 11 — "the" from *P&T*

P. 258 / L. 3 — "Here, permit me to remark . . . He went on to say:" The *Times* account has this passage coming after the sentence that it here precedes, but both the sense of SAD's remark and the evidence of the *P&T* account make clear that the passage is properly placed as shown here.

P. 258 / L. 11 — "I should be exceedingly glad to know . . . must admit it into the Union.": from the *Times* report of the Freeport debate, the text given here.

P. 258 / L. 13 — "Gentlemen, your silence . . . exclusively your judgment." from *P&T*.

P. 261 / L. 8 — "least" from *P&T*; *Times* has "last."

P. 261 / L. 9 — "wield" from *P&T*; *Times* has "withhold."

P. 262 / L. 10 — "as to" from *P&T*.

P. 263 / L. 1 — "combining on" from *P&T*; *Times* has "continuing."

P. 263 / L. 22 — "the true intent . . . in their own way." SAD here quotes, probably from memory, the text of the Kansas-Nebraska Act.

P. 264 / L. 17 — "The recent legislation . . . WITHIN THEIR LIMITS.": the text given here is John Bassett Moore, ed., *The Works of James Buchanan* (Philadelphia: Lippincott, 1910), 10:81. The *Times* text differs only slightly, chiefly in its capitalization in the last sentence, which has been retained on the assumption that it represents SAD's emphasis.

P. 264 / L. 27 — "a" from *P&T*.

P. 265 / L. 10 — "If the inhabitants of any territory . . . forcing slavery upon any community.": the source text is unknown. That of *Times,* given here, differs only in punctuation from the authoritative modern text noted in the annotation (see note 14, pp. 264–65).

P&T does not print this quotation, nor does it mention Jefferson Davis by name. It has SAD say: "And you will find in a speech delivered in Maine the same construction given to that thing that I gave in my Freeport speech." This would seem to indicate either that the *Times* incorporated it after the fact or that the *P&T*, for whatever reason, declined to print the Davis quote.

P. 267 / L. 4 — "and convulse it" from *P&T.*

P. 267 / L. 21 — "There are no ladies . . . fine chance of them back here." from *Times.*

P. 267 / L. 30 — "I told him that . . . prosecution of that war." from *Times.*

P. 269 / L. 7 — "which guarantees to the citizens . . . in the several states." from *Times.*

P. 270 / L. 5 — "—I said" from *Times.*

P. 270 / L. 13 — "It may be argued . . . stand as our standard.": AL read from his Chicago speech of July 10, 1858, presumably as printed in *P&T* on July 12, the text given here. Two verbal mistakes ("slaves" for "slavery" and "remain" for "stand") indicate that *P&T*'s report of the debate was based not on the printed text but the reporter's transcription. Except for a few differences in punctuation, the *Times* text conforms to that given here.

P. 270 / L. 28 — "this they meant.": the word "they" is not part of this phrase in the printed text of the original speech, but it appears in both *Times* and *P&T* accounts and presumably was added by AL on the platform.

P. 270 / L. 37 — "I think the authors . . . all people, of all colors everywhere.": the text presented here (with the exception of the added word noted above) is that printed in the *Illinois State Journal*, June 29, 1857. The *P&T* text for this passage contains evidence of having been stenographed, rather than copied from Lincoln's reading text.

P. 272 / L. 3 — "by the evidence he produces": emendation from AL's Debates Scrapbook (201), there inserted into the P&T text and probably adapted from the *Times* reading: "by such evidence as he produced." Note also that AL is reported as saying in the next sentence: "What is the evidence he produces?"

P. 273 / L. 6 — "And what is the foundation . . . until the year 1808." AL's source text is undoubtedly that contained in the letter to the *Times*, the text given here. Compared with the text of a standard edition of Clay's speeches available in 1858, most of the italicization shown here reflects that added by the letter writer or *the Times* to indicate emphasis. See *The Speeches of Henry Clay*, ed. Calvin Colton, 2 vols. (New York: Barnes, 1857), 2:386–87.

P. 273 / L. 20 — "I wish every slave . . . of his ancestors." from *Times.*

P. 273 / L. 23 — "I desire no concealment . . . *slavery among its elements.*" AL's source text may have been the Colton edition cited above and followed here, *The Speeches of Henry Clay*, 2:387. Because AL repeats this passage later in the speech, it seems most likely that he did utter the sentence omitted in the *P&T* report (see previous note). The italicization in the last sentence probably reflects AL's emphasis.

P. 273 / L. 27 — "These were the sentiments . . . among its elements.'" from *Times.*

P. 273 / L. 27 — "we have" from *Times.*

P. 274 / L. 5 — "in regard to the Declaration of Independence" from *Times.*

P. 274 / L. 26 — "I desire no concealment . . . among its elements." from the same source as cited above for this passage.

P. 274 / L. 28 — "from the Declaration of Independence, as applicable to this discussion and" from *Times.*

P. 274 / L. 30 — "where slavery exists" from *Times.*

P. 274 / L. 30 — "brought forth the Declaration of Independence to ask that" from *Times*.

P. 275 / L. 1 — "in this connection," from *Times*.

P. 275 / L. 4 — "Now, if you please, . . . that Springfield speech." from *Times*.

P. 275 / L. 12 — "I do not expect the Union to be dissolved-" from *Times*. As AL says he is speaking from memory, he may have simply forgotten this clause, but the presumption of the editors is that, inasmuch as the *Times* report includes it, the clause was more likely spoken and inadvertently omitted from *P&T*.

P. 275 / L. 17 — "We are now far into the fifth . . . North as well as South." While AL seems to be speaking from memory, the form of the text given here follows that printed in the *Chicago Daily Tribune,* June 19, 1858, and included by AL in his Debates Scrapbook.

His delivery text, which was reportedly printed from his manuscript in the *Illinois State Journal* on June 18, 1858 (see Basler et al., *Collected Works,* 2:461), seems to have reflected—at least in the early part of the speech, to which this passage belongs—the way AL laid it out for delivery, with each sentence being a separate paragraph, with an unusually heavy use of commas (to indicate pauses) and italics (to indicate emphasis). The *P&T* text, used by AL in his Debates Scrapbook, corrects some known errors in the *Journal* text and may well have been considered by AL as more suitable for readers. Slight differences in the *Journal* and *P&T* texts make it possible to see that, in the course of the debates, AL sometimes quoted from the *Journal* text (see pp. 298–99).

P. 275 / L. 20 — "He has never given it up, and" from *Times*.

P. 275 / L. 26 — "no more in the States, and" from *Times*.

P. 276 / L. 4 — "not" from *Times;* adopted by AL in his Debates Scrapbook, 203.

P. 276 / L. 11 — "of putting an end to slavery agitation . . . collateral one" from *Times*.

P. 276 / L. 30 — "and I have no disposition . . . Not at all!" from *Times*.

P. 277 / L. 11 — "but a tax or duty may be . . . ten dollars for each person" from *Times*.

P. 277 / L. 23 — "be" from *Times*.

P. 278 / L. 7 — "as" from *Times; P&T* has "is."

P. 278 / L. 9 — "In that sense, then . . . part slave and part free." from *Times*.

P. 278 / L. 15 — "it" from *Times*.

P. 278 / L. 27 — "I ask no more than that, and now" from *Times*.

P. 278 / L. 29 — "does he not do me injustice?" from *Times*.

P. 278 / L. 35 — "Now, I confess very frankly that" from *Times; P&T* has "I confess,."

P. 278 / L. 36 — "intend" from *Times; P&T* has "perceive"; adopted by AL in his Debates Scrapbook, 205.

P. 280 / L. 30 — "you": editorial emendation.

P. 281 / L. 13 — "the" from *Times;* adopted by AL in his Debates Scrapbook (205).

P. 283 / L. 35 — "it": editorial emendation.

P. 284 / L. 15 — "expressive" from *Times*.

P. 285 / L. 6 — "old serpent" from *Times; P&T* has "spirit." Here it appears that the *Times* reporter heard better than his counterpart on the *P&T*, for AL had used this expression "the same old serpent" earlier in the campaign. Compare this passage from AL's Chicago speech: " . . . this argument of the Judge is the same old serpent that says you work and I eat, you toil and I will enjoy the fruits of it. Turn it whatever way you will—whether it come from the mouth of a King, an excuse for enslaving the people of his country, or from the mouth of men of one race as a reason for enslaving the men of another race, it is all the same old serpent . . ." (Basler et al., *Collected Works*, 2:500).

P. 287 / L. 6 — "The back of his party is broken when abolitionism is withdrawn." from *P&T.*

P. 288 / L. 9 — "was" from *P&T.*

P. 291 / L. 31 — "niggers" from *P&T; Times* has "negroes." See pp. 4–5.

P. 291 / L. 33 — "niggers" from *P&T; Times* has "negroes." See pp. 4–5.

P. 293 / L. 4 — "marks" from *P&T; Times* has "makes."

P. 293 / L. 4 — "and" from *P&T; Times* has "of."'s

P. 294 / L. 19 — "I am told my time is up." from *P&T.*

GLOSSARY

PERSONS, ISSUES, AND EVENTS

abolitionism   A belief that slavery should be ended by legal prohibition. In its most radical form it called for the immediate and total eradication of the institution of slavery wherever it existed in the United States. At the time of the debates, AL, though antislavery, was not an abolitionist. He was distinguished from abolitionists in that he acknowledged slavery's protected status under the federal Constitution, and the Constitution's provision for a fugitive slave law. And he recognized that given political reality in the 1850s, slavery could not be prohibited by Congress or by constitutional amendment in states where it existed; it could only be prohibited in the District of Columbia or in the national territories where, before the Kansas-Nebraska Act in 1854, it was undisputed that Congress had jurisdiction. Though surely almost all members of the Republican Party in the 1850s were antislavery and some were abolitionists, few were radical abolitionists. However, SAD was inclined to accuse AL and other Republican leaders of adhering to the radical abolitionist position.

"another Dred Scott decision"   *Lemmon v. The People* was a case involving the right of a Virginia slaveowner to retain ownership of his slaves while bringing them through a free state (New York) en route to Texas, thus testing the principle underlying statutes that had been passed by almost all Northern states affirming the freedom of slaves brought through them by their masters. AL doubtless knew of this case, which was working its way through the judicial system in 1858, and how a Taney-dominated court might decide it would have seemed obvious to him.

Anti-Nebraska   A political stance of opposition to the Kansas-Nebraska Act and its repeal of the Missouri Compromise. Adherence to this position united many political activists in 1854 and 1855 who might otherwise have been divided by their earlier allegiance to the Whig, Democratic, or Free Soil parties.

Ashmun, George (1804–70)   A Whig congressional opponent of the Mexican War from Massachusetts. As chairman of the Republican National Convention in 1860, he would head the Republican delegation that notified AL of his nomination for the presidency.

Baker, Jehu (1822–1903)   An attorney and Republican activist from St. Clair County in southern Illinois. He would serve several terms in Congress and in a diplomatic post after the Civil War.

Banks, Nathaniel P. (1816–94) Originally a Democratic politician in Massachusetts, he opposed the Kansas-Nebraska Act during his first term in Congress. Successively a Know-Nothing and a Republican, he was the first Republican Speaker of the House of Representatives, and he had a checkered Civil War military career.

Bigler, William (1814–80) A Pennsylvania businessman, legislator, and governor, and supporter of the Buchanan administration, he was a Democratic member of the U.S. Senate from 1856 to 1861.

Bissell, William H. (1811–60) An Illinois legislator, congressman, and Mexican War hero, Bissell was also the first Republican to be elected governor of Illinois, and was serving at the time of the Lincoln-Douglas debates.

Black Republican Party A designation of Republicans by SAD and other Illinois Democrats, intended to remind Illinois's basically racist voters of the relatively charitable position taken by the antislavery Republican Party toward African Americans and thus to make their position seem more extreme than it was.

Blair, Francis Preston Jr. (1821–75) A scion of the politically prominent Blair family, Frank Blair represented Missouri in Congress in the 1850s as the only member from a slave state opposed to the extension of slavery. He was a strong advocate of the emancipation of slaves and the colonization of freedmen.

Breese, Sidney (1800–1878) A long-time Democratic political and judicial figure in Illinois. In 1858 he was offered as a candidate for the U.S. Senate by the small Illinois Democratic faction that opposed Douglas's stance on the Lecompton Constitution and was allied with the Buchanan administration.

Brooks, Preston (1819–57) A two-term Democratic representative from South Carolina best known for his caning of Charles Sumner in the Senate chamber after Sumner delivered his speech on "The Crime against Kansas," May 19–20, 1856.

Brown, Benjamin Gratz (1826–85) A member of the Missouri House of Representatives in the 1850s and editor of what became St. Louis's Republican newspaper, the *Missouri Democrat*. He was antislavery to the extent that he desired Missouri's slaves to be emancipated and replaced by free white laborers.

Browning, Orville H. (1806–81) A Whig member of the Illinois senate, 1836–43; prominent Quincy, Illinois, lawyer; and a founder of the Republican Party in Illinois. Long a political friend of AL's, he was appointed to the U.S. Senate to fill the vacancy left by the death of SAD in June 1861.

Buchanan, James (1791–68) Fifteenth president of the United States. In his inaugural address, Buchanan seemed to prepare the nation to accept the forthcoming *Dred Scott* decision's solution to the slavery crisis. As a result, AL accused him, along with SAD, former President Pierce, and Chief Justice Taney, of conspiring to nationalize slavery.

Calhoun, John C. (1782–1850) A representative and senator from South Carolina, and vice-president of the United States during Andrew Jackson's first term. He is best remembered for his support of slavery and states' rights. He died during the deliberations leading to the Compromise of 1850.

Campbell, Thompson (1811–68) An antislavery Illinois Democratic politician and one-term congressman from the Galena district, he was appointed U.S. land commissioner for California by President Pierce. Though as AL suggests he was still a Democrat in 1858, he eventually became a Republican.

Carlin, William H. (1815–) An attorney in Quincy, Illinois, and Illinois state senator in the 1850s. In 1858 he ran for reelection to the senate on the National Democratic ticket. His father, Thomas Carlin, had been governor of Illinois when AL was a member of the Illinois House of Representatives.

Casey, Zadok (1796–1862) A long-time Democratic politician from southern Illinois. A greatly venerated figure by 1858, he served several terms in the Illinois General Assembly, as lieutenant governor, and ten years in the U.S. House of Representatives.

Cass, Lewis (1782–1866) A Democratic senator from Michigan, cabinet member, and presidential candidate in 1848, who served during the congressional deliberations leading to the Compromise of 1850.

Chaffee, Calvin F. (1811–96) A Massachusetts physician, and Know-Nothing and Republican congressman who married the widow of Dr. John Emerson, the former master of Dred Scott, who claimed freedom on the basis of his residence in Illinois and Wisconsin Territory.

Chase, Salmon P. (1808–73) An antislavery activist from Ohio who served in the U.S. Senate in the 1850s as a Free-Soiler. He was very critical of the Kansas-Nebraska Act in the Senate, and he spoke against it in Illinois in the summer of 1854. He later would be AL's secretary of the treasury, and AL's appointee as chief justice of the U.S. Supreme Court following the death of Roger B. Taney.

Chase amendment (1854) Senator Salmon P. Chase's proposed amendment to the Kansas-Nebraska bill, which would specifically allow the voters of the territories to exclude slavery. That amendment was not adopted.

Cincinnati platform (1856) The platform adopted by the Democratic Party at its 1856 convention in Cincinnati, where James Buchanan was nominated for the presidency. Among its major provisions were endorsements of the Kansas-Nebraska Act and its affirmation that questions relating to slavery belonged to the states and territories and not to Congress.

Clay, Henry (1777–1852) A long-time member of the U.S. House of Representatives and Senate from Kentucky, leader of the Whig Party, and an architect of the Compromise of 1850, which briefly deferred the sectional crisis over slavery and its extension. AL called Clay his "beau ideal of a statesman," while SAD emphasized the common nationalism of the Whigs under Clay, and the Democrats.

Codding, Ichabod (1811–1907) A Congregational minister in northern Illinois who was an antislavery lecturer in the state between 1854 and 1858, and, as is indicated in these debates, a founder of the Republican Party in Illinois.

Compromise of 1850. Acts of Congress in response to the Wilmot Proviso controversy and California's application for admission to the Union. It also defined the status of the remainder of the Mexican Cession, which effectively deferred the sectional crisis until 1854. Representing concessions to both proslavery and antislavery forces, these acts allowed the admission of California as a free state, thereby creating a majority of free states in the Union, the organization of Utah and New Mexico territories without reference to slavery there, the assumption of Texas's debt in exchange for that state's relinquishment of claims to New Mexico and other areas, the abolition of the slave trade in the District of Columbia, and a controversial new fugitive slave law that was much more stringent than its predecessor.

Cook, Isaac (Ike) (1810–86)   A Chicago entrepreneur and politician who became postmaster in that city at SAD's behest, only to be removed by James Buchanan, and then to be reappointed as a sympathizer with Buchanan after SAD and the president broke over the Lecompton Constitution.

Corwin, Thomas (1794–1865)   A Whig senator from Ohio between 1845 and 1851. In the Senate his opposition to the Mexican War was especially emphatic. He was Fillmore's secretary of the treasury, and would be AL's appointee as American minister to Mexico.

Crittenden, John J. (1787–1863)   A Whig, Know-Nothing, and Unionist U.S. Senator from Kentucky who was thought of as Henry Clay's successor. He considered the Kansas-Nebraska Act unwise and later opposed the Lecompton Constitution. As a result, he favored SAD's reelection to the Senate "as a rebuke to the administration."

Crittenden-Montgomery bill (1858)   A substitute to the Lecompton Constitution bill moved first in the U.S. Senate on March 23, 1858, by John J. Crittenden of Kentucky. The bill would require the Lecompton Constitution to be resubmitted, with no stipulations concerning the existing status of slavery, to a popular vote in Kansas. If the constitution were thus rejected, a new one should be drawn up. Crittenden's substitute failed, whereupon the Lecompton Constitution passed in the Senate. On April 1, 1858, the same substitute to the Lecompton Constitution was offered in the House of Representatives by Congressman William Montgomery of Pennsylvania. The substitute bill passed in the House, but the Senate refused to concur in it. The English bill was thereupon drawn up and passed as a compromise between the two houses.

Curtis, Benjamin R. (1809–74)   An associate justice of the U.S. Supreme Court, 1851–57. He dissented from the Court's ruling in the *Dred Scott* case that Scott was not a citizen and that the Missouri Compromise was unconstitutional. He resigned from the Court shortly thereafter.

Davis, Jacob C. (1820–83)   An attorney in Warsaw, Illinois; Illinois state senator; and briefly a member of Congress in 1856–57. He was a National Democratic candidate for the Illinois legislature in 1858.

Davis, Jefferson (1808–89)   A Democratic congressman and senator from Mississippi, Mexican War veteran, secretary of war under Pierce, and president of the Confederate States of America. As late as 1858 he enunciated what amounted to Douglas's Freeport Doctrine, doubtless hoping to assuage Northern fears of an aggressive Southern slave power.

Denio, Cyrenius B. (1821–85)   A three-term Whig and Republican member of the Illinois House of Representatives from Galena, in far northern Illinois. President Lincoln rewarded his partisan loyalty by appointing him to a patronage position in California.

Dougherty, John (1806–79)   A lawyer and state legislator from Union County in far southern Illinois. He was active in the small pro-Buchanan administration and anti-Douglas Democratic faction in Illinois in 1858, opposing SAD's position on the Lecompton Constitution.

Douglass, Frederick (1817–95)   A black abolitionist who escaped from slavery in Maryland in 1838 to develop a career in the North as an antislavery journalist and lecturer. He spoke against the Kansas-Nebraska Act in Illinois in the fall of 1854.

Dred Scott **decision (1857)**   Chief Justice Roger B. Taney wrote the majority opinion in this decision, which ruled that under the federal Constitution Dred Scott, as a Negro, could not be a U.S. citizen and thus could not sue in federal courts, and that Congress, as it had undertaken to do in the Missouri Compromise, could not exclude slavery from U.S. territories. Scott's residence on free soil in the state of Illinois and Wisconsin Territory did not therefore entitle him to freedom; the Missouri Compromise was therefore deemed unconstitutional; and slavery could thus be legitimately carried into the national territories. As this was only the second time in American history that an act of Congress had been declared unconstitutional, AL considered the decision to be "unsettled doctrine," and he spoke of finding a way to reverse it. Ultimately, AL argued that the decision was evidence of a conspiracy on the part of Presidents Pierce and Buchanan, Chief Justice Taney and SAD, to perpetuate slavery in this country and to make it a national institution.

Egypt   The nickname attached to southern Illinois, a region most conspicuously inhabited in the nineteenth century by settlers or their descendants from the upland South, and overwhelmingly anti-Negro and Democratic in politics. The name probably derives from the availability of grain and livestock in southern Illinois after the severe winter of 1830–31, just as grain had been obtainable in pharaonic Egypt during a Mediterranean famine in biblical times.

English bill (1858)   A final effort by supporters of the Buchanan administration to secure the admission of Kansas to the Union under the Lecompton Constitution. The bill's primary author was Congressman William H. English of Indiana. The bill would couple Kansas's admission to the Union with a land grant. If the grant was accepted by Kansas voters, statehood would follow under the Lecompton Constitution, regardless of the territory's population. Were the grant not accepted, Kansas statehood would be deferred until the territory had population equal to the minimum required of a congressional district, which in 1858 was 93,420. SAD ultimately opposed the bill, arguing that "when there are inducements on one side [the land grant] and penalties on the other [the requirement to wait for a certain population], there is no freedom of election." As did most congressional Republicans, AL opposed the English bill as a mere "contrivance." Nonetheless, the English bill passed both houses of Congress, and under its terms the Lecompton Constitution was eventually and finally rejected by Kansas voters on August 2, 1858, by 11,812 to 1,926.

Farnsworth, John M. (1820–97)   A radically antislavery Republican congressman who represented Chicago for two terms (1857–61) prior to the Civil War, and five more terms after service in the Union Army. His name was a byword for antislavery extremism.

Ficklin, Orlando B. (1808–86)   A Democratic legal and political associate of AL's, from Coles County in eastern Illinois. He served in the Illinois General Assembly in the 1830s and 1840s and in Congress in the 1840s and early 1850s.

Fillmore, Millard (1800–1874)   Thirteenth president of the United States and a Whig who came to the White House after the death of Zachary Taylor. His influence in behalf of the Compromise of 1850 contributed significantly to its success. In 1856 he was the nativist American Party's candidate for president.

Freeport Doctrine (1858)   SAD's answer to AL's second question posed to him at the Freeport debate on August 27, 1858. With implicit reference to the *Dred Scott* decision's determination that neither Congress nor a territorial legislature could prohibit slavery in the national territories, AL asked if a territory's citizens could thus in any way exclude slavery before the formation of a state constitution. SAD responded that slavery could only exist in a territory if it had popular support and was protected by local police regulations and legislation. This answer was popular in Illinois for it seemed to lend hope to antislavery immigrants to the territories, but it was anathema to Southern Democrats. SAD had publicly affirmed the same position previously, and he reiterated it several times during these debates; similar positions had been taken by Southern congressmen as late as 1858. But the context of SAD's Freeport declaration was different from that of his earlier ones. By August 27, 1858, after SAD's tacit cooperation with Republicans against the Lecompton Constitution and the English bill, his standing with Southern Democrats was greatly diminished. AL found SAD's doctrine an "absurdity," saying that it claimed "no less than a thing may be lawfully driven away from where it has a lawful right to be."

Free Soil   A doctrine of opposition to the extension of slavery into the national territories, first enunciated after the acquisition of new territory as a result of the Mexican War. Adherents to this position, of whom AL was eventually one, acknowledged that slavery was constitutionally protected in the states where it existed. The Free-Soil political party, which was dedicated to these principles, was short-lived but influential in the presidential election of 1848. AL opposed that party because it threatened to divide the Whig vote in the North that year.

Fugitive Slave Law (1850) One of the most controversial portions of the Compromise of 1850. According to its terms, should a claimant establish proof of ownership of an African American captive before a special commissioner, he could take possession of that captive. The prisoner had no recourse to the right of habeas corpus or to normal due process such as a jury trial or a judicial hearing. The law further entitled the special commissioner to a ten-dollar fee if he decided for the claimant, but to only five dollars if he freed the prisoner. The law also authorized federal officers to call on citizens to help enforce its provisions. To many Northerners, the law seemed to be an invitation to the kidnapping of Northern Negroes by Southern slave catchers. AL found the law distasteful, but since the return of fugitive slaves was required by the federal Constitution, he did not call for its repeal.

Garrison, William Lloyd (1805–79) A radical Massachusetts abolitionist, editor of the *Liberator*, and a founder of the American Anti-Slavery Society. He would be a supporter of AL during the Civil War.

Giddings, Joshua R. (1793–1864) An abolitionist member of the U.S. House of Representatives from Ohio, and messmate of AL's when the latter served in Congress. He spoke against the Kansas-Nebraska Act in Illinois in the summer of 1854. SAD capitalized on Giddings's notoriety as an abolitionist when addressing Illinois's generally Negrophobic audiences.

Hale, John P. (1806–73) A Free Soil and then Republican member of the U.S. Senate from New Hampshire, he was contentious in Senate deliberations on slavery and active in floor debates on the issue of Kansas statehood.

Harris, Thomas L. (1816–58) A Democratic lawyer, congressman, and Mexican War hero who represented AL's home district in central Illinois during the 1850s. He was the principal supporter of SAD's position on the Lecompton Constitution in the lower house of Congress.

Henry, John (1800–1882) A long-time political figure from Jacksonville, Illinois, he served in the Illinois House and Senate as a Whig, and for one month in early 1847 in the U.S. House of Representatives. He filled the seat lately occupied by Edward D. Baker and which would be taken by AL in December of that year. His brief voting record in Congress, especially on the Mexican War, was sometimes confused with AL's.

Hope, Thomas M. (1813–85) A sometime mayor of Alton, Illinois, and a prominent National Democrat (anti-SAD) leader there in 1858. In 1842 he had been one of James Shields's seconds in Shields's aborted duel with AL.

Illinois and the rights of blacks Illinois's Constitution of 1848 asserted the rights of "all men" to life, liberty, and property, and forbade the presence of slavery. However, it limited the voting franchise and militia service to white males and instructed the state legislature to "pass such laws as will effectively prohibit free persons of color from immigrating to and settling in this state . . .," which the legislature did in 1853. Elsewhere, Illinois statutes forbade testimony in courts by African Americans against whites, or jury service by them. Most of these disabilities were repealed by statute at the end of the Civil War, or by the Fifteenth Amendment to the federal Constitution.

Illinois senatorial election of 1855   Encouraged by the Anti-Nebraska majority that was returned to the Illinois General Assembly in November of 1854, AL undertook a run for the U.S. Senate as a Whig, to replace SAD's Democratic ally, James Shields. AL's bid was thwarted by the opposition of five Anti-Nebraska Democrats in the legislature who refused to vote for an Anti-Nebraska Whig. To insure that Shields's successor would be Anti-Nebraska, AL threw his support to Lyman Trumbull, who was thus elected.

Johnson, Richard M. (1780–1850)   A congressman and U.S. senator from Kentucky, and vice-president during the administration of Martin Van Buren. He became notorious for his common-law marriage to a mulatto woman who was also his slave, and for fathering two mixed-race daughters.

Judd, Norman B. (1815–78)   While an Anti-Nebraska Democrat member of the Illinois legislature in 1855, Judd refused to vote for AL during AL's first run for the U.S. Senate. He later became a prominent Republican and was chairman of the Illinois Republican State Central Committee in 1858. Judd presented AL's letter proposing these debates to SAD on July 24, 1858, and he nominated AL for president at the Republican convention in 1860.

Kansas-Nebraska Act (1854)   Promoted by SAD and passed in May of 1854, this act of Congress provided for the creation of two new territories north of latitude 36° 30' in the Louisiana Purchase, the opening of which was deemed essential to the construction of a transcontinental railroad. SAD claimed that a new precedent for territorial organization had been established by the creation of Utah and New Mexico territories from the Mexican Cession in 1850, when the choice of forbidding or adopting slavery was left to the citizens of those territories. Hence he included a similar provision in the Kansas-Nebraska Act, although the Missouri Compromise of 1820 had banned slavery from the area in question. An additional provision specifically repealing the Missouri Compromise was probably essential to attract the Southern congressional votes needed for the passage of the act, though this provision, and the "popular sovereignty" provision allowing territorial citizens to make their own choices concerning slavery, insured that the Kansas-Nebraska Act would be controversial, for it reopened the possibility of slavery being extended into an area previously closed to it. From it stemmed frontier warfare in Kansas between proslavery and free-state factions, the collapse of the Whig party over the slavery issue, the establishment of the antislavery Republican Party, and the perpetuation of the nation's sectional crisis over the extension of slavery.

Know-Nothings   Members of the nativist American party, which came into existence in opposition to the heavy immigration from Ireland and Germany in the early 1850s. The party stood for restrictions on immigration and limits on the political activity of immigrants, among other things. Because of the semi-secret early character of the party, its members, when asked about it, were said to reply that they knew nothing.

Koerner, Gustave (1809–96)   After fleeing from a revolt in Germany in 1833, Koerner settled in Belleville, Illinois, practiced law, and entered politics. As a Democrat, he served on the Illinois State Supreme Court and as Illinois's lieutenant governor. Eventually becoming a Republican after the Kansas-Nebraska Act, he participated in AL's 1858 and 1860 campaigns and was an effective emissary between President Lincoln and German Americans.

Lanphier, Charles H. (1820–1903)   The editor and proprietor of the Democratic *Illinois State Register* in Springfield, one of the oldest newspapers in the state and SAD's principal journalistic supporter in central Illinois.

Lecompton Constitution (1857–58)   Proslavery activists were able to dominate the political machinery of the territory of Kansas after the first elections there in 1855, and though declining in numbers to an obvious minority, they called a state constitutional convention, which met at Lecompton (the territorial capital) in October 1857. The convention prepared a constitution that would have committed Kansas to retaining slavery for several years after statehood, and which could be ratified only through a device allowing the slaves already in Kansas to remain there. The Lecompton Constitution was thus an instrument prepared by a minority faction, which would have imposed an unwanted institution upon the territorial majority. Though the constitution appeared to be ratified in a referendum on December 21, 1857, many antislavery Kansans simply boycotted the election; others had already been effectively disfranchised. SAD denounced the constitution and its mode of submission as "a system of trickery and jugglery to defeat the fair expression of the will of the people," though he expressed indifference toward the outcome of a fairly administered territorial election on slavery. Nonetheless, his opposition estranged him from President Buchanan, who made support of Lecompton a test of Democratic party loyalty and who needed to placate Southern members of his party. Though Republicans also opposed the Lecompton Constitution, AL reminded them that the issue of the possible extension of slavery into the territories under terms such as those in the Kansas-Nebraska Act still remained in dispute between them and Douglas. The Lecompton Constitution was eventually and finally rejected by Kansas voters in an election on August 2, 1858, which was called for as a provision of the English bill.

Lovejoy, Owen (1811–64)   An abolitionist, Congregationalist minister, and congressman from Princeton in northern Illinois, whose antislavery editor brother Elijah was killed by an anti-abolitionist mob in Alton, Illinois, in 1837. He was openly involved in the Underground Railroad and a founder of the Republican Party in Illinois. His name was a byword for antislavery activism.

Maine Law (1851)   Maine was the first state to prohibit the manufacture and sale of alcoholic beverages. Its law became a model for similar prohibitory legislation in other states and countries.

Matheny, James H. (1818–90)   A Sangamon County, Illinois, Whig and Republican politician and lawyer who was groomsman at the wedding of AL and Mary Todd. In 1856 he delivered a speech alleging an agreement between AL, Lyman Trumbull, and factions they led, to divide the spoils after the Anti-Nebraska political victory in Illinois two years earlier.

Mayo, Edward L. (1807–77)   A county judge and newspaper proprietor in DeKalb County in northern Illinois. A Democratic supporter of civil rights for blacks in the 1850s, he was an unsuccessful candidate for Congress in 1854, and he failed in his run for the Illinois legislature in 1858.

McLean, John (1785–1861)   A long-time associate justice of the U.S. Supreme Court who cited historical and legal precedents in dissenting from the Court's ruling in the *Dred Scott* case on black citizenship and Congress's power in the territories.

Minnesota Enabling Act (1857)   In his first annual message, President Buchanan expressed the hope that that act of Congress, which stipulated that Minnesota's new state constitution should be ratified by the people, would be a precedent for all future similar situations.

Missouri Compromise (1820)   A congressional compromise that allowed the admission of Missouri to the Union as a slave state, but which otherwise prohibited slavery north of a line defined by latitude 36° 30' in the Louisiana Purchase. When the Missouri Compromise was repealed by the Kansas-Nebraska Act in 1854, allowing slavery to enter an area from which it had been previously banned, AL returned to politics and attacked SAD for authorizing the repeal of an intersectional agreement on slavery that SAD himself had shortly before described as "canonised in the hearts of the American people." The Missouri Compromise was declared to have been unconstitutional by the *Dred Scott* decision in 1857, with slavery thus in theory to be allowed to spread into national territories regardless of the wishes of the citizens of those territories.

Molony, Richard S. (1811–91)   A physician and politician in Boone County in northern Illinois. Though opposed to the extension of slavery and the Fugitive Slave Law, he was successful in his run for Congress as a Democrat in 1850, and was a delegate at the Democratic convention in Baltimore in 1852.

National Democrats   A faction of the Illinois Democratic Party whose adherents objected to SAD's opposition to the Lecompton Constitution in 1858, and who remained loyal to the Buchanan administration. Many were federal officeholders in Illinois. SAD insisted that they were in league with Illinois Republicans, and that they labored in behalf of a victory by AL.

Nebraska bill (1854)   *See* Kansas-Nebraska Act.

"Negro equality"   In speeches at Chicago, Springfield, and elsewhere during the 1858 senatorial campaign in Illinois, SAD maintained that AL's insistence that blacks were entitled to the natural rights enumerated in the Declaration of Independence was more than merely that. He asserted that in espousing such a doctrine, AL betrayed his conviction that blacks and whites were equal, and in believing that, AL and the Republicans also favored Negro citizenship (which AL in fact repeatedly insisted that he opposed), which could only lead to racial intermarriage and amalgamation.

Nelson Samuel (1792–1873)   An associate justice of the U.S. Supreme Court, 1845–1872. He concurred with the majority in the *Dred Scott* decision, arguing that a slave had no right to come before the court.

"new Dred Scott decision"   *See* "another Dred Scott decision."

Northwest Ordinance of 1787   A statute enacted by both the confederation and federal congresses that provided for the administration and progress toward statehood of the national territory northwest of the Ohio River. The ordinance excluded slavery from that territory.

Norton, Jesse O. (1812–75)   An antislavery northern Illinois Whig and Republican lawyer, state legislator, and circuit judge who served two terms in Congress during the 1850s and another during the Civil War.

nullification   A doctrine originating as early as the Virginia and Kentucky resolutions of 1798, that an act of Congress may be declared unconstitutional and thereby null and void, by state action. It was founded on the assumption that the federal government was a creature of the states, which retained their sovereignty after the federal government's establishment. The nullification issue came to a head in 1832 when a South Carolina convention declared the federal tariffs of 1828 and 1832 to be null and void in that state.

old line Democrats   Followers of Andrew Jackson and his successors who hewed to the traditional Democratic line of opposition to banks, corporations, and federally supported enterprise, and of support of the sovereignty of the states, and of the deposit of federal funds in a national subtreasury. Though riven somewhat in Illinois, as these debates reveal, the Democratic Party in 1858 had yet to be significantly divided over the slavery issue and thus remained a party with a discernible national identity.

old line Whigs or old line Clay Whigs   Members of the Whig party before its disintegration in the mid-1850s, who were suspicious of a strong executive and tended to favor such nationalizing economic developments as the establishment of a national bank, a protective tariff, and internal improvements (roads and canals) to be built at federal expense. The Whig Party had a strong presence in both the North and the South until the Mexican War and the subsequent Wilmot Proviso controversy reintroduced nationally the divisive issue of slavery.

Ordinance of 1787   *See* Northwest Ordinance of 1787.

Orr, James L. (1822–73)   A Democratic congressman from South Carolina in the 1850s and Speaker of the House in the 35th Congress. In a House speech in 1856 he anticipated what became SAD's Freeport Doctrine, probably intending to mollify opponents to the extension of slavery by asserting that the institution could not be sustained where it was not wanted.

Palmer, John M. (1817–1900)   An Illinois legislator who was one of the Anti-Nebraska Democrats who stood in the way of AL's election to the Senate in 1855. A year later he had become a Republican and presided over his new party's first convention in Illinois. He would be a Union army general and, after the Civil War, governor of Illinois and a member of the U.S. Senate.

Peck, Ebenezer (1805–81)   A Chicago-based Illinois legislator and jurist who after a long career as a Democrat became a Republican after the passage of the Kansas-Nebraska Act. As president, AL would appoint him to the U.S. Court of Claims in 1863.

Phillips, Wendell (1811–84)   An effective radical abolitionist orator who was based in New England. During the Civil War he was outspoken in his criticism of AL for tardiness in acting against slavery.

Phoenix, John (George Horatio Derby) (1823–61)   A lieutenant in the U.S. Army's Topographical Corps in the 1850s who was also one of California's first humorists. While stationed in California, he supplemented his army pay with surveying jobs.

Pierce, Franklin (1804–69)   Fourteenth president of the United States who, because of his pro-Southern policies and because he supported and signed the Kansas-Nebraska Act, was accused by AL of conspiring with SAD, former President Buchanan, and Chief Justice Taney to nationalize slavery in the United States.

popular sovereignty (1854)   The major underlying concept of the Kansas-Nebraska Act, that (in SAD's words as stated in the body of the act) "it was the true intent and meaning of the act not to legislate slavery into any State or territory, nor to exclude it therefrom, but to leave the people thereof perfectly free to form and regulate their domestic institutions in their own way, subject only to the Constitution of the United States." An early enunciation of this doctrine, that territorial citizens might themselves adopt or reject slavery, was spelled out by Lewis Cass in 1847 in a letter to Tennessean A. O. P. Nicholson. AL was appalled by this doctrine, "invented in these degenerate latter days," he said, "to cloak the spread of slavery."

Reynolds, John (1789–1865)   A long-time Illinois Democratic warhorse, as judge, legislator, governor, congressman, and U.S. senator. He actively opposed SAD in the latter's break with the Buchanan administration in 1858, as a speaker, and as editor of an anti-SAD newspaper which he established in Belleville, Illinois.

Scott, Dred (1795–1858)   A Missouri slave who sued for his freedom, claiming entitlement to it from having resided on free soil in Illinois and Wisconsin Territory. The case became the basis for Chief Justice Taney's controversial ruling against the Missouri Compromise.

Scott, Winfield (1786–1866)   The long-time general-in-chief of the U.S. Army, Scott was a hero of the War of 1812 and the Black Hawk War, and commander of American forces in the Mexican War. He was the Whig presidential candidate in 1852.

Seward, William H. (1801–72)   An outspokenly antislavery Whig and Republican U.S. senator from New York, he would be AL's chief rival for the Republican presidential nomination in 1860 and, after the presidential election, AL's secretary of state.

Shields, James (1806/1810–79)   An Illinois Democratic state politician, Mexican War hero, and U.S. senator whose seat was contested by AL and Lyman Trumbull in 1855. He later served in the U.S. Senate from Minnesota and Missouri, the only person ever to represent three different states in that body.

Singleton, James W. (1811–92)   A lawyer and state representative from Brown County and later Adams County in western Illinois. Originally a Whig in politics, he became a Democrat in the 1850s and was a strong advocate of intersectional peace during the Civil War. During the 1858 senatorial campaign Singleton undercut AL's professed devotion to Henry Clay by pointing out his opposition to Clay's nomination for the presidency in 1848.

slavery in Illinois Territory   Though slavery had been prohibited in the Northwest Territory, in which Illinois was included, during Illinois's territorial period de facto slavery existed through provisions permitting earlier slaveholding citizens to retain their slave property, and allowing a form of indentured servitude. Slavery was constitutionally prohibited when Illinois became a state, but even that prohibition was prospective and did not significantly change the status of slaves or "servants" already present. Slavery only disappeared from Illinois after several Illinois Supreme Court decisions in the 1840s.

Smith, Samuel A. (1822–63)   A three-term Democratic congressman from Tennessee, and state agent to collect arms for the Confederate army during the Civil War. He anticipated SAD's Freeport Doctrine by asserting that slavery, to survive in a territory, needed laws to protect it as well as to establish it.

"spot resolutions"   On December 22, 1847, after the Mexican War was effectively won, Congressman AL introduced a series of resolutions addressed to President Polk and demanding to know whether the spot on which American blood was shed in a skirmish with Mexican troops in April 1846 was indeed on American soil, as the president had alleged. The resolutions made AL notorious as "Spotty Lincoln" among congressional Democrats and other proponents of the Mexican War at home in Illinois. Though SAD alleged at Alton that the resolutions had been read to Mexican soldiers in the field, the fact that military activity had ended seems to make such an event unlikely.

Springfield resolutions controversy   SAD confronted AL at the Ottawa debate with a series of radical resolutions that he maintained had been adopted by a Republican state convention in Springfield on October 4, 1854, and for which AL therefore must claim responsibility. AL denied knowledge of the resolutions and professed but little sympathy with some of their more extreme positions. It was almost immediately revealed that the resolutions, though falsely published as a local matter in Springfield's Democratic *Illinois State Register,* were adopted not at Springfield but at a district Republican convention at Aurora, Illinois, in September 1854. Taken unawares by it at Ottawa, AL several times in the debates raised the issue of this "forgery" with SAD.

squatter sovereignty   A contemptuous title frequently given by AL and other Republicans in 1858 to the doctrine of popular sovereignty promoted by SAD in the Kansas-Nebraska Act and later.

Stephens, Alexander H. (1812–83)   A long-time Whig member of the House of Representatives from Georgia about whose oratorical talents Congressman AL had been enthusiastic. During the Civil War he was vice-president of the Confederate States of America.

Sumner, Charles (1811–74)   A founder of the Free Soil Party and Free Soil and Republican senator from Massachusetts from 1851 until his death. On May 22, 1856, he was caned in the Senate by Congressman Preston Brooks of South Carolina, after giving his speech on "The Crime against Kansas." In that address Sumner fiercely attacked slavery, South Carolina, SAD, and Brooks's relative, Senator Andrew Butler of the Palmetto State.

Sweet, Martin P. (1806–64)   An attorney and itinerant Methodist minister from Stephenson County in northern Illinois. He was an unsuccessful Whig candidate for Congress in 1844 and again in 1850.

Taney, Roger B. (1777–1864)   The successor to John Marshall as chief justice of the U.S. Supreme Court, Taney is probably best known for his authorship of the *Dred Scott* decision, which led AL to accuse him, SAD, and Presidents Pierce and Buchanan of conspiring to nationalize slavery.

Taylor, Zachary (1784–1850)   A career soldier, hero of the Mexican War, and twelfth president of the United States. His early death made the Compromise of 1850 possible, as he had advocated statehood for California, New Mexico, and Utah without recognition of the claims of critics of those measures.

Texas annexation (1845)   The joint resolution of Congress that provided for the annexation of Texas allowed the former Republic of Texas to be divided into as many as five states, more than one of which (because it lay south of the Missouri Compromise line) could have permitted the existence of slavery.

Toombs, Robert (1810–85)   A Democratic member of the U.S. Senate from Georgia, serving from 1853 until he resigned in February 1861, in support of the Confederacy. He strove to find an intersectional compromise on the Kansas issue in Congress in 1856.

Toombs bill (1856)   An unsuccessful effort to provide for Kansas statehood, which was sponsored by Senator Robert Toombs of Georgia. The bill would provide for a territorial election of delegates to a constitutional convention in Kansas, and upon the framing of a constitution, Kansas would be admitted to the Union according to its terms regardless of the territory's population. The original version of the bill seemed to provide that the constitution should be submitted to a popular vote in the territory, but this provision was removed by the Senate

Committee on Territories, whose chairman was SAD. This removal was to haunt SAD in 1858 when both Lyman Trumbull and AL accused him of hypocrisy in attacking the Lecompton Constitution as a device to be foisted upon an unwilling Kansas electorate, after having already cancelled Kansans' right to vote on another constitution two years before.

Trumbull, Lyman (1813–96)   An Illinois state politician and U.S. Senator whose first term in the Senate (1855–1861) was won at AL's expense. Trumbull in the 1850s was an Anti-Nebraska Democrat who became a Republican, and he was actively involved in AL's 1858 senatorial campaign.

Turner, Thomas J. (1815–74)   A lawyer and newspaperman from Freeport, Illinois, and a sometime Illinois legislator and congressman. He was speaker of the Illinois House of Representatives when AL was defeated by Lyman Trumbull in his run for the Senate in 1855. Originally a Democrat, he became a Republican after the passage of the Kansas-Nebraska Act.

Washburne, Elihu B. (1816–87)   A long-time Whig and Republican congressman from Galena, Illinois, who was a convert to the new Republican Party as early as the fall of 1854, much sooner than AL was. He was a loyal congressional supporter of AL during AL's presidency.

Webster, Daniel (1777–1852)   A representative and senator from New Hampshire and Massachusetts, renowned as a persuasive orator and Whig leader, whose speech on March 7, 1850, helped insure the enactment of the Compromise Measures of 1850.

Wendell, Cornelius (1811–70)   The public printer at different times for both houses of Congress in the 1850s. In 1858 he became proprietor of the *Washington Union*, the Buchanan administration's mouthpiece in the nation's capital.

Wentworth, John (1815–88)   The longtime proprietor of the *Chicago Democrat* and an attorney in Chicago, "Long John" served four terms in Congress as a Democrat, then to become a Republican mayor of Chicago, and erratic AL partisan following the Kansas-Nebraska Act.

White, Horace (1834–1916)   The young Republican journalist who covered the Lincoln-Douglas debates for the *Chicago Press and Tribune*. He later wrote a chapter on the debates for the second edition of the Herndon-Weik biography of AL.

Williams, Archibald (1801–63)   An Illinois Whig and Republican lawyer and political leader who served in the state legislature in the 1830s and during the Taylor administration was U.S. attorney general for Illinois. As president, AL would appoint him to a federal judgeship in Kansas in 1861.

Wilmot Proviso (1846)   An amendment to a congressional appropriations bill introduced by Democratic Congressman David Wilmot of Pennsylvania early in the Mexican War. The proviso stipulated that "neither slavery nor involuntary servitude shall ever exist in any part" of any territory acquired by the United States from Mexico. The proviso was reintroduced a number of times in the House of Representatives, and though passing there, it never passed in the

Senate. AL claimed to have voted forty times for the proviso during his term in Congress. Agitation over the proviso contributed to the intersectional tension that led to the Compromise of 1850.

Wilson, Henry (1812–75)   A shoemaker who became a Republican U.S. Senator from Massachusetts. He would later serve as vice president of the United States under Ulysses Grant.

Yates, Richard (1818–73)   A Whig and Republican Illinois lawyer and politician who served in the Illinois legislature in the 1840s and in Congress, 1851–55. He would be Illinois's Civil War governor.

INDEX

RODNEY O. DAVIS and **DOUGLAS L. WILSON**
are codirectors of the Lincoln Studies Center at
Knox College and coeditors of *Herndon's Informants:*
Letters, Interviews, and Statements about Abraham Lincoln
(1998) and *Herndon's Lincoln* (2006).

**THE KNOX COLLEGE
LINCOLN STUDIES CENTER SERIES**

Herndon's Lincoln
William H. Herndon and Jesse W. Weik;
edited by Douglas L. Wilson and Rodney O. Davis

The Lincoln-Douglas Debates
The Lincoln Studies Center Edition
Edited by Rodney O. Davis and Douglas L. Wilson

The University of Illinois Press
is a founding member of the
Association of American University Presses

Composed in 10.5/13.5 Adobe Minion Pro
with Copperplate Gothic display
by Jim Proefrock
at the University of Illinois Press
Designed by Copenhaver Cumpston
Manufactured by Thomson-Shore, Inc.

UNIVERSITY OF ILLINOIS PRESS
1325 South Oak Street   Champaign, IL 61820-6903
www.press.uillinois.edu